TRUE STORIES
ROCK & ROLL NIGHTMARES

VOLUME 2

BY

STACI LAYNE WILSON

Copyright © 2023 by Staci Layne Wilson

Published by Excessive Nuance in paperback
ISBN-13: 978-1-7375139-4-0

Also available via e-book & audio

OTHER
ROCK & ROLL NIGHTMARES

ALONG COMES SCARY ('60s EDITION)
DO YOU FEAR LIKE WE DO ('70s EDITION)
GORY DAYS ('80s EDITION)
TRUE STORIES: VOLUME ONE
ROCKTAILS (DRINK RECIPES)

COMING SOON

28 (SPECULATIVE FICTION)
DEATH NOTES
LOVE STINKS
BAD BLOOD
KILLER NIGHTCLUBS
& MANY MORE!

PRAISE FOR ROCK & ROLL NIGHTMARES

"MTV's Headbangers Ball meets Tales from the Crypt—perfect entertainment for anyone who's ever played Stairway to Heaven backwards to hear the mumbled phrase 'Here's to my sweet Satan.'" (Variety)

"There's gallows humor galore but it's tempered with Wilson's empathy, ability to see several sides of a situation, and her obvious love of classic rock music and the people who created it."
(On the Rock Block)

"I loved this book and couldn't put it down once I started. Staci Wilson has a wonderful writing style, lean and expressive."
(5-star Amazon review)

"I really, really thought going into this book I'd know most of the stories. Not even close! I learned something new every page if not every paragraph about the mad excesses, personal tragedies or just bad luck that legendarily befalls musicians."
(5-star Amazon review)

CONTENTS
TRUE STORIES VOLUME 2

INTRODUCTION TO ROCK & ROLL NIGHTMARES: TRUE STORIES, VOLUME TWO

"It's been a long time since I rock and rolled."
—Led Zeppelin

Some say today's music has all the sparkle of a fizzled firework; the mystique is gone, and the creativity...? Kaput. Thanks to autotune, music-writing software, songs easily accessible (and disposable) with a single click, and publicists running artists' social media accounts... how do we even know what we're really listening to, or who we're actually seeing?

Are we delusional old coots, or are we onto something? According to music historian Ted Gioia in his 2022 essay, *Is Old Music Killing New Music*, "Old songs now represent 70% of the U.S. music market. Those who make a living from new music—especially that endangered species known as the working musician—should look at these figures with fear and trembling. But the news gets worse: the new-music market is shrinking. All the growth in the market is coming from old songs," he wrote. "The current list of most-downloaded tracks on iTunes is filled with the names of bands from the previous century, such as Creedence

Clearwater Revival and The Police." Even young people, Gioia concludes, are listening to music made long before they were born, and they are loving it.

Music may be presented and consumed differently, but the power of a great song always has been, and I suspect always will be, more profound than any other medium. We have songs for falling in love, wedding songs, driving songs, relaxing songs, breakup songs, and funeral songs because music can be anywhere we are, whether we're cruising down the boulevard with the top down or hunkered down in an office, hard at work. A disc of vinyl, a spool of tape, or a digital sequence can contain tears, laughter, love, lust, enlightenment, or darkness all at once. The lyrics were *about* something, whether it was personal or topical... there were no A.I. lyric-generators then.

In 1973, Led Zeppelin had their own jet—with a freaking *fireplace* in it! There were full bedrooms inside, and mini-skirted stewardesses serving champagne and caviar. When they disembarked, it was to a clamor of fans and sold-out concerts. Guys wanted to *be* them, and girls wanted to be *with* them. They truly lived that life—it wasn't a set rented out for Instagrammers.

But just a couple of years later, there was a backlash and stadium rockers were suddenly considered "uncool" by fans and music journalists who extolled the virtues of spare, no-frills underground artists like Patti Smith and the MC5. In the 1960s and '70s, being popular meant you were uncool—you were a sellout. (Imagine that today, with our desperate need for followers, likes, and verified-checkmark status.)

Back in the golden days, rock music was the bestselling form of entertainment—for a time, album and concert revenue outshone movies, books, and plays. The men (and they were mostly male) who made the music were the superheroes of the day. But in the end, they were human, and vulnerable to addiction, disease, death, and everything in between.

As an informal student of psychology, it's these dark nights of the soul that make me want to dig deeper into their backstories. You get the idea—the word "nightmares" is right there in the title, so this book isn't all rainbows, lollipops, limos, and #1 hits. Right now, there's no genre more popular than true crime but tragedy has been the seed of storytelling since ancient times and as humans, we view sad stories as cautionary but also as things that happen to other people, not us.

When asked by *Rolling Stone* how he felt about The Beatles' manager Brian Epstein's premature death at the age of 33, John Lennon said, "There is a sort of little hysterical, 'hee, hee, I'm glad it's not me' or something in it, that funny feeling when somebody dies. I don't know whether you've had it... I've had a lot of people die on me. And the other feeling is, 'What the fuck? What can *I* do?'"

While the tales you'll find herein are indeed fascinating, they are on the exploitative side. So, in order to keep my karmic checks and balances in harmony, I'm donating a portion of the profits from sales of this book to the Sweet Relief Musicians Fund. I first heard about this extraordinary organization when I went through them to help my friend, Danny Amis (aka, Daddy-O Grande of Los Straitjackets) when he was felled by a serious illness—and seriously expensive medical bills. The Sweet Relief Musicians Fund has been rockin' since 1994 and it supports career musicians who are experiencing sickness, disability, or age-related problems. They provide financial assistance to pay medical bills and for food, shelter, and other basic necessities. It's truly wonderful and so very needed.

To paraphrase Jim Croce, we can't save time in a bottle but we can damn well try to contain it in the pages of a book. *Rock & Roll Nightmares: True Stories, Volume Two* is a capsule of a different time—a time when rock ruled the earth. I hope you'll be entertained, educated, and maybe even moved by the array of stories in this book.

CHAPTER ONE: PSYCHO KILLER

"Some people never go crazy. What truly horrible lives they must lead."

—Charles Bukowski

While depraved devotees with murderous minds are the stuff of horror novels and scary movies, such scenarios have happened in real-life. From Tejano sensation Selena being shot in the back by the president of her fan club to YouTube cover-queen Christina Grimmie getting gunned down at a meet-and-greet; many famous folks have real reasons to fear their fans.

The most prominent musician to die at the whim of a so-called admirer is undoubtedly John Lennon. There have been entire books written on this murder alone, dissecting it from beginning to end and beyond. It's a tragic, fascinating case that was eerily foreshadowed by the victim himself. When still with The Beatles, John was asked how he expected to die. He jokingly replied, "I'll probably be popped off by some loony." Just before his murder, the "Imagine" singer said he wanted his new album to go to "Number one, with a bullet."

The erstwhile Beatle and his wife, avant-garde artist Yoko Ono, were big believers in a mental technique called manifestation. Manifesting is based on the idea that you can think your dreams into reality—it was the basis behind the bestselling book, *The Secret* by Rhonda Byrne, which was heavily touted by talk show host and all-around money-magnet Oprah Winfrey when it was published in 2006. But long before that book's worldwide recognition, manifestation was the bedrock of the hippie mindset.

According to celebrity journalist and crime writer Vicky Sheff, who profiled the Lennons and wrote about the aftermath of the "Revolver" icon's murder, John was excited about the release of his new album *Double Fantasy* and wanted to see it rise quickly in the rankings. Vicky wrote that she was at the couple's largest Dakota apartment (they owned six units in the famed Manhattan building) interviewing them in late November 1980 when their assistant, Fred Seaman, entered the room with copies of *Billboard* and *Cashbox* so the couple could peruse the Top 100. John "grabs a red pen and circles the entry: Number 25 with a bullet," Vicky wrote. "With the marker's bold line, he draws an arrow from the number 25 slot to number one, putting a line through Barbra Streisand's album *Guilty*. 'We're on our way,' he laughs."

However, the initial reaction to the album and its first single "(Just Like) Starting Over" was not great and they were nowhere near the top. That is, until December 8, 1980, when John Lennon, 40, was blasted with four bullets fired by 25-year-old Mark David Chapman, and his "manifestation" came true posthumously. (It seems there's something to the adage, "Be careful what you wish for.")

The "Instant Karma! (We All Shine On)" singer spent his last day working and promoting his album. After a breakfast of eggs benedict and cappuccino at Café La Fortuna, he got a haircut. Then he and Yoko did a photo shoot with famed photographer Annie Leibovitz—resulting in the iconic image that later appeared on the cover of *Rolling Stone*, showing the couple lying in bed; she fully clothed and him naked, clinging to her. After that, radio reporter Dave Sholin interviewed the ex-Beatles baritone for three hours. While a wide range of subjects was discussed, one soundbite stands out as particularly tragic: "We're either going to live or we're going to die. I consider that my work won't be finished until I'm dead and buried—and I hope that's a long time [from now]."

At about 5 p.m., he headed home and signed autographs for fans waiting just outside the arched entryway to The Dakota—among them was Mark David Chapman, clutching the *Double Fantasy* LP in his trembling hands. Someone snapped a photo of the killer and his prey. "He was very kind to me," Chapman later said in an interview. "Ironically, very kind, and was very patient with me. The limousine was waiting... and he took his time with me and he got the pen going and he signed my album. He asked me if I needed anything else. I said, 'No. No sir.' And he walked away. A very cordial and decent man."

After a brief stop at home, John and Yoko took a cab to The Record Factory where they began recording a song called "Walking on Thin Ice." When the couple returned to The Dakota close to 11 p.m., Mark was still there, waiting in the shadows. But this time, he wanted something far more precious than an autograph.

Yoko went on ahead and was through the gates when the psychopath called out to a straggling John, saying "Mr. Lennon," to get him to stop. Mark then proceeded to fire four hollow-point bullets from a Charter Arms Undercover .38 Special into the musician's back, with a fifth projectile missing its mark and shattering a nearby window.

The fatally wounded "Help!" co-composer was able to crawl up the steps toward the lobby crying out, "I'm shot!"

The concierge whipped off his jacket to staunch the bleeding, while the doorman apprehended the shooter. Someone called 911 and an ambulance was dispatched immediately but it wouldn't be there for at least 10 minutes.

"Are you John Lennon?" one of the policemen on the scene asked the victim. John was able to croak, "Yes," but had lost so much blood—both his subclavian artery and lungs were punctured—that he passed out on the spot. NYPD Officer Peter Cullen later recalled that John was lying face-down, bleeding profusely. The cops decided to get the former Beatle to the hospital as quickly as possible, getting him into a black-and-white. "We treated it like a cop was shot," Officer Tony Palma later told *Inside Edition*.

Surgeon Dr. David Halleran worked on his patient—whom he didn't recognize at the time—at Roosevelt Hospital, performing an emergency thoracotomy, but the injuries were too severe and John Winston Lennon was soon pronounced dead.

The dum-dum bullets used had been specially designed to cause maximum physical damage and that is why, the assassin revealed, he'd chosen them: "To ensure John Lennon would die." When law enforcement arrived at the scene of the crime two minutes after the shooting, Mark was being held fast by The Dakota's doorman, Jose Perdomo, who'd disarmed him and kicked the gun away. The killer was casually reading a paperback of J.D. Salinger's *The Catcher in the Rye* he'd purchased earlier that day, and did not resist arrest. The pudgy, pig-eyed blond man calmly told police he killed John Lennon because "he was so famous" but was "a poseur," living a different lifestyle than the one he espoused to the public.

But there was more to it than that. Mark started out as an admirer of The Beatles, but when John said, in 1966, that The Beatles "were more popular than Jesus," something clicked in the budding religious fanatic's mind and he made it his mission to silence that sort of blasphemy forever. He later said he gave no thought to Yoko, or to John's two sons, teenage Julian (from his first marriage) and five-year-old Sean, who was away with a nanny at another residence when the murder took place. Mark planned to kill himself after shooting his former idol, but "I was too much of a coward." Instead, three Beatles fans committed suicide following the tragedy, prompting his widow to issue a public statement asking that no one else do the same.

Born in Texas on May 10, 1951, Mark David Chapman grew up in Decatur, Georgia, and had a rough time of it at the hands of his abusive father who also beat Mark's mom. This led to the boy's delinquency and drug use; he later talked about living on the streets for weeks at a time starting at the age of 14. He wanted to murder his dad but could never work up the courage.

Around this time, Mark became a born-again Christian and was incensed by John's freewheeling lifestyle and his years-old remark about The Beatles being "more popular than Jesus," while the lyrics of songs like "God" and "Imagine" grated on him. A former classmate,

Miles McManus, later said that Mark would sing the lyrics, "Imagine... John Lennon *dead*."

The troubled teen eventually moved to Hawaii, where he got a job as a security guard—and became a freelance minister of sorts. It was there that he met his future wife, Gloria Abe, a travel agent. She'd been raised as a Buddhist but quickly converted to Christianity—as such, she does not believe in divorce and she remains married to the murderer to this day. In fact, the pair have enjoyed regular conjugal visits over the past four decades as Mark's pleas for parole have been denied time and time again.

As his mind turned increasingly warped, Mark cultivated a series of obsessions including the artwork and music of Todd Rundgren and the controversial novel, *The Catcher in the Rye* (which, incidentally, was released in the same year as his birth). Chapman contemplated killing other public figures, including Paul McCartney, Johnny Carson, Ronald Reagan, and Elizabeth Taylor, but it was Lennon who remained consistently in the crosshairs of his craziness. He later told journalist James R. Gaines that he read the book *John Lennon: One Day at a Time* (by Anthony Fawcett) in 1980, and that's when "his 10-year obsession with The Beatles congealed into a hatred of John Lennon in particular."

Almost needless to say, Chapman's signed copy of the *Double Fantasy* album has become a macabre collector's item. It was initially found on the morning following the murder by a groundskeeper in the shrubbery at the entrance to The Dakota; he duly handed the vinyl over to police as evidence, and it was later returned by prosecutors to him with a letter of thanks from the district attorney. The employee, whose name has never been released, became the de-facto owner of the artifact. The album cover is in black and white and features a close-up of John kissing his wife; the signature, along with the year scrawled underneath, appears on the image of Yoko's neck. The record also bears Chapman's forensically enhanced fingerprints along with the police evidence marker, WJ-T2. It was first sold by the finder in 1998 for $150,000 and then that collector got $850,000 for it 12 years later. It was auctioned off again in 2020, selling for an undisclosed amount to an unnamed investor.

That's not the only ghoulish memento that's made the rounds; Mark David Chapman has signed and sold copies of *The Catcher in the Rye* from behind bars. Worse still, while John Lennon's body was still warm on its slab at the morgue, an attendant snapped photos and sold the gruesome images to tabloids that slapped them on their front covers. In 2009, Yoko, who still lives at the murder site, began displaying her husband's bloodstained clothes and gore-spattered glasses as museum exhibits. In 2016, The Dakota's former concierge, Jay Hastings, sold the white shirt he was wearing as part of his uniform when he got smudged trying to help the fallen music hero in the aftermath of the attack. He also put up his own autographed copy of Double Fantasy—"To Jay, Love, John Lennon and Yoko Ono"—on the auction block. Fred Seaman, the assistant, kept working for Yoko after John's death so that he could secret out mementos and paperwork to use for his own gain and to aid in writing his tell-all exposé, *The Last Days of John Lennon: A Personal Memoir.*

When John Lennon was a young musician just starting, he was a fan of the American R&B singer, Sam Cooke—who was shot dead in 1964. Eleven years later, John recorded "Bring it on Home to Me," for his solo album of covers, *Rock 'N' Roll.* Like John, Sam had a hit in the wake of his death. "Shake" was recorded at his last studio session at RCA Studios in Hollywood, California, and was released 10 days after he was killed, in a historic double-sided single that also featured the epic "A Change Is Gonna Come," a song that would become forever entwined with the Civil Rights Movement.

By the time he was killed on December 11, 1964, 33-year-old Samuel Cook, known professionally as Sam Cooke, was one of the most successful singers in America. Sam was born on January 22, 1931, one of eight children, in Clarksdale, Mississippi, but the family moved to Chicago, Illinois, where he began to sing as a child. He belted out spirituals onstage at church, then at the age of 19, Sam was chosen to take over lead vocals for the Soul Stirrers, the most famous gospel group of its time. He went solo in 1957, releasing a string of chart-toppers, including "You Send Me," "Cupid," "Chain Gang," and "Twistin' the Night Away."

Sam was intellectual, well-read, and a canny businessman who retained the rights to his work and built a publishing company—showing shrewd foresight rare for a musician in those days. But he didn't just look out for himself; Cooke was a great proponent of his peers, boosting the careers of other would-be legends including Aretha Franklin, Al Green, Curtis Mayfield, Stevie Wonder, and Marvin Gaye. He also helped bring the music of Otis Redding and James Brown into the mainstream. What's more, he leveraged his popularity with Black *and* white audiences to fight for equal rights.

Sam Cooke was married twice. His first wife was singer-dancer Dolores Elizabeth Milligan Cook, who performed under the stage name "Dee Dee Mohawk." They divorced in 1958 and that same year, he married his second wife, Barbara Campbell. Dee Dee was killed in a car crash a year later. Barbara and Sam had three kids; Linda, Tracy, and Vincent, who drowned in the family swimming pool as a toddler. He also fathered at least three other children out of wedlock. Despite his pious upbringing, Sam was a libidinous womanizer whose philandering ultimately led to his death.

It happened on Friday, December 11, 1964, at about 3 a.m., while the "Another Saturday Night" singer was engaged in a tryst with a

Chinese-American call girl at the Hacienda, a seedy, run-down maison de pass plunked in the Watts area of South-Central Los Angeles (L.A.). The attractive 22-year-old, Elisa Boyer, did not disclose her profession upon meeting the famous singer—she said she and Sam had a chance encounter at the chic Hollywood hotspot, Martoni's Italian Restaurant, and that he drove her to the $3-a-night no-tell motel against her will after she asked to be taken home.

According to the testimony she later gave, things got out of hand once they got behind closed doors. After being stripped down to nothing but her slip by Sam, Elisa said she seized the opportunity to escape when her captor went into the bathroom. She grabbed her clothes, and most of his, then ran from the room. She tried to get help at the manager's office but her pleas were ignored so she made her way to the nearest payphone and called the police.

The thwarted lothario, wearing only his dinner jacket and one shoe, gave chase. Now in a rage, he made his way to the night manager's office and began pounding on the door, demanding, "Where's the girl?!"

The Hacienda's manager, Bertha Franklin, was on the phone with the motel's owner, Evelyn Carr, asking what she should do, when the guest forced his way inside by busting the door open. He looked to be in a drunken rage so Bertha, who kept a firearm handy for protection, shot at him three times—two bullets missed but the third hit the soul singer square in the heart. Evelyn, having heard all this, hung up and called the police. (At the autopsy, the victim's blood-alcohol level was measured at .16, which was twice the legal driving limit.)

When uniformed officers arrived, Bertha Franklin told them that she started defending herself by kicking the man, whom she did not recognize, then, "I tried to bite him through the jacket. I was fighting, biting, scratching, everything." They tussled, and Bertha said her attacker was trying to hold her still by grabbing both of her wrists, one in each of his hands, in a viselike grip. "Finally, I got up... I ran and grabbed the pistol off the TV, and I shot, at close range, three times." According to the 55-year-old motel manager, Sam said in a perplexed tone, "Lady, you shot me," then went after her again. She hit him in the head with a broomstick, at which point he fell and died. Bertha later testified in court that being confronted by an irate, pantsless man wearing one shoe had terrified her to the point that she feared for her life.

But her story didn't add up. Sam Cooke had been shot with a .22 pistol, but the gun registered to Bertha Franklin was a .32. The bullet that passed through his body was taken into police evidence but somehow went missing. Other guests at the Hacienda told the police that they never heard gunshots. Or maybe they were just inured to the sound—it was a rough area and even the police were unmoved by the multiple homicides they investigated there.

(The neighborhood went up in flames during the Watts riots in the summer of 1965.)

Elisa Boyer's story didn't quite come together, either. There are inconsistencies between her version of the events and details recalled by diners at Martoni's who saw the couple earlier that night. Al Schmitt, Sam's close friend and longtime producer, said the singing star was hard to miss in his posh Sy Devore suit while flashing cash for all to see. Hence, some suggested that Elisa went willingly with Sam to the motel, then slipped out of the room with his pants to rob him—not escaping an attempted rape. However, a police search of her purse following the incident turned up nothing but a $20 bill. In Sam's red Ferrari, they found a money clip with $108 in cash—a far cry from the thousands he reportedly had in hand at the restaurant. His discarded pants were found on the motel's premises but his credit cards were missing and never turned up.

Both Bertha Franklin and Elisa Boyer passed polygraph tests and their testimonies presented at the coroner's inquest were believed; forensic pathologist Dr. Cyril H. Wecht used the term "justifiable homicide" and closed the case.

But questions remained.

Sam's friend and fellow icon, Etta James, was one of many mourners at the funeral in Chicago on December 18, 1964. Stretching across five city blocks, some 200,000 fans queued up to view the body but Etta was one of the select few who had a private, up-close audience with the corpse before the main ceremony. She wrote in her memoir *Rage to Survive* that Sam's head was "practically disconnected from his shoulders. That's how badly he'd been beaten. His hands were broken and crushed. They tried to cover it with makeup but I could see massive bruises on his head. No woman with a broomstick could have inflicted that kind of beating against a strong, full-grown man." None of the injuries Etta said she saw were noted in the autopsy report.

Several discrepancies have led to speculation of conspiracies—was the "Wonderful World" singer assassinated by some shady branch of the U.S. Government to silence his voice in the Civil Rights movement? After all, Sam was a prominent voice for Black rights and had attracted the ire of racists when he refused to perform at segregated venues. The characteristically outspoken boxer Muhammad Ali said, "If Cooke had been Frank Sinatra, The Beatles, or Ricky Nelson, the FBI would be investigating."

Some theorists believe that if there is treachery, then Sam's manager, Allen Klein, a notoriously ruthless businessman, was behind it. He was the owner of Tracey, Ltd., and following the shooting, he became the rights-holder of all of Sam's recordings. But no evidence has ever been found that could tie the music mogul to the case, and since his client's star was on the rise, he stood to make even more money with Sam Cooke alive.

The aftermath of the whole sordid situation got even stranger.

It came to light that Bertha Franklin, a former madam with a criminal record, had actually shot *another* patron of the Hacienda six months before she killed Sam. In the wake of her most awful act, she was forced to quit her job at the motel after receiving death threats from some of Sam's more outraged fans. She filed a $200,000 lawsuit against the Cooke estate for punitive damages and injuries but was awarded only a fraction of that amount. Sam's widow, Barbara, countersued the ex nookie-bookie, seeking $7,000 in damages to cover Cooke's funeral expenses (she lost the case). Bertha decided it was best to leave town so she moved to Michigan, where she died a year and a half later of a massive coronary.

Elisa Boyer was picked up a month after Sam Cooke's death for soliciting an undercover cop for $40 a pop. Over the years, she shuffled multiple aliases like so many playing cards— Lisa Boyer, Lisa Lee, Crystal Chan Young, Elsie Nakama—acquiring a rap sheet longer than John Holmes' schlong until her final arrest in 1979. Elisa was convicted and put in prison for 25 to life after she was convicted of manslaughter for shooting and killing her boyfriend.

Although he sang like an angel, Sam had "the devil in him," according to an anonymous female dalliance. He "couldn't resist bad girls," his friend and fellow crooner Robert "Bumps" Blackwell said, adding, "Sam would walk past a good girl to get to a hooker." Within a period of just five weeks in 1952, three women each gave birth to a daughter fathered by Sam... and that was only the beginning of a barrage of paternity suits that were filed up until his death. Nowadays, Cooke would be labeled a sex addict and probably would have gone to rehab for it; or maybe he'd be canceled. But back then he just dealt with the consequences... until the consequences were dealt to him.

The charismatic tenor's wife was well-aware of Sam's naughty nature and likewise, she gave as good as she got. The pair had met when she was a precocious 13-year-old, and he was 18. At the time her husband was killed, Barbara was having a torrid affair with a bartender—as well as 21-year-old Bobby Womack, Sam's protégé. In a fuel to the fire move, friends and family were shocked when she brought her young lover to the L.A. funeral (one wasn't enough for a superstar of that stature) and saw that he was wearing a ring and watch Sam had on when he was killed.

Mere months after the burial, Barbara and Bobby tied the knot. But not many were happy about the union; they got hate mail, including a parcel containing a baby doll in a coffin, and were booed when they went out on the town together. They had a son, named Vincent after the baby who had drowned (he committed suicide in 1986 at the age of 21).

Bobby Womack, who had gotten a career boost when The Rolling Stones covered his song "It's All Over Now" (and achieved their first #1 in 1964), was suddenly a pariah, echoing the song's title. As the years went on, Bobby turned to drugs and even began a sexual relationship with Sam and Barbara's eldest child, Linda, when she was 17. Barbara found them in bed together in 1970, and she shot at Bobby—the bullet only grazed his temple and she was never charged. Not surprisingly, they divorced that same year. As if that wasn't bizarre enough, Linda later married Bobby's younger brother, Cecil. (One wonders how awkward Thanksgiving dinners must have been at the Womack household.)

Even Sam Cooke's flashy Ferrari has a footnote. Shortly after marrying, Barbara and Bobby needed money to start their new life but the will was taking too long in probate, so the dead man's ride went to Hollywood Sport Cars to be sold to the highest bidder. Dennis Wilson from The Beach Boys, a fan of Sam's music and a car connoisseur, bought the crimson 1963 Ferrari 250 GT Berlinetta Lusso for $10,000 cash and proudly drove it everywhere—he even towed his boat with it. After changing hands a few times, the red roadster was sold to a collector for an undisclosed world-record sum and its whereabouts are unknown.

House of Freaks was a two-man, minimalist post-punk Americana band that formed in Richmond, Virginia in 1984. Bryan Harvey played guitar and sang, while Johnny Hott played percussion. Harvey and Hott foreshadowed more popular rock duos like the White Stripes and Black Keys, and while they never hit the big-time, they did get some radio play with their songs "Rocking Chair" and "When the Hammer Came Down" (a title that would prove chillingly ironic).

"We got shit all the time about not having a bass player," Bryan bitterly told *Rolling Stone* in 2004. "I mean, it was *our* fucking band. Did people hassle Flock of Seagulls for not having a guitar player?"

The pair eventually broke up but still played music together, and separately as parts of other groups.

Still Richmond-based, Bryan Harvey performed on New Year's Eve of 2005 with his band NrG Krysys, then went home to his wife Kathryn and their two young daughters, Stella and Ruby. They were to host a New Year's Day party and of course, Johnny Hott was invited.

Johnny pulled up at about 4 p.m. and parked in front of his former bandmate's unassuming two-story house. He was the first to arrive and noted that the quiet neighborhood seemed to be lazing and enjoying the last vestiges of holiday cheer—Christmas trees could be seen through windows and colored lights still decorated the houses. Oddly, none of the neighbors seemed to have noticed that the Harvey home was on fire.

The shocked percussionist called 911 and fast-moving, siren-blaring firetrucks were soon squealing to a stop at the scene. First responders dashed inside and found the source of the blaze: the basement. Inside the smoke-filled room were four prone bodies. Immediately, firefighters rushed the victims outside and into the fresh air in hopes of reviving them... but in the late afternoon sun, they saw that all four had been bound, gagged, and murdered. Their bodies were so viciously wounded that cops and firemen reportedly cried at the scene. A knife from the family's own kitchen was used to stab them and slash their throats, while a claw hammer taken from Bryan's toolbox did the rest.

Who would do such a heinous, horrible thing? The Harveys had no enemies. The 49-year-old musician was well-liked, and his wife, 10 years younger, owned and operated World of Mirth, a popular toy and novelty shop where locals came to play and marvel at the ever-changing arty displays. Stella was nine, and Ruby was just four.

As it turned out, the quadruple murder was a random crime of chance. Early on that first morning of 2006, Bryan Harvey had carelessly left the front door ajar after fetching his newspaper and the gap was spotted by an evil opportunist. Most days it wouldn't matter; the neighborhood was safe. But at that fateful moment, an innocent oversight gave a killer carte blanche. People were wondering not only who, but why? Why savagely slay an entire family for what amounted to very little? Were a computer, a wedding ring, and a basket of cookies worth four lives?

There was a memorial for the family, where Bryan's musician friends played a mournful, moving version of George Harrison's "All Things Must Pass." But there was no sense of closure; not when the maniac was still out there.

On January 3, a couple living in Chesterfield County, Virginia, was robbed by two men and a woman who got into their house by pretending to ask for directions; fortunately, they were left unharmed. Now law enforcement assumed that they were looking for more than one perpetrator in the Harvey slaying. A few days later, another family was found dead in their home, murdered.

Richmond residents were on edge but they wouldn't have to worry much longer. The police were tipped to a pair of possible suspects by a concerned caller, and by January 7th, relatives Ricky Javon Gray and Ray Joseph Dandridge, both 28, were in custody. Gray, the uncle, and Dandridge, his nephew, had only recently been released from prison. Their records boasted a myriad of small-time crimes and drug-related charges but now they were accused of far worse and faced the death penalty.

Ray's girlfriend Ashley Baskerville assisted the duo as an accomplice during their murder and robbery spree... until she became a victim herself. The 21-year-old was part of the second family found dead; she, her mother Mary Baskerville-Tucker, and stepfather Percyell Tucker were slain days after the Harvey homicides. The Gray/Dandridge death spree had begun one month earlier, when they brutally beat and suffocated Ricky's wife of six months, Treva, and hid her in a shallow grave. From November 2005 until they were caught in the first week of January 2006, the callous criminals killed eight people.

Ricky Gray's trial commenced nine months after he was caught. The Medical Examiner, Dr. Darin Trelka, testified that Bryan Harvey was struck six times in the head with the hammer and that his neck was cut in a sawing motion no less than eight times. His body also had "very severe" burns in several places. Kathryn's half-brother, actor Steven Culp (famous for playing Rex Van De Kamp on the TV series *Desperate Housewives*), wept as the doctor described the injuries to her body and many in the courtroom sobbed openly when he went on to describe the "overkill" suffered by the defenseless little girls.

Other heartbreaking details came out— apparently, Kathryn had a chance to escape and save herself but she did not take it. When the family was initially forced into the basement by the PCP-pickled perpetrators, Stella was at a friend's house. But she needed to be home for the New Year's Day party, so her playmate's mom, Kiersten Perkinson, drove her. Rather than just dropping her off, Kiersten walked the nine-year-old to the front door to make sure she got inside safely. Little did she know, inside was the *least* safe place for the doomed child. Hearing the doorbell, the offenders untied and ungagged Kathryn. They ordered her to answer as if nothing was amiss, then bring her daughter back down to the basement. Kiersten testified that she had a "brief exchange" with the "pale and ashen" Kathryn but didn't realize anything was wrong; maybe she thought she was hung over from too much New Year's Eve partying. It was surmised that after doing as she was told, Kathryn was tied up, and so was Stella. Shortly after, Ricky and Ray murdered the entire family in the most heinous, painful manner imaginable, then set the place on fire.

Ricky Gray had the nerve to plead not guilty, using the "abuse excuse." His defense team tried to argue that their client did what he did because of his own physical and sexual mistreatment as a child—they even showed jurors a cute photo of him as a little boy wearing a sailor suit—but it didn't work. Ricky was convicted and sentenced to death. Ray Dandridge, rattled, decided not to go to court; he changed his plea to guilty and was given life in the penitentiary.

Just before Ricky Gray was executed by lethal injection on January 18, 2017, he was asked if he had any last words. He replied "Nope," and that was that.

British guitarist Dave Rowbotham was another musician felled with a hammer, but his killer has never been caught. The axe man was well-respected in the Manchester music scene, having played with the likes of Happy Mondays, Simply Red, and Mothmen. Friends and colleagues described him as "funny," "bohemian," and "friendly" but by the time he met his end at just 34 years of age on November 8, 1991, Dave had lost touch with his music connections and spiraled into an abyss of alcoholism and drug addiction.

His girlfriend, Kathleen Griffiths, became worried that she hadn't heard from him in a while, so she went to his Burnage, Manchester, flat and got inside. She found her man dead on the living room floor in a pool of congealed blood, his head laid open by blows from a lathe hammer (different from the more common claw hammer, this implement has a hatchet blade on one side with a small, lateral nick for pulling nails).

It was a shocking murder but details remain sketchy to this day—it's not publicly known if the weapon was left at the scene, what sort of forensic evidence was gathered, or even whether there were (or are) any viable suspects. Since the "One More Weapon" guitarist had fallen in with drug dealers and other shady figures, we'll probably never know who did it or why. In his memory, his former Happy Mondays bandmates wrote a song called "Cowboy Dave," which was released on their album *Yes Please!* in 1992.

American rock drummer John Gary Driscoll might not be as famous as some of his contemporaries but sadly, his name is at the center of one of the most bizarre unsolved murders in music history.

Gary, who never went by his first name, performed on the heavy metal scene with vocalist Ronnie James Dio in a few bands, including Elf, and he was featured on Rainbow's first album in 1975. The self-titled vinyl includes the legendary classic headbanging barnburner, "Man on the Silver Mountain." Surprisingly, Rainbow's leader and guitarist Ritchie Blackmore fired Gary because he wasn't happy with his sound—Gary played in an R&B style, which you'd think would have been known when he was hired... nonetheless, he was sacked and summarily replaced by the harder-driving British percussionist, Cozy Powell.

After Rainbow faded from his résumé, Gary drifted on to a few other bands. Unfortunately, none of them were particularly successful and he was forced back to his hometown of Ithaca in upstate New York, where he took a day job in order to make ends meet. The *Ithaca Journal* published his obituary, which stated he was a "self-employed tile installer."

The 41-year-old was found dead in his home on June 8, 1987. Hard facts of the case are almost nonexistent but there's plenty of speculation and rumor. Some say it was a drug deal gone wrong, while others toss Satanism into the mix because the body was allegedly dismembered and flayed. According to lore, there was a suspect who fled the country after being questioned by police. Sadly, the case remains open to this day. But you never know… due to advances in DNA technology, even the most nebulous murders can be solved many decades later.

Fred "FREAK" Smith was a multi-instrumentalist who left his indelible mark on the crucial 1980s hardcore punk scene of Washington, D.C., but when he was found stabbed to death in Las Palmas Park in San Fernando, California, on August 8, 2017, he was thought to be just another homeless, middle-aged man in the wrong place at the wrong time. Without any I.D. on him, it took several days for the victim to be identified.

The lifeless body was found in a secluded area behind the park's softball field by the Los Angeles Fire Department, which had been responding to a cardiac arrest call. San Fernando Police Chief Tony Vairo told the *El Sol Newspaper* that FREAK was known to them because the recovering addict had been a resident of the Blake House, a sober-living group home in the area.

When he was finally named, that didn't end the questions—in fact, the mystery deepened. Why would a once-lauded music mover-shaker wind up like that? "Fred didn't fit in the world," said Ian MacKaye, founder of Dischord Records, the label that signed the musician's first and best-known band, Beefeater. "He lived the way he wanted to live." Others pointed to the high cost of living in even the most rundown areas of L.A., and the paltry pay offered to musicians lucky enough to snag stage time in the city's dwindling live-music venues. Still others wondered if the attack was racially motivated, as San Fernando is a predominantly Latino and gang-infested area.

As an African-American in a starkly Caucasian scene, FREAK stood out as a punk rocker. "When I first heard someone refer to me as the 'negro Lemmy,' I was floored," he told *Maximum Rocknroll* in 2010. But the "boisterous" axe man wasn't completely alone as a minority in the D.C. hardcore scene: Dag Nasty singer Shawn Brown, Void guitarist Jon "Bubba" Dupree, and Bad Brains were there, too. "It was very strange to be these 'token' negros playing in front of predominantly all-white audiences," FREAK said.

The bald-headed powerhouse left Beefeater to join Strange Boutique, a different kind of band that had a sinister, goth-infused sound. After they broke up in 1994, he moved to Los Angeles, where he played in several other bands and had his name legally changed to FREAK, caps and all.

By 2011, FREAK was a vagrant, and, said Strange Boutique's drummer Danny Ingram, the eccentricities that had once made his bandmate charming now chafed. He realized this when he met up with his old friend on a visit to West L.A. "We went out one night and we went from bar to bar to bar, until we finally settled on a place where Fred felt comfortable," Danny recalled. But even then, "he would jump up and accost every single passerby. He would tell them the most horribly inappropriate jokes." When Danny found out that FREAK was sleeping on buses and showering at the YMCA, "I couldn't believe it. I offered to give him money but he didn't want to [take] it."

Although his personality had shifted in his later years, friends and associates eulogized him fondly, saying that FREAK was a lively, funny, selfless, and generous man who always had time for those in need of anything from a kind word to a guitar lesson.

L.A. County Supervisor Sheila Kuehl took an interest in FREAK's death and offered a $10,000 reward for any information leading to the apprehension and conviction of his killer. "He paved the way for African-American musicians in the punk genre," she said, adding that DNA found on the scene has been entered into a national database.

But still, the senseless murder of 55-year-old Fred "FREAK" Smith remains unsolved.

While this next murder is also still unsolved, we do finally know the name of the victim: it's Frank "Frankie" Little Jr., a short-term guitarist for the famous soul outfit, The O'Jays. It took 39 years, but the partial human remains discovered in a garbage bag in

Twinsburg, Ohio, on February 18, 1982, were finally identified, due to the DNA Doe Project. The outfit, which specializes in tracking hard-to-find genealogical profiles, got a match through one of his relatives and confirmed it was, indeed, the "Oh, How You Hurt Me" guitarist. By the time the body parts were discovered in the early '80s, they were already at least a couple of years old and no one ever suspected it was him. The family just thought they'd lost track of him and he was never reported as missing.

"Frankie was a guitarist and songwriter in the very early O'Jays," said the group in a joint statement released in December of 2021. "He came with us when we first ventured out of Cleveland and traveled to L.A., but he also was in love with a woman in Cleveland that he missed so much that he soon returned to Cleveland after a short amount of time. That was in the mid-1960s and we had not heard from him after then. Although this sounds like a tragic ending, we wish his family and friends closure to what appears to be a very sad story."

American-born bassist John Francis Anthony "Jaco" Pastorius III was known for his four-string prowess in several genres including jazz, fusion, folk, rock, and pop. The long-fingered, lanky strings man can be heard on albums by Weather Report, Blood, Sweat & Tears, and Joni Mitchell, to name but a few. He toured with Herbie Hancock and made a few critically-acclaimed solo albums before his time on earth was cut short.

Jaco's talent stood out first and foremost but he was also known for his eccentric, erratic behavior. For the most part, it was all in fun and his friends and family accepted his quirks as just another dimension of his gregarious personality. He had long, straight dark hair which he topped with a bandana reminiscent of the hippie days, and a hugely welcoming, infectious smile.

Before his life started to circle the drain, Jaco was a well-respected innovator. When he was coming up in the '60s and '70s, bassists traditionally stayed still, stood back, and kept the beat... not him—he played like a virtuosic frontman, fast and loud, as he vocalized and even did flips onstage or lay on his back, picking the instrument as he poised it above his head. The self-taught "Punk Jazz" bassist perfected many unorthodox and complex techniques and he also brought the fretless bass into the spotlight when he modified his 1962 Fender Jazz sunburst. He did this in true mad scientist style, using a butter knife to pry out each thin bar of metal, then sealed the fretboard with Plastic Wood and applied several coats of Petite's Poly-Poxy to top it off. Because of its distinctive booming growl, Jaco nicknamed his instrument the "Bass of Doom." Although Bill Wyman of The Rolling Stones was playing a home-converted fretless instrument himself as early as 1961 it's Jaco's Bass of Doom that became famous—it was all about *that* bass!

The "Birdland" bass man was described by his friends and peers as fun and freewheeling but they saw his moods grow increasingly mercurial when, thanks to a bandmate's casual encouragement, he started drinking hard liquor. Jaco's father, also a musician, had been a lush and Jaco vowed never to be like him. But sadly, his jovial social drinking devolved into hardcore alcoholism and before long, Jaco lost everything dear to him. His wife, Tracy, walked out on him and took their two kids with her. He even lost his beloved Bass of Doom. During an argument, he smashed it into shards. It was painstakingly rebuilt only to be stolen from a park bench in New York City's Central Park never to be seen by its owner again.

"By 1980, Jaco was always angry and drunk," said Weather Report's keyboardist, Joe Zawinul. "He began to try to out-macho me. To outdrink me, like a competition. Sure, I drank and occasionally did a little blow, but I liked myself too much to hurt myself. Jaco did everything to indulgence. Then his music began to slip. It was still perfect, but it wasn't fresh. It was like a circus act; Jaco relied on tricks he had done before."

Too late, a doctor diagnosed Jaco with "manic depression" (a condition now known as bipolar disorder). Cyclic peaks in brain activity bestowed creative intensity on Jaco but when he came down, he dove to the bottom of the nearest bottle. When he came up for air, he was violent and impossible. In 1982, he pleaded guilty to threatening a police officer following an argument with his second wife, Ingrid, who was pregnant with twins at the time. Jaco was sentenced to probation, which he violated by making a spectacle of himself, riding on the hood of a pickup truck while blotto and in the buff. His drunken antics onstage soon gave him the kind of reputation no musician wants. He was committed to the psychiatric ward of Bellevue Hospital in New York and prescribed Lithium but it caused hand tremors, so he stopped taking it.

After Ingrid filed for divorce in 1985, Jaco met his last love, Terry Nagell, whom his family later described as an alcoholic with a temper; not exactly girlfriend material. Witnesses said he took to wandering the streets in a haze, wearing torn, filthy clothes and unlaced sneakers, carrying a bass guitar under one arm. The once-lauded musical genius spat at passersby, ranting at them. He bounced between New York and Fort Lauderdale, committing petty crimes such as breaking and entering, and theft. Jaco couldn't stay out of his favorite bars, even after he was banned from most of them, which led to his ultimate downfall.

On the last day of his waking life, September 11, 1987, Jaco Pastorius called up Terry, who'd broken up with him some months before—he was too much, even for her. They had lunch together, then Terry invited Jaco to go to a Santana concert at Sunrise Musical Theater in Sunrise, Florida, with her and her new boyfriend. The erstwhile bassist agreed and seemed fine with it, but he showed up at the gig bombed out of his gourd. He staggered his way onstage and tried unsuccessfully to blend in with the band. He was forcibly removed and kicked off the premises by security. On his way out, he said to Terry, "I hope you and your blond boyfriend are happy together," adding, "I'm dead."

At about 1:30 that morning, Jaco called Terry at home, screaming obscenities. At some point after that, he made his way to the Midnight Bottle Club in Wilton Manors. He'd been permanently barred from the establishment sometime before and was still irate about it. After reportedly kicking in a glass door, Jaco got into a violent confrontation with the club's security and doorman, 25-year-old Luc Havan, a Vietnamese refugee who was a martial arts expert with a third-degree black belt in karate.

As the once-brilliant musician lay unconscious in a widening pool of his own blood, a bystander called for the police and an ambulance. As far as everyone on the scene knew, the prone man was a random vagrant—a troublemaker who'd apparently messed with the wrong dude.

Jaco's skull was fractured, both eyes were swollen shut with the right ruptured and torn from its socket, his teeth were broken, he was branded with the impression of a ring on his cheek, his left arm was badly injured, and there was massive internal bleeding. He was carted off to the nearest hospital where he lay comatose in the intensive-care unit for nine days, unrecognized until the bruising and puffiness went down, and, completely by chance, he was spotted by the obstetrician who had delivered his children. Once identified, local newspapers ran the story and his loved ones rushed to his side. But there was nothing they could do to save him.

Thirty-five-year-old Jaco Pastorius died on September 21st, without ever regaining consciousness. He was surrounded by his parents and brothers, his two ex-wives, his four children, and his friends. Terry Nagell was not on the approved visitor list.

Midnight Bottle Club's bouncer Luc Havan faced the very serious charge of second-degree murder if he stood trial, so he pleaded guilty to manslaughter and was sentenced to 22 months in prison and five years of probation. After serving just four months, he was paroled for good behavior. Following his shockingly early release, Ingrid remarked that "he served one month for each child he left fatherless." Luc stayed in the area and stayed in the bar biz, but he didn't stay out of trouble—he's been arrested for assault and battery in recent years.

Though his life and career were relatively brief, Jaco Pastorius' influence lives on. He's been credited with inspiring musicians around the world, is the subject of a documentary film, and has been described as "arguably the most important and groundbreaking electric bassist in history" by *Guitar Player* magazine. Oh, and the missing Bass of Doom? It was M.I.A. for decades before turning up in a music store. A fan recognized it, and after some some legal wrangling and help from Metallica bassist Robert Trujillo, the instrument is now in the hands of Jaco's son, bassist Felix Pastorius.

The Pacific Northwest has spawned some of the most innovative guitar-rock sounds of all-time—from boisterous garage rock epitomized by bands like The Ventures and The Sonics in the 1960s to the heavy fuzz and doom-and-gloom lyrics brought forth by Nirvana and Soundgarden. Perhaps because the weather is so wet and cold, it forced people to stay indoors and find ways to feed their souls... like playing music.

But the dark skies and storms also provide the perfect cover for evildoers. Resident serial killers Ted Bundy and Gary Ridgeway hid the bodies of their victims in the rain-nourished forests and foliage, while other bad guys, such as Kenneth Bianchi and Jesus Mezquia, fled from warmer climes to sleety Seattle to continue their crimes.

Kenneth Bianchi made up half of the Hillside Stranglers team—the pair left a trail of gore across Southern California in the 1970s—

before going solo in the Seattle suburb of Bellingham, where he killed two women before he was caught.

Jesus Mezquia was part of the Mariel Boatlift of the early 1980s, in which Cuban dictator Fidel Castro allowed tens of thousands of his country's citizens, including criminals and mental patients, to escape to the U.S. by boat. In the early '80s—Jesus sailed in with an extensive criminal record and the hits just kept on coming.

He was arrested in Dade County for attempted solicitation, resisting arrest, kidnapping, indecent exposure, and carrying a concealed weapon, so he fled to Southern California, where he ran afoul of the law yet again. There were battery and assault convictions in 1986 and a battery-of-a-spouse conviction in 1989. He was sentenced to four years in prison, but the sentence was suspended and he was put on probation, which he violated in 1991 when he was accused of exposing himself in public. The inaptly-named Jesus made his way to Seattle in 1992.

Rather than turning over the proverbial new leaf, the felon fell into even darker deeds— including his first murder (that we know of). Jesus, who was described by acquaintances as "striking"—with hawkish features and standing a lanky six-foot-four, with a penchant for piling on gold chains, bracelets, and multiple rings— didn't exactly blend into the wallpaper. A neighbor said he had "an intensity" about him, and an icy cockiness some found attractive but that others found chilling. "The room drops about 10 degrees when he's in it," said King County Senior Deputy Prosecutor Tim Bradshaw.

On July 7, 1993, Jesus was trolling the dark, deserted streets of Seattle's Capitol Hill residential district in the middle of the night, in search of a likely victim. Charismatic local singer Mia Zapata was no victim—the 27-year-old was strong-willed, alert, and a staunch feminist who stood up for herself—but she had been drinking. And she was tired, following a successful West Coast tour with her band. She was further stressed, having recently split from her boyfriend, musician Robert Jenkins. After drinking in a bar, then hanging out at a friend's apartment, the "Here's to Your Fuck" singer set out on foot at about 1 a.m. in hopes of hailing a cab. Unfortunately, she caught the eye of the sex-obsessed, violent predator and never saw the light of day again.

Mexican-American Mia was born in Chicago and got into music while growing up in an upper-middle-class suburb of Douglass Hills in Louisville, Kentucky, with her media executive parents and two siblings. By the time she was nine, she had taught herself how to play the piano and the guitar, and she filled up notebooks with song lyrics. She got serious about music as a career following her parent's divorce and while attending a liberal arts college in Ohio. She loved punk but was also influenced by jazz, blues, and R&B singers like Bessie Smith, Billie Holiday, Jimmy Reed, Ray Charles, and Sam Cooke.

In 1986, she formed her band, The Gits (the name was inspired by a Monty Python skit with the phrase "sniveling little rat-faced git" running throughout). There was frontwoman Mia, guitarist Joe Spleen (née Andy Kessler), bassist Matt Dresdner, and drummer Steve Moriarty. Their music had the energy and aggression of punk, but the musicianship was more in line with the emerging grunge sound. Mia's powerful voice sounded like a combination of Janis Joplin, Courtney Love, and Joan Jett, but it was uniquely hers. People who saw her perform said she had a potent allure—however, offstage, she could be shy and, true to her Gen-X birthright, she was both frustrated and in love with the world.

She was a slim five-foot-eight, blonde-haired, and often wore small braids or mini dreadlocks. One of her calves bore a tattoo of a hen in honor of her childhood nickname, "Chicken legs," and it would be the identifying mark that changed her toe tag from Jane Doe to Mia Katherine Zapata.

After moving to Seattle in 1989, the band occupied the "Rathouse," an abandoned structure in the Capitol Hill district where they rehearsed and lived. They all worked regular jobs between gigs, with Mia waitressing while keeping her eye on getting that one lucky break.

The Gits were local darlings with a small but hardcore following who loved that the music was impossible to pigeonhole; some said they were punk, others thought grunge, and many assumed Mia was part of the "riot grrrl" movement. After a small, underground label released their album *Frenching the Bully* in 1992, The Gits were finally finding their footing. In a few days, they would launch a cross-country tour starting in New York. The brass ring was within reach when it all came to a bloody, violent end.

The summer of 1993 was a particularly deadly one in Seattle but Mia woke up on the morning of July 6, 1993, a sunny Tuesday, without any idea she would be homicide victim #33. She rolled out of bed at around 11 a.m., got dressed in rolled-up blue jeans, a black hoodie with "Gits" emblazoned on the back, and put on some boots. She went to a Thai restaurant for lunch with her dad, Richard Zapata (who'd remarried and relocated to Yakima, a two-hour drive from Seattle). Afterward, they went to Tower Records and the Seattle Art Museum. Father and daughter got together once or twice a month; Richard reportedly did not condone the "musician lifestyle" and he worried for her, making sure he visited often.

"She was very naïve about the life she chose," he later said in an interview with the *Seattle Times*. "Mia was the best of our family; she had a complete and total social conscience. She cared about people. She would see people on the street, homeless, and tell us that it wasn't their fault."

At about 3 p.m. he dropped her off at home, where Mia did laundry, walked her dog, and chatted briefly with one of her roommates. At 6:30 p.m., she made her way to the Winston Apartments on Capitol Hill; in the back was a makeshift rehearsal studio, dubbed "Pancreas." She rehearsed with Hells Smells, the band that her ex, Robert Jenkins, was a member of and with whom she often sang backup vocals. She and Robert, who was 21 years older than she, had been in love enough to consider marriage but soon after their split he began dating someone else and Mia was stung by how quickly he'd moved on.

After rehearsals she walked over to the Comet Tavern, a watering hole a block away on East Pike Street, where she and the rest of The Gits could often be found—she joined friends and fellow musicians from the band 7 Year Bitch and had a few drinks, on top of the ones she'd reportedly downed at the studio. Talk turned to the Bitch's co-founder and guitarist, Stefanie Sargent, who had died at the age of 24 one year earlier after a night of heavy drinking and shooting heroin. Lesson not learned apparently, because Mia suggested they do shots for the memorial toast. By midnight, she was flying high—and *really* upset with Robert. According to her friends, Mia said she was going back to Pancreas to give her ex a piece of her mind.

But Robert had left the premises by the time she circled back. Mia decided to go upstairs to the second-floor to see their mutual friend, 34-year-old Tracy Victoria "TV" Kenly. TV also sang for Hell's Smells. They talked, and TV remembered the "Precious Blood" singer was upset, distracted, and mumbling nonsense. At one point, a still-inebriated Mia bolted from the apartment without saying anything, then returned a few minutes later, apologizing. TV offered her a place to crash for the night but Mia begged off, saying she would catch a cab at the nearest gas station—she didn't have a driver's license and often took taxis to get from place to place. She put on her headphones, found a tune on her Walkman, and made her way down the stairs and out of sight. It was 2 a.m.

One hour and 20 minutes later, and almost two miles away, a sex worker stumbled upon the dead body of a young woman lying in a Christ-like pose—ankles crossed, arms out—on the pavement of 24th Avenue South, a dead-end between South Yesler and South Washington. The 27-year-old streetwalker, who called herself Charity, was trolling the area behind Catholic Community Services in the Central Area when she spotted something that looked like a bag of garbage... but not quite. When she got closer to see what it was, she realized it was a female, lying face-up, partially clothed, and seemingly dead. Charity ran a block and a half to a fire station and asked for help, which was immediately dispatched.

The victim showed no signs of life but she was still warm, so medics worked to revive her. The sweatshirt she wore was pulled up and bunched underneath her arms with the hood strings tied tight across her face and knotted under her throat. The paramedics observed abrasions on the exposed parts of her body, including what would later be identified as bite marks alongside her nipples. Her underwear and torn bra were found stuffed in the pocket of her jeans. She was declared dead at 3:35 a.m. on July 7, 1993, and sent to the morgue as a Jane Doe to await the medical examiner. Legend has it the deputy coroner was a fan of The Gits and it was he who first identified her as Mia Zapata.

The autopsy report is particularly horrifying. She was forcefully raped, punched in the gut so many times that her liver was lacerated, savagely bitten on her breasts, then garroted with the cords of her hooded sweatshirt. The M.E. noted that even without the strangulation, Mia would likely have died from the blunt force trauma to her abdomen. Though Mia had injuries to her vaginal and anal area consistent with rape, no semen was found. Thinking there could be traces of saliva from the bites, the coroner swabbed the area. DNA testing was still in its infancy, so the evidence was optimistically saved for future use.

Investigators later surmised that the attacker came up behind Mia while she was listening to music through headphones and grabbed her, throwing her into a vehicle where he assaulted and killed her, then dumped her like so much trash on a squalid street only addicts and prostitutes dared to tread.

Robert was an immediate suspect—it's always the boyfriend, right? After all, he was decades older than Mia, a Vietnam vet, and something of a rudderless soul. But he was cooperative; he passed two lie-detector tests, gave blood and hair samples, and had a solid alibi. Someone floated the theory that she might have been a victim of the then-unidentified Green River Killer but since Mia was not a sex worker nor homeless, and she wasn't dumped by the water, she didn't fit the victimology or *modus operandi* at all. Could it have been an obsessed fan or a stalker? A sleepless sex offender stumbling upon a crime of opportunity?

"In the beginning, everyone was a suspect," said Gits bassist, Matt Dresdner. He and his bandmates organized a series of benefit concerts to raise money for an investigative fund—Nirvana, Pearl Jam, Soundgarden, and many others performed—raising $70,000. Joan Jett and Bikini Kill frontwoman Kathleen Hanna co-wrote a song, "Go Home," and donated the proceeds. But the funds dried up and so did the leads. The case went cold. The Gits disbanded.

But people didn't forget. Conspiracy theories whizzed around, and of course, Mia's lyrics were scrutinized to the letter. Many of her songs were dark, but "Sign of the Crab" was especially chilling: "Anything to get me in and then get me killed/Go ahead and slice me up, spread me all across this town/'Cause you know you're the one that won't be found/Maybe I've pushed my luck one too many times."

Mia was buried in Louisville, her grave marker describing her as a "Cherished daughter, sister, artist, friend, Git." Every August 25th, her birthday, her favorite flowers, yellow roses, were brought to the gravesite. For years, those who loved her mourned, knowing that whoever murdered Mia was still out there... somewhere.

In 2001, the Seattle P.D. was working on various cold cases, giving priority to the ones that had tangible evidence. They sent swabs to the Washington State Patrol Crime Laboratory for additional DNA analysis, then entered the results into the National Database. In December 2002, they nailed him: Jesus Mezquia, a felonious fisherman who'd been arrested in Miami and was obliged by law to give a cheek swab, was Mia Zapata's killer.

Mia's friends and family were relieved—but stunned. They'd never seen, or even heard of, the dangerous criminal in their midst. Capitol Hill wasn't exactly the safest place to be but given the savagery of the attack, there was always the thought that the killer must have had it in for Mia and specifically targeted her. But instead, it was surmised that Jesus, whose girlfriend was out of town, had free rein to stalk and terrorize someone... anyone. In her intoxicated state, Mia had no chance against the six-foot-four, 235-pound murderous misogynist.

Jesus denied ever laying eyes on the "Second Skin" singer, let alone laying hands on her. According to his neighbors in Seattle, the Cuban was superstitious and placed garlic in corners to ward off wicked spirits—obviously, it didn't work against his own evil. He ditched his live-in girlfriend, who later testified that he was scary and abusive, shortly after the murder and hightailed it to California. He then took his U.S. journey full circle, settling in Marathon, Florida, where he married and had a daughter. Jesus did odd jobs but he couldn't stay straight; he was arrested several times for petty crimes, including burglary. After he was nabbed in the Sunshine State, he was sent to Pierce County, Washington, to face the music.

A woman by the name of Valentina Dececco came forward to allege that the convict assaulted her six months after Mia's homicide. In January 1994, around 4:30 a.m., she was leaving her downtown Seattle apartment for a morning jog when a tall, swarthy man approached her out of nowhere. He knocked her to her knees and she felt pain at her throat. She managed to run away but upon returning home, she saw the man she later identified as Jesus Mezquia staring at her from around the corner of her building while masturbating. She did not report the incident at the time it happened and tried to forget about it. But when she saw his photograph in the newspaper after he was charged with the Mia Zapata homicide, she called the police. Valentina did not testify at the trial but the DNA had Jesus dead-to-rights.

After a month-long court case, the jury convicted him of first-degree felony murder and he was sentenced to nearly four decades in prison. In 2005, the coldblooded killer filed an appeal against his "excessive" sentence, arguing in part that he should have been allowed to present other suspects, including Mia's former boyfriend, and a cab driver who knew Mia, Scott MacFarlane, as part of his defense. He further argued that DNA evidence obtained from Florida should not have been admitted in a Washington case. But Robert Jenkins' own DNA had already exonerated him and although the cabbie had supposedly made some "incriminating statements" about Mia's murder in the months that followed, the court denied the killer's outrageous request. On January 29, 2009, Judge Sharon Armstrong once again penalized Jesus for raping and murdering Mia, this time putting him away for 36 years. Still stubbornly maintaining his innocence, a remorseless Mezquia died at the age of 66 in Pierce County hospital on January 21, 2021, from undisclosed causes.

While she is not a household name, Mia Zapata is far from forgotten. Several bands, including 7 Year Bitch, have dedicated songs and albums to her. Joan Jett had the last word, reminding us that it all comes down to the music: "Her legacy should be beautiful, strong punk-rock music coming from a woman's perspective because that's who she was."

Saxophonist Donald Myrick came to fame with the bestselling and beloved band Earth, Wind & Fire. They pioneered sexy R&B that mixed harmonizing vocals, big-band horns, Afro-Latin rhythms, and stylish showmanship. Don went on to rock fame with former Genesis vocalist and drummer, Phil Collins—that's his sax you hear soloing during the 1985 smash hit, "One More Night."

Sadly, Don was killed on July 30, 1993, while police were serving a search warrant based on a tip from a drug informant—Officer Gary Barbaro fired one shot square in the sax man's chest after mistaking a butane lighter for a firearm.

He was in a bad way at the time of his shocking death. Recently separated from his wife of 26 years, he'd been diagnosed with leukemia, was between music gigs, and was reduced to sharing a small apartment in a run-down area of Palms, a suburb of the more affluent beach city of Santa Monica.

An internal investigation was going on even as Don was laid to rest at the Inglewood Park Cemetery in Inglewood, California. "We'll find out what happened and we'll rectify it," said singer-songwriter Oscar Brown Jr., while talking to the press at the funeral. "But that don't bother Don, because he's gone to join a bigger band." As the body lay in a casket beneath floral arrangements decorated with black quarter notes and white doves, Louis Satterfield, a bassist and trombonist who'd grown up with Don in Chicago, told reporters that his friend never would have pulled a gun on anyone. "The only weapon he ever had was a weapon of peace: the saxophone."

Sergeant Gary Gallinot gave a press conference following the fatal shooting, explaining that the vice squad was on the trail of a dial-for-drugs ring that operated out of two addresses on the Westside—one was Don Myrick's residence. Don's friends denied that the musician was involved in the drug trade but Gallinot confirmed that detectives had identified his apartment as a place where couriers would pick up rock cocaine for delivery to customers who'd placed their orders by telephone.

Early on the morning of July 30th, police officers surrounded the "Shining Star" musician's home, covering the back door while Officer Gary Barbaro knocked and demanded entry at the front. No one answered so he opened the door with a key supplied by the management of the Oakwood apartment complex. He then entered and caught sight of the occupant, who was holding "a black metal object." Barbaro immediately drew his weapon and shot to kill.

Sergeant Gallinot said his officer feared for his life because the seven-inch butane lighter resembles a firearm known as a pencil gun. The sergeant added that the gun had been recently featured in police training bulletins and added that the lighter was the type commonly used to heat cocaine.

It was later revealed that one of Don's roommates was arrested for drug-related crimes so it was probably him running the illegal business. Don's widow, Barbara, and their three daughters, Shirika, Shani, and Lauren, were awarded $400,000 after settling their wrongful-death lawsuit against the City of Santa Monica.

Jack Russell was a wild young man in 1978, just 18 years old but already deep into the sex, drugs, and rock & roll lifestyle—the California-born blond was the randy frontman for a hard-driving band that would later become Great White, but at that time fame was far away and money was scarce, so he turned to robbery.

When Jack and a friend broke into a Whittier drug dealer's home to steal cocaine, things quickly escalated beyond control and he nearly became a killer. A PCP-addled, revolver-armed Jack got into an altercation with the live-in maid, but she managed to break free and locked herself in a bathroom. He gave chase and shot blindly through the door, miraculously hitting her square in the chest. Even more miraculous, the "Once Bitten... Twice Shy" singer remembered years later, was how the hapless housekeeper avoided certain death:

"The bullet hit a St. Christopher medallion by her heart and went into her shoulder, saving her life and mine. I wake up on my knees looking at a door with the gun between my legs and I'm like 'What the hell? Where am I? I had no clue [because of the PCP]."

Cops were called, the victim survived, and Jack Russell dodged a legal bullet by being sentenced as a youth, serving just 11 months in prison. His bandmates welcomed him back into the fold and the rest is heavy metal history.

There was no "Jail Break" for AC/DC drummer Phil Rudd when he was arrested at his home in New Zealand on November 6, 2014, and charged with attempting to procure a murder by hiring a hitman, as well as threatening to kill two people himself. For good measure, they also got him on possession of methamphetamine and cannabis, which were found in his pockets during the raid.

Apparently, it all started when Phil's 2014 solo album *Head Job* tanked. The colossal failure made him so mad that he reportedly fired most of his staff, including a personal assistant who had nothing to do with the making of the album. According to a transcript of the charges, the "Dirty Deeds Done Dirt Cheap" drummer phoned an unnamed associate and offered them a choice of money, a car, a motorcycle, or a house if they would murder his especially-hated former employee.

The following day, the angry Aussie made several threatening phone calls to his former assistant, even going so far as to say, "I'm going to come over and kill you." He reportedly added that he'd also do away with the man's young daughter.

Phillip Hugh Norman Rudd became AC/DC's drummer in 1975 when he was 21 years old and he stayed with the band until 1983. The death of AC/DC's iconic vocalist Bon Scott in 1980 had apparently put a strain on Phil, making him snappish and hard to work with. He routinely clashed with his bandmates, particularly rhythm guitarist Malcolm Young. Phil's drug use was also a factor in his dismissal. After getting the boot, Phil moved to New Zealand where he got married, fathered five children with his wife, raced cars, and owned a few businesses. But the "Rock 'N' Roll Damnation" drummer couldn't stay away and managed to reunite with his hard-rocking brethren in 1994. He was with them up until his arrest, whereupon he was replaced with another former AC/DC drummer, Welshman Chris Slade.

The charges of ordering a hit were ultimately dropped due to lack of evidence, but on April 21, 2015, the sexagenarian pleaded guilty to possessing drugs and the verbal death threat. Two months later, he was sentenced to eight months of house arrest and was ordered to pay NZ$120,000 (about $75,000 USD) in reparation after his appeal to be discharged without conviction was rejected. It wasn't a bad sentence, though—he *had* faced up to seven years in prison.

In 2017 he said in an interview that he was seeing a psychiatrist on a weekly basis and had given up the so-called "crazy shit." In 2020, Phil Rudd was back on the AC/DC drum throne, keeping the beat and keeping his nose clean.

CHAPTER TWO: BEEN CAUGHT STEALING

"Ah, hell...he [Bob Dylan] just stole from me. I steal from everybody. Why, I'm the biggest song-stealer there is."—Woody Guthrie

There's a popular meme showing two close-up photos of the same man. In the first, he's smiling in pure bliss. In the next, his expression has changed to convey utter shock and dismay. The text says, "When you think you're listening to 'Under Pressure' and you realize it's 'Ice, Ice Baby'." Yep. We've all been there!

To even the most untrained ear, the rip-off is unmistakable. Pop rapper Vanilla Ice, who turned out to be a one-hit-wonder, came out with "Ice, Ice Baby" in 1990 and rock fans immediately took him to task for lifting the bass line from Queen and David Bowie's 1981 song "Under Pressure." Uncredited and irate, Queen and Bowie both filed lawsuits against Robert Van Winkle (aka, you-know-who).

The bleach-blond rhyme-spitter tried to argue that there was a difference in one note but the court ruled in favor of the earlier composition and the original artists were added to the writing credits for the song. But there's a twist! A few years back, Ice revealed that he actually *bought the rights* to the song which, at the time, was cheaper than paying lawsuit damages. "Like Michael Jackson owned The Beatles catalog, I own 'Under Pressure,'" he said in an interview on the Dan Patrick Show. That means royalties are paid directly to the "Cool As Ice," rapper every time "Under Pressure" is played through a streaming platform, on the radio, on television, in a movie, or even in an elevator!

When rap and hip-hop was wending its way into the mainstream, rock and pop fans learned a new word: sampling. It's old hat now but back in the '80s there was a landmark Supreme Court case regarding 2 Live Crew's use of all of the music from Roy Orbison's "Oh, Pretty Woman." It was more than just a sample but not quite a cover. Because they rapped over the original music with different words, the use was seen legally as "transformative," which is also a form of criticism, which in turn qualifies it for Fair Use. This is exactly how the comedian Weird Al Yankovic can get away with his schtick, whether the target of the send-up likes it or not.

While a lot of early rock tunes are basically standard three-chord progressions and blues licks, rock & roll pioneer Chuck Berry initiated one of the first major plagiarism punch-ups in pop history when he sued The Beach Boys. He claimed that they nicked ideas from 1958's "Sweet Little Sixteen" and put them into "Surfin' USA" five years later. Brian Wilson took sole credit for the upbeat surf ditty but eventually, Chuck got his rightful shared credit.

Imitation has been the sincerest form of flattery for eons. Poets say, "Bad poets imitate; good poets steal." Authors say, "If you steal from one author, it's plagiarism; if you steal from many, it's research."

Some musicians aren't so generous in their assessments, though. Madonna Wayne "Pogo" Gacy, who played keyboards in Marilyn Manson's band from 1989 until 2007, took to social media to blast the late Nirvana frontman, Kurt Cobain, for fraud. The "Irresponsible Hate Anthem" composer hopped onto his socials to post a link to Blue Öyster Cult's song "Godzilla," then wrote a caption stating: "Burn in hell, Kurt." The pugnacious Pogo then posted another link to a Killing Joke track called "Eighties," with text adding: "And this is why you kill yourself... because you're a fucking thief." (Gacy took the posts down but of course, Facebook is forever.)

Let's look at the latter, first. The single "Eighties" was released in 1984. "Come As You Are" hit the airwaves in 1992. Kurt himself acknowledged that his composition sounded like the Killing Joke tune and there were some ruffled feathers when the grunge anthem was released and became a massive FM radio staple, staying on the *Billboard* Top 100 chart for months.

In the book, *Eyewitness Nirvana: The Day-By-Day Chronicle*, the band's manager Danny

Goldberg said, "We met to discuss what *Nevermind's* second single would be. We couldn't decide between 'Come as You Are' and 'In Bloom.' Kurt was nervous about 'Come as You Are' because it was too similar to the Killing Joke song but we all thought it was still the better song to go with. And, he was right: Killing Joke later did complain about it."

Killing Joke's management wrote a letter to Nirvana's reps but they didn't go ahead with a lawsuit because of financial and personal reasons. There's no doubt that legal fees can break the bank but what were the "personal" reasons? Some have said getting on the stand might have been too close for comfort, as Killing Joke's "Eighties" also sounds a lot like The Damned's 1982 track, "Life Goes On."

The riff really has made the rounds. A lesser-known band called Garden of Delight released a song in 1984 called "22 Faces," which has the same trippy guitar sound. So does a 1981 song by Bauhaus called "Hollow Hills." You'd have to take your time travel machine all the way back to 1968 to hear it again in what could be its first incarnation, "Baby, Come Back" by The Equals, which showcases a faster version of the refrain.

When all was said and done and the years dulled emotions, Killing Joke and Nirvana's Dave Grohl patched things up. Killing Joke bassist Paul Raven gave an interview to *Rolling Stone* in 2003, saying, "Yeah, Dave and I had a few laughs about that over the past year or so.

He mentioned it to me when I met him backstage at a Pantera show a couple of years back." Killing Joke's singer Jaz Coleman performed "Requiem," from their 1980 self-titled debut album, with Foo Fighters onstage, and the guys have since collaborated on a couple of other projects.

Now to BOC's "Godzilla" and Nirvana's "Smells Like Teen Spirit." No cease-and-desists there, but Kurt did say that while he agrees to the musical influence, he was going more for a Pixies feel. In 1994, he told *Rolling Stone*, "I was trying to write the ultimate pop song. I was basically trying to rip-off The Pixies. I have to admit it. When I heard The Pixies for the first time, I connected with that band so heavily that I should have been *in* that band—or at least a Pixies cover band. We used their sense of dynamics, being soft and quiet and then loud and hard." Kurt also said that when he was a kid, he listened to his dad's record collection which included Boston's "More Than A Feeling," which also inspired the grunge great.

A year after "Smells Like Teen Spirit" came out, the prince of parody, Weird Al Yankovic had an MTV smash with his video, "Smells Like Nirvana." While technically, he does not need permission, the polite parodist usually sends a request first—he got Kurt on the horn and asked if he could do a send-up of Nirvana's biggest hit. At the time, the comedian really needed a big hit of his own. His movie *UHF* tanked at the box office and he was feeling lower than Barry White's baritone. He got the band's blessing and the rest is marble-mouthed history.

"Bitter Sweet Symphony" by The Verve was released in 1997 and it was a bona fide smash. We heard it everywhere—on the radio, pouring from the neighbor's stereo speakers, MTV, the nationwide Nike commercial, the popular movie *Cruel Intentions...* it was everywhere all at once. Since The Verve had already released two albums that didn't garner much attention, the Britpop lads were over the moon... until they were in court.

The kerfuffle was over its use of five little notes from The Rolling Stones' composition, "The Last Time." It wasn't even from the better-known rock version; it was one with strings and horns recorded in 1965 by the Andrew Oldham Orchestra. What's more, that portion was written by arranger David Whitaker, who was never even credited on *any* of the recordings.

But The Verve were no thieves—they'd dutifully and legally negotiated a license to use the sample in advance. However, when their dreamy track went viral, former Stones manager Allen Klein (who owned the copyright to the band's 1960s catalog) got greedy. He decided to sue, claiming that The Verve broke the agreement when they allegedly used more of the song than they said they would. ABKCO Records, Klein's holding company, filed a plagiarism suit on behalf of himself and songwriters Mick Jagger and Keith Richards.

Then Andrew Loog Oldham, another former Stones manager who owned the actual recording that was sampled, piled on and sued the band for $1.7 million in mechanical royalties.

The Verve opted not to fight an expensive and protracted legal battle with the legendarily wily and cunning music moguls. It was just too much, so they signed away 100% of their rights, plus gave Mick and Keith writing credit for the whole song. In short, The Verve were stripped of their ownership, lost the ability to make any decisions (frontman Richard Ashcroft has said he never would have agreed to his song being used by Nike), and got bupkis in royalties. As the song says: "It's a bittersweet symphony, that's life/Trying to make ends meet, you're a slave to money then you die."

Fortunately, the ultimate outcome wasn't as dark as those lyrics. The "Lucky Man" singer finally got lucky when, on May 23, 2019, a decade after Allen died, Mick and Keith decided to sign over the rights to him. Richard Ashcroft now has sole writing credit and will receive all future royalties.

Guitarist and songwriter George Harrison was the first Beatle to snag a solo #1 on the *Billboard* charts. He did it with his catchy hymn, "My Sweet Lord." Regardless of religion, everyone was humming along to the earworm... much as they had been to the Chiffons' 1963 hit "He's So Fine." That's because both songs sound very much alike. The late songwriter Ronnie

Mack's publisher, Bright Tunes Music Corporation, filed a plagiarism suit against the pious Hare Krishna in February 1971 and the case finally went to trial five years later. The judge ruled that George was guilty of "subconscious plagiarism" but the penalty phase was delayed for yet another five years. He was then ordered to pay a huge chunk of change, but—guess who's back?—Allen Klein bought the Bright Tunes Music Corp's catalog and cut the ex-Beatle a break. The two had history since The Fab Four were once Klein's clients. Despite the discount, George was still on the hook for half-a-million bucks, so he kept the litigation party train going until 1998, making it one of the longest legal skirmishes in music history. The settlement ultimately awarded the rights to George in the U.K. and North America. Allen didn't live to see the outcome, but his estate was awarded the use of "My Sweet Lord" everywhere else in the world.

Huey Lewis & the News were everywhere in the 1980s and whether you liked it or not, you would inevitably find yourself singing along with head-bopping hits like "Hip To Be Square," "This Is It," and of course, "I Want A New Drug." Two years after the latter song came out, Ray Parker Jr., released his *Ghostbusters* theme song and toes were tapping to the same beat. No, really: the *same* beat. Rumor has it that the temp music used in the rough cut of the film was actually "I Want A New Drug" and somehow the tune burrowed its way into Parker's subconscious. Sounds legit. Regardless, Huey filed suit. The case was settled out of court with both parties agreeing to keep the settlement secret but several years later, Huey let some details slip during an interview for *MTV's Behind the Music*. Ray retaliated in court and prevailed.

The folks at Frito-Lay clearly didn't know who they were dealing with when they approached the notoriously maverick artist Tom Waits about using his song "Step Right Up" for a snack commercial—not only did he deny their request but he added that the lyrics are clearly "an indictment of advertising." So what did the multimillion-dollar conglomerate's suits do? They created a soundalike jingle and thought they could get away with it. No such luck. Frito-Lay laid out anything *but* "Small Change" when they lost the claim to the tune of $2.37 million.

Ah, Led Zeppelin... where do we start? So many songs stolen! Yes, lots of British blues-based bands that started in the '60s "paid tribute" to the American blues artists they loved and were influenced by but they sure didn't want to pay any royalties. The Rolling Stones, The Yardbirds, The Who, and so many more, got their creative juices flowing thanks to guys like Robert Johnson, Blind Lemon Jefferson, and Willie Dixon to name just a few. And let's face it: music copyright laws were murky then and many of those borrowed songs were greatly enhanced and altered. So where does homage end and theft begin? In some cases, it would take decades to get the answers.

Led Zeppelin did give some credit here and there but in at least a dozen instances, they neglected to do so. "We took some liberties, I must say," founder and guitarist Jimmy Page admitted in an interview with *Rolling Stone*. "As far as my end of it goes, I always tried to bring something fresh to anything that I used [but lead singer] Robert [Plant] was supposed to change the lyrics, and he didn't always do that, which is what brought on most of the grief." Robert was more philosophical about it all, telling *Musician* magazine in 1990, "Well, you only get caught when you're successful. That's the game."

Most of the issues stemmed from the band's first two albums, in their formative years when they were finding their musical footing and experimenting with different sounds. One simple blues tune they turned into a heavy metal masterwork is "You Shook Me," wherein Jimmy introduced his backward echo recording technique—and on that song, Willie Dixon *was* given credit. However, he was not given his due for another tune, "Bring It On Home" (a version recorded by Sonny Boy Williamson). Far from being lost in the mists of time, that song was only three years old when *Led Zeppelin I* was released in 1969. Zep was sued over a few more songs and settled the cases out of court—no doubt giving their accountants a case of the blues.

But when the sharks started circling their megahit and most career-defining song, "Stairway to Heaven," Jimmy and Robert decided to fight it out. The nearly eight-minute opus was never released as a single but that didn't stop it from becoming incredibly popular. It has been the backbone of rock radio for over 50 years, making *Led Zeppelin IV* one of the biggest-selling albums of all-time to this day. It took a while but in 2014 the lads were accused of plagiarizing the opening riff from a little-known song called "Taurus" from the psychedelic band, Spirit. The case was brought by the estate of Spirit's late frontman Randy Wolfe, who went by the name Randy California. (The singer-songwriter had died in a drowning accident in 1997.) Led Zeppelin prevailed but the case was revived on appeal in 2018. A court of appeals upheld the original verdict in 2020 and that effectively closed the case.

Nineties alt-rock band Radiohead was sued for copyright infringement in connection with their breakthrough smash "Creep" when The Hollies claimed that it stole from their 1974 song "The Air I Breathe." Songwriters Albert Hammond (father of Strokes guitarist Albert Hammond, Jr.) and Mike Hazelwood walked away with an undisclosed percentage of the publishing rights and royalties in an out of court settlement, and are credited as co-writers on "Creep."

Things took an ironic turn in 2017 when Radiohead's reps claimed that "Get Free" by

Lana Del Rey (co-written with Rick Nowels and Kieron Menzies) sounded an awful lot like "Creep." The alt-pop singer confirmed a possible lawsuit but denied any wrongdoing, taking to Twitter to say so. "Although I know my song wasn't inspired by 'Creep,' Radiohead feels it was and wants 100% of the publishing. I offered up to 40% over the last few months but they will only accept 100. Their lawyers have been relentless, so we will deal with it in court."

Radiohead's label issued a statement refuting the supposed suit, saying they were in talks but no legal action had been initiated. "As Radiohead's music publisher, it's true that we've been in discussions since August of last year with Lana Del Rey's representatives. It's clear that the verses of 'Get Free' use musical elements found in the verses of 'Creep' and we've requested that this be acknowledged in favor of all writers of 'Creep.' To set the record straight, no lawsuit has been issued and Radiohead have not said they 'will only accept 100%' of the publishing of 'Get Free.'" The case has yet to go to trial, and to date, no settlement has been reached between the two parties.

In the summer of 2022, Professor and folklorist Bruce Jackson criticized the rock duo of Johnny Depp and Jeff Beck for stealing lyrics from a convict. He publicly asserted that their rollicking blues song "Sad Motherfuckin' Parade," which appeared on the 2022 album *18*, borrowed heavily from an old toast. The spicy stanza was recited to him by an incarcerated man whom he interviewed in 1974, and the Prof put it into his book, *Get Your Ass in the Water and Swim Like Me* (and the corresponding album of the same name which came out two years later).

The rhyme is called "Hobo Ben" and the following lines appear in both works: "I'm raggedy, I know, but I have no stink/God bless the lady that'll buy me a drink" and "What that funky motherfucker really need, child, is a bath." Making matters murkier, the poem, being American folk, does not have a definitive author—the ribald refrain was related to the author by Slim Wilson, an inmate at Missouri State Penitentiary, but he's not the original writer, either.

After being publicly panned, Johnny and Jeff filed a lawsuit against the author for unspecified damages and legal fees, plus asked for a formal declaration that they did not commit copyright infringement. Their lawsuit claims that Bruce Jackson "owns no copyright in the words" to the poem, only his own recordings or transcript, which the pair insist they did not infringe. Language in their suit described Jackson's allegations as "an old-fashioned shakedown."

The complainant clapped back with his own lawsuit. "They didn't write a word of 'Sad Motherfuckin' Parade' and they are suing the person they stole it from and who caught them doing it," he told *Rolling Stone*. "From my point of view, this is like a burglar suing a homeowner because he cut his hand on the kitchen window he broke getting in."

Bruce Jackson's suit goes on to explain that he sent a letter to Depp and Beck in August of 2022 alleging that "nearly every single word" of the song was "copied from 'Hobo Ben,' including the title." He also suggested that the "inflection, tonality and rhythm" mirrored the recording he made of Slim Wilson performing the toast in the 1960s and that the dishonest duo sampled his recording to "construct portions of the vocal track." He went on to call their claim a "publicity stunt" and clarified that he did not make "formal financial demands" of the pair, adding, "any settlement monies would be donated directly to organizations that further [my] lifelong commitment to preserving African American culture and traditions." (The dueling grievances are still in their infancy as of this writing so there's no resolution to report.)

And now to the most ridiculous plagiarism lawsuit in music history: When John Fogerty was sued for sounding too much like John Fogerty! In 1985, the former Creedence Clearwater Revival frontman signed on with Warner Bros., and released a hit solo album, *Centerfield*. The LP yielded two Top 10 singles; the title track, and "The Old Man Down the Road," which was reminiscent of the Bayou-tinged rock & roll he'd become famous for in the '60s.

Saul Zaentz of Fantasy Records, who owned the rights to several CCR songs, including "Run

Through the Jungle," heard a similar sound between John's legacy material and the new tune... not to mention the sound of a cash register if his claim could be verified by a judge.

John brought his guitar to court and strummed his way to victory by demonstrating the key differences between the two songs. The "Fortunate Son" singer won the case, and his legal fees to boot.

Parliament-Funkadelic's George Clinton, along with his label, currently faces a lawsuit stemming from his claim that his band were merely hired guns and not entitled to any royalties. He, along with contemporaries James Brown and Sly Stone, created a unique form of funk music during the 1970s and George has been inducted into the Rock & Roll Hall of Fame for his singular contribution.

The estate of the late keyboardist Bernie Worrell argues that since the inception of P-Funk, the band members were integral contributors, not work-for-hire musicians under George's orchestration. What's more, a few former players allege that the impresario got them hooked on drugs so he could manipulate them into accepting substances in substitution for cold cash.

The complaint contends Clinton, through Thang, Inc., pocketed 100% of the royalties, advances, and performance fees rather than share the wealth with "the other musicians, artists, and producers who collaborated with him to write, create and record the music."

It goes on to say that "Clinton has a history of fraud, deceit, and delinquency when it comes to the performance of contracts that he has entered into on behalf of himself or his companies." There's also a reference made to the 2016 music documentary *Tear the Roof Off: The Untold Story of Parliament-Funkadelic*, in which some perturbed players (sans Bernie, who didn't participate in the film) accused their boss of plying them with drugs and then deducting the amount from their paychecks. While it's unclear how the frontman paying band members with dope instead of dollars factors into the Worrell complaint, the suit says, "Apparently, Clinton did this despite many band members not wanting drugs and needing money to provide for their families. Drug use was encouraged and pushed by Clinton." (The matter has not yet gone to trial at the time of this writing.)

There's another pending trial happening as I write, regarding handwritten lyrics stolen from Glenn Frey and Don Henley of Eagles fame. The theft occurred in the 1970s but the pages are just now turning up in connection with a case involving a curator for the Rock & Roll Hall of Fame.

Curator Craig Inciardi, rare book dealer Glenn Horowitz, and auctioneer Edward Kosinski were charged on May 12, 2022, over allegedly illegally possessing a cache of 100 handwritten notes and pages of lyrics by co-lead vocalist and drummer Henley, which has been appraised at more than $1 million. All three are accused of being involved in a conspiracy that sought to sell the ephemera, including lyrics from "Hotel California," "Life in the Fast Lane," and other songs, to potential buyers. Conversely, the defendants' attorneys claimed their clients were innocent and would "fight these unjustified charges vigorously."

Don said he has been trying to recover his property ever since it was allegedly stolen decades ago by a would-be biographer, Ed Sanders, who sold them to Glenn Horowitz in 2005. Officials said that Horowitz kept mum about his ill-gotten goods until recently when he allegedly brought his co-conspirators on board and attempted to sell the documents to high-end auction houses, including Sotheby's and Christie's—at the same time, he was trying to "coerce" Henley into buying back the property that lawfully belonged to him in the first place.

"The manuscripts were originally stolen in the late 1970s by an author who had been hired to write a biography of the band," reads the L.A. District Attorney's press release summarizing the indictment. "Despite knowing that the materials were stolen, the defendants attempted to sell the manuscripts, manufactured false provenance, and lied to auction houses, potential buyers, and law enforcement about the origin of the material."

According to *Rolling Stone*, the New York District Attorney's office began investigating the matter prior to Eagles' founding member Glenn Frey's death in January of 2016, "claiming that Horowitz hatched a plan to claim the documents had belonged to Frey, making the criminal investigation against the men fall apart. He allegedly wrote in an email that 'identifying [Frey] as the source would make this go away once and for all.' In addition to all three men being charged with one count of conspiracy in the fourth degree, which carries up to a four-year prison sentence, Horowitz faces a first-degree charge for attempted criminal possession of stolen property and two counts of hindering prosecution. Inciardi and Kosinski were also charged with first-degree counts of criminal possession."

Eagles manager Irving Azoff issued a statement saying, "This action exposes the truth about music memorabilia sales of highly personal, stolen items hidden behind a façade of legitimacy. No one has the right to sell illegally obtained property or profit from the outright theft of irreplaceable pieces of musical history. These handwritten lyrics are an integral part of the legacy Don Henley has created over the course of his 50-plus-year career."

Anyone who's seen the Led Zeppelin movie *The Song Remains the Same* will remember the dizzying, unexplained montage of news footage from the band's 1973 tour when a whole lotta loot was stolen from them while they were performing in New York City at Madison Square Garden on July 29. The incident headlined the papers and the nightly news, but the case remains unsolved to this day.

According to the police report, several stacks of $100 bills, plus passports and credit cards, had been stored in a safe-deposit box behind the desk at the Drake Hotel on Park Avenue at 56th Street, where Led Zeppelin, their management, and entourage were staying. This was standard procedure and the money was multiplying by the day as they were playing three consecutive shows at MSG in order to get enough footage for their film. Tour manager Richard Cole discovered the theft at 7:30 p.m. the night of the final gig. Everything except the passports was spirited away without a trace.

The band laid low in nearby apartments while Richard got rid of the drugs—bud, coke, and smack—in their hotel rooms. After that little bit of housekeeping, the cops were called. "New York City police and the FBI moved in to investigate, but so did the paparazzi," wrote Bob Spitz in his 2020 book, *Led Zeppelin: The Biography*. Peter Grant, the band's pugilistic and protective manager was arrested and charged with robbery and harassment for allegedly having struck a *Daily News* photographer, Charles Ruppman, and forcing him to turn over his film.

The Post reported that it was "the largest-ever hotel cash robbery in New York City," so "Some detectives wondered privately why the band had cashed its Garden-receipts check and taken the 1,800 $100 bills to the hotel," said the *New York Times* in 1973, "but a publicity man for the group, Danny Goldberg, said that the banks had been closed over the weekend and that some of the cash had been needed 'to pay off debts.'"

When it came to light that Richard Cole had the only key to the strongbox, he became the de-facto suspect in the crime. "It certainly looked to the cops like an inside job," Bob Spitz wrote. "He was interrogated and fingerprinted. Cole also said that he had taken and passed a lie-detector test. Nevertheless, he remained a primary suspect, as did a bellman."

The vintage *New York Times* story went into better detail about the hotel's security procedures and posited a different theory:

> *Detectives spent Sunday night and yesterday swarming through the elegant, red-carpeted Drake lobby at 440 Park Avenue at 56th Street questioning hotel employees and members of the band and their adoring train of groupies who might have attended the party.*
>
> *They were also exploring the possibility that the strongbox lock had been picked or that an employee had a complete set of keys. The boxes are made so that only a guest with his key*

and a hotel employee with a hotel key together can open the box.

Mr. Cole told the police that he had deposited the money in new $100 bills in the box on Friday and Saturday nights, after two concerts by Led Zeppelin at Madison Square Garden. At 1:20 a.m. Sunday, he reportedly said, he withdrew $1,200 for various band expenses. At 7:15 p.m. Sunday, prior to the group's last concert here, Mr. Cole said he returned to the box and found the money missing. The figure was erroneously given initially as $202,600.

Because the strongboxes stand along a wall in a cashier's area behind a counter, detectives presumed that a hotel employee was present when the box—#51—was opened. However, there was said to be no signature record which is usually required of anyone opening his own box.

The hotel refused any comment on the theft. Questions addressed to the management were referred to Philip Miles, vice president for public relations, who said he would have no statement during the investigation.

A spokesman said the theft would not change Led Zeppelin's plans, although detectives were unhappy at losing the chance to question the group more thoroughly.

The Spitz book went on to shine a harsh light on Led Zeppelin's manager: "No less than five sources close to the band told this author that Peter Grant had admitted to spiriting the Drake money away," he wrote. According to lore, the ridiculously rich Robert Plant and Jimmy Page just "laughed" about the missing money. "In the scheme of things, a loss of $200,000 was pocket change to Led Zeppelin, but it sure didn't look that way to the outside world."

While suspicion of Peter Grant amounts to little more than an unsubstantiated claim, there have been countless court cases against artists' managers who've embezzled every last dime from the very people whose interests they have been hired to protect.

It's a story as hoary as "that old-time rock & roll." The Beatles signed a recording contract that earned each member only one-fifth of a penny for every early single sold, and so did The Who. Badfinger founder and lead vocalist Pete Ham committed suicide in 1975, leaving behind a note that blamed the band's business manager Stan Polley for his despair, with a postscript calling the man a "soulless bastard."

Young David Bowie learned about the realities of the business the hard way after he signed a cockamamie contract with Tony Defries which reportedly gave the music manager more than 50% of the "Space Oddity" singer's earnings. The pair called it quits in 1975 but they were still entwined, with Tony snagging a share of the hitmaker's substantial income for the next seven years. While the manager certainly deserves some credit for the artist's early success, he also gets the blame for Bowie's considerable cocaine addiction in the mid-'70s. "We did mountains of cocaine, it looked like the Matterhorn, obscenely big," record producer Tony Visconti recalled in an interview. Basically, the two men were sentient lines of blow.

Wallowing in the financial fallout, the British superstar turned to drugs to numb himself from the seemingly never-ending distress. When checks started to bounce and Bowie realized he was broke, he did what any rock star would do: he took a jet from London to Bel Air, rented a mansion, and holed up for days and nights on end. His mind was a jumbled mass of manic panic and he became obsessed with the occult, burned black candles, and claimed to have seen bodies falling past his windows. He even went so far as to hire celebrity exorcist and witch Walli Elmlark to eradicate a resident demon from the backyard swimming pool.

Shunning the sun and ingesting pretty much nothing but illegal substances (plus a few red peppers and glasses of milk), David was reincarnated as the pallid, fashionable fascist, "Thin White Duke." Discarding his sparkling "Ziggy Stardust" persona and shedding the colorful "Aladdin Sane" character, Bowie began wearing monochromatic suits that draped elegantly over his scarecrow frame and he smoked German cigarettes with all the poise of a male Marlene Dietrich. The plastic bubblegum soul of his 1975 *Young Americans* LP was canned in favor of the eerie electronica of *Station to Station*—an album that he released in 1976 and later claimed to have no memory of making.

As it turned out, his old friend Iggy Pop turned things around when he checked into a Los Angeles mental institution to curb his own addictions. When Bowie visited the Stooges frontman, they agreed to help each other find the straight and narrow path back to health and wealth.

Nineteen-eighty-three's *Let's Dance* was David's first Defries-free record and it also became his biggest-selling album ever. He owned his recordings and set up an innovative bond deal that let him borrow money against income from future royalties, and lived happily-ever-after.

That is not the case for Tony Defries, who continues to fight lawsuits over his alleged questionable business scruples to this very day. In 2011, parties including Capitol Records LLC, EMI Music Inc., and Jones/Tintoretto Entertainment Co, LLC, sued him and MMRX (his legal business entity) for willful copyright infringement of musical compositions and recordings by artists including David Bowie, Iggy Pop, and John Mellencamp. The plaintiffs claim that Defries sold their songs through Amazon, iTunes, Spotify, and Napster, even though he did not own the distribution rights.

Tony lost the suit but didn't pay the piper so he was called back into court in 2019, where a New York judge ruled that he was still responsible for paying the $9.5 million judgment. The defiant rock & roll manager (who is also an attorney) vowed he'd take the case all the way to the Supreme Court if he had to.

Singer-songwriter Harry Nilsson knew everybody who was anybody; in the late '60s he'd commanded the respect of The Beatles who claimed he was their all-time favorite American musician and he was awarded GRAMMYs for "Everybody's Talkin'," (the standout song in the Academy Award-winning 1968 movie *Midnight Cowboy*), and for Best Male Pop Vocal in 1972 following the release of "Without You." Harry wrote the song "One" which was made famous by Three Dog Night and enjoyed success after success throughout the following decades. His face was on the cover of *Time* magazine and he achieved millionaire status before age 30 by landing a $5 million record deal that at the time was among the biggest ever seen.

Fast-forward to January 15, 1994, when the 52-year-old died flat-broke amid a flood of financial chaos resulting in foreclosure notices, a flurry of demand letters from no less than 75 creditors, and numerous dire warnings from the Internal Revenue Service (IRS).

Three years prior to his death due to heart failure, Harry discovered that his business manager, Cindy Sims, had been embezzling his money. Harry and his wife were forced into bankruptcy. "We went to bed one night a financially secure family of eight and woke up the next morning with $300 in our checking account," Nilsson wrote in a letter filed in court. He said that the sneaky Sims even went so far as to remove foreclosure notices from his front door so he wouldn't guess anything was amiss.

"I'm scared," Harry wrote in the court letter. "I never believed this could happen. It was my greatest fear growing up and it's still my greatest fear. I used to tell Cindy the worst thing that could happen to me would be to not have money again." The "(Put the Lime in the) Coconut" singer was forced to borrow money from friends (including Ringo Starr) so that he and his family could move into a more modest home in Agoura Hills, California.

Cindy Sims pleaded guilty to three counts of grand theft and served two years in state prison before being paroled in June of 1994, just a few months after Harry's heart gave out.

One of the most egregious instances of lowdown, shameful managerial behavior is that of Kelley Lynch, the woman who oversaw the fortunes of influential poet and folk singer Leonard Cohen for 17 years. She not only stole millions from him, but she also left several death threats on his voicemail after he sued her for the return of his own money. Leonard sued Kelley in 2005, a year after he had fired her as his manager, claiming she stole $5 million from his personal accounts and investments, leaving him with nothing.

Kelley reacted to her dismissal by calling the "Hey, That's No Way to Say Goodbye" singer repeatedly. "It started with just a few [phone calls], but it eventually accelerated to 20 or 30 a day," he testified in court. "It makes me feel very conscious about my surroundings. Every time I see a car slow down, I get worried."

The court ruled in his favor and ordered her to pay him $9.5 million, but cagey Kelley never repaid the money or faced criminal charges. Before being brought on as his manager, she had been a longtime family friend and was even a brief paramour. Although she seemed trustworthy, giving her unbridled access to the finances proved to be a major mistake—the saying "Love of money is the root of all evil" proved to be all too true.

The malicious manager was duly found guilty by a court of law but the matter wasn't over. Kelley made no payments and even went on the run, continuing to pester the "Hallelujah" songwriter from afar. So, he sued her again—this time for stalking. She was found and served, then compelled to return to L.A. to face her fate or suffer even worse legal consequences. Through the course of the proceedings, Leonard's lawyers showed the jury no less than 10 binders of printed emails and played them recordings filled with foul language and death threats. (Many of these vicious voicemails can be heard at: kelleylynchfactcheck.com/evidence.html)

Kelley's defense in the ensuing harassment case argued that the messages were "cries for help" following the 2005 court finding that she had embezzled millions because the action had "destroyed her reputation."

After winning that case as well, Leonard made a statement in his trademark poetic prose: "I want to thank the defendant, Ms. Kelley Lynch, for insisting on a jury trial, thus allowing the court to observe her profoundly unwholesome, obscene, and relentless strategies to escape the consequences of her wrongdoing," he said. "It is my prayer that she will take refuge in the wisdom of her religion, that a spirit of understanding will convert her heart from hatred to remorse, from anger to kindness, from the deadly intoxication of revenge to the lowly practices of self-reform."

The loss of his entire fortune following an enviable career that produced indelible classics like "Chelsea Hotel #2" and "Suzanne," prompted the shattered 75-year-old to go on the road again after spending a half-decade at the Zen Buddhist monastery and being basically retired. Fortunately, Leonard's ceaseless tours of Europe, North America, and Australia were massively popular, helping to get his retirement fund close to where it had been. (*Billboard* reported that the 2009 world tour alone earned nearly $10 million.)

Although Leonard Cohen passed away on November 7, 2016, his law team has reported continued harassment from Kelley Lynch as they stay on the case to collect the judgment against her on behalf of the estate.

Leonard Cohen proved that money can be replaced but when it comes to a musician's instrument being lost or stolen, it's akin to losing a limb.

There are few guitarists more closely connected to an iconic instrument than Peter Frampton and the fabled Gibson Les Paul he nicknamed "Phenix" when it rose from the ashes 32 years after being spirited away from the burning embers of a deadly plane crash. The tragedy happened on November 4, 1980, while Frampton was on tour in South America. The band's gear was put on a cargo plane in Venezuela, en route to Panama, but the aircraft bit the dust right after taking off from Caracas International Airport.

Peter later told *NPR,* "Basically I'm thinking, 'It's gone.' But the thing is, I'm also sitting in a restaurant where I can see the pilot's wife. She's waiting in the hotel for her husband, who, unfortunately, didn't make it. So we were all overcome because people lost their lives as well as our complete stage of gear."

When Peter's guitar technician went to Caracas a week after the tragedy to see what was left for insurance purposes, he learned that the tail of the plane had broken off and that there was some salvageable equipment inside. He also saw pictures of other gear that was totally burned up so it was assumed that the

Gibson Les Paul Custom was among those ruins.

He'd had the guitar for 10 years at that point, having acquired it during a four-show stint at Fillmore West as a replacement instrument. When Peter found that his current guitar wasn't up to snuff, a local musician, Marc Mariana, gave him a loaner—a three-pickup 1954 Les Paul Black Beauty that its owner modified with a few bells and whistles, transforming it into a one-of-a-kind custom model. The "Natural Born Bugie" strings man fell in love and offered to buy the Black Beauty on the spot, but Marc insisted his new friend accept the guitar as a gift. Peter played it on almost every song he recorded until the fateful year it vanished.

The ebony axe was featured on some of the musician's most memorable and multi-million-selling LPs including Humble Pie's last album, *Rock On,* sessions with John Entwistle and Harry Nilsson, and of course, his own solo smash, *Frampton Comes Alive!* The guitar was prominently featured on the cover of the latter, making it one of the most recognizable six-strings in rock history.

Since it is so familiar, it boggles the mind that whoever "rescued" the guitar from the smoking hulk of the cargo plane managed to keep it hidden for so long. No one knows who that was but eventually, the guitar found its way into the hands of a musician on the

Caribbean island of Curaçao, who proudly played it in public for many years.

At some point, it needed a tune-up so the anonymous guitarist's son took it to a local luthier for service. He just happened to find Donald Valentina, a Curaçao customs agent who repairs guitars in his spare time. Valentina immediately recognized Peter's prized Les Paul due to its unusual three-pickup configuration and put it all together when he spotted old burn marks marring the body. For the next few years, Donald, along with Ghatim Kabbara, CEO of The Curaçao Tourist Board, tried to convince the owners to sell the instrument. They refused all offers until November 2011 when they finally agreed to part with the guitar for $5,000. (Their names have presumably been withheld due to a confidentiality agreement.)

The guitar was reunited with Peter one month later. "It's sort of a matte black now," he told *NPR* at the time. "It's not shiny so much anymore." In the end, the British fret master decided to limit repairs on the instrument to "whatever needs to be replaced on it to make it just playable. But it must retain its battle scars."

The famous guitar was most recently featured in the 2022 book *Immortal Axes* by premier rock guitar photographer, Lisa S. Johnson. In the foreword, she wrote that taking pictures of Phenix "was one of the most cosmic experiences ... Peter's breath of life glinted off its restored sheen, telling the story of joy, sorrow, pain, and the resurrection of a soul mission still unfolding with its master." Lisa went on to sum up the feelings of so many other young music heads in the mid-'70s, writing, "I remember holding the *Frampton Comes Alive!* album cover in my hands, imagining what it would be like to cradle that gorgeous Gibson Les Paul in my arms."

When Canadian rocker Randy Bachman's guitar was stolen from his hotel room in Toronto in 1976, he probably thought he'd never see it again—especially as the years, turning into decades, ticked by.

It was the guitar of his dreams: a beautiful bright Western Orange 1957 Gretsch 6120, the same rare model famously played by three of Randy's most revered idols: Chet Atkins, Duane Eddy, and Eddie Cochran. Randy remembered being a teen in the early 1960s and spending his weekends standing outside a music store in his hometown of Winnipeg, Manitoba, trying to figure out how to get the $400 purchase price. He spent hours mowing lawns, washing cars, and doing every odd job imaginable so that he could one day afford to buy the Gretsch. Finally, at the age of 19, he had saved up enough. "It was years and years of dreaming about buying that guitar," Randy said.

Randy wrote anthems like "American Woman" and "No Sugar Tonight" for The Guess Who on the instrument, and the Gretsch was his songwriting partner in his next band, Bachman-Turner Overdrive, which had hits with "Takin' Care of Business" and "Let It Ride."

Needless to say, the guitarist was devastated when his beloved instrument went missing while he was recording in Toronto. It happened at a Holiday Inn and was doubly upsetting because he "always" shackled his instruments with a lock and chain when they were in his rooms... but "just that one time," it was left briefly unattended by a member of his crew. The trusted road manager reportedly put the instrument in his own room for safekeeping with the rest of the luggage while he checked out of the hotel. Within five minutes, Bachman said, his most prized possession was pilfered.

When he was told the Gretsch was gone, "I cried for three days; it was part of me," he said in a 2022 interview. "Because when you play a guitar, you hold it close and it feels your heartbeat and your breathing." Randy amassed a collection of over 350 lookalikes as he searched for "the one" but none of them matched the distinctive imperfection of his original instrument, which had a dark, circular knot in the wood.

In 2020, a diligent fan named William Long decided to play internet sleuth on Randy's behalf, and, after using special photo-enhancing software and memorizing every nick and blemish on the missing guitar, he immersed himself online. "I just got totally fascinated by this guitar," said William, who, though already semiretired, had extra time on his hands thanks to the COVID-19 pandemic-related quarantine. "Some people do jigsaw puzzles," he told the *Washington Post*. "I prefer doing real-life puzzles. I'm pretty good at going into corners of the Internet and scraping. I felt completely confident that I was going to find it."

William dove deep into every website, social media platform, and message board he could find that might have something about Gretsch guitars. "I became completely obsessed with it," he said. "I had a great time looking for it. It was fun." Within just a few weeks, he traced the instrument to the website of a music shop in Tokyo, Japan. The listing noted that the Gretsch had been sold in 2016 but it was soon traced to a guitarist named TAKESHI. The musician has produced several hit songs for Japanese pop stars and has also done scores for films, as well as TV commercials. (Incidentally, TAKESHI was born in the same year that Randy's guitar was stolen.)

William got in touch with Randy's son, Tal, whose fiancée, Koko Yamamoto, is fluent in Japanese. After some negotiation, TAKESHI agreed to return Randy's axe in exchange for a "twin sister" guitar made during the same week with a close serial number. There are fewer than 40 of those guitars in existence now, but Randy found one in perfect condition.

"I owned it and played it for only eight years and I'm extremely sad to return it now," TAKESHI admitted. "But [Randy] has been feeling sad for 46 years, and … I felt sorry for this legend." He went on to explain that the guitar really *is* special. "When I first strummed this guitar at the music shop in Tokyo, it spoke to me like no other guitar I've ever played," he said in a statement to the *Washington Post*, which was translated by Koko. "I'm so honored and proud to be the one who can finally return this stolen guitar to its owner, the rock star, Mr. Bachman, who was searching for it for nearly half a century."

The two musicians met up on July 1, 2022, (Canada Day) in Japan to exchange instruments. The pair, with their twin guitars, performed BTO's "You Ain't Seen Nothin' Yet" followed by "Rockin' Down the Highway" to an appreciative audience at Tokyo's Canadian embassy. It was Randy Bachman's first performance in the land of the rising sun since a 1995 show he did with Ringo Starr. The guitarists told the press they plan on making a documentary about the long-lost guitar, in which they will perform a new song, written by Randy, called "Lost and Found."

Another famous stolen guitar is that of California-born rocker Randy Rhodes, who wowed heavy metal lovers with his virtuosity when he performed first with Quiet Riot, then with Ozzy Osbourne. Sadly, he perished in a plane crash in 1982 when he was just 25 years old.

The Rhoads family held onto his instruments and gear and displayed them in the Musonia School of Music, an institution in

North Hollywood, California, founded by Randy's mother, Delores Rhoads. On Thanksgiving night in 2019, Randy's first-ever guitar (a 1963 Harmony Rocket), and a rare prototype signature Marshall head (an amplifier without a speaker) were appropriated from the premises by persons unknown. Various other memorabilia and gear were also taken—including a Peavey amp used by the "Crazy Train" guitarist during his time with Quiet Riot—but soon recovered from a nearby dumpster.

Following news of the theft, singer Ozzy Osbourne announced a $25,000 reward for the return of the property. "As you can imagine, the items that were stolen, including Randy's first electric guitar, are irreplaceable to the Rhoads Family. I am heartbroken that these treasured physical memories of Randy and Delores have been taken from the family."

It would take well over a year for the prized guitar and amp to finally be reunited with the family but the happy day came in May of 2021 when an anonymous person hand-delivered the irreplaceable items to the North Hollywood Police Department and did not ask for the $25,000 reward. There's been nothing published or posted by Randy's family with further information but a few instruments are still unaccounted for, including a Great Depression-era trumpet. So far, police have not made any arrests in connection to the case.

Legendary bassist Jaco Pastorius went from the highest of highs to the lowest of lows during his storied career—and the same can be said of his prized instrument, a custom-modified 1962 Fender Jazz model that he dubbed the "Bass of Doom." After it was stolen from a Manhattan park bench in 1986, it did indeed seem to be doomed to oblivion. No one saw so much as a string from it until 20 years later when the guitar turned up in a small shop on Manhattan's east side. Shockingly, the owner of the store refused to return it to the Pastorius family, and protracted legal squabbles followed for almost two years.

When Metallica bassist Robert Trujillo heard about this horrible situation, he decided to wield his star power and began a campaign to settle the case and get the de-fretted Bass of Doom back into the hands of its rightful heirs. When asked about his getting involved, Robert commented, "I felt a strong sense that it was the right thing to do for Jaco, and the family, whatever it took."

To thank him for his help, they gave custody of the bass to Robert with the agreement that if the family ever wanted it back, he would return it. In a 2013 interview with a Fender reporter, Robert revealed, "I played it for the first time at Yankee Stadium [a few months ago]. It was the first time in many, many years that it had been played in front of a New York audience." The Pastorius family was in attendance, and Trujillo chose to pay tribute to Jaco *and* the late Metallica bassist, Cliff Burton, by playing the band's iconic metal tune, "For Whom the Bell Tolls." Robert said, "That was a very special moment in my life. It was also special to the family, and it was special to the instrument."

One night in 1969, British-born drummer Alan White was making himself some stew for dinner when he got a phone call, asking him if he'd like to join John Lennon's newly-formed Plastic Ono Band. Although Alan was established and well-respected, he couldn't help but think it was a prankster doing an imitation of the Liverpudlian legend. But it really was a dream come true: the next day Alan found himself in a whirlwind, hastily learning songs in the back of an airplane headed to a gig in Toronto with John, Yoko, Eric Clapton, and Klaus Voormann.

After that, Alan's association with John Lennon was cemented; that's him playing the drums on "Imagine," "Instant Karma," and "Jealous Guy," to name a few. He also pounded the skins for George Harrison on his well-regarded solo album, *All Things Must Pass*. Twenty-three-year-old Alan joined YES in 1972 and with only three days to learn the music (are you sensing a pattern here?), the prog-rock group debuted their newest addition at a show in Dallas, Texas, which kicked off their Close to the Edge Tour. He stayed with YES for decades, guest-starred with countless other famous bands over the years, and was inducted into the Rock & Roll Hall of Fame in 2017.

Like most musicians, Alan White kept certain instruments that had significance to him—his custom "Plastic Ono Band" Ludwig Silver Sparkle drum kit was among his most treasured artifacts so he kept it under lock and key in a temperature-controlled, high-security storage space near his home in Newcastle, Washington.

On March 24, 2022, while Alan and his wife Gigi were on vacation, squatters broke into their house and lived there for several days. With plenty of time on their hands and dishonesty in their hearts, the lowlifes rummaged through the couple's files until they hit the jackpot—before that, they had no idea whose home they had invaded.

Criminals Chad Briner and Frederick Estes Jr., (also known as "Shadow") found the information they needed to get into the Whites' storage unit so they could rob it. They dispersed the items among friends to sell but the police managed to recover a triple-platinum record, a silver electronic keyboard, a Ludwig drum case and drum stand, plus other music-related equipment... but the kit was nowhere to be found.

The Silver Sparkle's storied history includes the fact that the Foo Fighters' late drummer Taylor Hawkins once played it during a charity event, meaning that Alan and Gigi White received terrible news twice on the same day: "We found out on Friday, on March 25, that the kit was missing *and* that Taylor had passed. So we were a little numb, shell shocked," Gigi told Seattle's *King 5 News*. "Taylor was so loved. I don't know a person who knew him who did not absolutely love and adore him, including us." As for the kit, "It is part of Alan's heart. I mean, that's his history."

Alan White was devastated over the loss of his heirloom and his already fragile health took a sudden turn for the worst—he died in his home just two months later, on May 26, 2022.

The kit is still missing and so are the suspects, who've been charged but not apprehended.

In 2011, My Chemical Romance drummed out their drummer Michael Pedicone due to his alleged stealing. The band posted a statement on its official website:

"The relationship between My Chemical Romance and Michael Pedicone is over. He was caught red-handed stealing from the band and confessed to police after our show last night in Auburn, Washington. We are heartbroken and sick to our stomachs over this entire situation. The band has no intention of pressing charges or taking this matter any further than we have to. We just want him out of our lives. The people who play in this band are a family, and family should not take advantage of each other like he did. We are currently moving forward, and hope

*to have a new drummer in place for our show in
Salt Lake City, Utah. The show must go on."*

The sticky-fingered sticks man responded
on Twitter, writing, "What happened is more
complicated than it sounds but I did make a
mistake. It was never my intention to hurt this
band or all of you." Although speculation has
run rampant for years now as to what Michael
stole—Merch money? Drugs? Gerard Way's
guyliner?—whatever it was remains a mystery.

While some nightmare nannies are
notorious for stealing husbands' hearts, a temp
was accused by Skid Row frontman Sebastian
Bach of swiping his wife Suzanne Le's pricey,
diamond-studded wristwatch in 2016. The
couple hired the still-unidentified woman from
an agency to watch their three-year-old son,
Trace Rox, at a hotel in Memphis, Tennessee,
while they went out on the town. Suzanne said
she tucked the timepiece away in a drawer and
later discovered it was missing. A police report
was filed but it appears the Chanel J12 H1009,
valued at $16,000 was never recovered.

One of the most unique and ubiquitous
items ever stolen from a rock star was a private
and personal sex tape made by Mötley Crüe
drummer Tommy Lee and his then-wife,
Baywatch star Pamela Anderson. It happened
in late 1995 when a disgruntled former
employee named Randy "Rand" Gauthier
retaliated against the Lees following a dispute
over payment. Rand decided to get his money by

hook or by crook—and became the latter one night after sneaking into the couple's massive Malibu mansion to steal an entire safe. Without knowing what was inside, he left Tommyland toute de suite and, cracking the six-foot-tall Browning at home, Rand found some obvious valuables—jewelry, Pam's white wedding bikini, guns—but there was also a mysterious Hi-8 videotape. He later played the tape and got an eyeful of the it-couple doing "it" on their honeymoon.

Rand, who is the son of actor Dick Gautier (Hymie the Robot in the TV series *Get Smart*), had previously worked in the porn industry in front of the camera but by the mid-'90s, he was down on his luck. As such, he decided to go for the gold rather than do the right thing. Because of Rand's connections in the adult film world, Tommy and Pam's intimate home movies were released to the public.

The steamy video quickly went viral as pay-per-view websites showcased it and VHS dubs were sold for $59.99 a pop. Within just one year, an estimated $77 million in revenue came pouring in—a figure well above the $20,000 the couple owed the crooked contractor for his renovation work. Of course, Gauthier had to split that money with his shady partners, one of them being a dangerous, mafia-connected smut-peddler who distributed the world's first mainstream triple-X film, *Deep Throat*, in 1971.

The Lees tried to just ignore the whole thing until, according to *Rolling Stone*, they got a heads-up that *Penthouse* had the tape and planned on running screenshots in an upcoming issue. On March 26, 1996, the couple filed a $10 million lawsuit against the magazine, plus complaints against everyone they thought had the tape, including Rand Gauthier. According to an item in *Mail on Sunday*, the former *Playboy* model was "heartbroken and embarrassed" by the tape's release, which happened while she was pregnant with her first child (she'd miscarried a few months before the theft of the tape).

Surprisingly, their legal complaints were thrown out of court by a judge after *Penthouse's* lawyer argued that since the couple often talked about their sex life to the media, and because Pam had posed nude before, the Lees had "forfeited their privacy rights." Of the 54 minutes caught on tape, only eight of them show the pair having sex. "We made it for ourselves on our honeymoon. We got home and put it in the safe. It wasn't something we discussed with anyone. It was just for fun, for us," Tommy said.

After a long and rocky road of fighting, giving in, and even trying to join forces with a distributor, Pam and Tommy maintain that to this day, they've never seen a dime for their pilfered performance. The Lees divorced (and later reconciled, then split) and oddly enough, Pamela went on to marry (and divorce, and remarry) movie producer Rick Solomon, who is most famous for co-starring in celebutant Paris Hilton's "leaked" sex tape in 2004.

Beginning in the mid-1980s, and continuing off and on for decades, Lewis Peter "Buddy" Morgan stole the identities of Eagles band members in order to sample the rock star life. When he started pulling the fast one there was no Internet, no smartphones, and few ways for the average person to verify his whoppers. At first, he tried Don Henley on for size—but the singer's successful solo career and MTV music videos made Buddy think twice. Especially after he got pinched. He somehow raised the $50,000 bail and went on the (long) run.

Next, he decided to be Eagles bassist and singer Randy Meisner, who left the band in 1977 and was, by all accounts, the shyest member (to the point that he sang his signature hit, "Take It to the Limit," off to the side of the stage, as close to darkness as he could get). Randy had been keeping a low post-Eagles profile, so not many people remembered or knew what he looked like.

Throughout the years, Buddy finagled guitars to sell or pawn from luthiers and manufacturers, grifted cash from Eagles fans with a concert ticket scheme, got free dinners out of music lovers, and conned women not only out of money but their clothes as well.

A cleverly titled *San Francisco Gate* exposé, "Fake It to the Limit," was written by Jack Boulware in 1998 and delved into the personal side of the scams. "The voices of [his] female victims resonate with unspoken humiliation.

The tones of their speech seem to ask questions they don't necessarily put into words, but undoubtedly have asked themselves: *How could I let my self-esteem plummet so low as to go to bed with some guy twice my age, just because he had a hit song 20 years ago? Was I so eager to do it that I even loaned him money?*

"There is one creepy question, however, that most of the women do get around to asking out loud: *How many other women were involved?* The only single person who could know the answer to that question has probably forgotten because each of these women represents only a small sliver of a life that has involved decades of grifting across the country."

After being sentenced to 16 months in California's San Quentin State Prison in 1998, the illegal Eagle insisted that the claims against him had been "fabrications," and that the monetary count was "inflated." But he was a longtime petty thief whose record stretched back to 1963, who stole and conned in order to fund his gambling habit.

San Francisco Police Department officer Curtis Cashen, who'd been after "Buddy" Morgan for four years, said, "If he had continued with Don Henley, I think people would have caught onto him a lot faster. To go to Meisner was an excellent choice." As Las Vegas historian Nolan Dalla, put it, "Meisner is certainly no Mick Jagger. He's not even a Bill Wyman." The real Randy Meisner released a statement at the time, saying, "I'm just so happy that they finally caught him. Hopefully, he'll learn his lesson and quit."

Buddy didn't quit; he was next spotted in his favorite gambling town, Las Vegas, in 2006. This time he had a young accomplice who was impersonating Mike McCready, the guitarist of Pearl Jam. (More than likely, it was a man named John Harlan, who had been arrested for impersonating McCready all over the nation.)

"Everyone was eating out of their hand," Nolan Dalla, who witnessed the swindle, wrote in his blog, "with no idea they should have been choking on lies." The fake Randy Meisner handed out guitar picks with "his" name on them, regaled gullible groupies with "insider" stories on the recording sessions for "Hotel California," and more. Nolan, who knew what was up, wound up scamming the scammer by inviting him to a fancy meal, then pulling the old "dine and dash" routine, sticking Buddy with the bill—a small but well-placed karmic kick in the nards.

There hasn't been a sighting of Lewis Peter "Buddy" Morgan (who would now be in his 80s) for several years... seems he's a prisoner of his own device.

CHAPTER THREE: I AM THE GOD OF HELLFIRE!
"Fire... bad!"—Frankenstein's Monster

Showman Arthur Brown and his band, The Crazy World of Arthur Brown, had a hit in 1968 with their frenetic psychedelic rock tune, "Fire." Putting his money where his mouth was, the frontman would wear a crown of flickering flames onstage, flirting with disaster in highly flammable grease paint on his face, which was decorated in black and white as a skull. The song began with a clarion call of, "I am the God of Hellfire!" then the music would come flooding in. Known as the Shaman of Shock-Rock, the British-born singer also wore flowing robes that were wont to catch fire while he gesticulated onstage—one time, in Windsor, his hellfire helmet went up in flames but bystanders quickly poured their beers over Arthur's head and he went on to finish the gig only slightly singed.

After Arthur came Gene Simmons of KISS, who also performed painted in black and white with flames flowing. But the man who was born Chaim Witz in Israel took things a step further by breathing fire like a character straight out of an old-fashioned freak show. During his debut of the now-famous stunt on New Year's Eve 1973, in New York City, the "Heaven's on Fire" singer accidentally spewed his kerosine against the wind and set his heavily-sprayed coif alight. It happened while the band was performing a song called, appropriately enough, "Firehouse." A quick-thinking roadie smothered the flare with a wet towel and Gene lived to see 1974. But the bombastic bassist kept on with his blazing belches and suffered many minor mishaps along the way. But hey, even Gene would say, "That's showbiz!"

Blackie Lawless of W.A.S.P. was "the" bad-boy of the 1980s—part hard rock, part glam, part hair-metal, part Marquis de Sade—but at some point, the platform-booted, leather-and-spandex clad frontman decided to ditch his trademark circular buzzsaw codpiece for one that shot fire. I mean, what could possibly go wrong with sizzling hot fireballs next to your... er, balls? As the old joke goes, "It worked in rehearsals," and it did, but Blackie neglected to take into account what might happen when compressed gunpowder met altitude. The band flew from the U.S. to Ireland, where they planned on unveiling the new gimmick onstage in Dublin. When the "Blind in Texas" singer pulled the cord, a blinding inferno exploded the codpiece, catapulting Blackie a foot and a half off the floor and igniting his trousers—giving a whole new meaning to the term "hotpants." Later, as he nursed his burns backstage, he winked at his bandmates and quipped, "If we wrote better songs, we wouldn't have to resort to stunts like this."

While W.A.S.P. didn't make the news for their errant inferno, there was nothing *but* international media coverage when Michael Jackson became a human sparkler during the filming of a Pepsi commercial at the Shrine Auditorium in L.A., on January 27, 1984. As he danced next to a fireworks display, the apparatus malfunctioned and sent a shower of sparks raining down on the singer's slick, pomaded Jheri curls. Laser-focused on his "Billie Jean" routine, Jacko was at first oblivious to the fact his skull was ablaze—but as the live audience of 3,000 fans gasped in horror, the Jackson band rushed to their brother and smothered the fire, which had spread to his sequined jacket after consuming his hair. MJ suffered second and third-degree burns and subsequently wore a hairpiece when collecting his GRAMMYs later that year.

Pepsi settled out of court, and Michael gave the $1.5 million award to the Brotman Medical Center, where he had been treated (prompting a change to the current name, Michael Jackson Burn Center). Still, that didn't stop the King of Pop from endorsing the soda pop—he later signed another publicity pact—not for a measly $700,000 though... this time he took home $10 million. Advertising exec Phil Dusenberry, who was the endorsement deal conduit, jokingly titled his memoir, *Then We Set His Hair on Fire: Insights and Accidents from a Hall of*

Fame Career in Advertising. It's no joking matter, though, that this painful accident is what set Michael on his path to pill addiction.

Metal mavens Metallica usually let their guitars do the screaming but when lead vocalist James Hetfield found himself too close to one of the 12-foot towers of flame meant to impress the audience, you can bet he was cursing a blue streak. It happened during the band's Wherever We May Roam tour at Montreal's Olympic Stadium on August 8, 1992, where they were headlining along with Guns N' Roses. Fortunately, his guitar shielded him from the brunt of the blaze. But the fire engulfed his left side, burning his hand, arm, eyebrows, face, and hair. The "Master of Puppets" singer suffered second and third-degree burns and was rushed to the nearest hospital.

The audience was freaked out and restless, so tour promoters called Guns N' Roses' manager asking if he could get them to start their set early. They did, but fussy frontman Axl Rose had a hissy fit over sound issues and left the stage, causing a full-on riot from the 53,000-strong audience. "I go and light myself on fire," James later said, "and he upstages me."

Rammstein formed in Germany in 1994 and before long, their unique blend of dark, driving techno and industrial metal was taking headbangers all around the world by storm. Not to be outdone by guys who've only set their hair on fire, frontman Till Lindemann is a licensed pyrotechnician who spends entire songs shrouded head-to-toe in flames. Band brother Christoph Schneider has revealed that the process is not without danger, though: "Till gets burned all the time, but he likes the pain." So metal.

As many documentaries and in-depth reports attest, Woodstock '99 was a dumpster fire. Literally and figuratively. There were many dumb decisions made, but perhaps the most boneheaded was when organizer Michael Lang (who also fronted the original Woodstock 30 years earlier) handed out candles and matches to an already angry and angsty audience at the tail-end of the three-day debacle. That was the last, but not the first, flameout; Haitian rapper Wyclef Jean was playing with fire on day two of the festival when he decided to channel Jimi Hendrix by setting his guitar alight after playing "The Star-Spangled Banner." Unfortunately, he inadvertently used his fingers as kindling. Worse, Wyclef flubbed the tribute—Jimi's famous sacrificial Strat fire happened at the Monterey Pop Festival, not Woodstock. Whoops!

While filming the music video for "Famous Last Words" in 2006, My Chemical Romance drummer Bob Bryar came close to uttering his. In a scenario straight out of *This is Spinal Tap*, the band was posed amidst glowing embers in an atmospheric wasteland when Bob's pants caught fire. (MCR has gone through a half-dozen drummers so maybe there *is* a *Spinal Tap* connection, after all.) The injury required skin grafting and the wound got infected, forcing the guys to cancel three shows while the "Black Parade" drummer healed. Four years later, he retired due to chronic wrist pain and became a real estate agent.

One of the most horrible incidents of pyrotechnics gone wrong involves the hard rock band, Jack Russell's Great White. It happened at the Station Nightclub in Rhode Island, New York, on February 20, 2003, and by the time the dust settled, 100 people were dead, including the group's new guitarist, Ty Longley, who was just 31 years old and an expectant dad.

The original Great White formed in 1977 and were made superstars via MTV videos in the 1980s which sent their singles "Rock Me" and "Once Bitten, Twice Shy" into the stratosphere. That incarnation of the band stayed together until 2001, then was reimagined and renamed to put a spotlight on its frontman, Jack Russell. But their heyday was in the rearview mirror and they were reduced to playing small clubs. Station Nightclub had a 250-person capacity but an estimated 400 were packed full to the gunnels.

Just a few minutes after the band launched into their first song, "Desert Moon," pyrotechnics ignited by their tour manager, Daniel Biechele, caused a rising fire to lick the back of the stage. Jack, seeing the flames behind him, tried to douse them with cups of water but they weren't very effective. No one realized at the time that the foam soundproof insulation was shoddy and that the fire would spread as quickly as it did. At first, everyone was orderly; patrons headed for the front doors, and the band went through a fire exit near the stage.

The front doors were clear but as the flames rose, so did the terror. A bottleneck formed when a bouncer blocked patrons' egress through the stage door and since two of the four exits had been chained shut, there was nowhere else to go. People began to panic, screaming and trying to shield themselves from exploding liquor bottles and wood beams falling from the ceiling. Individuals caught fire and trampled others in their desperation to get to the open air. Unedited, amateur video posted on YouTube shows the whole horror from beginning to end— about seven minutes—from the last note played by the band to the final screams of the dying mingled with the sirens of approaching firetrucks.

The club owners reportedly used non-fire-rated packing foam for soundproofing and then sprayed it with toxic paint. There weren't any clear exit markers, there wasn't an automated sprinkler system, and the employees later testified that they hadn't received *any* fire or safety training. What's more, tour manager Daniel, who wasn't trained in pyrotechnics and didn't have a permit, used outdoor-rated fireworks inside the packed club.

One hundred people died, and 115 survivors were badly burned, maimed, or permanently disfigured. Guitarist Ty Longley initially escaped unscathed but he returned to save his guitar and apparently found himself in a fatal firetrap, where he perished. He left behind his wife Heidi, who was three months pregnant with the couple's only child. Their son Acey Ty Christopher Longley went on to become a musician, and he runs a charity for hospitalized children in his dad's memory.

Daniel Biechele eventually pled guilty to 100 counts of involuntary manslaughter and served two years of his 10-year sentence in a Rhode Island prison before being paroled. Lawsuit settlements totaling $176 million were paid out to survivors and victims' families by the manufacturer of the soundproofing foam, as well as by radio stations and alcohol brands that sponsored the venue. Jack Russell Touring Inc., agreed to pay $1 million to survivors of the fire and victims' relatives with the stipulation that they wouldn't admit to any wrongdoing. Charities raised $3.8 million to help.

While the horror of the Station Nightclub tragedy helped bring better awareness in the U.S. of the dangers of pyrotechnics in small, flammable venues, a similar tragedy happened in Bucharest, Romania on October 30, 2015. The club, Colectiv, had opened just a few months before, and the band, Goodbye to Gravity, was giving a free concert to celebrate their forthcoming album, *Mantras of War*. The metalcore band was formed a few deafening years earlier by vocalist Andrei Găluț, winner of a Romanian "Idol" type show called *Megastar*. Along with guitarists Vlad Țelea and Mihai Alexandru, drummer Bogdan Lavinius, and bassist Alex Pascu, he announced that the album release party and performance would include customized lighting, pyrotechnic effects, and scenic elements meant to "give life to the science fiction artwork" of the new album.

The fire, which turned out to be the deadliest in the country's history, was started by outdoor-only sparkler firework candles that ignited the club's flammable polyurethane acoustic foam. Along with 62 fans, four of the five members of Goodbye to Gravity died in the mishandled melee. Guitarists Mihai Alexandru and Vlad Țelea were pronounced dead on the scene, while drummer Bogdan Enache and bassist Alex Pascu perished shortly thereafter in the hospital. Thirty-one-year-old Andrei Găluț lived but he was severely injured with burns covering 45% of his body.

Some musicians saved the pyrotechnics for later... much later. Like, after they were dead. I'm not talking about your run-of-the-mill cremations. Gram Parsons, the charismatic young singer of L.A. country-rock outfits The Byrds and Flying Burrito Brothers, once told his road manager, Phil Kaufman (affectionately known as "the road *mangler*"), that he'd love a Native American funeral in the Mojave Desert, complete with a flaming pyre. He probably thought that day was far, far off, but when the 26-year-old died of an overdose in the desert town of Joshua Tree, California, on December 19, 1973, his wish came true—sort of.

When Phil heard that his friend's body was to be flown to New Orleans to be buried in the hated family plot, he put a plan into action that would honor Gram's wishes. The long-haired hippie got behind the wheel of an old, borrowed Cadillac hearse, and drove directly to the Los Angeles International Airport where the casket containing the "Sin City" singer was on the tarmac waiting to take flight to the Big Easy. Kaufman, who later recalled he was drunk on Jack Daniels and was wearing a rhinestone cowboy hat, somehow managed to convince the authorities that there'd been a change of plans and he would be taking control of the situation.

He and another friend of Gram's, Michael Martin, signed the release paperwork with fake names, and off they went with the coffin rattling in the back of the Caddy. "Our whole team was me and Michael, assisted by Jose, Jack, Jim, and Mickey"—meaning, Jose Cuervo tequila, Jack Daniel's whiskey, Jim Beam bourbon, and Mickey's Bigmouth beer—"We were pretty well-oiled," Phil recalled, years later. They hit a wall on their way out, garnering the attention of an airport cop who walked over to the car's driver's side window and tsked, "I wouldn't want to be in your shoes now," then let them go on.

The drunken duo stopped at a petrol station in Cabazon near the Interstate 10 dinosaurs, where they filled their tank and a gas can, then headed to Joshua Tree with Gram still secured in his coffin. They drove off into the chilly desert night, not stopping until they reached Cap Rock in The Joshua Tree National Monument, a landmark geological formation, where they unloaded their precious cargo at about 1 a.m.

"We opened the back of the hearse," Phil said, "and the casket dropped as Michael was pulling it out. Michael was really edgy but I decided we had to say goodbye to Gram, so I opened up the casket. And the hinges obviously hadn't been oiled, so it creaked really loud. Then there he was, laying naked, with surgical tape covering where they had done the autopsy. We used to do this thing, you know, when you're a kid, where you point to someone's chest, they look down and you go 'zip' up to their nose? Well, that was the last thing I did to Gram.

"Then I poured the gasoline all over him and said: 'All right, Gram, on your way...' I struck the match and threw it onto the gasoline. And when you do that, it consumes an enormous amount of oxygen and makes a big 'Whooomph!' As we were watching, the body actually bubbled, and then we saw his ashes flying up into the night. Then we saw some headlights approaching from across the desert. We thought it might be the park rangers so we beat it out of there."

The paranoid pair peeled out, quickly hightailing home to L.A., but they were involved in a car accident as soon as they arrived. A police officer who was on the scene noticed empty alcohol bottles in the hearse and handcuffed Phil and Michael to each other. They managed to escape and ran off on foot.

"When we got back to my house, I got somebody to cut the handcuffs off," the tour manager recalled in an interview that was later published by *LouderSound.com*.

The flaming coffin was inevitably discovered and the next morning's papers were full of stories suggesting that the "Hot Burrito #1" singer's body had been the victim of some sort of satanic ritual. But word soon got around about who did what. "As it happened, Arthur Penn and Gene Hackman were shooting some scenes for a film called *Night Moves* at my house," when Phil Kaufman was arrested. "As I'm being taken to the cop car, Hackman and Penn are standing watching and they asked [my girlfriend] what was going on. When she explained, Arthur Penn said: 'Gene, we're shooting the wrong movie here.' Later, when I was driven home, they stopped filming and everybody gave me a round of applause." (There was a movie made 30 years later—not by Arthur Penn—called *Grand Theft Parsons*, which starred Johnny Knoxville as Phil Kaufman.)

Phil and Michael appeared in court on what would have been Gram Parsons' 27th birthday, November 5, 1973. Since there was no law against stealing a corpse at the time, the faithful friends were charged with misdemeanor theft of the coffin, which was valued at $700. They were also slapped with fines totaling an additional $600.

Steve Marriott was small in stature but big in voice, personality, style, and talent. In 1965, when he and his also-diminutive friend Ronnie Lane were just 17, they formed a band they called Small Faces—the first part being self-explanatory, while "face" was slang for being a good mod; someone with the right clothes, the right haircut, and the right taste in music.

Years of toil and paying dues were not in the cards for the lads from London. Within a matter of weeks, the Small Faces were gaining a solid fanbase and they were signed to a management contract by the formidable Don Arden (Sharon Osbourne's dad) and had their debut album put out by Decca Records. The catchy tune "Itchycoo Park" was among their early hits.

Steve quit the band at the end of 1968, storming off the stage during a live New Year's Eve gig after yelling, "I quit!" Shortly after, he formed a new, harder-rock group, Humble Pie, with guitarist and singer Peter Frampton. Humble Pie had a good run, finally breaking up in 1975, leaving Steve free to pursue a solo career.

Marriott was revered by his peers—his colossal voice and six-string virtuosity were legendary—but the "All or Nothing" singer's difficult personality and penchant for booze and pills kept him from achieving major, sustainable success. Eventually, he lost everything and was forced to perform in small pubs to make ends meet. At one point in his life, the former chart-topper was reduced to recycling glass bottles for pocket change.

The "30 Days in the Hole" hitmaker fathered at least four children with various women but seemed to be settling down in the late 1980s when he married his third wife, Toni Poulton—what's more, his former bandmate Peter Frampton wanted him to play on an upcoming album.

But it was not to be. Forty-four-year-old Steve Marriott died on April 20, 1991, when a fire ignited by a cigarette he'd dropped in a drunken stupor swept through his 16th-century home in Arkesden, Essex. The series of tragic events was set in motion the day before when, while flying home from the U.S. where Steve and Peter worked on some songs, Steve started drinking and popping valiums to calm his comeback jitters. Toni later recalled that her husband fell into a foul mood and picked a fight while in flight.

After arriving in the U.K., a friend picked them up at the airport and they went to one of Marriott's favorite restaurants for dinner, where he drank to the point of being blotto. The couple returned to their friend's house and decided to stay overnight since it was late. But even while in bed, Steve continued to pick at Toni. She finally fell asleep but later woke to discover that her husband had taken a taxi home.

At about 6:30 the next morning, a passing motorist saw the roof of the Marriotts' historic cottage ablaze and quickly called the fire department. It was reported that four fire engines were needed to put out the raging inferno.

Assistant Divisional Fire Officer Keith Dunatis, who found Steve's lifeless body, gave a heart-wrenching account to the press: "It was a tough fight getting upstairs. We searched the bedroom areas and it was very hot, we knew immediately that no one could have survived the fire. We began to feel around the walls and discovered him (Steve Marriott) lying on the floor between the bed and the wall. I would say he had been in bed and tried to escape. As soon as I saw the body clearly, I knew who it was. I used to be a fan, so it's difficult to put my feelings into words. The scene was horrific in that corner of the room. I saw him lying there and thought what a pity it all was. I deal with many fires but this one was like walking down memory lane. We managed to salvage all his guitars and musical equipment. I feel a bit upset; all the firemen do. It was like seeing part of our lives gone forever."

Toni Marriott's life plummeted downhill from there. Three years after her husband's death, the 45-year-old was sentenced to five years in prison for drunkenly killing her passenger, Penny Jessup, 21, when she crashed her Vauxhall Astra GTE.

During sentencing, the judge told Toni Marriott that he had no option but to send her to prison. "By your irresponsible behavior, you abruptly brought to an end the life of a young woman of 21, causing those near to her, and in particular her parents, untold pain, suffering, and misery which they will have to live with for a very long time." He went on to chastise the rock widow for an earlier drunken driving incident that had killed her own sister, Joanna, just yards from the site of the second fatal crash. "Although that offense occurred over 10 years ago, I would be failing in my duty if I ignored it. You have shown yourself to be a menace and a danger to the public, brought about, in my view, because of your drinking problems." Toni was sentenced to time behind bars, plus banned from getting behind the wheel of a car for an additional 10 years.

Florida-born rocker Tom Petty moved to L.A. to record an album in 1974 and he never looked back. The "Learning to Fly" songwriter put down roots in the City of Angels but faced hellfire on May 17, 1987, when an arsonist attempted to burn his Encino mansion to the ground with him and his family inside. While Tom, his then-wife Jane, and their five-year-old daughter were eating breakfast and discussing how they'd celebrate Jane's birthday that afternoon, they started to smell smoke.

Following the scent, which included lighter fluid, Tom discovered a wooden staircase at the back of the estate engulfed in flames and got everyone out—his housekeeper suffered minor injuries when her hair caught fire but it could have been a lot worse.

According to the *Los Angeles Daily News*, the fire grew in ferocity because of the wooden accents and roof. It ultimately caused $1 million in damages but somehow, Petty's basement recording studio survived intact. Regardless, "He lost everything," publicist Mitchell Schneider said at the time. All his keepsakes, memorabilia, photographs, and even the family's clothes, went up in smoke. What a heartbreaker.

Tom, who never received any threats in advance, was rattled for years afterward, even as the house was rebuilt. Like all good artists, he took inspiration from the event and wrote a hit song, "I Won't Back Down." Refusing to be intimidated, he had a new home built on the exact same site, preserving the untouched basement studio.

When Tom and Jane divorced in 1996, she got the house but owed more than it was worth and she wound up filing for bankruptcy. The home went to the bank, then various owners and tenants (one of whom had to be evicted by a SWAT team). Fans got a peek inside the posh, rebuilt, remodeled sprawling, three-story estate through realty websites when it went on the market in 2013 (ultimately selling for over $2 million, then changing hands a few times, most recently with a nearly $5 million price tag).

There's fire, and then there's getting fired— an entire book could be devoted to rockers who've gotten the boot. The Beatles (Pete Best), the Stones (Brian Jones), Black Sabbath (Ozzy Osbourne), Metallica (Dave Mustaine), AC/DC (Brian Johnson), Pink Floyd (Syd Barrett), Fleetwood Mac (Peter Green), and many more have all said buh-bye to band members.

"Rock Star" isn't your run-of-the-mill 9-to-5 and you don't see many ads for the title on *LinkedIn* but nevertheless, if you are one, you've got to show up and do the work. Casual attire, drinking on the job, and playing loud music is encouraged but there is a limit to the licentiousness. Even guys who *started* their bands, like Brian Jones and Syd Barrett, who probably thought they'd be riding the gravy train with biscuit wheels forever and a day, have been given their walking papers.

Perhaps the most famous, and earliest, example of a band jettisoning one of its core members is that of The Beatles and their first drummer, Pete Best. He was there for the first two years, playing countless shows in England and Germany before hitting it big. After recording the single "Love Me Do" in 1962, the lads from Liverpool dismissed him and hired Ringo Starr. Rumors went around saying that Pete was given the heave-ho because he was better looking than the other guys, upstaging them with all his female fans. Producer George Martin poo-poohed the notion, stating that Pete just wasn't the best on drums.

Although he was a founding member and integral part of The Rolling Stones, multi-instrumentalist Brian Jones was let go in 1969 for his excessive drug use. I mean... if Keith Richards thinks you're taking too many drugs, you probably do have a problem. Sadly, Brian died just one month later, becoming an early member of the infamous 27 Club.

One of the most famous firings is that of vocalist Ozzy Osbourne from heavy metal forerunners, Black Sabbath. Even though he wailed on hits like "Paranoid" and "Iron Man," his wild ways eventually wound up showing him the door. Sabbath went on with various lead singers but Ozzy had the last laugh with a wildly successful solo career and major celebrity status that continues to this day.

Aussie rockers AC/DC paid their dues and worked hard with songwriter and vocalist Bon Scott year after year and were about to break big after their album *Highway to Hell* was released in 1979. But Bon died and Brian Johnson was brought on for their massive breakout record, *Back in Black*. Brian belted out the band's most killer tunes for decades but in 2016 he was let go because, a spokesman for AC/DC said, he was going deaf. His fellow bandmates didn't even tell him to his face; they did it via phone. Brian later told *Alternative Nation* that it was tough to hear (cue the rimshot). "It's like being shot on the battlefield, it's just your turn. The lonely feeling, a lot of it is self-inflicted. For me, I'll be quite honest with you, I went into my office and buried my head in a bottle of whiskey, good whiskey."

It could have been worse—the AC/DC powers-that-be kicked bassist Mark Evans to the curb in 1977 on his 21st birthday. The ax came down during a backstage party for him, complete with a decorated cake bearing his name. Shocked and devastated, Mark left the festivities without saying goodbye. "I bailed out from the party. I said, 'Fuck this!' and took off," he recalled in an interview years later.

Even though he bashed bass on some of AC/DC's best albums (*T.N.T., High Voltage, Dirty Deeds Done Dirt Cheap*, and *Let There Be Rock*) his former band brothers still had one nasty surprise for Mark. In 2002, when it was announced that the metal mavens would be inducted into the Rock & Roll Hall of Fame, the "Big Balls" bassist's name was included, along with the late Bon Scott... but six weeks later, his name was stricken without explanation and he was not invited to the ceremony on March 10, 2003.

It's bad enough to get the bum's rush on your birthday but imagine being fired in a mass execution on your 50th anniversary—Mike Love certainly didn't live up to his last name when he axed *three* Beach Boys O.G.s (Brian Wilson, Al Jardine, and David Marks) during their 2012 Silver Anniversary tour. The "Good Vibrations" musician attempted to explain himself through a press release sent to the *L.A. Times* but it wasn't well-received.

Brian Wilson responded with an *L.A. Times*-published missive of his own which read, in part, "While I appreciate the nice cool things Mike said about me in his letter, and I do and always will love him as my cousin and bandmate, at the same time I'm still left wondering why he doesn't want to continue this great trip we're on. Al and I want to keep going because we believe we owe it to the music. That's it in a nutshell; all these conversations need to be between the shareholders, and I welcome Mike to call me."

The cousins' Shakespearian scuffles date back to 1966 with the recording sessions for the classic album, *Pet Sounds*, which Wilson ruled with an iron fist. There is also the issue of who actually wrote the Beach Boys' songs—Brian gets the lion's share of the credit, which Mike says is "almost certainly the largest case of fraud in music history." Mike has taken Brian to court on numerous occasions and in 1994, he won a suit that gave him a $5 million payday and retroactive songwriting credits on 35 tunes, including the distinctive hit "I Get Around." He was also awarded the "Beach Boys" name which resulted in him having the power to fire Brian, Al, and David on that fateful day.

The notoriously noxious Dave Mustaine was the lead guitarist for Metallica for only a couple of years but his dismissal from the titans of metal was grand, to say the least. One day in 1983 he got on his bandmates' last nerves, so they grabbed him and his gear, chucked him into a car, and drove him to the Port Authority Bus Terminal in New York. They brought in former Exodus guitarist Kirk Hammet on the very same day—and he's still with them. Soon after, Dave settled in L.A., where he formed the hugely successful thrash-metal band Megadeth.

Scott Weiland was the lead singer of the grunge outfit Stone Temple Pilots off and on for decades until 2013 when he found out from a press release that he was out for good. The remaining guys in STP claimed that Scott sabotaged the band's 20th-anniversary tour by repeatedly skipping promo appearances, turning up late for concerts, and using them to boost *his* solo career. Scott OD'd two years later, dying at the age of 52.

Steven Adler, who drummed for Guns N' Roses from 1985-1990 was drummed out of the hard-rocking band for his excessive drug use and chronic inability to maintain the beat during live shows. A few years later, another band member got canned: On October 31, 1996, lead singer Axl Rose faxed the offices of MTV to announce that guitarist Slash had been fired due to disloyalty in favor of his side-project, Slash's Snakepit. Other GN'R guys have come and gone but as of 2022 the core members are all on tour and playing to sold-out crowds.

Michael Anthony played bass for Van Halen from their inception in 1974 until 2006 when

Eddie Van Halen decided to replace him with his 16-year-old son, Wolfgang, for their David Lee Roth reunion tour. The ultimate insult came later when Van Halen remastered and released their first six albums; of course, Michael played on all of them but the official website photoshopped him off the covers of *Van Halen* and *Women and Children First*. They even put Wolfgang's image where Michael's was, even though he was born 13 years *after* their first album's debut!

"I couldn't figure out what they were trying to do except to brainwash the fans into thinking I was never in the band," the miffed Michael told *Rolling Stone* at the time. "That bummed me out quite a bit. I'm proud of all my history with Van Halen, and maybe they feel otherwise."

One of Pink Floyd's most memorable album covers is 1975's *Wish You Were Here*, which was created by the legendary design agency, Hipgnosis. It bears a photo of two suited businessmen shaking hands on the Warner Bros. studio lot—and one of them is engulfed in flames. There was no photoshopping; stuntman Ronnie Rondell, Jr., was really roasting. He was protected by a fire-retardant layer underneath his suit, which extended over his head underneath a wig, but after being lit up and photographed for 15 frames, things started to sizzle. "The flames were blown back and ignited his real mustache for an instant," Hipgnosis co-founder and art director Storm Thorgerson later recalled. "A close shave, one might say."

Art rockers Pink Floyd famously fired their co-founder, the brilliant but troubled Syd Barrett, in 1968 after he fried his mind during countless LSD (lysergic acid diethylamide, also known as acid) trips. Roger Waters and David Gilmour, along with the rest of the groundbreaking band, brought their music to the masses in the '70s with bestselling albums like *Dark Side of the Moon* and *The Wall*. But it seems keyboardist Richard Wright hit a wall during the sessions for the latter album due to his escalating drug use. Or at least, that was the party line—according to Bob Ezrin, producer of *The Wall*, Richard was "a victim of Roger's almost Teutonic cruelty. No matter what Rick did, it didn't seem to be good enough for Roger" and he was pink-slipped. He did return to the band, but things were never the same. Wright went to "The Great Gig in the Sky" on September 15, 2008, after a battle with lung cancer.

Ex-Jane's Addiction guitarist Dave Navarro lasted a grand total of one album—1995's *One Hot Minute*—with the Red Hot Chili Peppers before being bounced due to "creative differences" and being so high during a rehearsal that he crashed into an amp. "I honestly couldn't play a fucking note," he later admitted. "I fell... like, I literally tripped into stacks of speakers and storage gear and whatever. [It was] pretty clear, that I wasn't going to be able to get it together so, they decided to go a different direction. And [guitarist John Frusciante, whom Navarro had replaced] was clean and wanted to get back in the band."

Don Felder was the lead guitarist of Eagles from 1974 until his termination from the band 27 years later. (With a hiatus in between when the band broke up before returning in 1994 for their Hell Freezes Over Tour.) Don had a hand in writing much of their music, as well (including the iconic and overplayed hit, "Hotel California"). The Eagles' easygoing, laid-back music and image were belied by their personal conflicts, massive egos, and notorious infighting. Don responded to his dismissal with litigation demanding a $50 million payout, was countersued, and the results of the settlement remain sealed and secret to this day. The strings man hasn't been crying over it, though; he's enjoyed successful collaborations with Foreigner, REO Speedwagon, and Styx, saying, "It's like a family [and] It's just fun rock & roll. There's no hissy-fits, drama, or egos."

Fleetwood Mac is another band beset by inner turmoil and multiple personnel changes. Guitarist, vocalist, and songwriter Lindsey Buckingham has been in and out so many times there might as well have been a revolving door in the recording studio. The "Go Your Own Way" guitarist joined the group in 1974 along with his then-girlfriend Stevie Nicks, but left in 1987.

He rejoined in 1996 for a reunion tour and hung in there until getting the axe in 2018 because, he said, he was told, "Stevie never wants to be on a stage with you again." Nicks fired back with a statement published through *Rolling Stone*: "It's unfortunate that Lindsey has chosen to tell a revisionist history of what transpired in 2018 with Fleetwood Mac. His version of events is factually inaccurate." The whole kerfuffle was settled out of court in short order, just a couple of months after Lindsay Buckingham sued.

Sammy Hagar was fired from Van Halen in the mid-'90s, shortly after they wrote a song for the disaster film, *Twister*. Although the announcement was made that he quit, the Red Rocker made no bones about the shocking situation in a 2022 interview with *Rolling Stone*. "I was fired. I was told that I quit by Eddie. It was Father's Day, Sunday morning, at 9 a.m. The phone rings and I'm laying there with my brand-new baby. He goes, 'You know, you always just wanted to be a solo artist, so go ahead and be one. We're going to get Dave back in the band.' And when he said that, I flew up out of bed like I'd seen a ghost." Wow. Way to ruin a man's holiday, Eddie. (Fortunately, the former bandmates patched up their hard feelings prior to EVH's death due to cancer on October 6, 2020.)

Bassist Kelli Garni was fired from Quiet Riot in 1978 after he fired a gun in the general direction of his bandmates. "Randy [Rhoads] and I argued over whether we should kick out [vocalist] Kevin DuBrow. People say that during that fight I tried to shoot Randy and that is not true," he said in an interview with *The Metal Voice*. "I fired a bullet through the ceiling. The bullet went nowhere near Randy Rhoads and in no way would I ever try to kill my best friend. And yes, a pretty good fistfight happened—a rather violent one. Randy left my house bleeding pretty badly and so did I. But that is what friends and brothers do; they roll around on the ground, beat each other up and that's all it was."

The fisticuffs resulted in Kelly's walking papers. "I was kicked out of Quiet Riot because of this," he said. "I have no problems saying that. Once I started to pull a gun out, the management said, 'He is out-of-control,' which I agree ... I deserved to get fired—totally deserved it."

All's well that ends well, even if it takes 43 years to get there; Kelli Garni happily shared the stage in Las Vegas with the current lineup of Quiet Riot on New Year's Eve in 2021.

CHAPTER FOUR: LUNATIC FRINGE

"One cannot accomplish anything without fanaticism." —Eva Perón

For every famous musician basking in the spotlight, countless nobodies are lurking in the shadows. Most are harmless but sometimes a fan becomes a fanatic. Madonna, Britney Spears, Shania Twain, Taylor Swift, and Lady Gaga have all dealt with stalkers but this petrifying pastime isn't limited to fixating on pop princesses.

Perhaps the most famous—and tragic—obsession is that of wannabe rock star Charlie Manson and his warped worship of The Beatles. When the crackpot cult leader was arrested in 1969 for his part in the heinous crimes known as the Tate-LaBianca Murders, he blamed the Fab Four, telling the district attorney, "It's The Beatles, the music they're putting out. These kids listen to this music and pick up the message. It's subliminal."

Charlie took *The White Album* title literally, believing it predicted an impending global race riot. And, like any good megalomaniac, he put himself at the center, saying that he alone held the key to world domination. When the uprising didn't happen, he hoped to push his agenda to fruition by ordering the deaths of the richest white folks he could find and then blaming Blacks for the crimes.

Charles Milles Manson was born November 12, 1934, in Cincinnati, Ohio to a 15-year-old juvenile delinquent, Kathleen Manson, and a married man, Colonel Walker Henderson Scott Sr., who had to be sued to acknowledge his bastard son (but the pair never met; Walker, an alcoholic, died of cirrhosis of the liver at the age of 44). After his mother was sent away for armed robbery, young Charlie spent his formative years in juvenile reformatories and in prison for crimes that included petty larceny, burglary, auto theft, pimping, and just like Mom, armed robbery.

When he was set free in 1967, the convict moved to the ultimate destination for peace and love, San Francisco, California, where he attracted a committed cluster of hippie followers who hung on his every word. They migrated to L.A. and by 1968, Charles Manson was the head of "The Family," a communal cult dedicated to sex, drugs, and rock & roll.

Ever since he was a boy, Charlie enjoyed writing songs and listening to music. More than anything, he wanted to be a singing sensation and he gave it a go when he was in L.A., connecting with The Byrds' manager, Terry Melcher. The music mogul strung the wannabe along, then reneged on his tacit promises to record him. So, the aspiring star set his sights on The Beach Boys as well.

After the band's drummer, Dennis Wilson, picked up a couple of Family girls hitchhiking, he was introduced to Charlie and eventually recorded one of his songs, "Cease to Exist" and put it on The Beach Boys' 1969 LP, *20/20*. However, they renamed it "Never Learn Not to Love," and changed the lyrics and arrangement to the point that they didn't feel the need to give the guru credit. An infuriated Manson felt so betrayed as a result, he ordered his girls to trash Dennis' home and steal everything they could carry. The "California Girls" composer got off easy.

Using fringe psychology and occult proclamations of doom-and-gloom—not to mention mind-numbing drugs and *The White Album* played over and over—the puppet master continued to preach about the coming of an apocalyptic race war that would devastate all except for The Family, who would be poised to take over the world and all its riches. Manson's followers claimed to have sent telegrams, written letters, and made phone calls to Apple Records to invite The Beatles to join them before the race war, but they didn't receive any response.

In August of 1969, chosen disciples of The Family carried out eight high-profile, sacrificial murders over the course of two nights. The most famous victim was the beautiful blonde actress Sharon Tate, who was the eight-and-a-half-months-pregnant wife of renowned film director Roman Polanski. The 26-year-old was tortured and stabbed to death in her rented Benedict Canyon home along with three guests—the house on Cielo Drive had only recently been vacated by none other than Terry Melcher. Another victim, 18-year-old Stephen Parent, was found murdered in his car; he'd been headed off the property when the killers arrived. Chosen at random, middle-aged married grocery store chain owners Leno and Rosemary LaBianca were viciously slain in their Los Feliz home the next night. Messages echoing song titles and lyrics from *The White Album* were written on the walls in the blood of the victims.

The Manson Family was responsible for two other deaths in the summer of 1969, those of guitar teacher and drug dealer Gary Hinman, and Donald "Shorty" Shea, a horse wrangler on the derelict movie ranch The Family called home.

The resultant trial of the counterculture cultist and his followers in 1970 attracted national attention. Although he wasn't present while the killings were carried out, the wild-eyed false prophet was sentenced to death for his coercion of the crimes.

As for The Beatles' take on the whole nightmare, they have all spoken out. "It has nothing to do with me," said John Lennon in a 1980 interview with *Playboy*. "Manson was just an extreme version of the people who came up with the 'Paul is dead' thing or who figured out that the initials to 'Lucy in the Sky with Diamonds' were LSD and concluded I was writing about acid."

Paul McCartney gave an interview in 2000 for the book *The Beatles Anthology* saying, "Charles Manson interpreted that 'Helter Skelter' was something to do with the four horsemen of the Apocalypse. I still don't know what all that stuff is; it's from the Bible, 'Revelations'—I haven't read it so I wouldn't know. But he interpreted the whole thing [and] arrived at having to go out and kill everyone. It was frightening because you don't write songs for those reasons." George Harrison added, "It was upsetting to be associated with something so sleazy as Charles Manson."

Ringo Starr knew Roman Polanski and Sharon Tate personally and expressed his distress over her awful death. "It was upsetting. I mean, I knew [them] and—God!—it was a rough time. And it stopped everyone in their tracks because suddenly all this violence came out in the midst of all this love and peace and psychedelia. It was pretty miserable, actually. And everyone got really insecure; not just us, not just the rockers. But everyone in L.A. felt: 'Oh, God, it can happen to anybody.' Thank God they caught the bugger."

When all was said and done, years after the fact, Charles Manson revealed in an interview that he really wasn't into The Beatles anymore. "I am a Bing Crosby fan," he said. (His favorite

song? It had to be "White Christmas.")
Following the abolition of capital punishment in California in 1972, Charlie Manson's sentence was commuted to life in the penitentiary. He was repeatedly denied parole and died in a Bakersfield prison on November 19, 2017, at the age of 83.

Over time, the cult of Manson stayed strong as his legend grew, catapulting him into the pop culture zeitgeist. His image could be seen on book covers and tee-shirts, and his lyrics lived on in the mouths of bands like Guns N' Roses, who covered "Look at Your Game, Girl," a ballad that was written in 1968. The song was recorded as a demo to play for Terry Melcher and it was ultimately released on Manson's post-murders debut album, *Lie: The Love and Terror Cult* (1970). When GN'R released the song in 1993 on *The Spaghetti Incident?* there was a backlash.

Detractors and fans alike felt that it was in poor taste and they worried that the convicted kook would profit from album sales; but Geffen Records made sure that the money went to Bartek Frykowski, who was 12 years old when his father, Voytek Frykowski, was stabbed 51 times, bludgeoned 13 times, and shot twice, in the Cielo Drive bloodbath. (In an eerie echo of his dad's death, Bartek committed suicide by blade in Lodz, Poland, on June 8, 1999, while he was a guest at the mansion of an actress, Karolina Wajda.)

One of Charlie Manson's most devoted followers was Lynette "Squeaky" Fromme—a waifish redhead whose seemingly harmless appearance hid a diabolical and murderous mind. Her most famous fixation made the news with her intent to assassinate the then-President of the United States, Gerald Ford. The 27-year-old was convicted and sentenced to life in prison on November 19, 1975, but earlier that spring when she was free and Led Zeppelin was on tour, Squeaky was writing disturbing love notes to "Stairway to Heaven" guitarist Jimmy Page. The band's publicist, Danny Goldberg, recounted in his memoir *Bumping Into Geniuses* that he threw the letters away and never showed them to Jimmy.

Page became the target of another stalker two decades later while on tour with vocalist Robert Plant in a post-LZ endeavor, aptly named Page & Plant. While Jimmy was playing "Kashmir" onstage at The Palace in Auburn Hills, Michigan, on March 31, 1995, a former fan wielding a Swiss Army pocket knife tried to slash his way through security but was quickly subdued. Still, 23-year-old Lance Cunningham Alworth cut two concertgoers on his way to the band from Section 223, which was located behind the stage. In the melee, the inept instigator accidentally wounded himself with the knife before being cuffed and taken into custody.

Cunningham's intentions were clear, according to Police Chief John Dalton. He told reporters the assailant "said he was going to 'off Jimmy Page,'" and added that before finding religion 18 months before, he'd been a fan of Led Zeppelin, whose music he now described as "satanic." (Apparently, murder was A-okay in the Michigan man's newfound spiritual beliefs.) The young man was charged with three counts of felonious assault and one count of aggravated assault.

Jimmy Page was oblivious to the would-be attacker's proximity at the time, only finding out about the assassination attempt after the concert. The "Trampled Underfoot" songwriter had seen his share of tragedy, not the least of which was the accidental overdrinking death of Led Zeppelin bandmate John Bonham on September 25, 1980, at Page's estate in Windsor, England, known as the Old Mill House. The 31-year-old skins man died of pulmonary aspiration when he vomited while passed out in an upstairs bedroom.

Sadly, John "Bonzo" Bonham was not the first person to die of misadventure at one of Jimmy's residences. Just a year and one month before, 26-year-old photographer and sometime house-sitter, Philip Churchill-Hale, died of drug-induced vomit inhalation at Page's stately Plumpton Place, a 58-acre estate in East Sussex, England, which included a home studio where Jimmy was mixing what would become Led Zeppelin's final studio album, *In Through the Out Door*.

The guitarist tried to dodge testifying at the inquest into his employee's death citing stress, but the coroner, John Dodd, wouldn't accept any excuses. The guitarist said that on the night of October 23, 1979, Philip and a friend came over and had a few drinks. The friend went home, and Jimmy said he left Hale to take a two-hour business call that lasted until 3 a.m. After that, Jimmy said he told his friend that he was going to go to bed and Philip asked him if he could stay the night. The impromptu houseguest brought his host a hot toddy and according to Jimmy, his last words were, "You're the most eccentric man I've ever met." With that, the photographer retired to one of the guestrooms.

Jimmy's housekeeper, Barbara Spencer, told the inquiry that she arrived at the moated Elizabethan manor to begin work at 9 a.m. Her employer was in the kitchen, but having been up for several hours, Jimmy decided to go back to bed shortly after her arrival. As far as Barbara knew, houseguest Hale was peacefully asleep in a bedroom known as "the Black Room." At around 2:30 p.m., the maid tried to wake Philip but found him unresponsive. Rather than calling for help, she went to the bar, poured Page a brandy, and woke him with the bad news.

The autopsy revealed high levels of cocaine, heroin, alcohol, and morphine in the young shutterbug's blood but his death was caused by inhalation of vomit and not an overdose. The coroner concluded that Philip Churchill-Hale "had everything to live for" and ruled out any possibility of suicide. Sadly, he was just another casualty hanging out on the rock & roll fringe.

Even before he was murdered by a so-called fan, John Lennon had his share of stalkers. In 1978, teenage brothers Greg and Ritchie Martello broke into John and Yoko's co-op apartment in the historic Dakota building, just hoping for a glimpse of their idol. Greg, now an attorney practicing in New York City, gave an off-the-cuff interview in 2018 to freelance entertainment reporter, Lauren LaMagna. He said that as he and his brother were roaming the halls looking for Lennon's 7th-floor unit, they were intercepted by Ono. Rather than calling the police, she offered the boys a job working in the office.

"It was my first day and I was the first to meet [John]. I saw him and he saw me and my jaw dropped," Greg remembered. "I went up to him and he charged at me, pointed a finger at me, and said, 'You're the guy that broke security!' I thought my idol was mad at me! But then he smiled and said, 'It's a pleasure to meet ya, kid. You got guts.' That's what I love about him. In his heart, he knew we were [just] kids."

In the beginning, the job consisted of opening fan mail, filing, and babysitting the couple's young son, Sean. Greg stayed on to work with Yoko after John was shot and killed. "It was terrible. There was a change in the air. In the beginning, we took away all the newspapers and turned off the TV because Sean didn't know and Yoko wanted to tell him her own way. There were thousands of fans chanting and singing outside and we lived in that for weeks; we tried to be there for them. Much less than employees but more as family. They lost a father and husband, the world lost an idol, and I lost a friend."

Greg worked for Yoko for a couple of years then went to law school. But they stay in touch. "I went with Yoko to Iceland for what would have been John's 70th birthday. We went to a light ceremony. Ringo was there and a lot of other celebrities. I get a Christmas gift from Yoko every year along with a *handwritten* Christmas card."

Beatle George Harrison didn't fare as well with his own break-ins. There were two separate incidents in December of 1999. The first stalker, 27-year-old Cristin Keleher, broke into his unoccupied Maui mansion on the 23rd, slipping in through an unlocked sliding glass door. George and his wife Olivia were not home at the time, so the brazen fan baked a pizza taken from the house's freezer, drank a bottle of soda, and called her mother in New Jersey. Her presence triggered an alarm, and the police were soon on the spot.

When the cops arrived, they found Cristin calmly doing her laundry. When asked why she had broken in, she replied that she "had a psychic connection with George" and thought it would be okay with him. She served four months in jail for the crime, which was the culmination of "years" of stalking the "Something" songwriter.

Sadly, Cristin struggled with untreated mental illness, became homeless, and died seven years later in a murder-suicide at the hands of her boyfriend, also a transient, Stanley Merchant, 48. Their shot-gunned bodies were found by a hiker in Truckee, California.

Only one week after the incident in Maui, another fan broke into George's Victorian mansion in Britain. George, his wife Olivia, and their 21-year-old son Dhani were all sleeping in their Friar Park home when the uninvited guest popped in for a visit. But this deranged dude didn't bring his laundry—no, he brought a knife with a wickedly sharp six-inch blade.

Thirty-four-year-old Michael "Mad Mick" Abrams said he had been receiving messages from a higher power, telling him to kill George Harrison. According to court reports, the perpetrator "believed that The Beatles were witches who flew around on broomsticks." Subsequently, George Harrison possessed him and he had been sent on a mission by God to kill him. He saw George as a sorcerer and a devil." What's more, the ex-junkie saw himself as "the fifth Beatle" and was convinced Harrison was the "Phantom Menace" (a figure from the writings of Nostradamus).

The paranoid schizophrenic bought a train ticket from his home in Liverpool to swanky Henley-on-Thames, a six-hour ride to the north, then made a beeline to the sprawling, wooded estate of the Harrisons.

"The mansion is a massive, curious, neo-Gothic Victorian built in 1889, comprising 62 eccentric acres of caves, grottoes, underground passages, an Alpine rock garden with a scale model of the Matterhorn and a multitude of garden gnomes that were used on Harrison's *All Things Must Pass* album cover photo," wrote John Steward, reporting for *The Day*. "After John Lennon's murder, a high-tech security system had been installed, monitored by guards based in a security booth at the front gate. The estate walls were topped with razor wire."

It was 3:30 a.m. on December 30th when Abrams scaled those walls, slipped by security, then got into the fortress by breaking a window with the wing of a statue of St. Michael sculpted by George's wife. The couple heard the noise, got up, and George peeked into the hallway to investigate. At first, Olivia later said, they thought maybe a chandelier had fallen and shattered.

The unstable stalker came out of the darkness, charged, and overpowered the "All You Need Is Love" guitarist. A quick-thinking Olivia called the cops, then she grabbed a handy fireplace poker and "hit the guy several times, and I could see the blood spreading down his blond hair, and then he got up, and he chased me. He had me around the neck and George got up and jumped on his back."

That's when the recently-released mental patient put his evil murder plan into action, throwing George Harrison to the floor and stabbing him mercilessly and repeatedly in the chest.

"I could feel the strength drain from me," the hitmaker later recalled. "I vividly remember a deliberate thrust of the knife into my chest." With a collapsed lung and a deep wound a mere two inches from his heart, he felt and tasted blood flooding his mouth. "I believed I had been fatally stabbed," he said, adding that he was terrified that he'd suffer the same horrible fate as his fallen bandmate.

Olivia continued to whack at the intruder and he leaped at her, waving the knife, carving a bloody gash across her forehead. But Mad Mick was weakening from the California-born artist's repeated blows and he finally collapsed, giving Olivia an opportunity to disarm him.

Responding to the emergency call just moments after it was made, two constables rushed into the house. They found a gory scene, items in disarray, and the victims in a state of shock. Olivia was clinging to the banister of the staircase, and George lay on the floor. An officer took the would-be assassin into custody as he helpfully screamed, "I did it! I did it!"

Paramedics arrived and rushed Harrison to the hospital. His injuries were severe, leading to the partial removal of one of his lungs. But he handled the situation with his customary grace and wit, telling reporters that the attacker "wasn't a burglar, and he certainly wasn't auditioning for The Traveling Wilburys." (They were a supergroup comprised of Harrison, Bob Dylan, Roy Orbison, Tom Petty, and Jeff Lynne.)

The ex-Beatles star had a tough time of it in his final years—just before the terrifying attack, he had had surgery for throat cancer and was treated for a brain tumor. On November 29, 2001, after searching for a cure in Switzerland and the U.S., George Harrison died of metastatic non-small cell lung cancer. The devotee of Hindu beliefs left the mortal coil in peace while surrounded by his loved ones in band brother Paul McCartney's L.A. home. He was just 58.

Michael Abram was determined "unable to stand trial by reason of insanity" after three psychiatrists diagnosed him with paranoid schizophrenia and psychosis. Still, he was found guilty of two counts of attempted murder and was committed to a medium-security psychiatric hospital for a relatively short period. Recalling the attack, he was contrite. "Afterwards, I was happy that I had done it. It was 'mission accomplished.' At that stage, I cannot say that I felt that I wanted him dead but I was glad that I had scared him.

"[Now] I am deeply embarrassed about the terrible thing that I did. I feel very guilty about it but I cannot turn back time and all that I can say is that I am very, very sorry. Given the chance, I would like to explain to him (Harrison) what happened to me so that he could understand. I do wish he could understand that it was not my fault. Physically, I did it but I was not in control of my mind. I tried to get treatment from the hospital but they turned me out. He (Harrison) is a very kind, caring, and understanding man. I would love to think that he might be able to see it from my point of view but I do not think he ever will."

According to the latest update, Michael Abram, a father of two, is still living in his hometown of Liverpool and has stayed out of trouble.

In her 1998 autobiography *Somebody to Love?* Jefferson Airplane songstress Grace Slick recalled two persistent stalkers she dealt with shortly after giving birth to her daughter with bandmate Paul Kantner. Baby China was born on January 25, 1971, in San Francisco. Although the trio lived in a safe, upscale neighborhood, two different men broke into the house on separate occasions, because, they claimed, they were China's real father.

"Sure, being famous can be fun, but when you have to resort to bodyguards, killer dogs, armored cars, and Fort Knox security systems, it makes you wonder," wrote Grace. "Today, my own home is situated so that there's no way to get to it except through an electric gate that closes behind anyone who enters. And if they look scary, I press a button and the gate becomes electrified, meaning that if you touch it, you're toast. Nice and friendly, but I was robbed three times in my relatively well-protected Mill Valley house. This time around, I've made a vow: no robbers, intruders, paparazzi, or nuts (except me) get in or out without searing results. Welcome to the modern world."

Serial stalker Karen Jane McNeil purportedly set her sights on Guns N' Roses frontman Axl Rose, Metallica drummer Lars Ulrich, and solo superstar Justin Timberlake. The 35-year-old began her obsession tour in April of 1995 when she boarded a plane from Ohio to California after hearing a "psychic call" from Axl. She found out where he lived in Malibu and set her phaser on "stalk." She illegally entered his home while the "Welcome to the Jungle" chart-topper was sitting in his kitchen, playing guitar. Karen might have thought the serenade was for her but the next thing she heard was police car sirens. However, that didn't deter the ardent fan, who violated restraining orders time and time again over the years and finally spent a year behind bars in 2000 for her trouble... and wrote him several letters from there. In 2009 Karen did double duty, harassing Justin Timberlake and Lars Ulrich simultaneously—both were granted restraining orders.

Former Zep singer Robert Plant got himself a girlfriend in 2010, though he'd never actually met the woman—Alysson Billings purportedly began telling friends that she was in a relationship with the "Tall Cool One" singer but things didn't turn dangerous until Robert started dating folk singer Patty Griffin in 2013. It took three years before a threat assessment triggered his request for a restraining order. That's when the miffed wannabe mistress started sending the star disturbing messages and strange packages that included hotel room keys and dead flowers. One note that was released to the public via court records read, "Your betrayal with another woman still stabs my mind," adding, "This woman is literally evil for you and your life. She's got you so pussy-whooped and henpecked, it makes me want to puke! You are about to fall for that evil old crotch. And I'm not joking: I cannot, will not, and shall not live this way anymore." The restraining order and beefed-up personal security did the trick and there's been no more stalking reported, even after Robert and Patty broke up.

Eleven years before he died tragically by his own hand in 2017, Linkin Park lead vocalist Chester Bennington was the target of a single-minded cyber-stalker who commandeered his online accounts, email, and PayPal, and phoned him and his wife at all hours of the night, saying things like, "I know where your kids are," and "I have complete control of your lives."

For months, the couple was harassed and so were all their friends and family, whose email addresses and phone numbers were stored in online address books. Talinda Bennington was taunted and called a "whore" by the stalker during relentless, middle-of-the-night phone calls. Passwords were changed and complaints were made, but law enforcement was of no help in catching the person the Benningtons called "Crazypants."

Finally, the couple turned to Konstantinos "Gus" Dimitrelos, a former Secret Service Agent with a black belt in judo and a school of hard knocks degree in computer forensics. The hacks and calls were quickly traced through an IP address to an employee workstation at Sandia National Laboratories, a highly secured nuclear weapons facility in Albuquerque, New Mexico.

Dimitrelos and his associates went directly to Sandia to confront the hacker. As it turned out, the villain was computer technologist Devan Townsend, 27, an obsessive and loopy Linkin Park fan who was the unwed mother of an infant son. When confronted, Devan said she committed the crimes and made the threats because she was "bored." Apparently, her Q-Level Security job at Sandia took about half an hour a day, and she was looking for other ways to pass the time. (I guess she never heard of Candy Crush.) When they found her, she was wearing a Linkin Park hoodie and had a band sticker in her work cubicle. A search of her home revealed a "shrine" to the band, and Chester in particular.

Devon confessed and laid out how she engineered the whole thing. The stalking started when she saw Chester's email address inadvertently cc'd in a mass mailing to promote a tattoo parlor he owned. Using Chester's birthday and zip code to access his Mac.com account, she took stabs at possible passwords until she found the right one which was his middle name: Charlie.

"Crazypants" suddenly had access to all of her idol's voicemails and messages and gathered other information from there, including private family photos of his young children. Townsend soon had everything at her fingertips: Social Security numbers, friends' emails and physical addresses, calendars, passwords, and more.

When she heard that Chester would be performing in Arizona, she got backstage through private information and "just happened to" meet him—she kept a snapshot of herself proudly posing with the unwitting "Numb" singer.

Even after Townsend's arrest, the heavily pierced and tattooed frontman stayed rattled and on edge. "When you find out some total stranger has personal pictures of your kids in the bath, has the phone numbers of your parents and close friends and every business associate, listens to every voicemail you've had for the last year, intercepts every email you've written or received … it fuels my desire to make sure this kind of action is viewed as criminal," he said in an interview with *Wired*.

Although she got too close for comfort, at least Chester's stalker was living in another state. That was not the case for R&B singer Cindy Birdsong, who became the target of a maniacal maintenance man that worked in the building where she lived. The beautiful and talented songstress rose to fame in 1967 when she left Patti LaBelle & the Bluebells and replaced co-founding Supremes member, Florence Ballard.

On December 2, 1969, the 30-year-old vocalist was kidnapped while unlocking the door to her Hollywood apartment. She was with her then-boyfriend (later husband) Charles Hewlett and their friend, Howard Meak, when they were forced inside at knifepoint by the intruder. The lovesick "long-haired hippie type" criminal made Cindy tie up the two men with electrical cords and their own neckties then forced her downstairs and into her car. Charles and Howard quickly got free and phoned the police.

Meanwhile, as the car sped down the highway, the terrified "Take Me For A Little While" singer managed to unlock the car door somewhere in Long Beach. When she sensed the driver slowing down she jumped out of the vehicle, which kept on going. She "raced along the freeway shoulder in the direction of oncoming traffic," according to an *Associated Press* article, and "was spotted within moments by California Highway Patrol Officers Jerry Miller and Ken Miles who placed her in their cruiser, where she fainted. Miss Birdsong was rushed to memorial hospital where she was treated for minor knife wounds and abrasions, then released."

Four days later, on December 6th, 28-year-old Charles Collier, who had a prior record, contacted the authorities from his hiding place in Las Vegas and turned himself in. A judge sentenced him to five years in prison for the kidnapping and theft of the car.

Cindy Birdsong continued her music career but eventually retired to become a nurse, where she worked at UCLA. She returned to singing briefly, then became a minister. She is currently in her 80s and still lives in the L.A. area.

Stevie Nicks came close to being kidnapped in 1998, after a deranged devotee—who'd recently been released from a Denver mental health facility—bought a ticket to her July 21st concert in Englewood, Colorado, and planned on taking more than just a souvenir home.

Despite being barred from going anywhere near the "Stand Back" singer by a Los Angeles Superior Court judge, 38-year-old Ronald Anacelteo turned up, ticket in hand, but security barred him and his ticket was refunded. Ronald believed that 50-year-old Stevie had supernatural powers and could cure his homosexuality and schizophrenia by carrying his child.

Sheriff's investigator Dan Davis told the press shortly after the averted crisis that "Anacelteo said he has stalked Nicks since the

1970s and has approached the stage several times. He believes that Nicks has the power to heal him and that he will be able to absorb this spiritual power if he is able to get close to her. He also said he wants to make babies with her."

On September 24, 2008, Christian Tarantino, a filthy-rich New York gym owner, was arrested for the dirty deed of orchestrating three murders—his former business partner, Vincent Gargiulo, was the last to go down. The victim, who was the brother-in-law of Twisted Sister's Dee Snider, was shot in the face by a hired hitman in August of 2003 as he walked to work at a construction site in Manhattan. It happened shortly after he'd threatened to expose Tarantino in two previous killings—and he was true to his word, even from beyond the grave, as his tape recording was anonymously mailed to NYPD homicide detectives a few months later. Dee supported his wife, Suzette, throughout the trial and the subsequent retrial, which took place in May of 2012. The malevolent mastermind was sentenced to life in prison.

Popular Detroit, Michigan, radio disc jockey and personality John O'Leary, 67, was found dead with multiple stab wounds outside his Highland Park home on November 21, 2021. The 40-year-radio veteran had been missing for about a week before his roommate, 38-year-old Sean Lamoureux, was arrested and charged with the killing. No motive was revealed but the alleged killer tried to hide the evidence of his crime by putting the body in the backyard and hiding it beneath shingles, sheets, and a wheelbarrow.

"John was just a guy who loved the music passionately," radio historian Art Vuolo said in an interview with *Click on Detroit*. "He was on the ground floor of what they used to call underground radio, progressive rock radio."

As of this writing, the murder trial is still pending.

Jacqueline "Jackie" Avant, the 81-year-old wife of music executive and Rock & Roll Hall of Famer Clarence Avant (aka, "The Black Godfather"), was killed during a brutal home invasion in Beverly Hills on December 1, 2021.

The beloved philanthropist was shot in the back by career criminal Aariel Maynor, who "laughed and bragged about" what he did, according to an article in *the Los Angeles Times*. A security video from a neighboring home "captured Maynor in dark clothing approaching the house with the AR-15-style rifle." After he killed Jackie, he fired at an unarmed security guard before fleeing in his Lexus. Somewhere along the way, he dropped a red glove that ultimately tied him to the murder.

The killer was caught that same night while trying to rob another family. Aariel later said that when the burglary at the Avant house failed, he went to a home in the Hollywood Hills to see what he could get there. But the 30-year-old, who has several facial tattoos and has been treated for mental illness, was caught by police after accidentally shooting himself in the foot with his own rifle.

"I'm going to get out of jail. I'll probably do like 20 ... 25 years, get out, you feel me?" the unconcerned killer declared during a recorded jailhouse phone call to a friend. As it turned out, Aariel Maynor was sentenced to 190 years in the penitentiary. (Just a slight miscalculation.)

District Attorney George Gascón said in a statement that the sentencing marked "the end of a tragic case that rocked our community. Given the sentence today, Mr. Maynor will be ineligible for early parole, and will spend the rest of his life in prison."

Harvey Miller, known on the airwaves as "Humble Harve," was a key player in KHJ's "Boss Radio" DJ team that transformed rock radio in the 1960s in L.A. "When the music was hot, so were we," he said in a 2003 interview with the *L.A. Times.* "We were right in the midst of the hottest place in the world, musically. This was the center of everything— all the recording studios were going 24 hours a day. We were right in the center of all that energy."

Humble Harve is so entrenched in pop culture that he's even immortalized in Quentin Tarantino's Oscar-nominated ode to yesteryear, *Once Upon a Time...in Hollywood.* After successful stints in other cities, he made his way to La-La Land and became a star. Harve was the top-rated nighttime disc jockey on KHJ for five years, and he also did commercials and voice-over work, in addition to narrating the 1967 counterculture documentary film, *Mondo Mod*.

The otherwise lauded DJ—who passed away at the age of 84 from natural causes on June 4, 2019—forever tarnished his legacy because of one rash decision he made at his Hollywood Hills home on May 7, 1971. During a fight with his wife, 35-year-old Mary Gladys Miller, he pulled a pistol and fired, killing her. According to court testimony, she had been unfaithful to him and was taunting him, saying, "If you don't like it, why don't you just shoot me?"

Before he was put on trial, Harve had to be found. Following the murder, the desperate DJ fled to a friend's house and hid out. That friend? None other than the gun-toting, future lady-killer, tune tycoon, Phil Spector. Although the platter-spinner did shave off his signature dark mustache and goatee, plus tinted his hair red, he knew he couldn't evade the law indefinitely. A couple of weeks later, he turned himself in to the authorities and was jailed.

He initially pleaded not guilty but changed his plea to guilty of second-degree murder, his lawyer arguing that Mary Gladys pulled a gun on him, and as he tried to take it from her, the weapon discharged, firing a single shot to her chest. Humble Harve expressed remorse for his actions and told the court, "She was my wife, my lover, my partner, and my companion for life. I swear to God, I never meant to harm her."

L.A. County Superior Court Judge Arthur L. Alarcon bought it and gave Miller five years to life, saying that the killing was a "situational crime" that could not reoccur, and recommended he be considered for parole halfway through the sentence.

While incarcerated at the California Institution for Men in Chino, Humble Harve taught radio skills to his fellow prisoners and lent his voice to recorded materials for the blind. The model inmate was released early for good behavior and soon returned to broadcasting, where he flourished for decades.

Robert George "Joe" Meek has been described as the British Phil Spector—a vanguard record producer, sound engineer, and songwriter responsible for introducing innovative and unique soundscapes into various artists' music. However, there would be more to their connection than just music... it's also murder meted out on a certain deadly date that ties them together in infamy.

Born on April 5, 1929, in Gloucestershire, England, Joe was a child prodigy who had a keen interest in tech and performance art. While undoubtedly bright, he never felt good enough because his mother made it plain that she'd wanted a girl instead of a boy. She dressed him according to her wishes for the first four years of his life but eventually, he was allowed to wear pants and tinker with electronics. The future music man assembled various items such as cameras and television sets from scratch to learn how they worked. He became obsessed with outer space and wondered if there was some way he could reach other worlds through his experiments.

As an adult, Joe, who was tone-deaf, defied the odds and got into music as a recording engineer; he made a name for himself through sheer audacity and using outrageous techniques to get certain sounds. He created his own studio in the London flat he rented, and the first major hit produced there was "Johnny Remember Me," a trendy death-disc ditty about a young man haunted by his departed girlfriend. Sung by John Leyton, the single reached #1 on the U.K. charts in July of 1961.

Joe Meek wrote the space-age instrumental "Telstar" for The Tornados the following year and it took off like, well, a rocket, quickly becoming a *Billboard* Hot 100 smash, making it the first single by a British band to score the top spot on both sides of the Atlantic. More hits started coming from the modest, unorthodox studio on 304 Holloway Road, where Joe encouraged musicians to play their instruments in the loo or staggered on the staircase as he manipulated their sound electronically.

Tornados drummer Clem Cattini recalled, "The studio was bizarre. I mean the drums were in the fireplace! But it was incredible, the sounds he could get out of that studio, the equipment he used, and what he recorded 'Telstar' with. Modern equipment could not get anywhere near it."

A year after "Telstar" was released, Joe was detained for cottaging—having homosexual relations with a hustler in a standalone public bathroom. (City toilets at the time were fashioned to look like cottages, hence the tag.) Just being gay was illegal in the U.K. at the time and the high-profile arrest was a major blow to the closeted producer. He was fined £15 at Clerkenwell Magistrates' Court after pleading guilty to "persistently importuning for an immoral purpose." (At least they didn't make him say it five times, fast.)

Even though his secret was out, Joe became a target for blackmailers. Then he clashed with London's most notorious dangerous gangsters, the Kray Twins—evidently, Ronnie Kray, who, incidentally, was also gay, demanded that Meek hand over management of The Tornados to him, and was refused.

As the musical landscape shifted in the mid-1960s, Joe couldn't keep up. The 30ish stuffed shirt pooh-poohed The Beatles, and advised a band in search of a vocalist to forget about hiring Rod Stewart. Not that he necessarily *wanted* to keep up—the acclaimed producer was becoming obsessed with the idea of communicating with the dead and that became his main focus. He would slip recording devices into cemeteries hoping to catch the voices of spirits floating around in the Great Beyond... but all he got was a cat's meow. An undaunted Joe became convinced that a human spirit was trapped in the feline body and the mews were in fact calls for help.

He was especially fixated on rock & roll singer Buddy Holly, whose death he claimed to have foreseen through a deck of tarot cards. Joe's failure to somehow prevent the plane crash that killed the "Peggy Sue" singer on February 3, 1959, weighed heavily on his fragile mind. As far as he was concerned, February 3rd was the most cursed date on the calendar—as it turned out, he was right... or, through a self-fulfilling prophecy, he *made* it so.

Clem Cattini, The Tornados' drummer, remembered an incident he witnessed that gave him pause. Apparently, Phil Spector called from America and after talking for just a few minutes, Joe flew into a rage and smashed the telephone to bits. He explained to Clem that Phil was stealing his unique techniques by employing Joe's landlady as a spy... or maybe the Wall of Sound whiz was eavesdropping from the studio's bathroom via supernatural intervention. He couldn't decide but he knew for sure his rival was trouble. Even though the band knew of their engineer's eccentricities, bassist Heinz Burt left his hunting rifle with Joe for safekeeping.

One thing after another toppled Joe's life like so many dominoes of disaster. His financial backing was pulled; he was involved in a lawsuit with a French film composer over the melody that defined "Telstar;" and he was beaten up by anonymous ruffians more than once.

Things came to a head when Joe was warned he'd be questioned about the headline-grabbing "Suitcase Murder" of 17-year-old Bernard Oliver—the boy had been raped, killed, cut into eight pieces, and then his remains were stashed inside luggage which was dumped into a field. Most believe that the two men had no connection whatsoever, while others say Bernard had worked off and on at Joe's studio as a tape-stacker. In any case, Scotland Yard publicly declared their intention to question every gay man they knew of in London, which would, of course, include Meek because of his prior arrest. As his fear blossomed and his mental health decayed, the musical maverick began to believe aliens were using him as a communication device and he was terrified that he'd say the wrong thing to the police.

On the morning of Friday, February 3, 1967, the eighth anniversary of Buddy Holly's death, Joe's studio assistant, Patrick Pink, went to work as usual. Tape-stackers were there, and Joe was busy burning letters, documents, and paintings in the bathtub. Rather than speaking, Joe communicated with Patrick by handwritten notes—he still thought his place was bugged and that his landlady was listening through the fireplace. The last note read, "I'm going now.

Goodbye." Patrick had no idea what the words *really* meant.

Once his tasks were done, Joe dismissed his tape-stackers for the day and he asked one of them to send the landlady, 56-year-old Mrs. Violet Shenton, up to the third-floor studio for a quick word. She resided elsewhere but worked in her retail shop on the ground level during the day.

Patrick, who was in the second-floor office below the studio heard them shouting, then Violet said, "Calm down, Joe." Her remark was answered by several loud bangs. The shocked studio assistant rushed from the room only to see Violet tumbling down the stairs with bullet holes "smoking" in her back. He then raced upstairs and caught a glimpse of 37-year-old Joe Meek disappearing into his control room. He heard the shotgun being reloaded and before he could wonder if the next bullets were for him, he heard his boss take his own life with Heinz Burt's single-barrel blaster.

Four years after his death, Joe Meek was found innocent of plagiarism and considerable royalties were paid to his estate. Precisely 36 years after his death, on February 3, 2003, Joe Meek's adversary, Phil Spector, shot and killed a woman after trapping her in the Alhambra fortress he called home.

Lana Jean Clarkson was a lovely, sunny California blonde who was born on April 5, 1962, in Long Beach, and when she grew up, she hoped to find her fortune as a model and actress in Tinsel Town. She made her big screen debut in 1982's *Fast Times at Ridgemont High* as the hot wife of nerdy science teacher Mr. Vargas (played by Vincent Schiavelli). She had said just one word, "Hi," but it got her into the Screen Actors Guild. Lana went on to star in B-movies directed by Roger Corman and John Landis, while her TV appearances included small roles on popular shows like *Night Court, The Love Boat, Riptide, Three's Company, Knight Rider*, and *Wings*. She was also in several major national commercials. While she worked, she also volunteered weekly to deliver meals for the charity, Project Angel Food. Like her idol Marilyn Monroe, Lana was a bombshell with a soft heart for those less fortunate.

Hollywood is an ageist town, to say the least, and Lana found her roles fewer and farther between when she hit her mid-30s. She wanted to be a comedian and even tried doing some standup but that didn't pan out and by the time she turned 40, a still-stunning Lana was working as a hostess at the popular Sunset Strip hotspot, the House of Blues. She'd only had the job for about a month when 64-year-old music impresario Harvey Phillip "Phil" Spector walked through the door and sealed her tragic fate.

Spector's chauffeur, Adriano de Souza, later testified in court how he had driven to several hallowed Hollywood haunts, including Trader Vic's and Dan Tana's, before winding up at the

House of Blues. Along for the ride were two different dates (both of whom bailed before the end of the evening) and at least one bottle of 150-proof tequila (which was consumed along the way, between bars). When the "To Know Him Is to Love Him" producer stumbled into the House of Blues, Lana didn't know who he was. In fact, the leggy, blue-eyed babe initially took the customer for an ugly woman before her boss set her straight and ordered her to treat him "like gold."

There is no doubt that Phil Spector was a legend in the music world. As a musician, he formed the Teddy Bears in 1958 with high school friends Marshall Lieb and Annette Kleinbard and enjoyed success before moving on to write and produce for his own company, Philles Records. The first single out of the gate was, the million-selling "He's a Rebel" by The Crystals. He changed the sound of Motown, pop, rock, and punk with equal aplomb. His 1989 induction into the Rock & Roll Hall of Fame gushes, "Layer upon layer of instruments and echoes come to a roaring climax in his compositions, often backing up his own brilliant lyrics." But toward the end of his life as a free man, he grew increasingly eccentric and audacious. He went out on the town wearing outrageous outfits topped with beehive wigs that brought his five-foot-five-inch frame up several notches, making a spectacle of himself.

Somehow, the maniacal magnate talked Lana Clarkson into going home with him after last call. Driver de Souza remembered the pair watching *Kiss Tomorrow Goodbye*, a 1950 film noir starring James Cagney, as they sat together in the back of the Mercedes S430 limousine which was headed to Spector's "Pyrenees Castle." The 33-room turreted 1925 French Chateau-style mansion was perched on a hill in the sleepy Los Angeles suburb of Alhambra, and neighbors later likened the hot-tempered New York native to a feudal lord among serfs.

Two hours after the couple went inside, de Souza said he heard a gunshot and saw his boss emerge from the mansion babbling, "I think I killed someone." Behind him, slumped in a high-backed, white Louis XIV replica chair, lay the body. Reduced to a film noir cliché: the blonde starlet was shot dead and a mystery wrapped in red herrings was spun for the armada of press and law enforcement that soon stormed the castle. They found the unresponsive victim fully clothed in her tight black minidress, with a gun near her feet, which were clad in low-heeled black Mary Janes. Her leopard-print purse hung from the chair's blood-spattered arm. A single gunshot had blown out her top row of teeth and they now littered the crimson carpet like jagged dice.

An agitated Phil Spector stood nearby with his hands shoved in his pockets. When the police asked to see his hands, he refused and was zapped with a taser for his obstinance and then taken into custody. He was recorded saying, "The gun went off accidentally. She works at the House of Blues. It was a mistake. I don't understand what the fuck is wrong with you people." Later, at the police station, he said she committed suicide.

The "Let it Be" showman seemed to be basking in a spotlight that had dimmed for him in recent years. He romanced the press, telling the dramatic tale of Lana's "suicide," saying that she "kissed the gun" before blowing off half her face with his ever-ready .38 Special Colt Cobra revolver. Later, he threw tantrums on the courtroom steps, donned bizarre, flamboyant hairpieces paired with pearl-buttoned rococo suits, and paraded his bodyguards before eager, snapping cameras. His high-profile lawyer, Robert Shapiro, was a celebrity in and of himself—as a member of the legal "Dream Team," Shapiro had managed to defend O.J. Simpson successfully in his own murder case, so naturally, the hitmaker thought he'd go free, too.

In 2006, amid the flurry of trouble and while out on bail, the self-styled "mad genius of rock & roll" married 26-year-old Rachelle Short, whom he spotted at his neighborhood Starbucks three years before. The pair got hitched just a few months after the heinous crime. The blonde wannabe singer, it was noted in the press, bore an uncanny resemblance to Lana Clarkson. They wed in the opulent, mirrored and chandeliered foyer where the murder took place. When asked how she could bear to be married in a murder house, and that room in particular, Rachelle rolled her eyes and replied, "Why wouldn't I? I sit in that chair all the time." The bride's lack of reverence was staggering to all who encountered her; she was also heard snickering in court when Lana's acting reel was played, according to *Vanity Fair* reporter, Dominic Dunne.

The whole thing turned out to be a win/win for the self-satisfied trophy wife—Phil was in prison for much of their marriage and she was free to spend his leftover millions like money was going out of style. In 2016 he filed for divorce citing irreconcilable differences, and accused Rachelle, who was living in the castle, of purchasing a $350,000 airplane, an Aston Martin and a Ferrari, getting plastic surgery, buying top-tier jewelry for herself, and buying not one, but two, homes for her mom, while allotting him a paltry $300 a month to survive on in jail.

The first trial ended in a hung jury and the second time around, Phil Spector's legal team was downsized to a single lawyer, Doron Weinberg. Toning things down didn't help—the Wall of Sound architect was sentenced to 19 years to life behind bars (and many walls).

While it was no secret that the father of five never met a gun he didn't like and there had been stories circulating about his hair-trigger temper, all dirt came to the surface during the media frenzy.

- During a recording session of Rock 'n' Roll in 1973, the producer pulled a gun on John Lennon, the barrel mere inches from the "Give Peace a Chance" songwriter's ear. He then shot a deafening bullet into the studio ceiling. "Phil, if you're going to kill me, kill me, but don't fuck with me ears," Lennon griped.

- When working with the poetical Canadian troubadour Leonard Cohen in 1976 on his album *Death of a Ladies' Man*, the pint-sized producer reportedly wrapped a comradely arm around Leonard's shoulder, then pressed a gun to his neck. "I love you, Leonard," he whispered menacingly through clenched teeth. "I hope you do, Phil," Leonard replied drily.

- Spector also held The Ramones at gunpoint... maybe. Bassist Dee Dee Ramone recalled, "Phil leveled his gun at my heart and then motioned for me and the rest of the band to get back in the piano room. Then he sat down at his black concert piano and made us listen to him play and sing 'Baby, I Love You' until well after 4:30 in the morning." Drummer Marky Ramone later refuted his bandmate's account, telling the *Miami New Times*, "It was an honor to work with a guy like that who had such a great reputation as a producer. Sure, he had different situations with different artists. He did pull out guns on different people, but not at us. We were all different personalities; we were all crazy in a sense. So it really was like a loony bin, but we did our job, we did it well, and that was the result: *End of the Century*." (Which turned out to be the highest-charting studio album of the group's entire career.)

Those threats of violence were shocking enough, but no less than five women testified at the murder trial to tell their tales of terror at the hands of Phil Spector. Fifteen years prior, his first wife, singing sensation Ronnie Spector (née Veronica Bennet), released her memoir, *Be My Baby: How I Survived Mascara, Miniskirts, and Madness*, and wrote that, while she couldn't deny her ex-husband's musical genius and boost to her career, he was violent and vindictive.

The "Breakin' Up" songstress stated that he had an arsenal of firearms all over their house in Beverly Hills and even kept a gold coffin in their basement, telling her that would be her final resting place if she ever tried to leave him. But with the help of her mother, Ronnie literally escaped in the middle of the night. "I can only say that when I left in the early '70s, I knew that if I didn't leave at that time, I was going to die there," she wrote.

Many people were outraged on January 16, 2021, when Phil Spector's COVID-19-related death brought forth a slew of obituaries bearing praise for his contribution to popular music by creating his signature Wall of Sound. Lisa King, Director of Communications and External Relations at Refuge, wrote an editorial, saying, "It is deeply troubling when men convicted of violence against women are celebrated in a way that is detached from their crimes. Perpetrators of violence and abuse often assume that their fame, power, and wealth will ensure immunity from public scrutiny, and use this as a weapon to silence their victims. The media has a duty to remember the lives of the victims too. Lana Clarkson's life was stolen through an act of extreme violence, and her name must not become a footnote in her murderer's obituary."

Lana Clarkson is immortalized at the famous Hollywood Forever Cemetery in a large glass display case bearing her glamourous publicity photos pinned against a leopard-print backdrop. Her ashes are entombed inside a white urn that's festooned with bas-relief cherubs and flower blossoms.

Alexandre Despallières was French, chic, stylish, handsome, and witty. There was just something about him that charmed otherwise intelligent and guarded wealthy people into opening their homes, hearts, and wallets to him.

He gladly took those gifts, and more—in some cases, he took their very lives.

A shameless name-dropper, Alexandre told everyone he met that he was a member of the Rothschild family, the nephew of former French President Jacques Chirac, and related to Elizabeth Taylor. He owned a movie studio, an I.T. company worth billions, and of course, several swanky estates all over the world. None of it was true. In actuality, he was from a small Paris suburb, Bois-Colombes, and was an aspiring pop star who, as a young man, recorded a single entitled "L'Amour à Mort" (Love Until Death) that went nowhere.

With his hopes dashed, the gigolo, who'd started his life of crime at the age of 12 by stealing his father's credit cards, began manipulating jet-setters to get the things he wanted. Soon he successfully, if duplicitously, made his way up in the world. Alexandre even convinced an elderly Beverly Hills billionaire widow to legally adopt him when he was 37 years old, despite the fact she already had adult children of her own. Marcelle Becker soon annulled the adoption after suspecting he'd tried to poison her.

"Handsome Alex," as he was called, had perfected the fine art of toxic mixes from a young age, beginning with the family dog, then his parents (who died within 12 months of each other), his grandmother, and, finally, wealthy Sydney-born music mogul, Peter "P.I." Ikin.

Peter and Alex, 22 years apart in age, were first romantically linked in 1987, after meeting at a music conference in San Francisco. But the relationship didn't last, due to the elder man's demanding schedule as a globe-trotting executive for Warner Music. He brought major acts like Fleetwood Mac, Elton John, George Harrison, Madonna, and Rod Stewart to Australia, and in 1983, he co-founded the country's annual music honors show, the ARIA Awards.

In the spring of 2008, the alluring, gorgeous-as-ever 39-year-old Alexandre Despallières reappeared, turning Peter's life "upside down," as he said in emails sent to his friends and relatives. Now retired, the 61-year-old was living in an apartment overlooking Sydney Harbor and looking forward to having some free time. Despallières countered, saying he himself was almost out of time for good, having been diagnosed with an inoperable brain tumor. But he wasn't out of money—a digital company he claimed to have created was estimated to be worth several billion euros. His dying wish, the French fantasist explained, was to marry his beloved "P.I." and leave him his fortune.

The pair wed in a small civil ceremony at the Chelsea Town Hall in London on October 10, 2008. One month later, on November 12, Peter died in a room at the four-star Abba Montparnasse Hotel in Paris.

The coroner concluded that the cause was hepatitis and heart failure—natural causes. Details later emerged that "P.I." had been admitted to a Paris hospital three times in the three days before he died, complaining of nausea and stomach pain. Two days after the autopsy, without consulting his late husband's family, the Gallic grifter had the body cremated and laid the remains to rest at Père Lachaise, the historic Parisian cemetery where Jim Morrison is buried.

Red flags were raised when the Ikin family realized that their loved one's final wishes were not honored—his will made no bones about burying him in his native Australia, and had also earmarked money for his favorite charities. What's more, Alexandre moved like lightning to collect his spousal inheritance, had shacked up with a much younger boyfriend in Peter's Victorian home in London's swanky Cheyne Place, and oh yeah... he didn't die of a malignant brain tumor after all.

The spendy spouse bought three Porsches (one for himself although he couldn't drive, and two for friends), Tiffany jewels, and Cartier watches. He rented a castle in Halifax, West Yorkshire, and flew in party guests via helicopter.

Suspicions mounted and Billy Gaff, a close friend of Peter's and Rod Stewart's longtime manager, demanded that Alexandre show him the will. The widower grudgingly produced a photocopy, which was not witnessed by a solicitor, but by ex-lovers of the beneficiary (they were both later charged with forgery and fraud).

Billy and another friend of Peter's, John Reid (Elton John's former manager), realized that although Peter's corpse had been cremated, some of the organs were still on ice at the coroner's—French law dictates that body parts need to be on hand for one year in case foul play is suspected. With only three days to spare, the pair funded a forensic examination of Ikin's innards. The resulting toxicology report revealed a fatal dose of paracetamol.

After he was charged with the crime, Alexandre Despallières went to jail to await trial but managed to get out on bail thanks to a high-profile lawyer paid for by yet another rich, lovesick mark. While free, he used his chiseled good looks to conceal his icy heart again and again—and in one case, he allegedly (unsuccessfully) poisoned another wealthy victim.

All the while, "Handsome Alex" protested his innocence. "I have plenty of flaws, but I've never hurt anyone. I didn't sleep for the money. And I never killed nobody," he stated in broken English, during a 2012 interview with the *Parisian*.

It took 11 years but finally, the cunning conman was jailed and set to go to trial for murder in the summer of 2022. It was not to be; the 52-year-old imposter escaped justice by dying on January 26, 2022, from the coronavirus... or did he? There was no post-mortem and his ashes have been scattered (disrespectfully, if you ask anyone), in the Père Lachaise cemetery.

When asked for a statement, Billy Graff scoffed. "COVID? There were so many people who didn't like him, I wouldn't be surprised if one of them had bumped him off. Good riddance! Alexandre Despallières didn't deserve the life he robbed others of."

Although we've learned about the dangers of picking up hitchhikers from horror movies like *The Hitcher* (1986), the practice used to be quite common and was safe enough. Usually. That was not the case for the hapless Second Lieutenant Willis Turner Allman, who was shot and killed by a lone man he and a fellow Army friend picked up on the outskirts of Norfolk, Virginia, on December 26, 1949. Willis and Second Lieutenant Robert Buchanan agreed to give the stranger a ride home but the passenger decided he wanted to take a detour to robbery-town. After directing them to an empty field in the middle of nowhere, he pulled a gun and ordered Allman and Buchanan out.

Buchanan, who survived the ordeal, later told police that he believed the bandit hadn't intended to harm them until Allman said, "Don't shoot us, buddy." As rotten luck would have it, the criminal's nickname was Buddy and he assumed he'd been recognized. "Too bad for you," Robert Buchanan quoted him as saying, "because you know my name." Willis Allman lunged for the weapon and was shot in the chest as his friend ran for his life, escaping the barrage of bullets that followed him into the darkness.

Robert "Buddy" Green, 26, was apprehended two days later with the murder weapon and the whopping $4.85 he got from the good man he murdered.

If there's any bright side to this awful tragedy, it's that Willis Allman had already fathered two sons, Gregg and Duane, who would go on to form one of the most unique, innovative Southern music groups of the late '60s/early '70s. The Allman Brothers band blended blues and hard rock with powerful jazzlike improvisation, yielding hits like "Whipping Post" and "Ramblin' Man." While Gregg lived until the ripe age of 69 and enjoyed a long music career, his elder brother Duane died at just 24 in a motorcycle accident on October 29, 1971, cutting short an already-brilliant stint in the music world.

When Jane's Addiction guitarist and fashionista Dave Navarro was a kid, his parents divorced. James Navarro and former model Constance Hopkins went their separate ways and young Dave bounced back and forth between their L.A. households. But, Dave has said, he had a pretty happy childhood and was very close to his mother, who doted on him.

On March 3, 1983, the 15-year-old was staying with his father—thankfully, Dave had made a last-minute change in his plans. If he'd been at Connie's condo in Westwood, he might have been caught in the crossfire that killed her and her lifelong friend, Susan Jory.

No one knew that anything was wrong until James Navarro, alarmed when he couldn't reach his ex-wife, went to her house and found the bodies upstairs. Connie was shot and stuffed into a hall closet, while Sue had been shot in the head and lay face-down on the bedroom carpet.

The perpetrator was Connie's ex-boyfriend, a small-time thief and big-time sociopath named John "Dean" Riccardi, who'd been booted from her bed the year before. He wasn't about to go quietly into the night, though; the jilted man stalked his ex brazenly and relentlessly. "There are no locks that can keep me out of your house," he sneered, not caring who else heard.

He was right about that and he almost got away with the cowardly crime but was apprehended after being on the run for several years, the TV show *America's Most Wanted* aired his story. In 1991, eight years after committing the double murder, Riccardi was convicted and sentenced to death in 1994; his sentence was later commuted to life without the possibility of parole.

In 2015, Dave Navarro produced and appeared in the documentary, *Mourning Son*, which is about coming to grips with the effect his mother's murder had on him—he even went to face "the demon," John Riccardi in prison for the first time. "I wanted it to make me feel scorn and anger and rage, and it just didn't," the "Been Caught Stealing" guitarist told the *New York Times*. There was no revelation, no histrionics, just "an awkward exchange. I almost was watching myself as an outside observer, so it took a minute to get my body and mind and emotional and spiritual stability all back in sync." Dave came to a somewhat comforting realization about his mother's murderer: "He's just some old dude dying in jail."

Fifty-two-year-old Andrea "Nebelhexë" Meyer just happened to be in the wrong place at the wrong time when a maniac with a bow and arrows fired into a crowd in Kongsberg, Norway, on October 13, 2021. The attacks started inside a grocery store, then moved to a nearby residential area. The murder victims all lived on the same street and were part of its thriving artists' community, Norwegian media reported.

German-born Andrea was a renaissance woman of many talents and she worked with several metal bands throughout her career. The Pagan muse performed a spoken-word piece on Satyricon's 1996 album *Nemesis Divina* but her most prominent contribution is on Cradle of Filth's 1994 debut, *The Principle of Evil Made Flesh*. Frontman Dani Filth posted a remembrance of the artist via social media:

"She will be sadly missed and our deep-felt love and sympathies go out to her kith and kin."

Though divorced at the time of her death, Andrea had been married to Norwegian black metal guitar god and multi-instrumentalist, Tomas "Samoth" Haugen, most famously with the band, Emperor. The couple had a daughter, Alva. (Not-so-fun fact: In 1994, Samoth was sentenced to 16 months in prison for burning Skjold Church in Vindafjord, along with Varg Vikernes. He was a session bass player on the infamous Burzum EP, *Aske.*)

The killer, Espen Andersen Bråthen, 37, was arrested after he fired arrows inside the grocery store and then moved on to the neighboring houses, where he stabbed random residents with a knife he'd brought. He killed five people and badly wounded four others before he was apprehended not far from the scene—he pled guilty to murder and attempted murder in court on May 18, 2022.

Espen had been in trouble with the law before, and some reports said he had been radicalized by an extremist Islamic terrorist organization five years before the headline-making attack. Though Espen pled guilty, the court found that he was unfit for punishment under Norwegian law due to chronic paranoid schizophrenia, and he was committed to a mental health facility instead of prison.

It hasn't been determined yet whether the Norway bow and arrow attack was motivated by politics, but there's no doubt that Ireland's

Miami Show Band were political pawns when three of them lost their lives on July 31, 1975, as they traveled home to Dublin following a gig in Banbridge.

Lead singer Fran O'Toole, trumpeter Brian McCoy, and guitarist Tony Geraghty were killed by loyalists in an ambush when their minibus was stopped at what appeared to be a military checkpoint on a dark, lonely stretch of highway. Little did they know, it was a trap. While the musicians were outside their vehicle being questioned, two soldiers sneakily placed a bomb-bearing briefcase in their van. It was set to go off a few minutes later but instead, it exploded almost immediately, decapitating both terrorists. The blast blew the band members into an adjacent field, where they were pursued by men with firearms.

Trumpeter Brian, 32, was the first to die, shot with a 9mm Luger pistol in the back and neck with nine rounds. Bassist Stephen Travers, 24, had been injured in the blast, and his band brothers Tony, 24, and Fran, 28, tried to move him to safety but in the melee, they dropped him. Singer Fran ran but was felled by a bullet. He was then machine-gunned 22 times, mostly in the face, as he lay on the ground, helpless, begging for his life. Tony was shot twice in the back of his head and several times in the back as he tried in vain to outrun the bullets.

Stephen survived by laying where he'd been dropped in the field, playing dead. Saxophone player Des McAlea, 24, was hit by the door of the minibus in the explosion but wasn't hurt that badly. He ended up in tall grass and wasn't seen by the attackers. Before long, help arrived. But the two survivors had a long way to go in the healing process, both physically and emotionally.

Enjoying "Beatles-like" popularity complete with screaming female fans, the Miami Showband (one of about 700 "showbands" touring in Ireland at the time—these groups did covers of popular songs and dance music) had been playing to large crowds all over the island. Made up of both Protestants and Catholics, the band members themselves were not political and didn't concern themselves with the religious beliefs of the people who made up their audience. They were just grateful to be playing music that made people happy in such otherwise turbulent times.

As it turned out, the attack was carried out by 10 members (two of whom died in the explosion) of the Ulster Defense Regiment, an infantry squad of the British Army. While several suspects were questioned, charges only stuck on three of the shooters: Lance Corporal Thomas Raymond Crozier, Sergeant James Roderick Shane McDowell, and John James Somerville.

In a retrospective published in the *Sunday Mirror*, journalist Colin Wills called the Miami Showband massacre "one of the worst atrocities in the long history of the Troubles." (The

Troubles refers to a violent sectarian civil conflict.) Sadly, the vicious attack crippled Northern Ireland's live music scene for some time, as both bands and music fans were understandably fearful of being attacked and were reluctant to go out.

While some incredible songs have been written about school shootings—"I Don't Like Mondays" by the Boomtown Rats, "Jeremy" by Pearl Jam, and "Pumped Up Kicks" by Foster the People, to name a few—they illustrate terrorism on a smaller scale and highlight one of the worst, fastest-escalating issues of modern times.

While most Americans remember the Columbine High School Massacre as opening the floodgates to this appalling trend, Brenda Spencer was just 16 years old when she killed two adults, wounded eight children, and shot a police officer in the neck, at Grover Cleveland Elementary School in San Diego in 1979—20 years before Columbine. (The first known school-based mass shooting in the U.S. happened on April 9, 1891, but no toe-tapping rock tunes came out of that one.) During a six-hour standoff, Brenda was asked by a reporter why she was shooting innocent kids. She quipped, "I don't like Mondays. This livens up the day."

On April 20, 1999, Columbine High School seniors Eric Harris and Dylan Klebold—who billed themselves as "the Trench Coat Mafia" shot and killed 12 students and a teacher, and wounded 24 others, before committing suicide. Poor parenting, easy access to automatic weapons, being bullied, and mental health issues were partially blamed but the press, government officials, and the Religious Right zeroed in on goth shock rocker Marilyn Manson (born Brian Warner) as the catalyst for the boys' crime. It was also noted that the carnage was carried out on Adolf Hitler's birthday and that Manson was a self-proclaimed fan of the dictator, whom he called "the first rockstar."

Although rumors that the killers donned Marilyn Manson band tees while on their shooting spree were proved false, fellow musicians piled on. "We want to challenge Marilyn Manson and the rap people with the bad lyrics to write some positive songs," Lynyrd Skynyrd guitarist Gary Rossington told the *Denver Post.* "You don't have to write about killing little girls. If they're making all this money, let them write about something good in their lives. I'm not blaming them for Columbine, but they have a gift where people listen to their music—try to help a little bit instead of hurt so much.

"If Marilyn Manson would write a song that says, 'Do your damn homework,' it would make the world a better place and it wouldn't hurt him at all," Gary suggested. "And if he doesn't like it, to hell with him. He can come fight us by the bicycle racks."

The "Antichrist Superstar" singer isn't the only musician to bear the brunt of false allegations in connection with heinous felonies. Mexican metalhead Morbid Blackstar (aka Pablo Vergara) was accused by internet sleuths of murdering a Chinese-Canadian tourist, 21-year-old Elisa Lam, on February 19, 2013, at the notorious Cecil Hotel in the Skid Row district of Downtown L.A. Missing for nearly three weeks, Elisa was finally found rotting in the antique hotel's rooftop water tank. No wonder hotel guests had been complaining to management about the foul-smelling "rust" coming from their faucets!

While the baffling and bizarre case was making headlines all over the world, Morbid was posting videos on YouTube inadvertently hinting that he might be a murderer. Anything to get more song downloads, right? The tease backfired when agitated armchair detectives went on the warpath, picking apart every pixel of his uploads.

A corpse-painted Morbid shot one of his videos at the Cecil (unsuccessfully "rebranded" with the name Stay on Main prior to the crime being committed) using photos of serial killer Ted Bundy and murder victim Elizabeth Short (aka, The Black Dahlia) as his backdrop. A video for his band Slitwrist's song "Died in Pain" shows a young woman running for her life until she's caught and murdered. Another composition, "China," has heavily sound-altered lyrics describing a victim's remains being laid to rest in water (the ocean), and the line, "I'm thinking China."

Before long, mainstream media ran with the sensational story and Morbid's face was being shown on Taiwanese TV as an "official suspect" in the case. He posted a video on his YouTube channel in response, declaring, "This is Morbid. I want to inform you that I didn't kill Elisa Lam. I am innocent." Regardless, the erstwhile Pablo Vergara's YouTube, Facebook, and Google accounts were all terminated, and the PFM (the FBI of Mexico) went to his home to question him about his alleged "blood sacrifices for the devil."

The accused complained about the ruinous scandal in the 2021 docuseries, *Crime Scene: The Vanishing at the Cecil Hotel.* "There was no escape. When you get so much hate and negativity, there's something that breaks in your mind. After a while, there's just so much you can take. I did try to take my life and woke up in a psychiatric hospital. The web sleuths go on with their lives like nothing happened, but they really turned my life upside down."

Even though Morbid was able to establish his alibi and was fully cleared by the Los Angeles Police Department, the skeptical sleuths who first put Morbid on blast weren't satisfied. Several online vigilantes publicly accused the LAPD of conspiracies and the coroner's office of a cover-up when it was officially concluded that Elisa's death was a suicide—probably accidental—brought on by bipolar disorder.

"When the news was released about her death being an accident, no one apologized to me," Morbid groused. "No one reached out to me, nothing changed. It's just wrong, people shouldn't get away with that. We have to be more responsible for what we say and do. What happened to me can happen to anyone. I survived it, but lots of people get cyberbullied and they don't make it." He went on to say that he's quit making music, adding that The Cecil Hotel is "a portal to Hell, in my opinion. Once you step in there, bad things happen. I've come to realize that I'm maybe another victim of that place, just in a different way."

While the artist formerly and currently known as Prince Midnight may not be a household name, he did manage to pull off an admirable viral story in 2021 with his homemade "Skelecaster" guitar. The punk performance artist, whose real name is (possibly; no one knows for sure) Yaago Anax and resides in (where else?) Florida, caught the attention of morbid metal fans when he began documenting the making of a guitar using human bones. And not just any bones, this was a family skeleton—literally.

Prince Midnight told *Guitar World* that the bones were those of his Uncle Filip who'd died in a motorcycle crash in Greece in 1996. The body was donated to science but after it had served its purpose, the corpse—now just a skeleton—was returned to the family. Filip's frame was sent to his nephew in the U.S. after the ambitious instrumentalist worked out the details with the cemetery in Greece and the U.S. state department.

"At first, (my mom) said it was sacrilegious and the work of the devil—you know how moms are," Prince Midnight said in the interview. "But I asked her, 'Uncle Filip was the biggest metal head of anybody. Where would he rather be? In the ground or shredding?'"

"It's pretty metal to play a guitar made out of a skeleton," the proud luthier added, having posted a popular video of himself playing it to the tune of Darkthrone's "Transylvanian Hunger."

CHAPTER FIVE: ROCK THE CRADLE OF LOVE

"I'd love to be a pop idol. Of course, my groupies are now between 40 and 50."—Kevin Bacon

There have always been groupies but they became a cultural phenomenon with the rise of so-called "cock rock" in the 1960s and '70s when men gripping phallic mics and stroking vibrating guitar strings started to become worshipped as gods. One of the prime prototypes was Robert Plant, the lead singer of Led Zeppelin, who performed bare-chested and wore his jeans so tight you didn't have to guess whether or not he was circumcised.

In the spring of 1975, the leonine blond was caught on camera standing on the balcony outside his penthouse suite at the "Riot House" on Sunset Boulevard, gazing down at a ginormous billboard for Led Zeppelin's new album *Physical Graffiti*, spreading his arms like a master of all domains. He jokingly shouted from the Hollywood heavens, "I am a golden god!" and thereby captured the elan of the archetypical rock star in a single moment. Incidentally, *Physical Graffiti* featured a song called "Sick Again," which was about how young the American groupies were—the lyrics are partially cautionary, partially celebratory.

The fall of 1975 brought disco diva Donna Summer's *Love To Love You Baby*, a "17-minute vinyl aphrodisiac filled with rapturous moans, groans, murmurs, and yelps," (*the Guardian*) to the airwaves but years before (appropriately enough, in '69), Robert Plant expressed his own orgasmic ecstasy on "Whole Lotta Love," the opening song on *Led Zeppelin II*.

As the so-called sexual revolution blossomed in the '60s with the advent of The Pill and the rise of the Equal Rights Amendment (ERA), rock music as we know it today was being birthed. Men and boys grew their hair long and shunned the military, while women and girls banished their bras and took control of their own sex lives. The music they listened to exalted the assets of freedom, fun, rebellion, sin, and sexuality. There's the aforementioned "Whole Lotta Love," in which the singer promises "every inch" of his love, which played in the same radio rock blocks as the Stones' "Let's Spend the Night Together," and The Beatles' "Why Don't We Do It in the Road?"

As the new decade dawned, albums and concerts were generating more money worldwide than any other form of art-related entertainment, including movies, books, and live theater. Pink Floyd's *Dark Side of the Moon* (1973) and *The Wall* (1979) charted for weeks, months, and *years* on end, while Fleetwood Mac's *Rumors* sold over 10 million copies within just one month of its launch. Led Zeppelin's albums all went multiplatinum and the band broke concert attendance records left and right. Thanks to the popularity of rock, there were more millionaires under the age of 30 than ever before, and their faces graced the covers of *Life*, *Jet*, *Newsweek*, and of course, *Rolling Stone*, *CREEM*, *Hit Parader*, and *Circus*.

Countless impressionable, hormonal schoolgirls saved their lunch money to buy LPs, singles, concert tickets, and magazines featuring their faves. They dreamt of being rock star arm candy, riding in flashy limousines and private jets, being treated to front-row seats, and getting an inside look at luxury hotel suites. A faction of starry-eyed latch-key kids known as "Baby Groupies" took decisive action to make those dreams come true, and the millionaire music men lapped it up like peaches and cream. (Let's just say there's a fine line between debauchery and daycare.)

When those little foxes knocked on their hotel room doors, the boys in the band could easily have said, "No thanks," but history shows that more often than not, the girls were invited in. (The prog-rock band Rush was an exception: When they toured with KISS in the mid-'70s, bassist Gene Simmons was amazed that the low-key Canadians stayed in their hotel rooms alone and read books. He said, "When you're in rock, even an ugly mug like me can get laid. The Rush boys didn't even try!")

There was no such thing as an "R-rating" for records or concerts to bar minors from mature content, and explicit songs like Donna Summer's "Hot Stuff" and Rod Stewart's "Tonight's the Night" titillated many a teen. The Rolling Stones' "Stray Cat Blues" (1968) was originally written referring to a 15-year-old groupie, but Mick Jagger dropped that number to 13 when singing it live in the sassy '70s. (At least Steely Dan waited until she was of age in their catchy ode to nubile nookie, "Hey 19.")

These teenaged temptresses were photographed on the Sunset Strip and in clubs like The Rainbow, the Whisky a Go-Go, and Rodney's English Disco, wearing fishnet tights, gold lamé hotpants, tiny tube-tops, and towering platforms; heavily kohled eyes, crimson pouts, and bountiful curls were coiffed to complete the come-hither look. There was even a short-lived magazine devoted to this lifestyle called *Star*, which produced five issues in 1973 before being banned by panicked parents. The columnists had names like Donna Goodbody and one article, for example, starts like this: "Hey, little sister. Yes you, foxy mama, you sly young thing!" while another goes on to extoll the voluptuary virtues of Jagger's "sensuous lips." A similar magazine, *Groupie Rock*, hit the stands in 1978 with helpful how-to articles about getting your favorite rock star to fall in love with you, and featured a "Grope of the Month" male centerfold.

Lori Lightning, who now goes by her given last name, Maddox, and is a fashion buyer, was one of the most notorious of the Baby Groupie batch—a posse that included rich kid Sable Starr on the West Coast and Ford model Bebe Buell in New York, with many more between. Lori laid down with rock royalty that included David Bowie, Randy California, Iggy Pop, Mick Jagger, and Jimmy Page. Noteworthy notches on the proverbial bedposts were a way of gaining status among one's peers for these young ladies—the bigger the star, the better her cachet.

"Super-Groupie" Pamela Des Barres (aka, Miss Pamela) remembered those days in vivid detail in her bestselling 1987 memoir, *I'm With the Band*. She tells the tale of how her rambling boyfriend, Jimmy Page, left her for a younger "woman." Miss Pamela was 24 at the time, and "he left me stranded in front of the Whisky like a floundering, faded Jezebel while he sleazed off with a 13-year-old nymphet called Lori Lightning."

In an interview with *the Guardian*, Lori talked of her relationship with Jimmy, who was 27 when they met, as "the most beautiful pure love I thought I could ever feel. I'd only had sex once before in my whole life [with David Bowie]. I felt like I'd won the lottery." In regard to her age, she said, "I never thought there was anything wrong with it, but maybe there was. I used to get letters telling me he was a pedophile, but I'd never think of him like that. He never abused me, ever."

While a rocker's kinky craving for super-young females falls into the category of statutory rape (even when the coupling is consensual and there may only be a scant few years between their ages, it's still called "rape" and is not legal) they are generally *not* pedophiles. Pedophilia is a serious mental disorder that comes with a compulsion to sexually abuse children who have not yet reached puberty (usually under the age of 10). The pedophile is often (but not always) someone who's been molested at a young age and is in a mental state of arrested development.

Perhaps those bygone rockers should be called ephebophiles, instead—but even that's not quite right, as the term strictly denotes "the *preference* for mid-to-late adolescent sexual partners, not the mere presence of some level of sexual attraction," according to the 2009 medical study, *Archives of Sexual Behavior.* Famous musicians weren't skulking around schoolyards but they certainly did contribute to the delinquency of minors; most of the guys were into women their own age but for whatever reasons—alcohol impairment, a cocaine high, or heady with hero worship—they couldn't resist the bacchanal buffet while on tour.

Although brunette Lori Lightning and blonde Sable Starr were besties and often prowled the scene together, the latter was vehemently protective of her conquests. When

Lori fixed her gaze on Bowie, Sable reportedly threatened through gritted teeth, "If you touch him, I will shoot you. He's *mine*." The warning didn't work; according to Lori, it was the Starman himself who took her virginity.

The song "Look Away" on Iggy pop's 1996 album *Naughty Little Doggy* waxed philosophical on his 1970 affair with Starr: "I slept with Sable when she was 13/Her parents were too rich to do anything/She rocked her way around L.A./Until a New York Doll carried her away." Iggy was referring to New York Dolls guitarist Johnny Thunders, then 18, whom the groupie started dating when she was 16.

Many studies have shown that girls mature faster than boys, and their brains are as much as two years ahead of a male's during puberty. Neuro-imaging reveals that the typical teen girl has a stronger connection between the areas of the brain that control impulses (the amygdala) and judgment (the prefrontal cortex). It is not until late adolescence or their early 20s that boys' brains catch up to those of their female counterparts—so, if 18-year-old Johnny Thunders is sleeping with 16-year-old Sable Starr, does that make them even? (According to the law, that's a resounding *no*.)

The King of Rock & Roll himself, Elvis Presley, was notorious for his affinity for young teenage girls, whom he called "cherries." According to the extensively-researched book *Baby, Let's Play House: Elvis Presley and the Women Who Loved Him,* by Alanna Nash,

"Elvis the Pelvis" felt insecure around women his own age, and would invite groups of pubescent female fans to his love shack for sleepovers where he would tickle and kiss them, and even instructed them on how to wear makeup the way he liked. Fearing that he might not measure up to a full-grown woman's expectations, Presley became paranoid about his bedroom skills, hence his predilection for virgins who would not demand sex and could not compare him to other lovers. (For the full-on Freud experience, read up on The King's connection to his mother, Gladys.)

The enlisted 24-year-old met his first and only wife, Priscilla Beaulieu, in 1959 while he was stationed in Germany and she was just 14—his previous girlfriend, Frances Forbes, was also 14. (Maybe that's what "Jailhouse Rock" was *really* about!) In any case, once the knot was tied and she gave birth to their daughter, Lisa Marie, in 1968, Priscilla was all but abandoned. She wrote in her memoir *Elvis & Me* that he "had mentioned to me before we were married that he had never been able to make love to a woman who had a child." He wasn't kidding. After the pair parted ways in 1972, the "Love Me Tender" singer began courting 14-year-old Reeca Smith, a friend of his stepbrother, Ricky Stanley. According to Reeca, her love affair with the 37-year-old hound dog lasted only a few months and never went beyond "sweet, innocent kisses."

Rolling Stones bassist Bill Wyman followed in The King's blue suede footsteps when he met a 13-year-old model named Amanda "Mandy" Smith on the London Club scene. Like a true gentleman, the 47-year-old waited until she was 14 before taking her to bed. Their relationship went public when time was on their side—16 is the legal age of consent in England, so shortly after the bony blonde blew out the candles on her milestone birthday cake, the couple was seen out on the town, flaunting their love. In Wyman's 1991 autobiography, *A Stone Alone*, he wrote, "Mandy was a woman at 13. Everyone accepted her as an adult without question." (Define "everyone," Bill.)

The pair tied the knot—while wags joked that the bridal registry was probably at Toys R Us—but their union lasted less than two years because, she later said, the "Sticky Fingers" strings man got fed up with her health issues. The bride suffered from candida, a condition that prevented her from having sex for weeks or months at a time, and Bill reportedly wasn't willing to go without. In a bizarre turn of events, Mandy's mother, Patsy, 47, married Bill's son Stephen, 30, making Stephen a stepfather to his former stepmother! (Patsy and Stephen's union also lasted for a mere two years.)

Ted Nugent was 30 and Pele Massa was 17 when they got "Cat-Scratch Fever" in 1978. The Motor City Madman, whose songs have titles like "Jailbait" and "I Am a Predator," adopted the teen and became her legal guardian with the permission of her parents. This legality was necessary for them to travel together without worry regarding varying State laws involving the age of consent. Why not just marry? Well... good ol' Ted was still married to his first wife at the time. As he said in an interview for VH-1's *Behind the Music*, "I got the stamp of approval of Pele's parents because they figured that Ted Nugent was better than some drug-infested punk in high school." Some may beg to differ, but his young lover described Nugent as "a very gentle and romantic person that every woman wanted to be with."

Maybe "The Nuge" got the idea from his fellow rocker, Steven Tyler of Aerosmith. In November of 1973, the 25-year-old "Screamin' Demon" began courting Julia Holcomb, who was nine years his junior. Even at such a young age, Julia had already suffered through a ton of tragedy. She had been severely injured in a car accident that killed her brother and her grandfather, her father had abandoned her mother, and her stepfather was a raging alcoholic. The rudderless young woman met a groupie who took her to an Aerosmith concert, and the rest is rock & roll history. Once guardianship was given to the flamboyant rock star, the lovebirds lived together for a few years. But Julia broke it off, she said, because "the rabbit done died" (meaning, she got pregnant) and Steven forced her to get an abortion.

Oddly enough, Julia Holcomb didn't even rate her real name in the scarf-obsessed singer's bestselling 2011 memoir, *Does the Noise in my Head Bother You?* He refers to her only as "Little Oral Annie" and says that they actually met at an Aerosmith show at the Paramount Theater in Seattle, when she, along with five other "nubile young chicks, one cuter than the next," was offered up as a titillating party favor by the local concert promoter. But Steven developed feelings for this particular groupie, and, he wrote, "I was so in love I almost took a teenage bride. [And] her parents fell in love with me, signed papers over for me to have custody, so I wouldn't get arrested if I took her out of state."

Steven's book described their sex life in salacious detail. "I lived with her for three years. She was a sweet, mysterious creature… very smart and she knew what she liked and what I liked. We took baths together. She wore skirts with no panties. We did it on the red-eye from L.A. to Boston… that kind of stuff. All the things that guys dream about." They did the deed in private, in public, and "tried positions the *Kama Sutra* has yet to come up with."

In the end, he said, they split because of their mutual drug addiction and because she, in a drunken stupor, almost burned down his apartment and wound up in the hospital with smoke inhalation. "That's when reality slapped me in the face" so he sent her back to where she came from.

Julia Holcomb went on to a career and a marriage that yielded six children. What's more, she became an outspoken pro-life activist. In late 2022, she filed a #MeToo-driven lawsuit against Steven (though he wasn't named specifically, he's among "Does 1-50" to cover all her bases), accusing him of sexual assault, sexual battery, and intentional infliction of emotional distress. The lawsuit was filed following California legislation that temporarily waived statutes of limitations for childhood sexual abuse allegations.

"I want this action to expose an industry that protects celebrity offenders, to cleanse and hold accountable an industry that both exploited and allowed me to be exploited for years, along with so many other naïve and vulnerable kids and adults," Julia said in a statement regarding her suit. "Because I know that I am not the only one who suffered abuse in the music industry, I feel it is time for me to take this stand and bring this action, to speak up and stand in solidarity with the other survivors."

Steven Tyler hasn't made any statements regarding the lawsuit as of this writing, but a few years back, the recovering addict (perhaps in a bid to balance his karma) opened a home for wayward girls. Janie's House, a nonprofit organization founded in 2017, provides housing, therapy, and medical care for disadvantaged young women. "The mission of Janie's Fund does my heart and my soul good," Tyler said in a statement. "This is real—to help even just one girl through Janie's House is a dream come true... just when the world feels over, you can turn into a butterfly."

When pop music and soap opera star Rick Springfield published his memoir, *Late, Late at Night*, in 2010, he candidly—and often comically—shone a light on his depression, insecurities, ego, and addictions. His sex addiction seems to have caused him the most grief over the years, but some of the memories were good; he, as a "penniless musician" was performing at the fabled Whisky a Go-Go in Hollywood one night when a cute, petite, bubbly and busty redhead showed up and they caught each other's attention. While he was an unknown talent, she was the "hottest young actress in movies" due to her starring role in the horrifying devil-possession film, The Exorcist (1973).

"She invited me to the Rainbow club up the street after I'm done with my last set and she says she and her sister Debbie will buy me a drink," Rick wrote. "I don't know how old she is but I soon learn she is only 15. I am 25." After spending time together at the hotspot, Rick and Linda went to his apartment: "Most specifically, my bed. I am her first lover and she is an enthusiastic learner."

After that, they were an item. "We share a love of dogs and sex—separately, not in combination. Most of the time we don't leave the apartment," which he said, mind-blew him because she was Hollywood's hottest, high-paid actress at the time, and he was living on ramen and hard-pressed to scrape together his $180 per month rent.

When they did leave Rick's rathole, it was "blindly and innocently to the media slaughter." In the "Hard to Hold" singer's opinion, the papers and gossip rags "shocked" him and Blair when they published "incensed articles in both teen and regular press about [our] affair."

Despite their compatibility, the May-August relationship didn't last. "Really the only reason that we didn't stay together is being in the industry, it's very difficult under the limelight," Linda said in an interview. "There's a lot of scrutiny."

Linda went on to sample the wares of many other musicians, including Deep Purple bassist Glenn Hughes, guitarist Neil Giraldo, Robin Zander of Cheap Trick, Tommy Shaw of Styx, and even the "Superfreak" himself, Rick James.

Rick Springfield and Linda Blair's friendship has continued throughout the years, and they are both advocates for animal welfare organizations, including a charity she founded, WorldHeart Foundation.

In 1979, The Knack rose to stardom with its mega-earworm hit, "My Sharona." Lead singer Doug Fieger wrote the song for the then-teenager who would become his long-term girlfriend, Sharona Alperin. "I was about 16 or 17 at the time," the name-checked "younger kind" recalled in an interview many years later. "He was nine years older than me. And within a month, he told me that, 'I'm in love with you,

you're my soulmate, you're my other half, we're going to be together one day.'" And they were; while their romantic relationship didn't last, they remained friends up until his death due to lung cancer in 2010.

Sharona said she was, and is, flattered that "My Sharona" was written for her—"Never gonna stop, give it up, such a dirty mind/I always get it up, for the touch of the younger kind"—so much so in fact, that she posed for the photo on the cover of the 45 rpm record sleeve, braless in a thin white "wife-beater" tee.

Anthony Kedis, who grew up wild in the streets of L.A. and was barely supervised by his actor dad who went by the name Blackie Dammett, formed the band Red Hot Chili Peppers in 1983 when he was 21. In his memoir *Scar Tissue*, the "Californication" singer spoke of meeting a Catholic schoolgirl while on the road in the South and taking her across state lines—a double-whammy when it comes to breaking the law.

"After [the band] got offstage, she came up to me and said, 'I have something to tell you: My father's the chief of police and the entire state of Louisiana is looking for me because I've gone missing. Oh, and besides that, I'm only 14.' I wasn't incredibly scared, because, in my somewhat deluded mind," Anthony wrote, "I knew that if she told the chief of police that she was in love with me, he wasn't going to have me taken out to a field and shot. But I did want to get her the hell back home right away. So, we had sex one more time."

Prince fell for 16-year-old belly dancer Mayte Garcia when her mother took her backstage after a concert in Germany. Prince later told Oprah Winfrey he remembered thinking "that's my future wife" when he first laid eyes on the exotic stunner. The Purple One moved her into his Paisley Park mansion in Minneapolis, Minnesota, and he became her legal guardian. (Sound familiar? These guys know how to play the law even better than they play guitar.)

Mayte claimed she couldn't "pinpoint when [their relationship] became romantic," but she said that when she was 19, Prince told her "it's time" for her to go on birth control. "It was a 'finally!' moment. I was 19. I was ready." In her 2017 memoir, *The Most Beautiful: My Life with Prince*, Mayte recalled him wanting to change her name to "Arabia" but she refused on the grounds that her mother would not approve.

The pair were wed on February 14, 1996, when he was 37 and she was 22. As a wedding gift, Prince gave his bride a 7,500-square-foot love-nest in Spain, which was outfitted with a professional hair salon, a fully decked-out music studio, and a master suite with a mirror mounted above the bed. They had a son, Amiir Nelson, but the tyke lived for only one week due to a severe genetic mutation called Pfeiffer Syndrome (it has no specific cause, and is not always detected in utero). The heartbroken couple divorced four years later, following a miscarriage and Prince's conversion to the Jehovah's Witness religion. (Prince died of an accidental drug overdose at his Paisley Park estate in 2016.)

Like Jerry Lee Lewis before him, Beach Boy Dennis Wilson married into his own gene pool. Dennis' cousin Mike's daughter Shawn Love was only 16 when she started feeling those "Good Vibrations" in 1981. The scandal reportedly didn't faze the perennial party boy, who was described as having a classic surfer's indifference to possessions, squandering millions on the mythical wine, women, and song.

Shortly before he drowned at the age of 39 in 1983, Wilson wed Love, then 18. The baby-faced blond was his fifth wife and she had given birth to his fourth child, Gage, in 1982. After his passing, Dennis' widow had to fight for a payout from Transamerica Occidental Life Insurance Company, which claimed they shouldn't have to pony up since the drummer was drunk when he drowned in Marina del Rey while diving from his moored boat. A court said otherwise, and also ordered them to pay punitive damages on top of the $1-million policy that the musician took out just a little more than a year before his death. (Shawn died in 2003 of liver cancer.)

Willie Nelson's first wife Martha Matthews was 16 when they married. But he was 19, so does that even count as statutory rape? (In some states, yes, it does.) Shotgun Willie's wedding was not, by the way, of the shotgun sort—it was for *amour*.

"It was love. My first full blast of love, the kind of love where you lose your mind and let your heart lead the way," he remembered, years later. After having three children together, the couple split in 1962 due to domestic abuse. The perpetrator was not him... it was her. The crossover country star described a dealbreaker incident in which Martha tied him up and beat him with a broom.

"The Redheaded Stranger" may have been married and divorced a bunch of times, but he always supported his families. "Along the way, you pick up wives and kids and you are responsible for them. You don't discard them. There is no such thing as ex-wives, only *additional* wives."

If you think you've read the last about Jimmy Page and his eye for pretty young things, think again! In 2014, the silver fox met and fell for redheaded poet and author, Scarlett Sabat, who is 45 years his junior. (And she just happens to have the first name of his first daughter, who was born to Jimmy and French model, Charlotte Martin, in 1971... Scarlett the girlfriend was born in *1989*. Gulp.)

Jimmy's first wife, a native Louisianan named Patricia Ecker, was working as a waitress in the French Quarter when he was on tour with the British rock supergroup, The Firm, in 1986. She was 18 years younger than him. In December of that same year, the couple got hitched. They had a son, James Patrick Page III (born in 1988), but their love didn't last. On January 16, 1995, Jimmy and Patricia filed for divorce, and he married brunette bombshell Jimena Gómez-Paratcha later that same year. Jimena was 28 years younger than the "Ramble On" guitarist when they walked down the aisle. The couple had two children, Zofia Jade (born in 1997) and Ashen Josan (born in 1999), then split in 2011. (Patricia Ecker Page died on October 30, 2020, at the age of 58, from an undisclosed cause.)

As Jimmy gets older, his girlfriends get younger. (If Scarlett doesn't last, what's next... a zygote?) Scarlett, who resembles a Pre-Raphaelite muse painted by John William Waterhouse, admitted in an interview with *Tatler* that she was made to feel bad about the nearly half-a-century age difference as soon as her relationship went public. "I guess some people will say I've made an unusual choice. At the time [when we first got together] it felt very uncomfortable. I felt like my life was going to be over; I had such a sense of shame about the whole thing."

The British-born beauty got over it and moved into the "Stairway to Heaven" guitarist's Holland Park home in west London and they have been inseparable ever since. "I'm in an amazing relationship," Scarlett said. "I think a lot of people make assumptions but Jimmy's an exceptional man, and beautiful. There are a lot of women of all ages who are excited to meet him." (You don't say, Scarlett!)

Lest you think it's only young women who were sexualized in the '70s, check YouTube for blond, baby-faced pop idol Leif Garrett as a contestant on *The Dating Game* on their 1971 Halloween episode—he's asking slightly naughty questions of the three girls who were vying for a date with him. The queries touch on kissing, bikini wear, making guys happy, and even using the word "sexy" to describe his hopes for them. He was 11 years old at the time. A few years later, at 15, the "I Was Made for Dancing" hitmaker appeared shirtless on the cover of *Tiger Beat*, gazing lustfully into the camera and out at his fans.

When *MTV* hit the airwaves in the early '80s, it wasn't just young girls as the "video vixens." In an artful but odd music video by The Tubes for their hit single "She's a Beauty," a prepubescent young man is strapped into a carnival car, held against the heaving bosoms of a dominatrix, and taken for the ride of his life. That video marked the first acting job for 12-year-old Alexis Arquette (then known as Robert Arquette), who, after seeing a spectacle of sexy mermaids, cavewomen, and a talented trapeze artist, winds up in a cage, corralled by a bevy of beauties.

Tubes lead singer Fee Waybill said he wrote the song (along with his bandmates) after an almost-hallucinogenic jaunt through San Francisco's red light district, where he discovered a nude woman dancing in a plexiglass cage—in order to keep seeing her and talking to her, Fee fed quarters into the slot. Originally, the "She's a Beauty" chorus was supposed to go, "You can talk to a naked girl," but the record's producer convinced the band to call her a "pretty girl" instead.

Young Arquette was cast in the video because of The Tubes' Toto connection: his sister Rosanna, namesake of the 1982 Toto hit, was dating Steve Porcaro of Toto, the bandmate of "She's A Beauty" co-writer Steve Lukather. Alexis, who was transgender, died from a heart attack on September 11, 2016, after battling HIV for 29 years. She played a trans sex worker in the film "Last Exit to Brooklyn" and a Boy George impersonator in "The Wedding Singer."

CHAPTER SIX (SIX SIX): RUNNIN' WITH THE DEVIL

"People who cease to believe in God or goodness altogether still believe in the devil."—Anne Rice

First of all, let's address the satanic elephant in the room: Ozzy Osbourne's hit song "Mr. Crowley" mangles the wizard of wickedness' name. That indelible 1981 metal mantra inadvertently set off a chain reaction of mispronunciation—everyone says it the wrong way now.

The eponymous English occultist, who was active in the early 20th century, apparently dealt with the issue a lot because he made up a rhyme for the tongue-tied to remember him by: "The name is Crowley, it rhymes with Holy. It isn't Crowley, that rhymes with foully."

He even went so far as to create a five-line poem:

> My name it is Aleister Crowley,
> a master of Magick unholy.
> Of philtres and pentacles,
> covens, conventicles,
> of basil, nepenthe, and moly.

The 1980s are well-known for the so-called "Satanic Panic," but the backlash had to come from somewhere, right? That somewhere would be the '60s and '70s, when Beelzebub ran rampant through mainstream entertainment with blockbuster movies like *Rosemary's Baby*, *The Exorcist*, and *The Omen*, and chart-topping earworms ranging from "Sympathy for the Devil" to "The Devil Went Down to Georgia."

While Ozzy Osbourne co-wrote a catchy tune about the historical figure who referred to himself as "The Great Beast" and "The Wickedest Man in the World" (Aleister probably had his tongue stuck in his cheek; he did have a cult to run and books to sell, after all) it's Led Zeppelin's founder and guitarist, Jimmy Page, who is most closely associated with Crowley fanboyism.

Thanks to the subversive, arty, underground films of auteur Kenneth Anger, the long-dead practitioner was brought back to life in the rock world. *Invocation of My Demon Brother* and *Lucifer Rising*—both inspired by Crowley's Ancient Egypt-based spiritual beliefs—had Jimmy Page, Mick Jagger, and Bobby Beausoleil involved in creating eerie, mystical scores.

While the Stones only dabbled in the devil-may-care philosophies of Mr. Crowley, Jimmy dove right in, horns first. In 1970, he bought the mage's former residence, Boleskine House, which is situated on the southern bank of Loch Ness, Scotland. The famous occultist allegedly carried out esoteric rituals aimed at summoning supernatural beings, and Jimmy asserted that the place was indeed haunted. "There were two or three owners before Crowley moved into it," the "In My Time of Dying" guitarist told *Rolling Stone* in 1975. "It was also a church that was burned to the ground with the congregation in it. Strange things have happened in that house that had nothing to do with Crowley. The bad vibes were already there. A man was beheaded there, and sometimes you can hear his head rolling down." (Jimmy sold the place in 1992, and it burned to the ground for the second time in 2015; it's since been restored by its current owner, Keith Readdy, the author of *One Truth and One Spirit: Aleister Crowley's Spiritual Legacy*.)

During the 1970s, Jimmy Page amassed the world's premier collection of original Crowley books and manuscripts and bought London's Equinox Occult Bookshop (named after the author's journals of magick) to showcase them. The store was shuttered in 1979.

Page's outrageous obsession with Aleister Crowley led to whispers that he and his fellow members of Led Zeppelin had made a Faustian bargain in exchange for their superstardom. And when he had the occultist's dictum "Do what thou wilt" ("do what you want") inscribed in the run-off groove of the original vinyl releases of *Led Zeppelin III* in 1970, it led to a great deal of speculation from the press and fans alike.

Recording engineer Terry Manning told *Goldmine* how the whole thing came about. "Working with [the band] Big Star, we had added some messages of our own on there. I mentioned this to Jimmy and said, 'Anything you wanna write?' and he said, 'Ooh, yeah.' We'd been talking about the Aleister Crowley thing, so he said, 'Give me a few minutes,' and he sat down and he thought and he scribbled some things out and he finally came up with 'Do What Thou Wilt Shall Be the Whole of the Law' and 'So Mote It Be.'

"Once he'd figured out what he wanted to say, I took this little metal pencil-like thing and wrote them very carefully on the vinyl because if you drop that thing, you've ruined your master. You can't touch the grooves, so you have to lean over. Very difficult to do, that's why they don't really like you doing that. But we did it."

In 1974, when Led Zeppelin started their own record label, Swan Song, the launch party was held on Halloween night at Chislehurst Caves, in Chislehurst, Kent, and the engraved invitation began with Crowley's credo, "Do What Thou Wilt." The freaky fete featured half-naked nuns serving libations on platters, while models lay in coffins and actors wrestled in dark corners.

When Led Zeppelin broke up following the tragic, early death of their drummer John Bonham in 1980, speculation ran rampant that the band's misfortunes were due to the devil coming to collect for his earlier endowment of superstardom. That decade gave way to the Satanic Panic and Led Zep was one of the first bands accused of backwards masking.

Backwards masking (or backmasking) is a recording technique in which subliminal messages are planted within a piece of music for the purpose of encoding hidden suggestions to be picked up by the listener's subconscious and making them think or do things they would not otherwise carry out.

Televangelist Paul Crouch of the Trinity Broadcasting Network made this allegation in 1982, claiming that, when played backwards, the "bustle in your hedgerow" lyric of "Stairway to Heaven" says, "Here's to my sweet Satan/The one whose little path would make me sad, whose power is Satan/He will give those with him 666/There was a little toolshed where he made us suffer, sad Satan."

Jimmy Page laughed about the whole thing on a talk show, saying, "It's hard enough to write a song one way 'round." Robert Plant poo-poohed the whole thing too, protesting, "Who on Earth would have ever thought of doing that?" Well, Aleister Crowley thought of that. In an early issue of *The Equinox*, he says that an ambitious magician should "train himself to think backwards by external means." The Great Beast offered further advice: learn to walk backwards, speak backwards, and "listen to records reversed."

David Bowie paid tribute to Crowley with his 1971 song "Quicksand," name-checking the mage and his infamous Golden Dawn religious sect. In a 1976 interview with *Rolling Stone*, David said, "Rock has always been the Devil's music. I believe rock & roll is dangerous. I feel we're only heralding something even darker than ourselves."

Another occult figure fawned over by some pop musicians was Anton Szandor LaVey, founder of San Francisco's Church of Satan. His hedonistic Pagan-based religion was a rejection of *all* religions, where a practitioner was "a carnal beast living in a cosmos that is indifferent to our existence."

Born Howard Stanton Levey on April 11, 1930, in Chicago, he supposedly made ends meet as a carny, forensic photographer, burlesque organ accompanist, and lion tamer (heavy on the "supposedly"). In 1966, the goateed, baldheaded huckster hit paydirt with his trendy new religion and many musicians followed him like the proverbial pied-piper. Sammy Davis, Jr., was perhaps the most famous member of the Satanic congregation. In an advanced excerpt from his 1980 memoir *Hollywood in a Suitcase* but edited out of the final release, he wrote of the Church of Satan, "It was a short-lived interest, but I still have many friends in the Church of Satan. I say this to only show that however bizarre the subject, I don't pass judgment until I have found out everything I can about it. People who can put up an interesting case will often find that I'm a willing convert."

Local San Francisco rockers also flitted in and out of the sulfur-soaked pews. One of the Manson murderers, Susan Atkins, had performed as a topless "blood-swilling vampire" in the LaVey stage show "Witches' Sabbath" before joining The Family cult.

Anton connected with Roman Polanski and was supposed to have a cameo in the director's 1968 horror film *Rosemary's Baby* but it didn't pan out. A year later, Manson Family members murdered Polanski's wife, Sharon Tate, and celebrity hairdresser, Jay Sebring (among others). Jay had been a member of LaVey's church at the same time as Sammy, and was, in fact, the singer's stylist. According to a 50th-anniversary article about The Church of Satan published by *SFGate.com*, after the Manson murders, "LaVey's dark star began a long, slow decline that occasional talk show gigs couldn't reverse. Even welcoming rock star Marilyn Manson into the fold in the early '90s didn't help much. Besides, he despised rock & roll—even satanic metal he found distasteful. Instead, he favored romantic tunes of the 1940s."

One of Anton's daughters, Zeena, headed an experimental rock collective, Radio Werewolf, from 1988 to 1993. In 2016, *Classic Rock* magazine ranked them at #4 on their "25 Weirdest Bands of All-Time" list.

Rock & roll's alias as "the Devil's music" was meant to be an insult—though the genre was not the first to wear that tag. Men who played the blues (Robert Johnson), jazz (Jelly Roll Morton), and even classical hundreds of years before (Niccolò Paganini), were denounced as Satan's musical marionettes. Even religious rock & rollers like Elvis Presley (who grew up singing in church) and Jerry Lee Lewis (whose cousin was the Reverend Jimmy Swaggart) did not escape the wrath of the pious. Needless to say, straitlaced society's condemnation of their favorite music only drove teenagers' fandom further, leading directly to John Lennon's legendary 1966 quote, "The Beatles are more popular than Jesus." In 1967, Aleister Crowley appeared as one among the sea of the faces on the iconic cover of The Beatles album, *Sgt. Pepper's Lonely Hearts Club Band*.

Also in 1967, a group of Chicago-based musicians started a heavy, psychedelic proto-metal band called Coven. Vocalist Esther "Jinx" Dawson, lead guitarist Chris Neilsen, bassist Greg "Oz" Osborne, keyboardist Rick Durrett, and drummer Steve Ross, donned occult garb and sang the praises of you-know-who. In fact, Coven has the distinction of being the first-ever to "throw horns"—a defiant yet celebratory hand gesture that is still so popular to this day, there's even an emoji for it—as seen on their debut album, *Witchcraft Destroys Minds & Reaps Souls*. While performing onstage, Jinx would do the benediction of the Black Mass in Latin, followed by the Crowley quote, "Do what thou wilt shall be the whole of the law," and ending in a full-tilt scream of "Hail Satan!"

The first Coven LP ended with a 13-minute opus to dark forces, accompanied by a warning inside the gatefold: "To the best of our knowledge, this is the first Black Mass to be recorded, either in written words or in audio. It is as authentic as hundreds of hours of research in every known source can make it. We do not recommend its use by anyone who has not thoroughly studied Black Magic and is aware of the risks and dangers involved." Incidentally, the first track on the Coven album is called "Black Sabbath," and while they did have "Oz" Osbourne on bass, there is no relation to the British metal band Black Sabbath, with John "Ozzy" Osborne on lead vocals, that formed in 1968 (their first album, *Paranoid*, was released in 1970).

Birmingham's Black Sabbath didn't take its name from anything satanic—it was, in fact, the third name for the group previously known as Polka Turk, and Earth. A cinema across the street from the band's rehearsal space was showing the 1963 Gothic horror film *Black Sabbath* starring Boris Karloff, and noticing how many people lined up to see the fright flick, bassist Geezer Butler observed that it was "strange that people spend so much money to see scary movies." This prompted Ozzy and Geezer to write a song called "Black Sabbath." The tune featured the notorious musical tritone (an interval made up of three tones, or six semitones), also known as "the Devil's Interval" because it's inherently unsettling to the human ear. Judas Priest frontman Rob Halford has called it "probably the most evil song ever written." Inspired by their new sound, the band changed their name to Black Sabbath and set out to produce the musical equivalent of horror films.

Bands like Cream, The Yardbirds, Deep Purple, Mountain, and The Jimi Hendrix Experience are generally credited with developing the bombastic drumming, intense basslines, and distorted guitar sounds that differentiate heavy metal from other blues-based rock but if you had to pinpoint one band as being the godfathers of the genre, it would be Black Sabbath. They leaned into the hellish trappings heavier than most but they weren't the first, nor the most famous.

The Rolling Stones not only sang "Sympathy for the Devil," they demonstrated it with satyr-like sexuality, drug-downing, and naming their 1967 album *Their Satanic Majesties Request*, which marked the first time Old Scratch had been called out in the title of a major pop release. Their 1969 album *Let it Bleed* featured the song "Gimme Shelter," with the repetitive chorus, "Rape, murder, it's just a shot away." (Which is actually an anti-war protest.) Of "Sympathy" Keith said, "It's an uplifting song. It's just a matter of looking the Devil in the face. He's there all the time. I've had very close contact with Lucifer—I've met him several times."

But for most of those bands, it was showbiz Satanism; a tinseled swindle to sell records and keep themselves in the headlines. KISS supposedly stood for Knights in Satan's Service, while AC/DC was Anti-Christ/Devil's Child. Alice Cooper tapped veteran horror actor Vincent Price to record the mid-song narration for "Devil's Food," which appeared on his 1975 hit record, *Welcome to My Nightmare*.

By the 1980s, it had become a full-on joke, with bands like Mötley Crüe and Twisted Sister taking shock-rock to the mainstream—but Christian evangelists are not known for their sense of humor and they weren't laughing when they started the whole anti-metal craze. Ozzy Osbourne, who'd gone solo by then, was one of their biggest targets. Going back to his Black Sabbath days, they condemned "Paranoid" for the lyric, "I tell you to end your life." But, whoops, they got it wrong. Ozzy's mush-mouthed words are actually: "I tell you to enjoy life."

The "Crazy Train" singer, who billed himself as "The Prince of Darkness," drew parallels between his addictions to drugs and alcohol and Satan. "I was convinced I truly was possessed by the Devil. I remember sitting through *The Exorcist* a dozen times, saying to myself, 'Yeah, I can relate to that.'"

One of his songs, 1980's eardrum-shattering "Suicide Solution" became the basis of a wrongful-death lawsuit four years after its release. Nineteen-year-old John Daniel McCollum shot and killed himself on October 26, 1984, while lying on his bed listening to the *Blizzard of Ozz* record at home in Indio, California. His parents went on to sue the singer.

"He's a perfectly normal kid there, who really doesn't show any signs of any depression at all, is happy, and all of a sudden, six hours, he's dead. No one could explain it, the only thing we know is he was listening to this music," said McCollum's father, Jack.

The lyrics "Made your bed, rest your head/But you lie there and moan/Where to hide? Suicide is the only way out" were the main point of contention when the McCollums sued Ozzy and CBS Records in 1986.

"The boy must have been pretty messed up before he ever heard an Ozzy record," said the singer in an interview. "I mean, I can't help that, you know? I feel very sad for the boy, and I felt terribly sad for the parents. As a parent myself, I'd be pretty devastated if something like that happened. And I have thought about this, if the boot was on the other foot, I couldn't blame the artist."

The title is not a reference to suicide being a solution to a problem, but rather it refers to alcohol as a liquid substance that can lead to death when abused. (More than likely, songwriter and bassist Bob Daisley was referring to Ozzy himself with the lines, "Wine is fine but whiskey's quicker/Suicide is slow with liquor."

The McCollum case was dismissed by the State of California in 1988, but the family of another young fan, Michael Waller, filed a lawsuit against Osbourne that same year. They didn't go for the lyrics, though—they asserted that the subliminal messages hidden within "Suicide Solution" made Michael kill himself on May 3, 1986. Their case was thrown out as well.

The year before, in 1985, a bipartisan committee known as the Parents Music Resource Center (PMRC) was formed to fight what they considered dangerous or satanic music—everyone from W.A.S.P. to Madonna was on their shit list. The board was founded by four women known as the "Washington Wives": Tipper Gore, wife of Senator and later Vice President Al Gore; Susan Baker, wife of Treasury Secretary James Baker; Pam Howar, wife of Washington realtor Raymond Howar; and Sally Nevius, wife of former Washington City Council Chairman John Nevius.

The Washington Wives argued that albums should be rated, just like movies. But instead of issuing "G" to "R" guidelines, the PMRC demanded content-based ratings: "X" for profane or sexually explicit lyrics, "O" for occult references, "D/A" for lyrics about drugs and alcohol, and "V" for violent content. Stickering became such a sticking point that the Senate's Committee on Commerce held a hearing at which Frank Zappa, Twisted Sister's Dee

Snider, and even clean-cut "I'm a Country Boy" pop singer John Denver, testified against the proposed censorship.

Ultimately, the Record Industry Association of America did agree to labels stating: "Parental Advisory: Explicit Lyrics." Which probably only served to boost sales for many records. In 1986, Motely Crue released a "special limited-edition X-rated package" version of their single "Girls, Girls, Girls." Their album of the same name became one of the band's bestselling records.

The 1970s yielded so many genres of rock and pop—maybe more than any other 10-year period in music history—there was soft rock, hard rock, acid rock, singer-songwriter, glam, prog-rock, yacht rock, bubblegum-pop, punk, disco, hip-hop, electronica—but metal was the baddest of them all, setting precedents in landmark lawsuits. (But it wasn't just rock's head that rolled; the popular nerdy pastime Dungeons & Dragons was also targeted, with one litigator accusing the role-playing game of using "demonology, witchcraft, voodoo, murder, rape, blasphemy, suicide, assassination, insanity, sex perversion, homosexuality, prostitution, satanic type rituals, gambling, barbarism, cannibalism, sadism, desecration, demon summoning, necromantics, divination and other teachings" to defile young minds.)

All of this happened in the thick of the Satanic Panic. Ozzy Osbourne later said he figured he was doing the televangelists a favor simply by existing. "I've kept them in jobs," he said. "One time they were picketing [my] gig with this 'Antichrist' thing and I joined them at the end of the line with a broomstick and stapled 'Have a Nice Day' and a smiley face on it. They didn't know I was there."

Judas Priest's KK Downing reasoned, "Think about it. If armies of teenagers were spending all that money on beer, tee-shirts, petrol, albums, and concert tickets, then that's all money that could potentially be going other places—like the church. And it was no coincidence that areas of the U.S. where we ran into the most opposition were the very areas where organized religion was most powerful."

One of the few metal mouthpieces for Jesus was a band called Stryper. Stryper came of age on the same sacred ground as so many hair bands of the day did: the Sunset Strip in Hollywood. While they were a curio, they've proved to be no flash in the collection plate— their records have gone platinum, they've played stadiums, and, despite ups and downs over the decades, they're still making honest-to-God music with brothers and founding members Michael Sweet on vocals and guitar, and Robert Sweet on drums.

Their scripture-inspired name came from a passage in Isaiah 53:5, "By His stripes we are healed." It also stands for "Salvation Through Redemption, Yielding Peace, Encouragement, and Righteousness." The Bible boys fit in fine with their flashy brethren, wearing striped bumble-bee colored spandex onstage, coiffing big, teased hair, and stomping around in platform boots while tossing "the good book" out to their devout audiences.

The 2021 oral history, *Nöthin' But a Good Time: The Uncensored History of the '80s Hard Rock Explosion*, tells the epic story of glam metal and includes the unusual rise of Stryper. Michael Sweet recalled, "Around 1983… that's when we had a few of our friends in the music world, who had changed their lives, came into our rehearsal studio and told us about God. And that's when the light went on for us. And Oz [Fox, guitarist] had grown up in a Christian family. Tim [Gaines, bassist], his dad was a preacher. And Robert and I came to know God through Jimmy Swaggart. My brother started watching him on television when we were kids, like I'm sure a lot of people at the time did."

But it wasn't all fun and grace. Back in the day Stryper opened for mainstream bands like RATT and Bon Jovi, leading some fans and critics to claim that they were not good Christian rockers. Even their inspiration, the Reverend Jimmy Swaggart, was against the boys in yellow-and-black. The sweaty sermonist said that when the band gave out copies of the New Testament at their shows it was akin to "casting pearls before swine."

While Stryper is still spreading the gospel through screaming guitar solos, Swaggart was defrocked by the Assemblies of God in 1988 after a sex scandal involving prostitutes (and was caught with his hand in the cooch cookie jar again in 1991).

Like Black Sabbath, the band Judas Priest was from the industrial city of Birmingham, England. They formed around the same time, 1969, but its iconic, operatic-voiced lead singer, Rob Halford, didn't join the fray until the early '70s. With its distinctive dual-guitar screams, studs, leather, and Harley-Davidson onstage antics, not to mention international sales of over 50 million records, Judas Priest was *the* heavy metal poster band of the Reagan Era. Standout songs like "Breaking the Law," "Living after Midnight," and "You've Got Another Thing Comin'" put them in the spotlight… and America's crosshairs.

The band and their label, CBS Records, were sued by the grieving mother of a young man who shot himself in a failed suicide attempt after listening to the 1978 Judas Priest album, *Stained Class*, on loop. On December 23, 1985, Sparks, Nevada, residents Ray Belknap, 18, and James Vance, 20, spent six hours drinking, smoking weed, and listening to Judas Priest. Once they'd heard enough, they picked up a 12-gauge sawed-off shotgun (James owned several firearms) and walked to a nearby church playground, where they planned on killing themselves.

Ray was the first to go. James recalled, "I could see him but I couldn't see his eyes. He held the gun up against his throat and was talking with it pressed up against his throat. And he said, 'I sure fucked my life up.' Then he pulled the trigger, dying instantly."

Seeing what he saw, and still thinking the idea was a good one, James picked up the smoking, blood-slicked shotgun. "There was blood everywhere [but] I was going to shoot myself." Through a slobbering, gaping hole that had once been his mouth, the horribly disfigured young man recounted the awful incident in a 1992 PBS documentary about the case, called *Dream Deceivers: The Story Behind James Vance vs. Judas Priest.* "It was like I had no control over it. I didn't want to die. But I shot myself."

The badly wounded James and his dead best friend were found the next morning by a horrified passerby, who immediately called 911. From the hospital, James, whose eyes were thankfully spared, wrote to Ray's mother, Aunetta Roberson: "I believe that alcohol and heavy metal music such as Judas Priest led us to be mesmerized."

James Vance lived for three years after the suicide attempt, but his face was so badly disfigured that hospital bills amounted to more than $400,000 in trying—but not succeeding—to repair the devastating damage. After undergoing 150 hours of surgeries and suffering from constant pain, James slipped into a coma in 1988 and died within a few days. His attorney speculated that the 25-year-old committed suicide by overdose because he was so depressed over what Judas Priest's music had allegedly caused him to do. He left behind a one-year-old daughter, and parents who were still upset enough to charge ahead with the multi-million-dollar lawsuit that had already been filed.

While the case against Ozzy Osbourne didn't go to trial, the one against Judas Priest did—for six long weeks, beginning in July of 1990. One song, in particular, was considered to be the main culprit: "Better By Me, Better Than You," a cover of a prog-rock Spooky Tooth number. The prosecution homed in on an imagined invitation to suicide, arguing that the repeated phrase "Do it" was buried backwards in the track.

"Judas Priest and CBS pander this stuff to alienated teenagers," said Kenneth McKenna, the lawyer for Mr. Belknap's family. "The members of the chess club, the math and science majors, don't listen to this stuff. It's the dropouts, the drug and alcohol abusers. So our argument is, you have a duty to be more cautious when you're dealing with a population susceptible to this stuff."

When speaking to *Rolling Stone* about the case, Judas Priest's frontman said they were "baffled by some of the things that were coming out in the courtroom." They'd heard of backwards masking before in connection with The Beatles and Led Zeppelin but it wasn't something they'd ever even thought of doing. The band's manager cynically retorted, "If we were going to do that, I'd be saying, 'Buy seven copies,' not telling a couple of screwed-up kids to kill themselves."

The trial in Reno was the quintessential media circus, with supporters on both sides acting outrageously outside the courtroom, holding up signs, and getting into verbal altercations. The newspapers bore attention-grabbing headlines like, "Judas Priest: Subliminal Criminals!" The band listened to the maimed man's pre-recorded testimony and witnessed their albums being picked apart by attorneys and experts hunting for hidden messages.

"Further to the written documents, there was a filmed deposition of one of the youths— the one who survived but had shot most of his face off. It was just gruesome and disturbing to see that he had to wear a baby's bib because of his injuries. And because he now didn't have a nose, they had grown one upside down on his forehead and then turned it around," KK Downing wrote in his autobiography, *Heavy Duty: Days & Nights in Judas Priest.* "It was an awful sight, and one that made the gravity of the situation hit me."

The band's attorney, Suellen Fulstone, dug up the young men's troubled pasts, which included truancy, drugs, and arrests for petty crimes. James had a history of violence that included two assaults on his mother, Phyllis Vance. So the attorney argued that Belknap and Vance clearly were troubled young men, and it was not the group's music that resulted in their deaths. "I remember one of the terms I learned in the course of trying this case was the term 'dysfunctional family,'" she said, adding that Judas Priest bandmembers "felt bad for the family, but didn't feel they were in any way responsible for what happened."

"We weren't saying the band was some kind of Svengali who hypnotized them into doing this, but these two boys were in the suicide zone," said Timothy Post, who was representing Vance's estate. "We never said they were Presbyterian Sunday school teachers, but they were up on the bridge teetering and Judas Priest said 'jump.' This was a product liability case, and they were putting hidden poison in their product."

Gary Wright, who had a big hit in the 1970s with his song "Dreamweaver," wrote "Better By You, Better Than Me" in 1969 for his band, Spooky Tooth. When interviewed by *Pop Dose* in 2009, the singer and keyboardist revealed that he had been deposed by the Nevada Court when the lawsuit was filed. "It was one of those nuisance lawsuits that the family of the kids who committed suicide were trying to blame Judas Priest and saying it was their fault, when the kids were screwed-up, you know? How can you blame somebody that wrote a song that had nothing to do with suicide, on this? It was so absolutely out-there, you know? There is a generation, when I do that [song], they say, 'Why do you play a Judas Priest song?'"

Ultimately Judge Jerry Whitehead ruled that while there might have been subliminal messages in Judas Priest's record, they were buried too deep in the mix to be detected by a normal listener. It was the first time there had been a judicial determination on whether subliminal messages were or were not protected speech under the First Amendment and the nitty gritty of the judge's ruling was that music can't make you kill yourself. The case was finally dismissed.

The thrash-metal band Slayer was sued by the parents of a murder victim in connection with the 1996 satanic sacrifice of 16-year-old Elyse Pahler, in Arroyo Grande, California. David and Lisanne Pahler claimed that the band's songs "Postmortem" and "Dead Skin Mask" gave their daughter's three killers explicit instructions on how to "stalk, rape, torture, murder and commit acts of necrophilia."

The real culprits were the young members of a fame-seeking heavy metal band called Hatred. With brimstone-blackened souls, the three teens came up with a fiendish plan to get noticed. Instead of, you know, practicing their instruments and writing some kickass tunes, they decided to kill an innocent girl. Royce Casey, 17, Jacob Delashmutt, 16, and Joseph Fiorella, 15, stalked Elyse for weeks. Then, on July 22, they lured her to an out-of-the-way eucalyptus grove where they strangled, stabbed, and stomped her, then left her to bleed out. A 2009 supernatural horror film called *Jennifer's Body* was supposedly loosely based on the case—rock band sacrifices virgin—but the similarities end there. The true facts are far more alarming. After Elyse died, the boys came back and took turns having sex with her cold corpse, according to an article in the *San Luis Obispo Tribune*.

The case would go unsolved for eight months before Royce himself contacted police and led them to the partially mummified remains. Court transcripts revealed that the fledgling band members said they needed to commit a "sacrifice to the devil" to give them the "craziness" to "go professional" and "to receive power from the devil to help them play guitar better."

Royce admitted he chose Elyse because "she had blonde hair and blue eyes and, because she was a virgin, she would be a perfect sacrifice for the devil." Joseph told police that Slayer's music "started to influence the way I looked at things." To the contrary, Jacob told *The Washington Post*, "That's not why Elyse was murdered. She was murdered because Joe [Fiorella] was obsessed with her and obsessed with *killing* her."

Scott Harrington, attorney for Slayer and the Sony Music label American Recordings, was confident that the case would not go to trial. "There's not a legal position that could be taken that would make the band responsible," he said. "Where do you draw the line? You might as well start looking through the library at every book on the shelf." That case was thrown out, so the despairing parents tried again, claiming in another lawsuit that Slayer "knowingly distributed harmful material to minors." This case too was dismissed, with Judge E. Jeffrey Burke stating, "Slayer lyrics are repulsive and profane. But they do not direct or instruct listeners to commit the acts that resulted in the vicious torture-murder of Elyse Pahler."

Allen Hutkin, attorney for the prosecution, said, "It's tragic all around because not only did you lose Elyse who was this incredible, wonderful person, but you had these three boys who changed the course of their life by the horrible things they did by following these lyrics."

All three were convicted of first-degree murder. Royce Casey, who was granted parole in 2022 when he was 42 years old, told the board that he finally understood "how immense the suffering is that I caused, that Elyse doesn't have her life anymore because of me. She had to feel so much pain and terror while I was murdering her," he added. As Elyse was being murdered, she begged for help, calling out to her mother and to Jesus. "I'm ashamed by the person that I was then, and I'm disgusted by the person that I was then. I'm ashamed that I took her entire future away." His conscience "broke through the denial that I had, and those things helped me to be able to see that there was something deeper I needed to look at to understand that it was my defects that led me to this—not my co-defendants, not music, not drugs."

Many rock and metal musicians have been demonized due to a select few of their fans having carried out heinous crimes. Richard "The Night Stalker" Ramirez was one of the most depraved serial killers of his time, sadistically butchering 13 people in their Los Angeles County homes between June 1984 and August 1985.

A diehard fan of Judas Priest, Black Sabbath, and AC/DC, the homeless, self-proclaimed Satanist left an AC/DC baseball cap at the scene of a home invasion and was spotted wearing various band tees by witnesses. After he was apprehended, a story came out asserting that Richard was especially inspired by the AC/DC song "Night Prowler" which appeared on their 1979 album, *Highway to Hell*. The band members were mortified by their connection to such appalling acts, which included animal sacrifice, rape, and pedophilia. "It sickens you to have anything to do with that kind of thing," lead vocalist Brian Johnson told VH1.

Richard was sentenced to death on November 9, 1989, whereupon he remarked, "Dying doesn't scare me. I'll be in hell, with Satan." While looking forward to his fate on San Quentin's death row, the Night Stalker beat the system by dying of natural causes (liver failure) in 2013, at the age of 53.

Heavy metal-loving teenagers Damien Echols, Jessie Misskelley, and Jason Baldwin of West Memphis, Arkansas—now famously known as the "West Memphis Three"—were accused of murdering three prepubescent boys in 1994. They were arrested, and convicted, based largely on small-town prejudices, targeting their taste in music, Pagan religious beliefs, and the fact they wore their hair in "long mullets." (That haircut is a misdemeanor at best.) There was no DNA evidence, no witnesses placing them at the scene, and no personal affiliations to the victims at all.

The triple murder was, indeed, horrific. On May 5, 1993, best friends Steven Branch, Michael Moore, and Christopher Byers—all in the second grade—went missing. The next day, the boys' battered bodies were found in a drainage ditch in Robin Hood Hills Park. All had been stripped naked and hogtied with their own shoelaces, and Christopher's genitals were mutilated.

About a month later, the teenagers were brought in and interrogated after someone said that law enforcement should be looking at 18-year-old Damien Echols because he wore a black trench coat and listened to a lot of Metallica. Seventeen-year-old Jessie, whose IQ was reportedly only 72, was questioned for hours on end without legal counsel, and without his parents—he cracked under the pressure and falsely confessed, also implicating Damien and Jason.

Jesse was convicted of one count of first-degree murder and two counts of second-degree murder on February 5, 1994. The judge sentenced him to the maximum penalty—life in prison, plus 40 years. Damien and Jason were tried together and were convicted of three counts of capital murder. Jason got life in prison without parole, but Damien was sentenced to death by lethal injection.

Documentarians Joe Berlinger and Bruce Sinofsky's Emmy-winning 1996 documentary *Paradise Lost: The Child Murders at Robin Hills* made waves in the legal and music communities, as it shone a harsh light on the shoddy, prejudiced process that made icons of the West Memphis Three. Metallica licensed the use of their music at no charge to Joe and Bruce, which ultimately led to the pair directing Metallica's documentary, *Some Kind of Monster* (2004). Two more high-profile films followed, *Paradise Lost 2: Revelations* in 2000, and *Paradise Lost 3: Purgatory* in 2011.

The documentaries sent shockwaves through a worldwide audience, striking terror in the hearts of all who were considered "different." Henry Rollins of Black Flag stepped up to help prove the boys' innocence because, he said, "I saw a lot of myself in the three of them." Metallica frontman James Hetfield agreed: "The way you dress, the things you listen to... I can basically speak for myself, growing up, that that was just a sign of wanting to be creative and different."

Jason Baldwin was grateful for the documentaries, saying, "They wanted to overwhelm us, convict us, condemn us, and sweep us under the rug. And no one would be the wiser." He added that he was grateful that the films brought the situation to those outside the Bible Belt where they were convicted.

Lawyers, journalists, activists, and several major music stars—Eddie Vedder, Lemmy, Iggy Pop, Johnny Depp, Joe Strummer, Guns N' Roses, Natalie Maines of Dixie Chicks, and of course, Metallica—took up the fight for justice in a campaign known as "Free the West Memphis Three." Undoubtedly, their support aided in the court's decision to reverse the convictions and release all three wrongly convicted men. But there were some strings attached. On August 19, 2011, Echols, Baldwin, and Misskelley entered Alford pleas—a declaration of innocence while acknowledging that there's evidence to convict. After spending more than 18 years in prison, they were sentenced to time served plus 10 years suspended.

"So many people formed a chain and if one single link in that chain was gone, they would have killed me," Jason told *E! News* at the time. "You know just for example, the DNA testing that eventually led to us getting out, we couldn't even afford to get that done. Henry Rollins went on a tour just to raise the money to do the first round of DNA testing. If the media doesn't care, if the world doesn't care, if people don't look at it, they'll still kill you no matter how much evidence there is [to the contrary]."

Damien Echols is still trying to prove his innocence beyond a shadow of a doubt by petitioning for new DNA tests on the ligatures used to bind the three little boys. Prosecutors claimed everything had been lost or destroyed in a fire, but they were lying; in December of 2021, the ligatures and other associated items were found intact inside the West Memphis Police Department's evidence locker room. On June 22, 2022, Crittenden County Circuit Court Judge Tonya Alexander denied a petition by Damien to have advanced DNA testing done.

To this day, the murders of Steven Branch, Michael Moore, and Chris Byers remain unsolved.

Art imitated life in 2022 when the popular Netflix TV series *Stranger Things* introduced a pot-smoking, horn-throwing, B.C. Rich guitar-slinging antihero named Eddie (after "Eddie the Head," Iron Maiden's mascot). In the show's '80s-set storyline, the long-haired teen is accused of murder and has to save his skin by playing a blistering version of Metallica's "Master of Puppets."

As you may have noticed, there's been little mention of female rockers—aside from Coven's Jinx—having much interest in the devil's music.

While Debbie Harry did say she wrote the Blondie song "Do the Dark" about Satan, the most notable early example of a witchy woman is Stevie Nicks. After the vocalist joined the already-established blues-rock band Fleetwood Mac in 1974, she changed their image and their sound, forever linking them to the ethereal, dreams, and a certain Welsh witch named Rhiannon.

Stevie's rich, husky contralto conjures up magic all on its own but what she wore also had a lot to do with giving the press and her fans notions of bohemia and witchcraft—her flowing, soft pastel scarves, and her voodoo-inspired top hat and tailcoats brought about a lot of speculation. The inky-black top hat is one of the main symbols of voodoo's go-to deity, Papa Legba. He's a master linguist, a trickster, a fighter, and a messenger of destiny. Marie Laveau, the powerful, iconic voodoo queen of New Orleans who flourished in the early 1800s, was seen wearing a top hat and, like Stevie Nicks, she wrote her spells (lyrics) in a grimoire (notebook).

Stevie bought a storied, vintage house in the foothills of Hollywood and surrounded herself with loyal female friends, bringing to mind a coven. Her first solo album was called *Bella Donna*, named after a poisonous flower often used in witchcraft and magical rituals. Also known as Deadly Nightshade, the plant was used by wise-women in ancient times as a "flying" ointment; it was soaked in fat and then slathered onto the skin, producing a hallucinogenic sensation of flying or astral projection.

The acerbic and sexist music critic Lester Bangs once wrote an article about her, titled: "Stevie Nicks: Lilith or Bimbo?" But her female fans were undeterred—the 1970s was, after all, the era of the ERA, a sexual revolution, and mysticism in the mainstream. The talented, beautiful, mysterious, wealthy, and famous "Dreams" singer was everything many young women aspired to.

Pop singer Madonna raised the ire of the Religious Right in the 1980s with her subversion of Catholic imagery in her heavy-rotation *MTV* videos for "Like a Prayer" and "Papa Don't Preach." Her 2006 Confessions Tour was condemned as a "blasphemous challenge to the faith and a profanation of the cross" by Cardinal Ersilio Tonini, speaking with the approval of the then-pope, Benedict XVI. Ten years later, in 2016, her Rebel Heart Tour stage show featured pole dancers decked-out as naughty nuns, causing the Archbishop of Singapore to proclaim, "There is no neutrality in faith. One is either for or against. Being present [at Madonna's concerts] in itself is a counter-witness. Obedience to God and His commandments must come before the arts."

In February of 2017, baroque-pop singer-songwriter Lana Del Rey raised eyebrows with a Tweet she sent, urging her fellow witches to take part in a communal spell against then-President Donald Trump. "At the stroke of midnight... Feb 24, March 26, April 24, May 23... Ingredients can be found online," she wrote. The dates referred to the waning crescent moon, which occult devotees believe is the optimum time to get rid of stress and negative energy. Many of her fans took part in the mass occult ritual but The Donald remained in office until the end of his term.

When asked about the spell by *Billboard*, Lana said, "I'm in line with Yoko [Ono] and John [Lennon] and the belief that there's a power to the vibration of a thought. Your thoughts are very powerful things and they become words, and words become actions, and actions lead to physical changes. I really do believe that words are one of the last forms of magic and I'm a bit of a mystic at heart."

Some of the most profound and well-documented religious conversions in rock are those of George Harrison (his band may have been "more popular than Jesus" but the so-called Quiet Beatle gave his heart to Hare Krishna in 1966), Cat Stevens (following a near-drowning death in 1976, the "Wild World" singer converted to the Muslim faith, changed his name to Yusuf Islam, and got rid of all his guitars), Randy Bachman (who converted to Mormonism at the behest of his second wife—he ditched the bride but kept the religion), and Bob Dylan (in 1978, the cynical, Jewish-born Bob Zimmerman became a humble born-again

Christian after having a vision of Christ in a Tucson, Arizona, hotel room).

While George stayed true to his fervent philosophy (not the celibacy part, though), and Bachman is still a Latter-Day Saint, Bob and Yusuf softened up a bit; the Bard of 4th Street returned to his Jewish roots in the mid-1980s, and Yusuf added "Cat Stevens" to his name and resumed his music career in 2006.

Those are more well-known examples but there are some seemingly unlikely religious awakenings in rock and metal that may surprise you.

The Godfather of Shock-Rock, Alice Cooper, has been an outspoken and unabashed cheerleader for his lord and savior for many years. In fact, he started out life as Vincent Damon Furnier, the son of a preacher in The Church of Jesus Christ. Alice was active in the church during his preteen years but then he discovered rock & roll. While his act was provocative and spooky, his family always knew it was just that: an act.

"My dad knew my sense of humor, my dad was very cool," Cooper said in an interview with *The Christian Post*. "He loved rock & roll. He said, 'I love the music, I can't abide the lifestyle.' He said, 'I know the character you're playing. He's comical. He's a villain but at the same time, he'll slip on a banana peel.' It took a while for people to understand that I was playing a character named Alice Cooper. I wasn't Alice

Cooper; I was playing that character. It was like a dark vaudeville."

The "Welcome to my Nightmare" singer decided to let go and let God in 1983, when his out-of-control alcoholism caused his wife, Sheryl Goddard (a pastor's daughter), to file for divorce. The couple is still married, going on 46 years as of this writing. Alice says he reads the Bible and prays every day. (And by night, rock's ringmaster gets onstage and mock-guillotines himself as skewered fake baby heads look on.)

Arthur Harold Kane, Jr. was the bass guitarist for the legendary proto-punk transvestite troop, the New York Dolls, which formed in 1971. Like so many in his orbit, "Killer" Kane fell prey to drugs and drink, and he was kicked out of the gender-bending band in 1975. He formed the short-lived Killer Kane Band with future W.A.S.P. frontman Blackie Lawless, then spiraled into an abyss of addiction.

In 1988, Arthur caught a glimpse on TV of his former Dolls bandmate David Johansen talking about his co-starring role in the hit movie *Scrooged* and lost his shit—he flew into a rage, beat his wife with cat furniture (!), then jumped out the window. Fortunately, it wasn't a long drop but it was enough to land him in the hospital. When two good-looking ladies from the Church of Mormon (now better-known as The Church of Jesus Christ of Latter-day Saints) sashayed into his room with free pamphlets, Kane decided to give the religion a try.

He gave himself over to the disciples of Joseph Smith and in 2004, the "Personality Crisis" bassist was back in the rock & roll fold. He rejoined surviving Dolls David Johansen and Sylvain Sylvain to rehearse and play a reunion concert in London—that turning point was the subject of a heartfelt 2005 documentary, *New York Doll*. Less than a month after the event, Kane got sick. He thought that he had caught the flu and went to the hospital, complaining of fatigue. The 55-year-old, who was described by band brother David as "nonjudgmental, bawdy, and holy," was diagnosed with leukemia, then died just a few hours later.

Arthur's religion became a point of contention for his wife, Barbara, when LDS elders officials refused to release his remains to her. She wanted to honor her late husband's wishes and bury him next to former Dolls, Johnny Thunders and Jerry Nolan. They were interred at Mount St. Mary's cemetery in Brooklyn, New York, which were *not* sacred grounds, according to the bassist's brethren. Church officials held onto the body until it had decomposed too badly to be flown from L.A.

"As far as they were concerned, everything that Arthur had belonged to the Mormon Church... They said nothing belonged to me," Barbara Kane said in an interview with *WENN*. "They even prevented me from accessing my husband's body out of the county morgue. All I wanted to do was kiss him goodbye but they stopped me from doing that." A month later, Barbara won her bid... but it was too late. "The mortician said, 'We're very sorry Mrs. Kane but we can't take your husband back east. He's too badly decomposed.' They poured embalming fluid over him and wrapped him in a piece of plastic and that was it. He laid there for over a month! They said the only thing they could do with him was to cremate him."

Killer Kane's former lead singer in the self-titled band, Blackie Lawless, went on to heavy metal heights with the outrageously over-the-top, oversexed W.A.S.P., which formed in L.A. in 1982. The wild-eyed, black-dyed, buzzsaw codpiece-wearing frontman continued the "lock up your daughters" fears throughout the decade and beyond, with a stage show to rival that of Alice Cooper. But W.A.S.P.—which stands for We Are Sexual Perverts—played up themes of BDSM and misogyny to a degree that would make the Marquis de Sade blush.

Blackie (born Steven Edward Duren on September 4, 1956) grew up a God-fearing boy and was born-again at the age of 11. He stayed with the church until he moved to L.A. and got into music. W.A.S.P. was well-known for their songs "Wild Child," "Blind in Texas," and "Animal (Fuck Like a Beast)." Several years into his career, Lawless decided to reexamine his upbringing. "I walked around for 20 years thinking I was mad at God," he said in a 2015 interview with *Ultimate Classic Rock*. "I realized I was not mad at God; I was mad at man for that indoctrination I received." For him, it's not about religion, but faith.

During the frontman's pious period, W.A.S.P. dropped the PMRC-denounced "Animal (Fuck Like a Beast)" from their set. However, Blackie started having second thoughts about that in 2022. In an interview with *SiriusXM*'s Eddie Trunk, Blackie said, "I don't know [if we will play that song]. There's a part of me that says it's already out there. You can't put the genie back in the bottle. Do I owe it to the fanbase to really make this a true retrospect of what we've done? If I had to give you an answer right now, I would say I'm leaning in the direction of doing it."

When Megadeth frontman Dave Mustaine became a born-again Christian in 2002, he refused to tour with bands he deemed "satanic." "When I got saved there were certain things I didn't know," he wrote in his self-titled memoir. "And it's like that old saying when you're cooking: 'When in doubt, leave it out.' As a new Christian, I spent a lot of time trying to get comfortable in my new skin. There were times when it felt smooth and right; there were times when it felt like I was suffocating. It wasn't until the summer of 2005 that I began to sense harmony between my spiritual and artistic lives."

Two-thousand-and-five also heralded a sea change for KoЯn co-founder and guitarist, Brian "Head" Welch. The nu-metal rocker's revelation came after years of addiction to

Xanax, alcohol, methamphetamines, and sleeping pills. But marrying his girlfriend Rebekah and becoming a father was the clincher. "I heard [my daughter] Jennea Marie singing a KoЯn song called 'Adidas.' It means 'all day long I dream about sex.' It's a party song. And I felt like a loser. I'm no good for this kid," Brian said.

"I really wanted God to take away my addiction to drugs," he went on. "I was like, 'Jesus, if you're real, take away my addiction.' I felt Him come into my life, and that's when everything changed." As soon as the "Freak on a Leash" guitarist found Jesus, he lost KoЯn. In 2005, he happily settled into a laid-back life, where he could raise his daughter off the road.

"I think it made the guys mad," Brian told *MTV News* shortly after his departure, "It confused them. I left at the worst possible time. We got off Sony, and all the money was there, we were going to own all of our songs, but I had to prove to myself that money wasn't my God," he said. "I talked to [frontman] Jonathan [Davis] and he said, 'I don't get it, man, you're all happy and we're sitting here grieving because our band is breaking up.' And I wanted to tell him, 'Well, for years, you guys were out partying while I was sitting on the tour bus wanting to die.'"

Little by little, "Sir Headly" began to play again and in 2012, he briefly reunited with KoЯn before embarking on a solo career. To celebrate, he got his right eyelid inked with

Hebrew words relating to God to express his Christian faith. He talked about his first album, *Save Me From Myself*, with the *Great Falls Tribune*. "I knew it was going to be nothing near as big as KoЯn, but I was proud of it. It's got some heavy riffs and it's got a lot more emotion than I've ever put in music. I'm an emotional guy (and) it was cool to be able to put it in there. It was cool how people were surprised by it. A lot of people thought I was gonna come out with some 'Kumbaya' Jesus music."

While Brian was able to strike out on a successful new lifepath, Rebekah was not. The pair divorced and he won custody of their daughter. (Rebekah OD'd at the age of 47 in June of 2021.)

Iron Maiden skins man Nicko McBrain didn't have any big thunderbolts coming down to show him the way and no substance abuse problems to humble him before the Lord. The British-born basher was living in Boca Raton, Florida, with his wife in 1999 and decided to go to Church with her one day. And that was it— he was hooked. His newfound faith didn't give him the patience of Job, though; Nicko was arrested in 2003 after angrily hitting and injuring a snippy valet with his car. He was charged with third-degree assault and second-degree reckless endangerment but didn't serve any time and continued to play for Iron Maiden.

Nicko is one of the few metalheads who hasn't let his personal faith mess with his setlist. Maiden still performs songs like "The

Number of the Beast" and "Children of the Damned" and has images of Old Scratch emblazoned on its merch.

As the booming voice of Judas Priest, Rob Halford sang on 16 of the band's 18 full-length albums and was anointed in the genre, rightfully earning the title: "Metal God." Although he grew up fully aware and accepting that he was queer, Rob struggled with both his sexuality and his faith as a young man coming up in the world of heavy rock. When Priest was picking up speed in the '70s and then became a freight train in the '80s, their music was macho on steroids. The world was terrified of Acquired Immunodeficiency Syndrome (AIDS) and it was, at first, vilified as "the Gay Cancer." What's more, headbangers thought God was uncool. So, Rob kept those things about himself under wraps and hidden away from all but those closest to him.

In 1998, six years after he left Judas Priest, Rob came out as a homosexual during an interview with *MTV* (which he says was unplanned) and broke down in tears saying, "It's a wonderful moment when you walk out of the closet. Now I've done that and I've freed myself."

Another six years passed, and Rob Halford was back in the band and back on God's bandwagon. The "Turbo Lover" singer's upbringing had been Christian but he dove back into divinity when he released his first heavy metal Christmas album in 2009. "I'm just into the basics really," he said of his own righteous path. "Try to be a good person, and treat others as you'd like to be treated. That stuff was instilled in me as a kid. I'm not much for labels, but I think there's a big difference between religion and spirituality."

His own devout stance notwithstanding, the Metal God denounced conservative evangelical activists for their anti-queer stance and outspoken discrimination in a 2019 interview with *NME*, saying, "Don't get me started on the Christian Right pushing the LGBTQ community under the bus."

CHAPTER SEVEN: LOVE HURTS

"I gave him my heart, and he took and pinched it to death, and flung it back to me."
—Emily Bronte

It's terrifying enough to think about murderous strangers lurking in alcoves with loaded guns or deranged men with bows and arrows taking out targets at random, but what about those closest to us who may be plotting our demise? According to the National Coalition Against Domestic Violence, nearly 20 people per minute are physically abused by an intimate partner in the United States (this equates to more than 10 million people per year). And it's not just our nearest and dearest—friends, neighbors, coworkers, and teachers are also at risk. No matter how many fans they had, or how many GRAMMYs were perched on their mantles, these shocking statistics have also applied to some of the biggest names in music.

Like her more famous sister Rita, Priscilla Coolidge loved to sing and started perfecting her craft at a very young age. Born in Lafayette, Tennessee, to a Cherokee Baptist minister and Cherokee-Scottish mother, the girls were not only strikingly beautiful they were abundantly talented. As teens, the dark-haired pair performed together as a folk duo all over the U.S., and eventually settled in L.A. where they each went solo.

Rita was an in-demand backup singer for the likes of Eric Clapton, Joe Cocker, Stephen Stills, Leon Russell, and many more, before marrying singer-songwriter Kris Kristofferson and winning two GRAMMYs with him; her biggest hit, "Higher and Higher," came in 1977 just as they were splitting up and their private lives were splashed all over the tabloids.

Priscilla married Booker T. Jones of Booker T. & the MGs in 1969 and he produced her first solo album, *Gypsy Queen*, the following year. Along with John Lennon and Yoko Ono, and Leon and Mary Russell, they were among the few interracial couples in the spotlight on the music scene. They collaborated as a duo on three albums: *Booker T. & Priscilla*, *Home Grown*, and *Chronicles*. Things came full circle when Booker produced his soon-to-be-ex's last solo album, *Flying*, in 1979. Although Priscilla was named *Billboard* magazine's Best Female Vocalist two years running, her career never took off in the same way Rita's did. She continued to sing but settled for a smaller spotlight.

In 1981, Priscilla married *60 Minutes* anchor Ed Bradley but they divorced just a few years later. Her third husband was also in television—Michael Seibert worked for several production companies and studios, including

20th Century Fox. While Michael wasn't a high-profile mover and shaker, he got famous for all the wrong reasons when, on October 2, 2014, he shot Priscilla in the head and then turned the gun on himself.

Sixty-six-year-old Michael killed his 73-year-old wife for reasons unknown—details are sketchy but their Thousand Oaks, California, neighbors reported a loud quarrel just before the shots rang out.

In her memoir, *Delta Lady*, Rita remembered talking to Priscilla on the phone on her birthday, which was only a matter of hours before her murder. "It was very painful to write, but she was such an important part of my life," Rita told the *Belfast Telegraph*. Priscilla "was like my twin. We talked every day. We wrote music together for decades. She was my best friend from the time I can remember anything, and to lose her at all would have broken my heart... but to have lost her at the hands of a crazy man with a gun made it unacceptable." According to Rita, Michael was "a con man" and always in financial straits—Priscilla was considering ending the marriage but she never got the chance.

"He was not loved by his family, who wanted nothing to do with his remains, so I had arranged to have his body cremated—I know that's what Priscilla would have wanted," Rita wrote in her book. "The ashes were delivered to my house, but I didn't want him inside the house. Initially, I put him out in the groves that border my property and put him under an avocado tree. I woke up on New Years' Eve Day realizing that they were still there. And I didn't want him on my land. I wanted to take care of it before the New Year came." She collected the box and drove out into the California desert, hoping for a sign. "And then I saw it—an actual sign that said: Trespassers will be shot on sight." She dumped the killer's ashes and drove off without a backward glance.

Sadly, that was not Rita Coolidge's first brush with a murderer. While on Joe Cocker's Mad Dogs and Englishmen Tour in 1970, she was dating "Layla" drummer and co-composer, Jim Gordon. One evening, out of nowhere, he hit her so hard with a closed fist that he left her with a black eye that lasted for weeks—she had to cover it with layers of makeup before going onstage. The incident not only embarrassed her, but it also shook her up. She never spoke to him again.

"If you stick around, you're just asking for more," she wrote in her memoir. "I wouldn't talk to him; I wouldn't accept gifts; I didn't want anything to do with him." Rita added, "I knew there was something wrong with him and I didn't want to be around it. I think I understood on some level that he was mentally ill."

Jim's violence toward Rita Coolidge foreshadowed something much, much worse—years later, he attacked his mother with a hammer, then stabbed her to death.

Suffering from undiagnosed schizophrenia, he heard insidious voices, including that of his mother, telling him to starve, stop sleeping, and quit playing drums. "I was the king of the universe but I had to make sacrifices, and I had to do what *they* said," he explained in an interview with *Rolling Stone* following the crime.

James "Jim" Beck Gordon was considered a genius musician—not only was he a brilliant drummer but that's him on the ivories at the end of Derek & the Dominoes' indelible anthem to forbidden love, "Layla." He was credited with writing the mournful piano coda for that track, but Rita Coolidge says *she* wrote it for a song called "Time" while they were dating. Many witnesses have come forward since, saying it's true. Bobby Whitlock, who played keyboards for Derek & the Dominoes, said, "Jim took the melody from Rita's song and didn't give her credit for writing it. Her boyfriend ripped her off."

Born July 14, 1945, in L.A., Jim was always drawn to music. His parents, both hard-working professionals, encouraged their son to follow his dream; he went on the road at age 17, backing the Everly Brothers, then was hired by studio drummer Hal Blaine of The Wrecking Crew. He performed on records ranging from The Beach Boys' *Pet Sounds* to Helen Reddy's "I Am Woman," played drums on the majority of Steely Dan's album *Pretzel Logic*, and performed on three tracks of *Alice Cooper Goes to Hell*.

Jim Gordon was married in the '60s, had a daughter, and divorced. He dated Rita Coolidge, ending their relationship with a single punch. His father died in 1973, which deeply affected him. He bought a Ferrari and wrecked it while driving drunk. He married and divorced again after just six months. His mental state deteriorated and he was in and out of the hospital. He choked a girlfriend, nearly killing her. Through it all, he played the drums and played them to perfection. Music was the only thing that held him together.

In 1978, a mutual friend recommended him to singer-songwriter Jackson Browne, who was about to go on tour. "It was pretty well-known that he had had a breakdown," Jackson said, "but I wanted him on the tour. You just wanted to root for him. He cut such a gallant figure, with his open white silk shirts and felt Borsalino hat, and he was such a good drummer. He'd get my attention with this great fill, really imaginative. He just rose to the occasion."

The impressive list of his accomplishments goes on and on but as the new decade dawned, the GRAMMY-winner's mind went dark. The burly blond had always heard voices but when he was a boy they were attributed to harmless imaginary friends. He'd been a drinker and drugger for most of his adult life but he could always be counted on to turn in a flawless performance whether it was in the studio or on stage. Then in the early '80s, everything slid into a bottomless abyss.

Jim would isolate himself for days on end as he succumbed to his demons. One of the worst demons was the imagined evil of his own mother; he believed that Osa Marie Gordon had killed comedian Paul Lynde and musician Karen Carpenter, and that she would be coming for him next.

Osa was threatened so many times that she sought a restraining order against her unhinged son but the bureaucracy was too much for her to follow through with it. Eventually, she decided it would be best to move to Seattle, and live with her other son and his family. She never got the chance.

On June 3, 1983, one of the voices told Jim to kill the 72-year-old former maternity ward nurse, and he obeyed. The "You're So Vain" drummer packed a heavy hammer and an eight-inch knife into a leather attaché case, then drove his Datsun 200SX the short distance from his modest Van Nuys condo to Osa's North Hollywood apartment. It was about 11:30 p.m., when he knocked on her door. "Jim," she said, letting him in—and before she could say anything else, the six-foot-three lunatic struck her with the hammer several times. As the elderly woman screamed and fell to the floor, he plunged the knife into her chest three times and then left it protruding from her stilled heart—

marking the spot that not only ended her life, but for all intents and purposes, his too.

Only after his arrest was Jim Gordon properly diagnosed with schizophrenia. (Hey, better late than never!) The following summer, he was sentenced to 16-years-to-life in prison. When interviewed by *Rolling Stone* following the crime, he said his brother's voice had taken over from their mother's, but "I really don't feel that crazy. I think I'm pretty normal." (The parole board begs to differ: Jim has pled for his freedom at least 10 times and has been summarily denied.)

At the time of this writing, the murderous musician is still serving his sentence at the California Medical Facility, a psychiatric penitentiary in Vacaville, California, where he plays in the prison band and continues to collect royalties for "Layla," and many other songs.

Jim Gordon isn't the only fan of killer riffs locked up in Vacaville—Manson Family fringe member Bobby Beausoleil is there, too. He's behind bars for murdering his guitar teacher, Gary Hinman. The 21-year-old killer mistakenly believed that Gary had $20,000 stashed somewhere in his modest Topanga Canyon, California, abode and he was going to get it one way or another. But all Gary had was $20 in cash and his life—Bobby took them both.

While Gary was known as a gentle Buddhist who liked to play acoustic guitar and share his knowledge with others—according to lore, he gave lessons to both Bobby Beausoliel and cult leader Charlie Manson—he also had a side gig dealing drugs. The 34-year-old, slight, slender man had graduated with a degree in chemistry and was continuing his education by pursuing a Ph.D. in Sociology but he wasn't doing much in that regard; like so many of his peers living in the canyons at that time, he was just going with the flow. A capable multi-instrumentalist who played guitar, piano, and trombone to name a few, Gary worked off and on in music stores but his real ambition in the summer he died was to travel to Japan, where he planned on seriously studying Nichiren Shoshu Buddhism.

Bobby Beausoleil was a reasonably accomplished musician on his way up when he fell in with the Manson Family cult in 1968. The drug-addled lothario (nicknamed "Cupid," he fathered at least three children before he was 21 and appeared in a skin-flick) drifted in and out of psychedelic bands including The Orkustra, The Milky Way, and The Grass Roots (headed up by vocalist Arthur Lee, and later known as Love).

At some point, the sleepy-eyed songster met the controversial author and experimental independent filmmaker, Kenneth Anger. Bobby nabbed a role in the auteur's upcoming opus. *Lucifer Rising* was a homoerotic fantasy about the gods of ancient Egypt and a fallen angel— but the film was delayed for years and he never got his close-up.

Led Zeppelin's Jimmy Page was eventually hired to write the *Lucifer Rising* score and he produced a dark, eerie, ritualistic soundscape but after a falling out over creative differences, an incarcerated Bobby got the job. To perform and record his score, he put together The Magick Powerhouse of Oz band while in prison—and continues to record and profit from his music to this day. Lady Gaga used a few seconds of Bobby's *Lucifer Rising* composition in her 2017 documentary, *Five Foot Two*.

By 1968, Bobby was rooming with the generous, trusting Gary Hinman in Topanga Canyon. By all accounts, Gary had an open-door policy and all were welcome in his home. When Bobby met members of the Family the following summer, he moved into their commune on the run-down Spahn Movie Ranch in Chatsworth, about a half-hour's drive from Topanga. Gary was invited as well but declined; Charlie was reportedly insulted by the snub.

While at the ranch, Bobby bonded with members of the Straight Satans biker gang— who were anything *but* straight; it was their desire for drugs that heralded Hinson's grisly end, which in turn sparked the Family's higher-profile massacres in August of 1969.

The details in Bobby's story have changed countless times over the years but basically, he was using Gary as his supplier, and when the Straight Satans said they wanted some mescaline (an organic hallucinogenic, as opposed to LSD, which is manmade), Bobby had just the guy. The bikers forked over $1,000 for 1,000 tabs and Bobby did the deal with Gary. However, the Straight Satans were not happy with the quality of the product and demanded a refund. Bobby consulted the almighty Manson, who ordered Bobby and two acolytes— Mary Brunner and Susan Atkins—to get the money back from Gary, plus a 20K windfall he'd heard about.

Gary said not only didn't he have the currency to refund the unhappy customers but he didn't have anywhere near 20 grand. After being threatened with a loaded gun, Gary showed the trio, whom he considered friends, that he only had $50 in his checking account, adding that his parents were paying for his trip to Japan. Following a brutal beatdown by Bobby, the budding Buddhist signed over the titles to his two vehicles... but it still wasn't enough.

Bobby used Gary's phone to call Charlie at the ranch and the diminutive self-proclaimed deity was there in a flash, with fellow Family member Bruce Davis as backup. Without saying a word, Manson produced a samurai sword and slashed the restrained, roughed-up guitar teacher across his ear and cheek. As the blood gushed, Charlie sneered at Bobby to "be a man" and left with Bruce in one of Gary's cars.

Hinman pleaded to be taken to the hospital but Beausoleil, Brunner, and Atkins said no. They stitched up his nearly detached ear with dental floss while the victim chanted and prayed. An entire night and day passed as Bobby worked up the courage to do what he felt he had to do. At some point on July 27, 1969, he stabbed Gary twice in the chest.

But the wounds were not immediately fatal. Gary lingered for hours until, finally, Manson's girls suffocated him with a pillow. After he finally died, they dipped their hands into his blood and wrote "Political Piggy" on the nearest wall, adding a cat's paw in hopes of implicating the Black Panther Party in the crime. Then they walked out the door, leaving Gary Hinman's corpse to rot for four days until it was found, with the prayer beads still clutched in one hand.

All Bobby and his babes got away with was $20, which they used to treat themselves to coffee and strawberry cake.

On August 6, 1969—three days *before* the horrific Manson-mandated murders of actress Sharon Tate and her friends—Bobby was taken into custody after being found asleep in Gary's other car, which was parked alongside the 101 Freeway in San Luis Obispo County. An on-site inspection found a knife stashed in a wheel well. Bobby protested that he bought the car from an unidentified Black man, but his story didn't wash. Eventually, he was arrested for the murder and on April 18, 1970, he was found guilty and sentenced to death. His sentence was commuted in 1972 to life imprisonment with the possibility of parole, but it's a slim possibility—Bobby Beausoleil, who has since converted to

Buddhism, has been denied freedom time and time again.

While the name Felix Pappalardi, Jr., may not ring a bell to the casual rock music fan, you've heard him as the bassist and co-lead vocalist of the proto heavy metal band Mountain, whose sludgy burner "Mississippi Queen" was blasting through FM radio speakers everywhere in 1970. Prior to that, he worked with Eric Clapton and Cream, helping to write, arrange, and produce their second album, *Disraeli Gears*. A respected multi-instrumentalist, Felix played viola, keyboards, and trumpet during those sessions.

During that time, he and his wife, Gail Collins, along with Eric, co-wrote the hit single, "Strange Brew." The lyrics repeatedly say, "Kill what's inside of you," and apparently Gail was filled with rage because when she found out Felix was cheating on her, she shot him in the neck with a pocket pistol he had given her as a gift.

At the time of his death on August 17, 1983, 43-year-old Felix's career was on the skids and his personal life was also a shambles. But even before that, there'd been marital discord. According to drummer Corky Laing, "When Mountain started out, Felix and Gail were a brilliant, creative team. [Gail did the artwork for several of Mountain's album covers.] But Gail got in big trouble with drugs. Gradually, people in the business who knew them, realized she was a witch. She was very talented, very smart, but evil. Gail claimed she loved Felix, but they were always fighting. Felix was not a big guy, and Gail would beat the shit out of him. Other times they'd get high, and shoot at the walls in their house."

According to friends, the couple had an open marriage so it wasn't the galivanting that galled Gail; it was the fact that Felix had fallen in love with his 27-year-old protégé, Valerie Merians. So, it was divorce by derringer—after the scorned wife shot and killed Felix, she shredded their marriage certificate and called her lawyer. In time, the police arrived on the scene—the couple's small but swanky apartment in Manhattan with an East River view—and when they asked the "World of Pain" co-writer what happened she replied, "Oh, it was an accident. Felix was giving me a shooting lesson."

During the court case, she also blamed their cat for startling her and causing the gun to go off. Throughout the sensational trial, which made headlines all over New York and the world, witnesses testified that both Gail and Felix were longtime "gun nuts" and it was highly unlikely that she would need a lesson— especially at 6 a.m., and with Felix in nothing but his underwear. She had been indicted for second-degree murder, but in the end, she was convicted of a lesser charge; she was thrown in the clink for criminally negligent homicide and served two of her four-year sentence.

After that, she all but disappeared until news of her death by suicide surfaced on December 6, 2013. Seventy-two-year-old Gail Collins, who'd been going by her middle name, Delta, was found hanging in her home in the Mexican village of Ajijic, Jalisco, a resort town where she had been getting experimental cancer treatments. Her landlord made the shocking discovery and notified authorities. Gail left a goodbye note stating that she wanted to be cremated, and that her cats should be euthanized immediately so their ashes could be mixed with hers.

Mountain's mountainous frontman Leslie West (née Weinstein) said it all when he said, "Buy your wife a diamond ring, some flowers, a pushup bra... don't buy her a gun."

One of the most important—and underrated—punk bands to emerge from Canada in the 1970s was Teenage Head. Gord Lewis, the founding guitarist of the lauded group that earned several certified gold records, died brutally at the age of 65 on August 7, 2022, when he was slain by his 41-year-old son, Jonathan. The pair were roommates—not harmonious ones, obviously, but what could have led to such a drastic outcome?

Jonathan was allegedly suffering from severe mental illness. In the days leading up to the patricide, an email account bearing the name "Jonathan Lewis" sent dozens of bizarre messages to various news journalists suggesting that Gord was involved in a conspiracy against him and that he (Jonathan) had been poisoned by anthrax.

One rambling diatribe stated that people would "make some noise knowing someone had all their rights taken away from them, was refused medical treatment, killed, and it was all covered up by the media." Another email, sent on Saturday, August 6, said, "Now I just want to get help for my sickness and give my Dad a proper burial. He didn't deserve this." One more desperate message was sent the following morning at about 11 a.m.: "Funeral people need to get here quick. My Dad is starting to decay."

Finally, someone decided to take action, and police and paramedics were dispatched to the apartment on Catherine Street in the port city of Hamilton, Ontario, where the "Blood Boogie" guitarist was found deceased. While the cause of death has yet to be released at the time of this writing, "injuries consistent with foul play" were noted, and Jonathan was taken into custody and charged with second-degree murder.

And for the flipside: There's a parental saying that goes, "I brought you into this world, and I can take you out." Apparently, singer Marvin Gaye's father, Marvin Gay, Sr., took it as gospel because he fatally shot his son during a heated argument on the morning of April 1, 1984. Like Felix Pappalardi, Jr., Marvin Gaye was wasted with a weapon he had given to his killer as a gift.

Marvin Sr., was a Pentecostal minister who grew up in a horribly abusive home with his 14 brothers and sisters and continued the tradition when he started his own family. By all accounts, the cross-dressing, alcoholic hothead beat and belittled his wife and four children for years on end, especially his namesake. No one knows why but Marvin, Jr., was singled out for the brunt of his father's white-hot rage. "He never wanted Marvin," his mother Alberta said, adding that he even went so far as to doubt the boy's paternity. "He didn't love Marvin, and what's worse is, he didn't want me to love Marvin, either."

"If it wasn't for mother who was always there to console me and praise me for my singing, I think I would have been one of those child suicides you read about in the papers," Marvin told his biographer, David Ritz.

Despite his rigid religious dogma, Marvin Sr., drank to excess, had numerous extramarital affairs, and even fathered a child with another woman. He was a transvestite and made no secret of it—in fact, he was dressed in drag at one of his son's appearances on the *Midnight Special* television show. When asked about this predilection, Alberta reportedly said, "Soft things of all kinds attracted him. He liked to wear my panties, my gowns, and even my nylon hose. Marvin [as a child] would see him like that sometimes."

Marvin Gaye—who added the e to the end of his last name in response to endless schoolyard taunts—found freedom in Motown Records and became a superstar whose indelible hits include "Heard it Through the Grapevine" and "Let's Get it On." The soulful singer was "blessed with an exceptionally wide range that encompassed three distinct vocal styles—a piercing falsetto, a smooth mid-range tenor, and a deep gospel growl" and won legions of fans all over the world, plus enjoyed crossover appeal. But still, he could not win the approval of his dour dad. The title track on his most personal album, *What's Going On*, goes, "Father, Father. We don't need to escalate," and pleads, "Don't punish me with brutality."

Marvin seemed to hold it together throughout the 1960s and into the '70s but the unhealed wounds of his childhood demanded salve and he turned to cocaine and womanizing. By the 1980s he was forced to move in with his parents following a losing battle with depression, drugs, and debt.

The stately Tudor mansion, which Marvin had bought for himself but gave to his parents to avoid foreclosure, was in the West Adams district of Los Angeles, and Marvin's brother Frankie lived in a guesthouse on the property. The "Take This Heart of Mine" singer described the vibe as "living with a king, a very peculiar, changeable, cruel, and all-powerful king." But, he thought, he would only stay there until he could get back on his feet. Unfortunately, he left the house feet-first after Marvin Sr., shot him three times in the chest during an altercation.

What was the argument about? Misplaced insurance papers. Marvin Sr., had been railing for a full day and night, loudly blaming Alberta for carelessness, and stomping around the house as he looked for the policy. Close to 1 p.m., on April 1, 1983, the day before Marvin's 45th birthday, his life was ended by anger and a .38 Special.

According to Alberta's eyewitness account, after Marvin yelled at his father to be quiet, Marvin, Sr., went into his bedroom, then entered his son's room, where the "Mercy Mercy Me" singer was sitting up in his bed. Without a word, the seething 70-year-old man raised the gun and shot his son once in the chest. That bullet was enough to kill but after Marvin crumpled to the floor, his father approached him and shot him a second and third time at point-blank range. The gunman then turned and left the room, walked down the stairs, and waited calmly on the porch for the police to come.

Afterward, he claimed self-defense but the subsequent investigation found no physical evidence of any such thing. Lieutenant Robert Martin, the lead detective on the case, said, "There was no indication of bruises... nothing like he'd been punched out or that kind of stuff." He initially faced first-degree murder, but the charges were reduced to voluntary manslaughter and he was given a suspended six-year sentence and probation. The slain soul singer's mom, who soon divorced Marvin Sr., died of bone cancer in 1987. The killer outlived them all, finally succumbing to old age in a nursing home 11 years later.

Pockmarked punk rocker Sid Vicious, bassist of the short-lived but infamous Sex Pistols, was allegedly shot up with heroin by his mother Anne Beverley on February 2, 1979, and he never woke up. Was it accidental? Was it a misguided mercy killing by a mom who didn't think her 21-year-old son would survive prison? Sid—who was born in London as John Simon Ritchie on May 10, 1957—was out on bail and set to face trial for the killing of his girlfriend, Nancy Spungen. So, his future was uncertain at best. But at least the "No Future" musician had one before whatever happened, happened. No one really knows what led to the fatal fix, and since Anne OD'd on smack herself in 1996, she's not talking. Sid was suicidal his whole life, so maybe he did it himself.

By all accounts, Anne was an awful mother—when Sid was a toddler, she used him as a mule to feed her heroin habit and after he died, she tried to cash in on his notoriety by fronting a punk band of her own, Road Rage, and performing her son's biggest hit, a cover of Frank Sinatra's "My Way." But it was her way or the highway, as Anne admitted to throwing her son out on the streets, penniless, when he was 16—the only thing she ever gave him was a drug addiction. Anne later told Jon Savage of *the Guardian*, "I remember saying to him: 'It's either you or me, and it's not going to be me. I have got to try to preserve myself and you just fuck off.' He said: 'I've not got anywhere to go,' and I said: 'I don't care.'"

Sid's life philosophy turned out to be the same—fortunately for him, the "I don't care" credo was perfect for the advent of punk in the mid-1970s. With his spiked hair, black leather, and bad attitude, the skinny scrapper was recruited into the Sex Pistols. Even though he didn't know how to play bass, he replaced Glen Matlock in 1977, joining vocalist Johnny Rotten, guitarist Steve Jones, and drummer Paul Cook. After learning a few chords while listening to albums by The Ramones, Sid was ready for primetime. But like a child, he was better seen than heard—legend has it, Steve actually played bass on the band's only album, *Never Mind the Bollocks, Here's the Sex Pistols*. What's more, there was often a roadie sitting behind the bass amp playing the live songs while Sid mimed the motions and lobbed loogies at the audience. The Sex Pistols LP was a smash but their U.S. tour bombed and the band broke up. Sid went solo.

The "God Save the Queen" bassist moved to New York with his blowsy, blonde American girlfriend, "Nauseating Nancy" Spungen, and the pair took up residence at the Chelsea Hotel in Manhattan. They'd been inseparable since meeting some months before, each seeing a kindred spirit in the other. Nancy had been arrested for drug possession and petty theft as a teen, then she dropped out of school to follow rock bands such as Aerosmith, The New York Dolls, and The Ramones. Along the way, she supported herself by doing odd jobs and engaging in prostitution. In 1977, Nancy flew to London with The Heartbreakers and met the Sex Pistols—from that moment on, she and Sid were together. Til death did they part.

Nancy seemed doomed from birth—she nearly died of oxygen deprivation after being choked by her umbilical cord during her delivery on February 27, 1958, in Philadelphia, Pennsylvania. At the age of three months, the infant threw temper tantrums that were so intense she was prescribed a liquid barbiturate by her pediatrician. After that, she attacked a babysitter with scissors and as a young teen, she slit her wrists. When she was 15, her psychiatrist diagnosed her with schizophrenia. At 16, she dropped out of school, and at 17, she ran away with rock bands. Despite her abrasive behavior, spotty schooling, and heroin habit, Nancy was described as "highly intelligent."

Soon after checking into the Chelsea Hotel—the site of many a rock & roll ruin—the couple "checked out" in a downward spiral of drugs and death.

No one knows for sure what happened behind the closed door of Suite 100 but on October 12, 1978, the 20-year-old groupie was found with a single stab wound to her abdomen, curled up underneath the bathroom sink wearing nothing but a black bra and underwear. The blade had been a gift from her to Sid, according to the *New York Daily News*, but other sources said Sid had bought it for himself because it was similar to one owned by Stiv Bators, the lead singer of Dead Boys. Sid was no stranger to blades; his thin torso was scarred by countless self-inflicted cuts. He once used a bare razor blade to crudely carve the words GIMME A FIX across his chest just before going onstage in Dallas.

The crime was not initially reported by Sid. The Chelsea's front desk clerk got an anonymous call from outside the hotel. The man said, "There's trouble in Room 100." A bellman was dispatched to check out the situation, but before he returned, another call came in. This time, it was from within the storied walls of the historic hotel—more specifically, it came from Suite 100. "Someone is sick," a different male voice reported. "Need help."

The bellman entered the room and after pushing his way past a TV set that was blocking the door from the inside, he saw the blood-smeared body of a female lying face-up on the bathroom tiles, her head positioned under the sink. A trail of blood led from the pale corpse to the gore-soaked, rumpled, empty bed. The employee called for an ambulance but upon arrival, paramedics concluded that the young woman was beyond help. New York's finest arrived on the scene and soon found a bloodstained hunting knife, plus the couple's drugs and works. Sid was wandering the hallways, crying, agitated, and higher than his mohawk. Sweaty and stuttering, he admitted that he and Nancy had had an argument and concluded, "she must have fallen on the knife."

Sid, tanked on Tuinal, was cuffed, booked, and jailed. "I did it because I'm a dirty dog," he confessed—then quickly recanted the damning declaration, saying he couldn't remember what happened.

According to witnesses, Sid's royalty payment had come in and Nancy was throwing $100 bills around at a party in a drug den earlier that night, attracting the attention of several lowlifes. Two of particular interest were a dealer known only as "Michael" who lived on the 6th floor of the Chelsea (but checked out the next morning, disappearing into the wind), and the couple's opportunistic, addicted friend, Rockets Redglare (aka, Michael Morra, a raconteur who appeared the in the '80s comedies *After Hours* and *Desperately Seeking Susan*). All that money was missing but the NYPD had only one suspect and that was Sid Vicious.

Some people said he was "sweet" but he did often live up to his nickname. The Pistols' original bass player, Glen Matlock, had a pet cat, and one day while he was out, Sid decided to kill the animal. Glen's roommate, Mark Helfand, who stood by and witnessed the horrific act of cruelty, later said, "It didn't last long, as far as ticks on the clock, but it seemed like an eternity. It was whining and fighting to get away. Just before it died, it urinated right on his feet. Sid was holding it in front of me. He put the cat in a plastic bag and took it down to the trash."

Although the "I Killed the Cat" singer (yes, he really did sing a song about it onstage, though he never released a record of it) had made a spectacle of himself by torturing cats time and time again, everyone who knew him agreed that he would never murder Nancy. Dysfunctional and mutually abusive as they were, it was true love and she was his reason for living.

Following Nancy's autopsy—which concluded it had taken a few hours for her to bleed out from the single stab wound—the peroxided punk, vilified in the press and made the butt of jokes on late-night TV, was quietly buried in her hometown. A few days later, Sid was released on bail with money put up by his label boss, Richard Branson of Virgin Records.

Reportedly screaming "I want to die!" Sid soon attempted suicide by slashing himself with a broken lightbulb, and following a fight with singer Patti Smith's brother Todd at the Hurrah nightclub, the pugnacious punker forfeited his bail and spent seven weeks in the prison on Riker's Island. While there, he sent a letter to Nancy's parents, which was published in the 1983 book by Deborah Spungen, *And I Don't Want to Live This Life*: "Her pain was just too much to bear. Because, you see, I felt Nancy's pain as though it were my own, worse even... I love her with such passion. Every day is agony without her. I know now it is possible to die from a broken heart. Because when you love someone as much as we love each other, they become fundamental to your existence. So I will die soon, even if I don't kill myself. I guess you could say that I'm pining for her. I could live without food or water longer than I'm going to survive without Nancy... [She] was too beautiful for this world."

Having said that, Sid wasted no time in finding a new squeeze. He'd met 22-year-old aspiring actress Michelle Robinson some months before but now they were hooking up and planned on being together after he (hopefully) beat the murder rap. Just like Nancy, Michelle was described as a groupie—but Nancy had been after any and all band boys, while Michelle, according to those in the know, was particularly "obsessed" with Sid Vicious.

The "Pretty Vacant" musician was released on bail pending trial on February 1 and that night he celebrated his freedom in Michelle's Greenwich Village apartment with his mom (who'd migrated to New York the previous year, around the time her son did), and a few assorted friends. By all accounts, Sid was in good spirits. He spun New York Dolls records, played air guitar, and talked about the future—his manager, Malcolm McLaren, wanted Sid to cover "I Fought the Law and the Law Won," and "YMCA" on his next album. He ate his favorite meal, spaghetti Bolognaise, then asked his mum for some heroin.

She obliged but the drug was stepped on, and weak. He then asked his friend, music scene photographer Peter Gravelle, to help out—so, Peter got his hands on the purest heroin around and the pair indulged.

Having been compulsorily clean while on the inside, the 90% pure smack caused Sid to go into convulsions. Nobody called for help, fearing consequences in regard to Sid's bail, so they did their best to revive him. "He was eventually okay when I left," Peter said years later in an interview with *Louder Than War*, "however, Michelle had given him four quaaludes to help him sleep. Now, taking two of them is bad enough but after shooting heroin, four is fucking mental. Sid was always persuasive and probably asked his mum for another hit on top of that. I had left at 2 a.m., and found out the next afternoon he was dead."

So what really happened? According to Michelle, after the party-favor-dispensing photographer left, she and Sid headed off to bed. They disrobed and were fooling around but the young man had his mind on other things; just having barely survived an overdose, Sid was already jonesing for another hit. What happened after that is hazy in terms of detail but Michelle later told police she left the room and summoned Sid's mom. Anne, a mainlining pro, accidentally overshot the mark and Sid went into immediate cardiac arrest and died.

Or *was* it by accident? Did Sid himself ask his mother to euthanize him? Many historians believe that punk-rock's Romeo and Juliet had a suicide pact but Sid fell down on his end of the bargain at the Chelsea Hotel and felt guilty about it. Finally, he was making good on his promise.

Without their prime suspect to stand trial, the State quickly closed its case against John Simon Richie. Anne Richie was not charged with the death of Sid Vicious. Anne later said she asked the Spungen family for permission to bury her son beside their daughter but was unequivocally shot down and told not to attempt contact again. So, she had Sid cremated and then flew to Philadelphia with the ashes, where she secretly sprinkled them over Nancy's grave.

The hardcore punk movement spawned by Sid Vicious and his ilk, in turn, gave way to even more anarchistic tunes. In the late '80s and early '90s a subculture of Scandinavian musicians inspired by the dark aesthetics of bands like Black Sabbath, Coven, and Motörhead converged to spawn the music genre now known as black metal. There are many different types of metal (doom, industrial, thrash, speed... the list goes on and on) but what sets *black* metal apart is not only its fast, chordal, tremolo-picked riffing and shrieked high-pitched vocals... it's also the words. Some of the most popular songs lyrically extol the virtues of apathy, self-mutilation, misanthropy, rape, murder, suicide, cannibalism, necrophilia... and things go downhill from there.

In their spare time, some of the more evil-minded musicians went after the God squad that "destroyed ancestral Scandinavian pagan religions" by bombing or setting fire to historic churches. And again: things went further down, specifically for the aptly named band, Mayhem.

Mayhem greatly influenced second-wave black metal but they are first in terms of infamy. The Norwegian band that took its name from the Venom song "Mayhem with Mercy" was founded in 1984 by guitarist Øystein "Euronymous" Aarseth, bassist Jørn "Necrobutcher" Stubberud, and drummer Kjetil Manheim (whose name was apparently cool enough on its own). Following a couple of personnel changes, Mayhem brought Jan Axel "Hellhammer" Blomberg and brash, blond vocalist Per "Dead" Ohlin into the fold.

Hellhammer said that Dead "was the first black metal musician to use corpse paint," but really it was just a continuation of what Arthur Brown, Alice Cooper, and KISS had started years before—and that, of course, was an offshoot of the ceremonial face markings worn by various native tribes in their ritualistic song and dance routines. To top off his zombified image, Dead would bury his stage clothes in the forest for a few hours before going onstage so he'd look and smell like he'd just come from a grave. While performing, the "Life Eternal" singer would cut himself with knives and broken glass—what's more, Mayhem's stage décor often included impaled pig or sheep heads poised on stakes.

As covered in detail in *Rock & Roll Nightmares: True Stories, Volume One*, 22-year-old Dead fulfilled his destiny by killing himself with a shotgun blast to the face. The show went on and a year later, Euronymous invited his young protégé, bassist Varg "Count Grishnackh" Vikernes to join Mayhem. The Count also kept his place in the band he founded, Burzum (which translates to "darkness" in a fictional language crafted by Lord of the Rings writer J. R. R. Tolkien). They recorded some music but the pair didn't fully bond until they took part in torching the Medieval-style wood-framed Holmenkollen Chapel in Oslo on August 23, 1992. "Through church burning and black metal music, we will reawaken the Norwegians' feelings of belonging to Odin," said Varg.

Count Grishnackh put out his first album, *Burzum*, through Euronymous' Deathlike Silence label, and another—*Aske* ("Ashes"), boldly depicting an eerie cover photo of one of the churches he burned—soon followed. But the musical partnership was far from harmonious and before long, the bromance was over. Nineteen-year-old Varg came to resent his mentor and his anger ate away at him day and night. As admiration curdled into acrimony, The Count saw Euronymous as a "poseur" because, he said, the "Chainsaw Gutsfuck" guitarist used satanic and Nazi-related imagery to bolster his persona without practicing what he preached.

But for some members of Mayhem, being truly hateful and racist *was* of paramount importance. "Black metal is for white people," Hellhammer declared. It seemed the band's founder was forgetting his roots and moving more into the business side of black metal, which didn't sit well with many of his peers. Years later, Mayhem's previous bassist, Necrobutcher, admitted to *Heavy Consequence* that he was plotting to murder Euronymous but was beaten to the punch.

Owed money and feeling disillusioned, Varg decided that he wanted out of his contract with Euronymous. So, on August 10, 1993, he took a long drive to his frenemy's apartment in the middle of the night to surprise and confront him. Along for the ride was their mutual pal, Snorre Westvold Ruch, from the band Thorns. Knowing that cigarettes were verboten by Euronymous, Snorre waited outside and smoked while Varg, armed with a foldup blade, made his way to the 4th-floor walk-up apartment.

He knocked on the door and Euronymous, clad only in his underwear, answered, complaining about being woken up. According to Varg, things soon spun out-of-control: his former friend lunged for a kitchen knife, then kicked him, so he produced his pocket knife and started chasing Euronymous, stabbing at his back and shoulders. Euronymous dashed for the front door and exited the apartment, making a racket, shouting, and frantically banging on adjacent doors as he fled, "like a coward," Varg sneered.

The pair scuffled and the barefoot, barely-dressed Euronymous lost his balance and fell on the stairs. He lay sprawled in the stairwell, suffering from several sharp-force wounds to his back. Varg speared him some more but was distracted when Snorre appeared, shocked and staring in disbelief at the scarlet scene. "By then Euronymous was back on his feet. He looked resigned and said: 'It's enough,' but he tried to kick me again, and I finished him off by thrusting the knife through his skull, through his forehead, and he died instantaneously," Varg wrote via a blog in 2004 on his website, Burzum.org. The account was matter-of-fact, devoid of any emotion other than indignation, and blamed the victim for his own death.

"The eyes turned around in his head and a moan could be heard as he emptied his lungs when he died. He fell to a sitting position, but the knife was stuck in his head, so I [pulled] him up, as I held onto the knife." When Varg wrenched his blade from bone, Euronymous fell and rolled down the next flight of bare metal stairs "like a sack of potatoes—making enough noise to wake up the whole neighborhood."

Varg and Snorre split the scene, then hid the gore-drenched clothes and murder weapon. The police had their suspicions and they questioned Varg but they had to let him go due to lack of evidence. Before long, the Thorns keyboardist cracked, confessing everything. He was taken into custody and soon after, Varg was apprehended and arrested for the ghastly crime.

"Initially it was self-defense," Varg later recalled, "but when he started to flee, I was no longer in a life-threatening situation so, at that point, it was no longer self-defense but voluntary manslaughter, and as I saw it a pre-emptive strike, to prevent him from getting a second chance to kill me." He went on to deny that the murder was premeditated, yet he went to the apartment wearing gloves and carrying a weapon. The brutal bassist maintained it was manslaughter at most. "That should have given me only eight to 10 years. Instead, I got 21 years, and Snorre got eight years for doing absolutely nothing!" he griped.

The self-defense plea was weak at best. Varg didn't have a scratch on him, while the "Voice of a Tortured Skull" guitarist suffered 23 savage stab wounds: two to his head, five to his neck, and 16 to his back. During his trial, Varg contended that most of Euronymous' injuries were caused by glass that was broken during the struggle.

News of the 25-year-old metalhead's death brought about mixed responses in their community. By then, his popularity had begun to slip and there were rumors that Euronymous not only encouraged Dead's suicide but used it to further his own agenda. Some saw the late Mayhem leader as a martyr to the cause, while others denigrated him as the engineer of his own downfall.

Mayhem's first studio album, *De Mysteriis Dom Sathanas*, was released in May of 1994, nine months after the murder. Songwriting had begun in 1987 but due to bureaucracy, Dead's suicide, and the killing of its leader, the delay is understandable. The surviving band members decided to preserve everything as it was intended, so the album featured Varg "Count Grishnackh" Vikernes on bass. Hellhammer, ever the vending-machine of quotable quotes, said, "I thought it was appropriate that the murderer and victim were on the same record." Nearly 30 years after its release, *De Mysteriis Dom Sathanas* is widely regarded as one of the most influential black metal albums of all-time and is ranked #40 in the genre by *Rolling Stone* magazine.

As for Varg Vikernes, he was sentenced to the aforementioned 21 years in jail for the killing, as well as four counts of arson. The young man was busy behind bars, releasing two albums, getting married to a French woman named Marie, and fronting a pagan neo-Nazi gang. Despite the fact he escaped custody briefly and highjacked a car at gunpoint, Varg was released from prison six years early. After going free, he legally changed his name to Louis Cachet to avoid conflict in public (but he still goes by Varg Vikernes in his personal life).

While on parole, the multi-talented convict continued to record as Burzum, became a popular YouTuber, wrote some books, and created a role-playing game. Along the way, Varg and Marie had eight children—and ran afoul of the law on suspicion of terrorism after she bought four rifles. No charges were brought then but in 2014, Varg was convicted by a French court of "inciting racial hatred" against Muslims and Jews in his blog posts—he was given probation and made to pay a hefty fine. He's been laying low but in 2022, shortly before his Twitter account was suspended, the artist formerly known as The Count tweeted that he "appreciated" being labeled a Nazi.

Ozzy Osbourne has done some crazy things in his life as one of the world's most outrageous rock stars and tiffs with his wife and manager Sharon Osbourne are par for the course. But according to the 2020 documentary *Biography: The Nine Lives of Ozzy Osbourne*, he literally tried to murder her on September 2, 1989.

Sharon said she was sitting on the sofa in the couple's living room in Buckinghamshire, England, when the "Crazy Train" singer stumbled into the room, drunk. That was an everyday occurrence but what happened next went beyond the pale. He sat down, looked at her, and very calmly said, "We've come to a decision that you've got to die."

"I had no idea who was sat across from me on the sofa, but it wasn't my husband," Sharon said. "He goes to a state where he gets a look in his eyes, they're shutters... shutters were down on his eyes and I couldn't get through to him."

The self-avowed "Prince of Fucking Darkness" then proceeded to violently throttle her.

Ozzy said the feeling he had just before placing his hands around his wife's neck was "the calmest I've ever felt in my life. It was like serenity. Everything was just peaceful."

"He was calm. Very, very calm and he lunged across at me," she confirmed. Somehow, the redheaded music mogul managed to press a handy panic button. "I felt the stuff on the table and felt the panic button and just pressed it. Next thing I know, the cops were there."

The former Black Sabbath frontman, who was 34 at the time, claimed he didn't remember anything until he woke up in a cell at the local police station. "I was in Amersham jail, and I asked the cop, 'Why am I here?' And he says, 'You want me to read your charge?' So he read, 'John Michael Osbourne, you have been arrested for the attempted murder of Sharon Osbourne.'"

Sharon dropped the charges. "I was looking at all the options left in my life. I was looking at everything. What is going to be the best for my daughter? What is going to be the best for me? I hated being without him." Ozzy was shaken by the incident, and grateful. "He definitely watched what he was doing. He frightened himself," she said.

The "Mama, I'm Coming Home" singer went into rehab but relapsed several times throughout the years and at times, returned to his wife-beating ways—however, Sharon was a fighter as well. "Ozzy and I used to 'beat the shit out of each other," she said in a 2021 interview with the *Daily Mail*.

Things have calmed down and the elderly rockers both say they have been alcohol and drug-free for years and live harmoniously. (It's about time they grew up!)

In honor of the couple's 40th wedding anniversary on July 5, 2022, Ozzy took to social media and posted a vintage photo of their white wedding in Maui, Hawaii, with the words, "40 Years Ago Today! Happy Anniversary My Love." Sharon responded with a new snap of them in all-black outfits, writing, "2022 is a special year for me. It marks 40 years of marriage to my darling Ozzy. We first met when I was 18, over 52 years we have been friends, lovers, husband & wife, grandparents, and soulmates. Always at each other's side. I love you, Ozzy."

In a 2022 interview with *Rolling Stone*, the Ozzman elaborated on why he thinks their marriage has survived. "I've got a good wife, I think. She's been in rock & roll all her life. But she loves me, I love her. I haven't been the exact perfect husband, but she's fucking right about a lot of things."

Sharon added, "I knew that I was marrying an alcoholic. So what did I expect other than a bumpy ride? We've had more good times than bad. I regret nothing."

CHAPTER EIGHT: STAGE FRIGHT

"I near die of fear before I go onstage."
—Johnny Rotten

"Dime bag" was once the term for a cheap bag of weed; about a gram, which sold for $10. Beloved stoner and groove metal god Darrell Lance Abbott's nickname was "Dimebag" because he refused to carry more than the smallest amount of the herb on his person, lest he be busted and jailed. The three-strikes law was no joke in Darrell's heyday—plenty of pot puffers are still serving mandatory life sentences for getting popped three too many times.

Darrell, who was born in Ennis, Texas, on August 20, 1966, came from a music-loving family; his dad, Jerry Abbott, was a country music producer. Darrell learned to play guitar when he was 12 and soon fell in love with the glam-rock scene—he and his brother Vinnie Paul were both avid aspiring musicians and they dreamed of one day having their own band just like their idols, Alex and Eddie Van Halen.

The amiable, long-haired teen loved flashy guitar solos and could bust out brilliant barnburners like "Eruption" (Ed Van Halen) and "Crazy Train" (Randy Rhoads) with ease. In those days, he went by the name "Diamond" Darrell (a nod to the KISS song "Black Diamond") but before long, he settled on "Dimebag" and a legend was sparked. The boys joined the metal group Pantera in 1981, and when they released their first album, *Metal Magic*, drummer Vinnie was 18, and Darrell was only 16.

Pantera climbed the charts again and again, earning several gold and platinum record awards, not to mention GRAMMY nods, and Dime himself was considered one of the best guitarists in metal. *Metal Hammer*'s Dom Lawson gushed that he was a "revolutionary" who "played as if the guitar was some magical vestigial limb, as the very essence of his being poured out of him as a bewildering array of ageless riffs and spinetingling lead breaks." The group's down-tuned sound was a relentless mixture of punk and speed-metal that garnered fans from all over the world.

Even though metal took a hit after grunge burst onto the scene, Pantera's 1994 album *Far Beyond Driven* debuted at #1 on the *Billboard* chart and their music was in-demand until they split up in 2003 due to infighting. Still, it was a good run and the future looked bright for the Abbott brothers.

From there, Dime and Vinnie formed a supergroup called Damageplan. It should have been onward and upward, but one deranged Pantera fan blamed the powerhouse guitarist for not only the breakup of his favorite band but other bizarre, imagined slights. He decided to hunt Darrell down and vowed that it would not end well for the "Cowboys From Hell" musician.

A mountain of a man at six-foot-three, an ex-Marine, and a former semi-pro football player, 25-year-old Nathan Gale was known to pet an imaginary dog and talk to walls while blaring Pantera's music at all hours of the day and night. Nathan told friends that the band had stolen his music and that he was going to get even. Sadly, no one took him seriously enough to think he'd actually try to do something about it.

Damageplan was promoting their upcoming debut album when Nathan decided to take a semi-automatic weapon to their gig in Columbus, Ohio, on December 8, 2004. (December 8 is an oddly cursed day for rockers; the phenomenon is covered in *Volume One* of this series.) When the dust settled, a total of five people lay dead inside the Alrosa Villa Nightclub.

That afternoon, Dime was in good spirits. The pair had played at the club before with Pantera and were grateful to have the chance to show off their new licks at the well-known rock venue. Having done a satisfactory soundcheck at the venue, the brothers hung out, then Dime and Vinnie watched one of the opening acts from the wings, Volume Dealer. Before them, another local act, whose name, 12 Gauge, proved to be an eerie precursor to the night's events, played their set.

"[Volume Dealer] were doing Parliament songs heavy metal style and they were all dressed up like G.I. Joes," Vinnie Paul Abbott told reporter Jon Wiederhorn in 2006. "We were back there doing shots and peeking out and cracking up about the whole thing. So, we were all in a good mood and we had a full house that night and went up on the deck. Right before we went on, Dime was warming up his hand and putting his lip gloss on. The last thing I ever said to him was 'Van Halen?' And he gives me five and says, 'Van fuckin' Halen!' That was our code word for letting it all hang out and having a good time. And that's the last thing he ever said to me, man."

At about 10:15 p.m., shortly into Damageplan's opening song, "Breathing New Life," Nathan Gale ran out from behind a wall of amps and strode purposefully across the stage with his Beretta 9mm handgun drawn. Without hesitation, the disturbed fan fired three shots directly into 38-year-old Dimebag Darrell's head as he shook his hair in time with the heavy riffs. It's likely that he never saw the threat coming. He sustained four gunshot wounds, including one to the right cheek, one to the back of the head, one to the left ear, and one to the right hand. He collapsed, his right leg twisted under his body, then slumped toward the crowd. Feedback screeched from his guitar as panicked patrons quickly realized that what was happening was not a stunt. The enraged gunman kept firing as members of the crew charged him. Nathan killed four and injured two more before putting Vinnie's drum tech, John "Kat" Brooks, in a headlock and taking him hostage.

That's when Officer James "Jim" Niggemeyer, responding to the 911 calls in less than two minutes, arrived on the scene. He approached from the rear of the club while other officers ran toward the front of the stage, fighting their way through the thick of panicked concertgoers trying to flee through the front and side doors.

"People were screaming, 'Get in there, get in there. He's killing people,'" said Officer Ricky Crum, who heard a cluster of gunfire as he approached the building.

Officer Niggemeyer quickly assessed the situation and raised his police-issued 12-gauge Remington 870 shotgun, maneuvered around the abandoned drum set, and killed Nathan Gale with a single blast of lead pellets to the face. "I knew from that distance I could shoot the suspect, as long as I aimed high enough and wouldn't hurt the hostage," Niggemeyer later told *MTV News*. "At that point, almost immediately, I fired."

"Jim prevented further injuries and deaths," Crum said. "The suspect wasn't going to stop unless someone stopped him." (Although he was an undisputed hero, Niggemeyer suffered from severe post-traumatic stress and anxiety which eventually forced him to quit the police force.) While most of the audience ran out of the club, some stayed behind to "curse and kick" the corpse of the murderer, Crum added.

Nathan's mother, Mary Clark, told Columbus TV station *NBC 4*, "I bought him that gun. I'll never, never be able to live that part down. And I still didn't understand the whole thing, but he came home with his medications, and I don't know if he took them or not." (An autopsy by the Franklin County coroner's office confirmed that there was no medication in his system.) "I don't know if he was afraid to, or ... ashamed to, or ... didn't believe [he was mentally ill]. I have such remorse for those families, and I am so sorry that they are losing their loved ones. Their sons, brothers, fathers."

Alrosa manager Rick Cautela remembered his last view of survivor Vinnie Paul. "He was wrapped in a blanket, and he was clutching Dimebag's guitar." The other victims were Jeffrey "Mayhem" Thompson, Damageplan's head of security who initially tackled Gale; Erin Halk, an Alrosa Villa employee who did the same; and metal fan Nathan Bray, who jumped onto the stage and tried to resuscitate Dime. Tour manager Chris Paluksa and the drum tech taken hostage were both transported to Riverside Methodist Hospital, and road crew member Travis Burnett was treated at the scene with minor injuries.

The incident stunned and scared other musicians who realized just how vulnerable they were while onstage. "After something like that happens to one of your best friends, how could you ever feel safe, anywhere, ever?" asked Anthrax rhythm guitarist Scott Ian. "The few times that kids have made it up onto the stage during our show, no matter how friendly the scenario, the first thing I think is, 'Dude, you should not be on this fucking stage. You should know better.' To me, everything changed after Dime was killed. The stage became off-limits for everyone but musicians. I don't give a fuck how much fun you're having. Stay the fuck off the stage."

Darrell Abbott was buried on December 14, 2004. Eddie Van Halen arrived with Darrell's favorite guitar of all-time, the famous 1979 yellow-and-black-striped "Bumblebee" Charvel electric guitar that appears on the inner sleeve of *Van Halen II*. It was a posthumous gift to Darrell and is buried with him.

Ed and Dime had only met once. "We had just seen Van Halen in Midland, Texas, a few weeks earlier, and that was the first time he ever got to meet Eddie," the metal star's longtime girlfriend Rita Haney said in an interview. "They hung out before and after the show. Dime even got to play Eddie's rig at soundcheck. He was like a kid in a candy store."

Vinnie recalled, "Eddie sent a limo to pick us up, which was very cool. And we came in, and he brought us right up on stage and hung out at soundcheck and everything. And the show was amazing. And I'll never forget it. We got on the plane, and when we were flying back to Dallas, my brother looked at me, and he goes, 'Man, you know what? If this plane was to go down in a crash right now, I'd be okay with it. I finally got to meet the dude that made me wanna play guitar.' It was really special."

At the service in Moore Memorial Gardens Cemetery in Arlington, Texas, Eddie told the mourners, "I'm here for the same reason as everyone else: to give some love back. This guy was full of life. He lived and breathed rock & roll." Then he held his phone to a mic so everyone could hear a voicemail from Dime that he'd kept, which said, "Thank you so much, man, for the most awesome, uplifting, euphoric, spiritual rock & roll extravaganza ever!"

Vinnie Abbott died on June 22, 2018, in Las Vegas at the age of 54 from severe coronary artery disease and an enlarged heart. The brothers are buried side-by-side, in KISS Kaskets donated by Gene Simmons and Paul Stanley; Dime was a member of the KISS Army and had a portrait of Ace Frehley tattooed on his chest in 1992. In late 2020, a blockade was put around the burial ground to thwart vandals because Dime's grave had been defaced by several people over the years—plus, there was concern that someone might try to get into the coffin to steal the guitar. Paul Stanley told the press that he thought the damage done to the graves was "disrespectful" and that he thought adding the barrier was a good idea.

On December 7, 2021, just one day shy of the 17th anniversary of the shooting, Alrosa Villa was demolished to make way for affordable housing. "We've seen stars born here, unfortunately, we've had stars pass away here, but the one thing that can never be taken away from us is the amazing memories we've all created along the way with magical people inside of this magical place," read the announcement on the venue's Facebook page.

The storied night spot had been active for 45 years upon its demolition and welcomed a wide range of musical acts on its stage over the years, including David Byrne, Slipknot, Dio, KoЯn, Quiet Riot, RATT, and more. It survived the 2005 lawsuit brought by the Abbott family and other injured parties, claiming "that there was inadequate security provided at the music venue given the nature and size of the crowd and previous incidents at the club involving criminal activity," the prosecuting attorney Gerald Leeseberg said. Alarosa Villa's owners settled out of court for an undisclosed sum.

While Dimebag Darrell was the first musician to be murdered while playing onstage, he wasn't the first to die in front of his fans. On May 17, 1996, 61-year-old Johnny "Guitar" Watson was performing at the Blues Café in Yokohama, Japan, when his number came up.

Some of rock's most famous guitarists, including Jimi Hendrix and Eric Clapton, credited Watson with inspiring them, and

Frank Zappa said that hearing the icon's 1957 song "Three Hours Past Midnight" began his interest in performing. While Guitar started off as a blistering blues player who was on the cutting edge of rockabilly in the 1950s, he easily reinvented himself and slid seamlessly into the laid-back funk sound that became popular in the early 1970s. "Ain't That a Bitch" and "A Real Mother for Ya," were among his most popular tunes, grabbing the ears of young soon-to-be rappers like Ice Cube and Snoop Dogg, who sampled his riffs in their own songs in the decades to follow.

Shortly after taking the stage and greeting his audience in Japanese on that final night, Guitar collapsed and died from what was later determined to be a heart attack.

Heart failure took out many more musicians over the years:

> **November 30, 1996:** While high-pitched singer and accomplished ukulelist Tiny Tim, 64, was hardly in any kind of rock genre, he was heartily embraced by the counterculture in the swinging '60s and had a novelty hit with "Tip-Toe Thru' the Tulips with Me" in 1968. He was still milking that tune for all it was worth and was, in fact, playing it at a benefit show for the Women's Club of Minneapolis, when he croaked following a massive coronary.

<u>Most ironic song title</u>: "Fill Your Heart,"
which appeared on his 1968 album, *God
Bless Tiny Tim*.

October 20, 2011: New Vagrants
drummer Joe Forgione, 59, died onstage
during the band's finale at the
Downtime Club, in New York.
<u>Most ironic song title</u>: "Expressway to
Your Heart," a hit Joe had with his first
band, the Soul Survivors, in 1967.

December 22, 2012: Rigor Mortis
founder and guitarist Mike Scaccia, 47,
was an innovator in the early days of
thrash and industrial metal. He joined
Ministry in 1989, and appeared on the
band's bestselling album, *Psalm 69: The
Way to Succeed and the Way to Suck
Eggs*. Mike remained friendly with his
former band brothers and on his fateful
final day, he was performing at a
birthday bash for Rigor Mortis' lead
singer, Bruce Corbitt, when he collapsed
and died.
<u>Most ironic song title</u>: "Welcome to Your
Funeral," from Rigor Mortis' self-titled
1988 LP.

July 27, 2013: Frontman Mick Farren,
69, was a proto-punk who burst onto the
scene with his U.K.-based band The
Deviants in the late 1960s. As a lyricist,

he lent his wit to Hawkwind, Motörhead, the Pink Fairies, and MC 5's Wayne Kramer. Too expressive to be contained to music alone, he wrote for *NME*, documenting the punk movement as it happened, and authored dozens of books. He collapsed during The Deviants set at the Atomic Sunshine Festival in London and died from what was later determined to be a heart attack.

<u>Most ironic song title</u>: "Death of a Dream Machine" from The Deviants' 1969 album, *The Deviants 3*.

July 3, 1999: Singer and multi-instrumentalist Mark Sandman, 46, was known for his chugging, spooky bass, and his deep, dreamy voice, which helped him rise to fame in the uniquely guitarless band Morphine. (They employed vocals, a modified 2-string bass, drums, and saxophone only.) The Boston-based baritone was one of the more literary rockers and said his lyrics were often influenced by authors like noir superstar James Ellroy and beat-icon Jack Kerouac. Mark's heart failed him three songs into the band's performance at a three-day outdoor music festival at the Giardini del Principe in Palestrina, Lazio, Italy. Mark Sandman had no pre-existing medical conditions, so the 100-degree, relentlessly sunny day is thought to have triggered the incident.

<u>Most ironic song title</u>: "Do Not Go Quietly Unto Your Grave" from Morphine's debut album, *Good*.

May 21, 2016: Drummer Nick Menza, 51, also died three songs into a set. He tasted fame while playing on some of Megadeth's most highly regarded albums, including *Rust in Peace* and *Countdown to Extinction*. But he liked all kinds of music genres and was in several bands over his lifetime so he could expand his repertoire. When he crashed his last cymbal, he was in OHM—an instrumental, progressive rock/jazz fusion power trio fronted by former Megadeth guitarist Chris Poland, featuring bassist Robertino "Pag" Pagliari of Uli John Roth's band, and German-born Nick sat on the drum throne. They were performing at The Baked Potato jazz club in Studio City, California, when Nick suddenly collapsed. Despite audience members delivering CPR and a quick call to 911, a heart attack claimed yet another middle-aged musician.

<u>Most ironic song title</u>: "Symphony of Destruction," from *Countdown to Extinction*.

March 22, 2017: They sang that they were "just another band out of Boston," but Boston was a lot more than that when the hard-working, hard rockers had their heyday in the '70s and '80s. Admirably-afroed drummer John Thomas "Sib" Hashian was at the kit when their 1976 self-titled debut album went multi-platinum. Seven million copies of their follow-up, *Don't Look Back*, were snatched up by their long-haired, pot-smoking fanbase and their popularity swelled into stadiums all over the world, where they entertained the masses with guitar-anthems like "Rock & Roll Band" and "More Than a Feeling." Sib left the band but was back playing iconic Boston tunes on the Legends of Rock cruise alongside fellow ex-Boston member Barry Goudreau—as well as Foreigner frontman Lou Gramm, The Grass Roots, and ex-Kansas singer John Elefante—when he buckled and went down. Ship medics quickly administered CPR and tried a defibrillator on the 67-year-old but it was too late. Sib's memorial service included several stars. Dwayne "The Rock" Johnson, who was engaged to Sib's daughter Lauren (they married in 2019), posted about the gathering on his social media, saying that the man he thought of as "a second dad" was hard to lose. The way in which he died was "heavy stuff but one of the silver linings was that the room was FILLED with love because Sib was playing in front of all his fans and family doing what he loved to do."

Most ironic song title: "Rockin' Away," a 2007 single by Delp & Goudreau.

May 1, 2017: Atlanta, Georgia, music maestro Bruce "Colonel" Hampton, 70, was performing at his own birthday celebration when he passed away. Talk about taking things full circle! The Colonel was a local legend, known as the "grand-daddy of the jam band scene" and as a practical joker who often hammed it up onstage. While virtuoso teen guitarist Taz Niederauer and members of Blues Traveler and Widespread Panic played "Turn on Your Love Light," Bruce was standing to the side of the stage by the amps, digging the tune. When he fell to his knees, banjo player Jeff "The Reverend" Mosier later said he thought that the birthday boy was giving a Wayne's World "we're not worthy" gesture to Taz. But no... Bruce Hampton's own love light had gone out as he suffered a myocardial infarction and died.

Most ironic song title: "Fixin to Die," a Bukka White cover that Bruce and his band, The Aquarium Rescue Unit, released in 1991.

September 17, 2017: Brazilian percussionist and former member of the band Chicago, Laudir de Oliveira, was 77 when he left the mortal coil during a concert in Rio de Janeiro. Laudir had been living in Rio for decades but he did venture stateside to reunite with his old band brothers when Chicago was inducted into the Rock & Roll Hall of Fame just a year before his death. Laudir dropped from a heart attack while performing on stage alongside another drummer, Jovi Joviniano "He had just rained on a spectacular solo, at the end of 'Fibra,' a composition by Paulo Moura. It was super applauded. It was his last applause," said Jovi. "It was a very beautiful energy, and soon we began to play 'Tenderness,' a samba-choro of the K-ximbinho. He was playing a beautiful ganzá, and I even closed my eyes. Suddenly we saw that his conga was down. I looked up and he was bent over, his face on the skin of the instrument. He made his way there, in a very beautiful way. Touching, doing what he loved, being applauded, and alongside his friends. If poetry exists in death, Laudir died in poetry."

Most ironic song titles: "Feelin' Alright," by Joe Cocker (1969) and "If You Leave Me Now" by Chicago (1979).

Most musicians have been surprised by an errant electrical current at one time or another. An improperly grounded microphone, loosely-connected amp, or steel-stringed guitar could easily become lethal. Les Paul, a pioneer in the invention of the solid-body electric guitar, knew the pitfalls all too well. "I was in the studio and I had just built a transmitter. I stuck one hand in the transmitter and the other was on my guitar. It was like being struck by lightning. I fell to the floor. I couldn't speak. I couldn't holler for help. And I couldn't open my hand. My grip just kept getting tighter and tighter. My whole chest was strained. Fortunately, my bassist came into the control room and saw me and threw the main power switch just in time."

Apparently, Jimi Hendrix was never zapped despite the fact he played the electric guitar with his teeth, used the mike stand for slide guitar, banged into the speakers for feedback, and set his axe on fire with lighter fluid in proximity to various plugged-in cables.

Stone the Crows guitarist Les Harvey wasn't so lucky. The young Scotsman joined the "27 Club" on May 3, 1972, after being electrocuted by an ungrounded microphone while tuning up for a performance at Swansea

Top Rank in Wales. Chances are, you've never heard of Stone the Crows. But at the time of his premature death, Les and his blues-rock band were positioned for stardom with support from members of Led Zeppelin, with whom Stone the Crows shared a manager, the inimitable Peter Grant.

Stone the Crows (which is an exclamation of surprise or, er, *shock*—before that, they were called Power... you can't make this stuff up) got together in 1969 and were comprised of Les on guitar, his fiancée Maggie Bell on vocals, James Dewar on bass and vocals, John McGinnis on keyboards, and Colin Allen on drums. While none of the musicians had ever written songs, they had an ace-in-the-hole thanks to Les' friendship with fellow Glaswegian Lulu, who was married to Maurice Gibb of the Bee Gees. "Maurice said: 'Leslie, you've got a guitar. Write the tune first and then put the lyrics to it,'" Maggie Bell recalled in an interview with *Louder Sound.* "That's exactly what we did." While they never had hit singles, their album sales were solid.

The band, which had replaced McGinnis and Dewar with Ronnie Leahy and Steve Thompson respectively, was touring in support of their third album, *Teenage Licks*, when Les lost his life. "It was a fluke," Maggie said. "The rest of us were standing at the side of the stage; we hadn't even started yet. Leslie said to the audience: 'There's a technical hitch,' and he touched the microphone and the guitar. And that was it."

"We heard this deep humming sound," Colin added. "Leslie had the microphone in one hand and his guitar in the other, they kind of went together, and then like an arc-shape appeared. I was up really quickly and kicked the guitar out of his hand as he was lying on the floor." But it was too late. The promising young musician died in front of 1,200 fans and his bandmates.

Another friend of Led Zeppelin's Jimmy Page, Yardbirds vocalist and harmonica player Keith Relf, also died due to electrical shock. The "Heart Full of Soul" singer died on May 12, 1976, at the age of 33 when he was playing an improperly grounded guitar in his home studio basement. While his death did not occur onstage, what happened to Keith is still considered one of the more tragic accidents to befall a major rock artist.

The handsome, blond lead singer was one of the best voices of the British Invasion but unlike some of his bandmates—Jimmy Page, Eric Clapton, Jeff Beck—his career faltered when the Yardbirds broke up. He helped originate songs that would go on to become acid rock staples, like "Dazed and Confused," which Jimmy wrote while he was still in the Yardbirds and Keith sang onstage before the song was recorded by Led Zeppelin with Robert Plant on lead vocals.

Keith was frail and beset with health problems, including asthma, which may have made his body less able to handle the charge that killed him. Apparently, he stood, barefooted, on an exposed gas pipe and the current quickly made its way to the steel strings. "His son found him lying on the floor with his headphones still on," recalled Yardbirds bassist, Chris Dreja. The young boy at first thought his dad "was just asleep because he often worked through the night, you know. It was very sad. The thing about Keith that I always think is, that hearing it in retrospect, how amazingly good his harmonica playing was." Keith Relf was inducted into the Rock & Roll Hall of Fame with the Yardbirds in 1992.

To the shock of his fans, folkie Bob Dylan "went electric" in 1965—but The Rolling Stones took it to a whole other level that same year. Fortunately, most errant currents do not result in death... Or maybe it's just Keith Richards—The Rolling Stones' co-founder, guitarist, and all-around poster boy for not dying—sustained not one, but *two* severe jolts just months apart.

The first zap nearly took out the whole band. As they embarked on a tour of Scandinavia, Britain's bad boys were doing a soundcheck at the Fyens Forum in Odense on March 26, when Mick Jagger grabbed the mic and received an electric shock that spun him around and into Keith Richards and Brian Jones. Brian then staggered into bassist Bill Wyman, who fell down, unconscious, onstage, obviously bearing the brunt of the body-hopping 220-volt electric shock. Photos from a quick-thinking photographer show Bill coming to, with his grave-faced bandmates surrounding him. The show's promoter later said that the bassist was saved by pure luck when Jagger accidentally pulled out the main plug while reeling from his own shock.

The second shock happened at the Memorial Auditorium in Sacramento, California on December 3, while the lads were playing their poppy radio hit, "The Last Time." Fortunately for Keef, it wasn't his own "last time" but when his guitar strings came into contact with a metal mic stand, it set off a shower of sparks to rival a fireworks display. The gangly axe man fell to the floor of the stage, seemingly lifeless. The crowd of 5,000 fans went completely quiet and watched in horror as the slumped Stone was carried out of sight by medics.

Bill Wyman remembered that Keith's guitar strings had "curled up, melted like fuse wire." Concert promoter Jeff Hughson said that the surge sounded so much like gunfire that he believed Richards was the target of an assassination attempt.

After being rushed to the nearest hospital, Keith recalled surfacing from unconsciousness and overhearing a doctor saying, "Well, they either wake up or they don't." He later surmised that he may have survived because of the thick soles of his brand-new suede Hush Puppies shoes, which terminated the electrical charge before the electrical charge could terminate him. The "Jumping Jack Flash" guitarist was back onstage the next night, none the worse for wear.

KISS has had its share of onstage mishaps including misdirected pyrotechnics and flight harnesses gone awry, but they nearly lost guitarist Ace Frehley while performing at the Civic Center in Lakeland, Florida on the night of December 12, 1976. The band had just played "Detroit Rock City" from a perch at the top of the stage and were being lowered for their next number when The Spaceman grabbed onto a metal rail to steady himself and his guitar also made contact, creating an electrical circuit. He was seized into a rigor but finally broke free and tumbled several feet to the hard stage below. "If I hadn't been able to let go, I would have died," Ace later told the *Lakeland Ledger*. "My life passed in front of my eyes." He was taken backstage, where he was feeling so scared and shaken, he didn't want to go back out. But then he heard the crowd chanting his name and he returned to a standing ovation. "I had no feeling in my hands. I don't know how I even did it. I guess it was all adrenaline." The incident inspired Ace to write the song "Shock Me," which came out a year later, on KISS' *Love Gun* LP and marked his debut as a vocalist.

While you might chalk such accidents up to old-school wiring, they still happen in present day. Twenty-one-year-old Argentinian rocker

Agustin Briolini died on stage in 2014 when his lips made contact with a faulty microphone. He was electrocuted during the band's opening song and died at the scene. Just three years later, an up-and-coming French singer, Barbara Weldens, 35, was performing at a church in the historical village of Gourdon, when she got zapped, collapsed, and died. She had recently released her first album, which garnered several awards.

In 1970, Led Zeppelin's U.S. tour grossed an estimated $1,200,000 and shattered the attendance record which was set by The Beatles five years before. They were especially popular in L.A. but not everyone loved them.

The police, in particular, were wary of the Zep boys and their fans. Jimmy recalled a particularly unsettling incident from that tour in a 2020 social media post: "[We] embarked across a tour of the South in America. Long hair was pretty unpopular in the late '60s and even 1970. The authorities appeared to be building up a head of steam over what they believed to be happening with the current movement within the musical manifestation of the time. They seemed intent to keep audiences seated. Indeed, news reached us of the unthinkable: the audience had been tear-gassed at a show at the Forum in L.A., in the very state where one assumed there was a liberal outlook to change.

"However, the South already appeared to be taking a far tougher right-wing stance. At the end of a rousing show, albeit one where the audience had already been somewhat intimidated by the police, the band went backstage to the dressing room fully prepared to play an encore for what was audibly a really enthusiastic crowd. At the point of exit from the dressing room, a burly policeman put an iron bar across the door to stop me from going out, with the phrase 'You go out there boy, and I'll break your head.' That night, we *didn't* play an encore in Nashville!"

Throughout the 1970s, Led Zeppelin was beset by enterprising fans who bootlegged audio (and sometimes video) of their concerts to sell on the black market. In that long ago, mist-enshrouded Jurassic era before billions of iPhone videos from concertgoers could be streamed online, these wily entrepreneurs got actual cash-money from selling illegal recordings of entire rock concerts. The most popular band to be bootlegged was Led Zeppelin and their Redwood of a manager, former wrestler Peter Grant, was *not* having it. If he spotted anyone recording, he would personally go into the audience to break their tapes or, as he did at the Bath Festival in 1970, throw a bucket of water on their recording equipment. The famously short-tempered, six-foot-five manager died in 1995 but can you imagine his reaction to the advent of fan-flown drones?

Philly may be called the City of Brotherly Love but it's always been a rough town, as Aerosmith found out on October 10, 1977, when a fan threw an M-80 firecracker onstage toward the end of their performance. "We were going back up on the stage to do the encore," guitarist Brad Whitford later told *Goldmine*. "I was going up the stairs right behind [singer] Steven [Tyler] and [guitarist] Joe [Perry], and I felt the concussion of the cherry bomb going off. Steven immediately covered his face and there was blood shooting up out of Joe's arm." Joe screamed, "Fuck you, Philadelphia!" as they were whisked offstage by security.

Steven's cornea was burned and Joe had a ruptured artery in his hand, which forced the band to take a break. They shied away from Philly for a while but returned on November 25, 1978. "Five songs into a sold-out show, someone threw a beer bottle from the balcony," Brad recalled in Aerosmith's collective 1997 autobiography, *Walk This Way*. "It hit the stage dead center, right in front of the monitor, and exploded, sending shards of glass into Steven's face. I think some glass went right through his mouth. That's it. Backstage, Steven's holding a towel to his bloody face, and he wants to go back on! The vote was four-to-one against, and we were in the limos two minutes later. Fuck this." What Brad neglected to mention is, the song Aerosmith was playing was "Sight for Sore Eyes." Maybe the fan thought it was a command.

An overly eager Rolling Stones fan got a sore head courtesy of Keith Richards after jumping up onstage during their December

18th, 1981, performance at the Coliseum in Hampton, Virginia. The band was closing their concert with "(I Can't Get No) Satisfaction" when the still-unidentified music lover leaped up and started charging toward an American flag-clad Mick Jagger. As he passed Keef, he was intercepted by a barrage of bonks with the guitarist's black Telecaster.

"The damn thing stayed in tune, and this is the greatest [advertisement] for Fender that I can give you," he later said. (Talk about a Fender-bender!) Not only didn't the guitar miss a note, Mick saw what was happening but just kept on singing and strutting. Security quickly swooped in and scooped the stunned stage-crasher up and called the cops.

In an interview post-incident, Keith Richards explained, "The only reason I did it was because security was not there—they were two steps behind. I am watching Mick's back. I don't know where this guy is gonna go... You know it's a kind of automatic, instinctive thing... I just watched my mate's back." What's more, he laughed, "I bailed [the fan] out afterwards. He didn't spend the night in jail... He still owes me 200 bucks."

It's not always the fans that sustain guitar-given head injuries. During their 1992 *MTV Video Music Awards* performance, Nirvana's "Lithium" ended in a grand finale in which six-foot-seven bassist Krist Novoselic flung his instrument 20 feet into the air and tried to catch it. He missed, but the bass didn't miss his noggin. Krist fell to the ground, writhing in pain, so vocalist and guitarist Kurt Cobain decided to punish his own instrument by jamming its headstock into the nearest amp. Drummer Dave Grohl recalled the incident on a talk show hosted by Dennis Miller, saying he was so worried about his bandmate that he ran backstage, looking everywhere frantically. "Finally, I find him and he's got this huge lump on his head but he's sitting there drinking straight from a champagne bottle with Brian May from Queen" with a huge smile on his face.

Just the year before, on October 19, 1991, Nirvana's frontman whapped a security guard on the head with his guitar while crowd-surfing during the band's cover of "Love Buzz" by Shocking Blue. It happened at Trees Club in Dallas, and the gig was booked around the time *Nevermind* was released. By the time the band took the stage at that small venue, their single "Smells Like Teen Spirit" had been released and was blowing up on the radio and *MTV*. About a thousand grunge enthusiasts were inside, while hundreds more clamored outside.

According to the promoter, Kurt was upset with the sound mix and started to smash the equipment with his guitar—but the monitors belonged to the venue, not the band. After that, the finicky frontman dove into the audience, and as the crowd pushed him back toward the stage, he hit a muscle-bound bouncer, Turner Van Blarcum, in the face with his guitar. Turner, bleeding profusely, punched and kicked the singer, then sent him skittering across the stage with a body slam. Kris and Dave immediately grabbed and subdued the angry employee, and Kurt escaped into the backstage area. After some coaxing by the Trees' management, the band went out and finished their set.

Turner Van Blarcum was still seething, so he waited in the parking lot in hopes of confronting the newly-anointed grunge gods before they could leave. They caught a cab in the nick of time, slamming the doors in Turner's face, who responded by running alongside and punching the window of the vehicle hard enough to break the glass.

Dead Boys and Lords of the New Church frontman Stiv Bators (born Steven John Bator) injured himself onstage with a chancy stunt—he'd been miming self-strangulation for years but one time when using the microphone cord, he took things too far, and died "for over a minute. If I hadn't pissed myself," alerting bandmates and crew members that something had gone wrong, he might not have made it. (The showman did die two years later, at the age of 40. On June 4, 1990, he was hit by a taxi in Paris, where he'd taken up residence. He apparently thought his injuries were minor so he went home to bed, but he never woke up. The cremains were sprinkled over Jim Morrison's grave by his grieving girlfriend, Caroline

Warren, who said she snorted a portion of Stiv's cinders so that she could feel closer to him.)

Alice Cooper also strangled himself onstage but it wasn't on purpose. The sultan of shock-rock has been mock-murdering himself since 1971, usually as a finale to his macabre tune, "Dead Babies." He's employed every means of execution from the guillotine to Old Sparky.

On April 7, 1988, at Wembley Arena in London, the piano wire that keeps the "School's Out" singer safely suspended during his gallows stunt suddenly snapped. Alice was able to slip his chin over the rope to save his neck from breaking. "Everything has its stress limit and after doing so many shows, I never thought about changing the wire. You know, I figured it'll last forever," he told *Entertainment Weekly*. "The wire snaps. I could hear the rope hit my chin and in an instant, I flipped my head back. That must've been a fraction of a second because if it caught my chin, it would have been a different result. It went over my neck and gave me a pretty good burn. I went down to the floor and pretty much blacked out."

While it's natural to assume that cherry bombs and falling bass guitars are going to do some serious damage, it probably never occurred to David Bowie to lookout for lobbed lollipops. But on June 19, 2004, a not-so-sweet Oslo, Norway, concertgoer chucked a sucker at the "Fame" singer, wedging it right into his left eye (which already had an enlarged and fixed pupil following a childhood fight). Bowie was unhurt and the show went on.

No one knows what flavor that lolly was, but it was probably citrus because three years later, Irish rockers U2 lived a real-life *This is Spinäl Tap* moment at Valle Hovin stadium in Oslo when the giant prop lemon they were supposed to emerge from didn't open, trapping them inside for several embarrassing minutes. During this tour, the band would re-emerge for their encores to a remix of their hit song "Lemon" while stepping out from a giant yellow mirror ball; everything worked perfectly until it didn't. After that, the lemon became, well, a "lemon"—in Las Vegas, as well as Tokyo, the contraption had to be wheeled off the stage with U2 still trapped inside. Frontman Bono was very Zen about it all, telling an interviewer, "It was a beautiful thing, being inside that lemon."

If it hadn't been for an appendicitis attack onstage, we might not have had Brian Johnson as the lead singer for AC/DC. The indelible Bon Scott had fronted the headbanging hard rock band from 1974 until his death in 1980 but guitarists Malcolm and Angus Young and drummer Phil Rudd decided to replace him. Not that he was "replaceable" but the band had paid their dues and then some, and their popularity was finally steadily on the rise. So, they started scouting talent and one gutsy talent, in particular, made an impression in the strangest of ways.

While Brian was mainly known for his glam-rock pipes as the frontman of minor hitmakers Geordie, Angus heard a certain quality in his voice that he thought would click with AC/DC. Not only that, he had a good reputation as a solid dude and had been highly praised by the late Bon Scott. But could he stand out onstage? "I remember Bon telling me the story of when he saw Brian singing with his band [in the 1970s]," Angus recalled in an interview. "He says to me, 'There's this guy up there screaming at the top of his lungs and then the next thing you know he hits the deck. He's on the floor, rolling around and screaming. I thought it was great, and then to top it off—you couldn't get a better encore—they came in and wheeled the guy off!'"

What Bon didn't know was that Brian was diagnosed with appendicitis later that night, which was the cause of his writhing and screaming onstage! Bon died in London on February 19, 1980, after a long night of drinking, just days before AC/DC was due to start writing for what became *Back in Black*. Brian stepped behind the mic and the rest is rock & roll history—the album went on to become one of the bestselling LPs of all-time, spawning classics like "Hell's Bells," "Givin' the Dog a Bone," and of course, the title track.

Seventies songstress Carly Simon suffered a strange case of spontaneous and copious vaginal bleeding while onstage in October of 1980. The "Anticipation" singer had suffered from lifelong panic attacks—which are far more intense than the usual jitters—that were so debilitating that in 1976, she became the first and only *Saturday Night Live* musical guest to appear via a pre-taped performance. But what happened in Pittsburgh, Pennsylvania, went beyond the pale. Onstage her heart palpitations went wild, and soon she found herself in the midst of a full-on panic strike. Unable to sing, she asked the audience to come onstage and help her.

"I had two choices," Carly later told the *New York Times*. "I could either leave the stage and say I was sick or tell the audience the truth. I decided to tell them I was having an anxiety attack, and they were incredibly supportive. They said, 'Go with it—we'll be with you.' But after two songs, I was still having palpitations. I suggested that I might feel better if someone came on the stage. About 50 people came up, and it was like an encounter group. They rubbed my arms and legs and said, 'We love you,' and I was able to finish the first show. But I collapsed before the second show with 10,000 people waiting.

"I couldn't get the words out," she recalled in her memoir, *Boys in the Trees*. "There was blood everywhere." She realized that she had mysteriously begun to bleed down her legs, soaking her pants with gore. The cause remains a mystery, as Carly never says in the book whether she had a miscarriage, spontaneous menstruation, or an anxiety-related hemorrhage. "In retrospect, the very idea of the tour was foolish," she said. "My marriage to James Taylor was breaking up, and my son, Ben, had been sick and had had a kidney removed, and I'd lost 25 pounds. I was in terrible shape, physically and emotionally." Fortunately, she recovered and has treated her fans to many live performances since then.

Performing onstage with wild animals is usually not the best idea. Just ask Siegfried and Roy. Or the soon-to-be-headless live bat tossed to Ozzy Osbourne by a fan during a 1982 show in Des Moines, Iowa. Alice Cooper has had several boa constrictors on tour with him over the years, and there have been a few mishaps, including escapes and one snake that came down with a bout of diarrhea in front of a crowd of thousands that included Alice's VIP guests, Johnny Rotten and Rob Zombie.

Those animal antics pale in comparison to ZZ Top's "Worldwide Texas Tour" which started in 1976 and concluded the following year. The idea was to take Texas to the people, which the trio did by employing a massive 35-ton Lone Star State-shaped stage, full-sized windmills, live cacti, and countless other props. Sharing the spotlight with "that little ol' band from Texas" was an indigenous animal menagerie including buffalo, Longhorn steer, a javelina pig, rattlesnakes, tarantulas, and vultures... what could possibly go wrong? Or as drummer Frank Beard recalled, "Some idiot, I can't remember which one of us it was, said, 'Hey, let's take a buffalo on tour.' And it went on from there."

The professional animal wrangler they hired, Ralph Fisher, assured them that he could "train anything with hair," and he did prep the animals to avoid catastrophe as best he could. "For months, we played loud rock music to them on a timer so it would come off and on during the night, along with a light show. I popped firecrackers near them, waved flags, anything to simulate what might happen in a concert," he said.

Regardless, some animals did misbehave onstage, and on November 28, 1976, the buffalo made a break for it while backstage in Fort Worth. Assistant set designer Michel Priest remembered the commotion in a 2014 interview. "As they were leading the buffalo onto the scissor lift for rehearsal, the animal jerked his nose-ring out, so he's throwing his head around in pain, snorting and wild-eyed. He sees this tall strip of light streaming in through the doors in the distance so he heads straight for it. Between him and the light, of course, are the limos with the drivers inside. He charges right between the first two, but then gets jammed between the next two. The driver wakes from his nap, looks over, and not five inches from his eye is the face of this insane buffalo, sneezing and blowing blood all over the window." The buffalo was caught and treated for his nose injury.

ZZ Top's lead guitarist and vocalist Billy Gibbons added, "The animal rights groups were always present to make sure that these critters were being taken proper care of."

In a vintage interview, the late Beard (the only band member without one) said that he had several buzzards perched around his drum kit every night, and "When I played a slow blues thing, they'd get real interested in me, you know? So, I'd move my arms around a lot more" to keep them from thinking he was a potential meal.

There are countless tales of performers tripping and falling onstage (and off the stage, sometimes dropping several feet and breaking limbs). But when the stage falls on the performer, that's rare. Funk and soul superstar Curtis Mayfield, whose 1970s hits included "Superfly" and "Pusherman" was warming up for a blustering, stormy outdoor show at Wingate Field in Flatbush, Brooklyn, on August 13, 1990, when a windswept lighting tower fell on his back.

Curtis' son Todd wrote about it in a 2016 biography called *Traveling Soul*. "Dad blacked out, came to, and discovered neither his hands nor arms were where he thought they were. He lay splattered on the stage, helpless as an infant. Then it rained. Big drops. Torrents poured from the sky; thunder exploded like shrapnel. [Drummer, Lee] Goodness rushed over to his bandleader. 'Are you all right?' he yelled into the rain. 'I think so, but I can't move,' my father groaned, sodden in the squall, powerless to take cover. He kept his eyes open, afraid that if he closed them, he'd die. Someone covered him with a plastic sheet, and everyone waited without breath until an ambulance arrived."

The 48-year-old musician was "rushed to Kings County Hospital. In the only stroke of luck that day, the hospital stood right next to the field. Paramedics saved his life, but not his body. After stabilizing him in traction, doctors told him the brutal truth—the stage light had crushed several vertebrae. Paralyzed from the neck down, he would never walk, let alone play guitar, again."

Things went from bad to worse—Todd describes his father's agonizing phantom pain, and a fire that burnt his house down, destroying many of Curtis' precious career artifacts. "Dad kept his old master tapes in the basement, and when the fire hoses extinguished the blaze, they also doused some of the most famous recordings in soul music history."

In 1994, Curtis Mayfield was honored by the GRAMMYs with a Legend Award. At the ceremony, he was wheeled onstage where he gave a short speech. Along with former bandmates from his first group the Impressions, he sang "Amen" in what would be his last public performance ever. He died on the day after Christmas five years later.

If you've never heard of Eagles of Death Metal, you've probably never heard them at all. Formed in the late '90s in Palm Desert, California, the band's nucleus was comprised of Jesse Hughes on vocals and guitar, with Josh Homme on drums (who's most famous for his other band, Queens of the Stone Age). The group rotates through a range of guest musicians who perform on their albums and at live shows. Eagles of Death Metal is a wink of a name—their music is light, fun, and combines, "bluegrass slide guitar mixed with stripper drum beats and Canned Heat vocals," according to Josh. So, not metal at all. While the retro rockers were performing their song "Kiss the Devil" at the Bataclan in Paris on November 13, 2015, Islamic terrorists stormed the venue with automatic rifles, grenades, and suicide-bomb vests. Close to 100 music lovers were murdered, but the band miraculously survived.

Some of the most notorious terror attacks at concerts have taken place in the U.S. Most of them, however, have not been during rock shows. Other music genres seem to be the incendiary ingredient when it comes to these things.

Soul band Jack Mack and the Heart Attack were performing at the Centennial Olympic Park bombing at the 1996 Summer Olympics in Atlanta, on July 27, when a homegrown terrorist's pipe bomb went off near the crowd, killing one spectator and wounding over a hundred others. A news cameraman died of a heart attack (oh, the irony) while running to cover the unprecedented episode. This incident led to a massive injustice against security guard Richard Jewell, who was accused of the crime when he was actually a bona fide hero. (The culprit was Eric Rudolf, a man who committed several other acts of terrorism and was finally jailed for life in 2005.)

On May 22, 2017, an Islamist extremist suicide bomber detonated a shrapnel-studded projectile as music lovers were leaving England's Manchester Arena following a concert by American pop princess Ariana Grande. The terrorist, 22-year-old Salman Ramadan Abedi, died at the scene as he took young fans and their parents with him—the youngest victim was an eight-year-old girl, Saffie Rose Roussos, one of 21 souls senselessly extinguished. Another 1,017 were injured, many of them children. Arianna visited the survivors in the hospital and says she still carries a lot of trauma as a result. In May 2020, the older brother of the bomber, Ismael Abedi, was charged with 22 counts of murder and a charge of conspiracy for helping to construct the bombing device—he left the country shortly after. According to an August 2022 item by *Sky News*, the convict is thought to be with his parents and siblings in Libya.

The deadliest mass shooting committed by an individual in United States history happened on October 1, 2017, on the Las Vegas Strip during a country music festival called

Route 91 Harvest. Jason Aldean, who's had 24 #1 singles on the U.S. *Billboard* Hot Country Songs and Country Airplay charts, was performing when over 1,000 shots were fired from a 32nd-floor window of the nearby Mandalay Bay Hotel and Casino. Jason survived but 60 people lost their lives that day. The lone gunman, 64-year-old Stephen Paddock, of Mesquite, Nevada, committed suicide in his hotel room before he could be apprehended.

Nineteen-sixty-nine was a pivotal year. It began with Richard Nixon assuming the U.S. presidency, and marked the beginning of the end for The Beatles. That summer, astronaut Neil Armstrong walked on the moon, and the Woodstock Music & Art Fair united music lovers as never before. The year ended with the arrest of the murderous Manson Family, and a disastrous San Francisco area performance headlined by The Rolling Stones.

When rock fans think of gigs gone horribly wrong, one word usually comes to mind: *Altamont.* The Altamont Speedway Free Festival was a counterculture concert, held on December 6, 1969, in Northern California—it was supposed to be the West Coast's answer to Woodstock's "three days of peace, love, and music" but sadly, it did not turn out that way.

Although not many remember or know that people *did* die at Woodstock in the summer of '69—two OD'd and one was run over by a tractor while cocooned in a sleeping bag—Altamont is thought of as far more deadly because of the violence and murder that sealed its bloodstained legacy.

The free concert was conceived by the Stones to counteract criticism that their ticket prices were too high—they'd had a successful few months touring the States and decided that a "thank you" was in order before going home to the U.K. Their reps found the location, they asked some of their favorite bands to open, and security was hastily hired... too bad it was provided by the Hells Angels Motorcycle Club. (The missing apostrophe is intentional; according to the organization, since there are many types of "hell," no punctuation is needed.)

The trouble started before the Stones even stepped onstage. For one thing, the location was announced less than a day in advance and none of the nearest businesses or residents were notified. Altamont was a desolate, barren space, and concertgoers were reduced to burning horrendous-smelling garbage for warmth and light as night fell. (The Rolling Stones wanted to perform in dramatic darkness.) Dick Carter, the manager-promoter of Altamont Raceway who'd offered the spot for free at the last-minute, was used to dealing with crowds of about 5,000 for demolition derbies—the concert attracted 300,000 music lovers and to say the venue was underequipped would be an understatement.

Jan Vinson, who piloted the Stones helicopter into the concert site, later vowed that he would never work a rock festival again, because of the "mass confusion and because I was put in a position which was dangerous to both me and the machine, and the crowd. Those people were messed up on everything—dope, wine, needles. They were higher than any altitude I've ever flown at. I wasn't about to get out of the chopper and talk to any of them."

As soon as the headlining band exited the helicopter, they were mobbed by zealous fans—mostly women, who wanted to give them presents or kiss them, but one fan promptly punched Mick Jagger in the kisser, yelling, "I hate you! I hate you!" The singer pulled his red cape around him and shrugged the incident off.

While they waited in safety, the opening bands bore the brunt of the Hells Angels' violent crowd-control tactics. The gang of 100 or so was tanked up on reds and red wine, and armed with sawn-off pool cues to be used as truncheons, plus several other more-concealable weapons. They were not discriminate; they beat women to bloody pulps for stage jumping or just crowding to the front, and even clocked Jefferson Airplane's Marty Balan to unconsciousness when he tried to intervene and save a fan from a biker's unwarranted wrath.

In an unrelated incident, one of the Airplane's sometime backup singers, San Francisco-based musician Denise Kaufman, was hit with a beer bottle, resulting in a fractured skull. She had to undergo emergency surgery to have a jagged chunk of bone removed from her brain.

"Somebody threw a beer bottle way up in the air and it came down on me and knocked me unconscious," she told *Rolling Stone*. Denise, who was in a pioneering all-female rock group called Ace of Cups, recalled that she had to be awake during the surgery because the position of the injury could only be treated under local anesthetic.

The Grateful Dead were scheduled to perform and even though they themselves had used Hells Angels as security for their own prior gigs, they were too spooked to go on and left by helicopter. Along with Santana and the Jefferson Airplane, the Flying Burrito Brothers and Crosby, Stills, Nash & Young, played their hits.

Among the 300,000-strong throng of humanity were teenagers Meredith Hunter and his girlfriend, Patty Bredehoft. As an interracial couple, the pair had endured their share of derision—but at the Altamont concert, some of the Hells Angels seemed particularly menacing. Partway through the concert, Patty was ready to call it a day, Stones or no Stones. But Meredith didn't want to go just yet, so he walked to the champagne-beige 1965 Mustang he'd borrowed and retrieved a pistol from the trunk that he'd brought "just in case."

According to Saul Austerlitz's book *Just A Shot Away*, the weapon was a long-barreled .22 Smith & Wesson revolver with a blue-steel barrel. Patty saw her boyfriend tuck the gun into his jacket pocket (the always-flashy dresser was decked-out in a lime green suit and matching hat). "Why are you getting that?" she asked. "It's just to protect myself. They're getting really bad," he told her. "[The Hells Angels] are pushing people off the stage, and beating people up."

The lads from London finally appeared onstage in all their satanic majesty, robed and rhinestoned, playing under the cover of darkness and a waning crescent moon. They did a few numbers in fits and starts, as the crowd and leather-cut-wearing Angels continued to rumble with agitation. While notes of "Sympathy for the Devil" rang from the inadequate sound system, a fight broke out 20 feet from the stage. The band stopped the song while Mick tried to figure out what was going on and how to stop it; he peered into the darkness and asked everyone to "cool it."

The Stones finished that song, then played a few more. During "Under My Thumb," 18-year-old Meredith Hunter was viciously stabbed by a 21-year-old Hells Angel named Alan Passaro, prompting the former to pull his gun.

But before any blood was drawn, Meredith had been accosted for getting too close to the stage—eyewitnesses said that an unidentified aggressor from the ramshackle security detail pulled the young man's hair and yanked on his ear while chuckling at his pain and surprise. A few more bikers joined the fray and escalated the violence, pulling Meredith to the ground in an attempt to pin him down. Sixteen-year-old Patty stood by, frozen with terror.

The young man wrested himself free from the bikers, found his feet, and ran as best he could through the thick crowd. He paused, pulled his pistol, and then held it in the air. His girlfriend shouted at him not to shoot. Hunter lowered his gun and resumed running.

"A short, stocky Angel named Alan Passaro, wearing a sleeveless light-brown vest with a 'FRISCO' patch over the left breast jumped on him from behind, grabbing at his arm," wrote author Saul Austerlitz in 2018. "The biker almost rode on his back as he raised his arm over his head and brought his knife down in a long, curving arc, stabbing Hunter twice. ... The Hells Angel stabbed Hunter no less than four more times, his knife repeatedly piercing his back. Hunter, wounded, dropped to his knees. The Hells Angel gripped him by the shoulders and kicked him in the face, over and over. The Angels surrounded him in a loose circle, pounding him with their boots until he collapsed face-forward. The Angels punched and kicked Meredith as they dragged him away from the stage and toward the scaffolding. Hunter fell to the ground and bumped against some part of the scaffolding, perhaps its pillars. Hunter softly told his attackers, his strength already beginning to fade, 'I wasn't going to shoot you.'"

Not satisfied, the murderous mob picked up a nearby trash can and bashed Meredith's skull with it. Alan Passaro then "stood on top of his battered head for a full minute before finally stepping back. 'Don't touch him,' he told a bystander who had been watching the fight. 'He's going to die anyway.'"

The gravely injured teen was taken to the nearest Red Cross medical tent by concerned bystanders but it was too late. Or, as Dr. Richard Baldwin said at the time, even if Meredith Hunter had been stabbed like that in an operating room, he wouldn't have made it because so many arteries were severed, and his nose was crushed so badly that he couldn't get enough oxygen to keep his heart beating.

Meredith Hunter died, and Mick Jagger sang "Street Fighting Man" at last: "What can a poor boy do/but sing in a rock & roll band?" The words hit home because there really was nothing the musicians could do as untold chaos reigned in the audience.

A film crew was on-site to capture the magic (and murder). The resulting two-hour movie, *Gimme Shelter*, was directed by Albert and David Maysles and Charlotte Zwerin, and it closely chronicled the last weeks of The Rolling Stones' U.S. tour. Cameraman Baird Bryant caught the murder on camera and it was shown in the documentary, which premiered at Cannes the following year.

Sonny Barger, the Hells Angels President at the time, said in a radio interview the day after Altamont that his motorcycle gang was only responding to what they were given. "People who call themselves flower children [shouldn't]. There is some of them lousy people ain't a bit better than the worst of us, and it's about time they realized it. They can call us all kinds of lousy dogs, and say that we shouldn't be there. But you know what, when they started messing with our bikes, they started it."

Carlos Santana, who was the first to perform on that fateful day, disagreed. "There were bad vibes from the beginning. The fights started because the Hells Angels were pushing people around. There was no provocation; the Angels started the whole violence thing and there's no fucking doubt about that."

Some blamed the hubris of The Rolling Stones, and Mick in particular of being on a "star trip," by insisting on having their moment in the spotlight. Or lack of spotlight as was the case, since they wanted to perform in dramatic near-darkness. The Stones' road manager, Sam Cutler, told the press not to blame the band or its frontman. "Mick didn't make the arrangements. I did. Put it on me."

Sam was just about the only person who did step up. Sonny Barger said, "Remember, the Angels were asked to be there. They were asked to guard the stage and they did it. In their mind, 'guard a stage' means <u>guard</u> it. That means if anyone comes near it, you do them in, and in the

Angels' style, if you do them in, you *do them in*. I don't dig everybody blaming the Angels. Blame is the dumbest trip there is; there isn't any blame."

Meredith Hunter wasn't the only one who never made it home from the concert. Three others died that day as well. Berkeley residents Mark Feiger and Richard Savlov, both 22, were killed by a hit-and-run driver as they sat around a campfire by the side of the speedway road. A massive Plymouth rolled over their chests, crushing them. Candy Sue Johnson, also 22, of Oakland, and James McDonald, 21, of Santa Cruz, both suffered head and internal injuries in the same accident. The driver fled the scene and was never brought to justice. The other death was listed by the coroner as "John Doe," who drowned after diving into an irrigation canal. The young 20-something was clearly high on hallucinogenic drugs and, after being warned not to by police, he slid into the water and drowned almost immediately.

As for how many were seriously hurt, there are no precise figures. The overall chaos made it impossible for medics to keep records, local hospitals did not release information to the media, and the injured were spread out in hospitals all over the Bay Area. Countless concertgoers later reported being dosed with LSD without their knowledge when offered sips of drinks, others were mugged, women were sexually harassed, cars were stolen, and an infant laying on a beach blanket in the crowd with his mother was reportedly trod on by a booted Hells Angel and nearly killed. (Speaking of which, there were no babies born during the Altamont concert—that fable was allegedly made up by the Stones' spin doctors to balance out the bad news.)

Guitarist Keith Richards' immediate reaction to the event was, "on the whole, a good concert." (Cringe.) But in fairness, the band was insulated by their entourage and rushed to their air transportation so quickly, they didn't know about the murder until the following day. They knew someone had been hurt but if you watch their real-time reaction in the *Gimme Shelter* film, they are just as confused as everyone else; details were much slower to emerge before the days of mobile phones, social media, and up-to-the-millisecond news coverage.

Mick Taylor, who'd joined The Rolling Stones just five months previously, was still shaken when he got home to London. "I was really scared," he said in an interview. "I was frightened for all of us, particularly for Mick because he had to be very careful what he said all the time, very careful. ... I've always heard about the incredible violence in America, but I'd never actually seen it. They're so used to it over there, it's a commonplace thing. They find it easier to accept. I've just never seen anything like that before. It was just completely barbaric."

Meredith Hunter's small funeral took place four days after his death and was held at

Skyview Memorial Lawn in East Vallejo, California. The Hunters could not afford a gravestone, so their son's final resting place was "unmarked for decades to come, a symbol of the forgetting already taking place," wrote Austerlitz. "Meredith Hunter's name would be a footnote to music history, but its link to the real young man who had lived, not just died, disappeared under the earth, with no marker to serve as a reminder." One wonders why The Rolling Stones didn't help pay for and mark the grave; maybe they were never told of the family's poverty and they certainly never asked. Only stage manager Chip Monck (who'd also worked at the Woodstock concert) paid his respects to Meredith's loved ones.

Too bereft to attend the subsequent trial of Alan Passaro for the assault, the Hunter family was not surprised by the acquittal—another Black man had died at the hands of a white man, and that was that. Alan drowned in Anderson Lake in Santa Clara County on March 29, 1985, under "suspicious circumstances."

Thirty-seven years after Meredith Hunter was buried, a short documentary called *Lot 63, Grave C*, was screened at various film festivals, leading to a flood of donations to buy him a proper headstone. His grave was finally marked in 2008 and it reads, simply,

In Loving Memory
Meredith Curly Hunter, Jr.
October 24, 1951 – December 6, 1969

Altamont was not The Rolling Stones' first brush with concert chaos. In 1965, they toured Germany, where the straight press referred to them as "cavemen" whose music was "primitive and unimaginative."

But the fans didn't feel that way. They were crazy for Mick, Keith, Brian Jones, and Charlie Watts. A sold-out show in Hamburg erupted into violence when thousands of ticketless young ruffians decided to take out their frustrations on streetlamps, benches, planters, and cars just outside the venue. The police responded with brutality and by the time the dust settled, 47 people were arrested and 31 were treated for injuries.

But that was a walk in the park compared to what happened the following day in West Berlin, where the Stones performed at the Waldbühne Woodland Stage. Once again, the concert was sold-out, and once again, fans who had not been able to get tickets turned up anyway. Since the venue was an open-air arena, they were able to break through the police cordon and get in. The eager teens rushed to the stage, inciting a riot. The band, afraid for their lives, stopped the music after just 20 minutes, fleeing the scene. Their abrupt exit prompted a melee that resulted in 87 injuries and left the concert hall in shambles. Eyewitnesses later recalled their terror, as the police whaled on everyone, even beating a group of young girls huddled and hiding under the stage, using hard rubber batons on them, then drenching them with high-pressure water hoses.

While one can kind of understand how the Stones could rile up a crowd, it was fresh-faced bubblegum-pop idol David Cassidy that roused the next major act of anarchy at a concert. David rose to fame on the television sitcom, The Partridge Family, which aired for four years and ended in 1974—the same year David was on tour to showcase his album, *Dreams Are Nuthin' More Than Wishes*. The star was performing in London at White City to a colossal crowd of screaming, crying, jeans-creaming teenage girls who were there to witness what the 24-year-old American had advertised as a final farewell before retirement (he wound up taking an 11-year hiatus from live performances).

The 35,000-capacity sports arena quickly sold-out and those unfortunates who couldn't somehow get a coveted ticket in their little perspiring palms went bananas. Many of the fans were on their feet for 12 hours, either vying for a top spot near the stage or hoping to snag a scalped pass. As the teens screamed and stampeded outside, the puka-shell-wearing, feather-haired dreamboat took the stage and caused a similar reaction inside. Fan-girls fainted and were trampled by mindless others as they rushed the stage, hoping for a smile or a drop of David's sweat. Hundreds were hurt and while 30 people were bad off enough to need medical attention, one unconscious 14-year-old, Bernadette Whelan, was rushed to west London's Hammersmith Hospital in dire straits.

"It was Beatle-Osmond-T.Rexstacy-mania all balled up into one," reported *Goldmine*, adding that "a souvenir album, *Cassidy Live*, would be along before the seats were even dry. Bernadette was one of the lucky ticket-holders, and her bedroom at her home in Stockwell Park, south London, spoke of her dedication to the star. A nearly life-sized poster of a gorgeous, glowering Cassidy dominated the wall above her headboard."

On May 30, 1974, four days after her comatose body was placed on life support, the schoolgirl passed away due to traumatic asphyxiation—or, as the coroner said, Bernadette was "a victim of contrived hysteria." The British Safety Council condemned Cassidy's White City show as a "suicide concert."

David was devastated but he did not attend the fan's funeral for fear of setting off more mania. He called her parents, and he sent an elaborate floral arrangement. "We don't blame David," a tearful Peter and Bridget Whelan said in an interview. "Bernadette would not have liked us to blame him."

David Cassidy's overwhelming fame set him on the path to substance abuse, multiple divorces, estrangement from his children, and bankruptcy. Sadly, he died of dementia and alcohol-related organ failure at the age of 67 on November 21, 2017.

Just a little over a year after losing their larger-than-life drummer Keith Moon to an overdose, The Who went on tour in support of their albums *The Kids Are Alright* and *Quadrophenia*, and debuted new sticks man Kenney Jones, formerly of Small Faces. They toured Europe and America to great success and acclaim but the mood soured on December 3, 1979, in Cincinnati, Ohio, when 11 fans—each holding an $11 ticket—were trampled to death by thousands more during a rush to get inside the Riverfront Coliseum. The show was "festival seating only" for many ticket-holders (meaning, no assigned seats; it was first-come, first-served).

The horror happened while Roger Daltrey, Pete Townshend, et al, were doing a late soundcheck. The crowd heard the music and mistook it for the concert starting without them and they stampeded. Part of the problem, it was later determined, was that the venue had relatively narrow doors leading inside, and they opened outward, creating even more of a challenge to get through. The staff did not want to unlock them too early, which caused several people to be crushed against the closed glass doors which cracked and buckled as the throng pushed and smushed. Survivors later described the terror and sense of helplessness they felt as the wind was knocked out of them; if they fell, indiscriminate feet simply stomped on them and kept going. Boyfriends and girlfriends, brothers and sisters, and friends were suddenly separated and unable to help each other.

One survivor, Pete B., later wrote that when he and his friends were in the melee, he fell three times and even lost his shoes—but he was in superior shape from playing high school football and managed to get back up each time. "The police stood around and watched. I was separated from my friends and watched the show alone and with blackened socks. When we reunited at the car, we had no idea anyone died. The radio said two had died, then three, then 11 the next day. The experience made me stronger. I have no fear of crowds and I consider myself a survivor because I did have to fight to escape. I don't feel that I touched any of the 11 that died, but I can't be sure. I remember girls screaming and crying, saying things like 'My friend is buried and can't breathe.'" Adding insult to injury, he added, "The show was okay. I never really cared for The Who."

Aside from the 11 lives lost, 300 were treated for injuries at local hospitals, the youngest victim being just 10 years old. In heart-wrenching news footage, you can hear The Who playing "The Kids Are Alright" as reporters give the grim statistics with prone bodies covered in sheets dotting the background.

The band didn't know about the incident until afterward—"We're totally shattered," Roger said in an interview the next day. The

Who's manager, Bill Curbishley, and supervisors at the venue reportedly decided to continue the concert as planned for fear of an even worse response from the agitated audience if they were made to leave without a concert.

Two fatal overdoses were also noted on *ITN's London News with Leonard Parkin*, with the anchor saying that the pair were "high on mary-wah-nah" and hallucinating, which supposedly led to their deaths. (Shades of *Reefer Madness*! It now is widely known that one cannot OD from smoking the usual amount of cannabis; there were probably other drugs at play.)

Strangely, in an interview for that same newscast, Pete initially blamed the fans and The Who's music (at least partially), for the violent outburst. "For us, it's deeply painful because we live off these kids, you know what I'm saying? They're our bread and butter. And to see the kids being taken out [not from the rush] but in drug overdose situations, it's deeply affecting. Eighty to 95% of our fans are male in the U.S.A., and they're usually rough and ready kids, and they like rock & roll. It's a very powerful music and ours is a very explosive music." He added, "We haven't used drugs since 1967. Roger Daltrey hasn't used drugs at all, I don't think. We like to show that you can work hard and you can get out of your brain, if you like, on the 'drugs' you've got inside your own head."

Members of the band moved on to the next show the following day but they did express their regret and sent flowers to the funerals. Much later on, the musicians visited the school where three of the victims attended classes and helped bring awareness to a memorial fund for Arts scholarships, which had been enacted in their names.

As a result of the high-profile tragedy, several procedures were changed in Cincinnati which filtered out into other cities in the U.S. "Won't Get Fooled Again," indeed. However, it should be noted that for at least three years before The Who's concert at the Riverfront Coliseum, concerned concertgoers and spectators for other events had been writing strongly-worded letters to the management and their local government about rampant negligence and the possible dangers of just such a disaster. While city council meetings did bring up potential problems at the venue, the powers-that-be were either too greedy or too lazy to take any preventative measures until they were forced into doing so. Three weeks too late, festival seating was banned in Cincinnati. Lawsuits were filed against the City, the concert promoter, and The Who, by survivors but they never went to court and insurance covered the damages.

The Who did not return to the scene of the tragedy for over four decades. They performed in Cincinnati during their "Who Hits Back" Tour on May 15, 2022. They included the community, victims' families, and survivors, in a unique performance that included an 11-minute instrumental introduction to "Love Reign O'er Me" along with a big screen projection showing photos of the 11 fans that lost their lives on that fateful day.

On June 14, 1986, one man died and three others suffered from serious injuries during an Ozzy Osbourne-headlined concert in Long Beach, California. John Loftus, 22, wound up at the morgue when, according to Lieutenant Bart Day, "he fell over backwards because he was probably overdosing, hit his head, broke his neck, and died." Paramedics rushed the young headbanger, already in full cardiac arrest, to St. Mary Medical Center at 9:20 p.m. on Saturday, and he was pronounced dead by doctors 10 minutes later of an apparently broken neck. While such a fracture isn't always fatal or even paralyzing, any trauma to the vertebrae can have serious consequences because the spinal cord, which is the central nervous system's connection between the brain and the body, runs through the center of the neck and backbone.

Ozzy got the blame but his opening act Metallica were actually the ones onstage when the four concertgoers took the plunge off the balcony onto the next level. "A lot of people were like slamming... you know, they get in a circle and hop, just hitting each other, bumping into each other, and it got too crazy," one of the injured teenagers said. "I just remember waking up at the hospital with a tube in my mouth."

According to the *L.A. Times*, paramedics and officials from area hospitals said they were swamped with emergency calls as a result of the Ozz-man's concerts, held at the 14,000-seat Long Beach Convention Center Arena on three consecutive nights. George Matson, the general manager of the venue, said the incidents were not out of the ordinary. "Normally, at an event of this size, we have 10 to 12 people treated for various things. On Friday we had 12, on Saturday, 19." When he was asked if they would book acts like Ozzy and Metallica again, he replied, "We provide facilities for entertainment. The people demand entertainment, we will book any event, whatever the people want."

Two *Appetite for Destruction* fans were killed during the Guns N' Roses set at the Monsters of Rock festival at Castle Donington, England, in 1988. Frontman Axl Rose, safely stationed onstage, helpfully suggested, "Don't fucking kill each other" when he saw the sea of humanity stream en masse toward him. Between being booked and appearing, Guns N' Roses had a massive worldwide hit with "Sweet Child O' Mine," which resulted in much more excitement to see them up-close than expected, and the organizers weren't properly prepared. With 107,000 in attendance at the rainy, mud-slicked outdoor show, it was impossible for Alan

Dick, 18, and Landon Siggers, 20, to avoid the undertow in the surge. They were crushed and suffocated just 15 feet from the stage and both were pronounced dead on arrival at the nearest hospital.

In 2020, guitarist Slash did an interview with *Kerrang!* and recalled the extreme highs and lows of that gig. It was a huge show with unprecedented fan support for the "Welcome to the Jungle" rockers, but when they were told what happened, their morale plunged. "[After the gig], we went to this bar, drinking—this little hotel we were at—I don't remember if we were sleeping there, or why we were there, but there were tons of kids there and it was a scene in itself. I ran into our tour manager at the bar and he was crying. That's when I found out that two kids had been trampled to death when we were playing. There was a bizarre shift from complete euphoria to going to this depressed state. The positive memory of the gig got washed away. It was heavy."

The event was canceled the following year and when Monsters of Rock returned in 1990, it did so with sounder safety protocols in place.

Guns N' Roses found themselves in the headlines again on November 29, 2022, when a fan was hit in the head by Axl's microphone during his traditional show-ender. For decades, the "Paradise City" singer threw his mic into the audience following the encore, but after the incident, which took place in Adelaide,

Australia, and hit Rebecca Howe flat in the face, he decided to call it quits on the custom.

Rebecca posted images of herself on TikTok, showing that she suffered from two black eyes and a cut, bloody nose. "He took a bow, and then he launched the microphone out to the crowd, and then bang, right on the bridge of my nose," she said, describing how she was left "hyperventilating and in a state of shock." Another fan caught the prize while she was helped out of the crowd by an off-duty police officer. "What if it was a couple of inches to the right or left? I could have lost an eye." She asked, "What if it hit me in the mouth, and I broke my teeth? If my head was turned and it hit me in the temple, it could have killed me." As of this writing, no lawsuit has been filed but it's probably inevitable.

Nineteen-ninety-six was an awful year for The Smashing Pumpkins. On July 12, they lost touring keyboard player Jonathan Melvoin to a heroin overdose and they subsequently fired longtime drummer Jimmy Chamberlain for his own reckless drug use (he was there when Jonathan died, shooting up the same smack).

Things had been on an upward trajectory for the emo rockers—frontman Billy Corgan, guitarist James Iha, and bassist D'arcy Wretzky were the nucleus of the band and they were finally enjoying the fruits of their labor. Their well-received 1991 debut album *Gish*, and its follow-up release, *Siamese Dream*, put them on the map. In 1994, they headlined

Lollapalooza, and the following year, they released their multiplatinum 2-disc CD, *Melancholy and The Infinite Sadness*. (But as the cliché says, "what goes up must come down" and we've all seen what happens when a pumpkin hits the pavement.)

The Pumpkins' first fall came on May 11, 1996, while they were performing in Dublin, Ireland. During the band's performance of "Bullet with Butterfly Wings," 17-year-old Bernadette O'Brien was crushed in the crowd. At around 10 p.m., she was smushed against the front of the stage as frantic fans pushed forward from a mosh pit, despite warnings from the band that people were getting hurt.

As Billy tried to articulate what was happening, he saw that he was getting nowhere and he threatened to end the concert. D'arcy interjected, "Listen! Listen! Don't fucking boo, do you fucking understand? Do you understand what he said? There are fucking people backstage dying. Do you care? I see people up here with smiles on their faces. It's not fucking funny."

The grievously injured Bernadette was pulled over the barricade by security staff and taken to a hospital, but she died two days later. The horrified band released a statement sharing their thoughts and sent flowers to her funeral. Their planned show in Belfast was canceled following the incident. Then, just two months later, they lost two of their own— Johnathan and Jimmy.

Denmark's annual Roskilde Festival is one of the biggest rock shows in the world and the biggest in Scandinavia. It usually goes off without a hitch but in 2000, headliners Pearl Jam helped to attract over 100,000 souls to the outdoor event, which included other popular rock acts like Iron Maiden, The Cure, and Oasis.

The site was deluged with rain and the resulting slick, squishy mud that suctions off shoes and brings even the mightiest of moshers to their knees. The tragedy unfolded in front of the Orange Stage on the night of June 30, while Eddie Vedder and company were blasting through their grungy greatest. Nine men died, and 26 were injured in a calamitous crowd crush.

The Seattle-based band knew something was wrong but it was impossible to work out exactly what was happening in the dark, swirling mass below. They paused in mid-song a few times. "There were still 40,000 people out there," Eddie recalled a few years later. "They were ready for the show to start again. They started singing, 'I'm still alive.' [asking for our single from the album *Ten*] 'Alive' was going to be the next song. That was when my brain clicked a switch." He saw one fan being laid out by security and, "They were blue. We knew immediately it had gone on to that other level. I knew I would never be the same."

The Cure, who was supposed to follow Pearl Jam, canceled their set and the entire festival concluded on a sour note. As it turned out, none of the people who died were under the influence of drugs and none were heavily impaired by alcohol, either. Although Pearl Jam made their live return just two months later with Sonic Youth, they opted not to play another festival until Reading and Leeds in 2006. In 2002, PJ released a memorial song, "Love Boat Captain" to remember the day they "lost nine friends we'll never know."

Love Parade 2010 was supposed to be a big deal to showcase the very best in EDM (electronic dance music) but it wound up being a big disaster. The free show was meant to accommodate 200,000 people but a mammoth 1.4 million fans wanted to get their dance on at the event, which originated in 1989 in West Berlin, Germany. The awful incident happened inside a tunnel underpass entry point leading to the venue. It was reported that attendees were falling off stairs and then trodden, resulting in 500 injuries and 21 deaths (15 people died at the site, then six succumbed in the hospital). Love Parade was dormant for years but revived as Rave the Planet 2022.

GRAMMY-nominated Travis "I'm not a hip-hopper" Scott organized and headlined the 2021 Astroworld Music Festival in his hometown of Houston, Texas, at NRG Park on November 5th. He thought he was doing a good thing for pandemic-weary music lovers by providing one of the first big live events following the nationwide lockdown but sadly, eight people were killed, 25 were hospitalized, and some 300 more were treated onsite for injuries when rampaging concertgoers surged toward the stage during the opening song—which just happened to be "Escape Plan."

Numerous concertgoers documented the incident, posting real-time phone videos and recounting their excruciating experiences on social media—a huge change from The Who's 1979 show, wherein city officials and the media tried to blame drug use and "the devil's music."

An injured ICU nurse attending the concert later told *CNN* that she passed out twice from pressure on her chest and back, and how the "feral" crowd continued to stomp screaming people on the ground in order to get closer to their idol. The youngest to die was nine-year-old Ezra Blount. He succumbed to severe damage to his brain, kidney, and liver after being "kicked, stepped on, and trampled, and nearly crushed to death," according to a lawsuit his family filed against Travis Scott and the event's organizer, Live Nation. Following the tragedy, the "Sicko Mode" rapper promised to cover the costs of funerals, medical bills, and to provide trauma counseling for those in need. However, a legal mess ensued that is still going on as of this writing.

Sometimes the violence spreads from the venue to the parking lot—which you might expect at a metal or punk show, but... Elton John? After his "Goodbye Yellow Brick Road" farewell concert in L.A. at Dodger's Stadium on November 17, 2022, pandemonium broke out as the venue's typical nightmare parking and exiting situation escalated into a full-on beatdown of an older couple following a minor collision. Video went viral (bystanders filmed but did nothing to help) showing six 30-somethings walloping a husband and wife in their 60s, resulting in unconsciousness and broken bones.

The footage clearly shows the male victim lying motionless on the ground, still being beaten by multiple assailants while the man's wife is seen being pulled away by her hair as she attempts to check on her spouse. News reports said that the wife later told police (who could not get to the scene in the tangle of traffic) that she tried to revive her husband for about 45 minutes, believing he had died, before he finally regained consciousness. The assailants fled the scene and the victims were interviewed at the hospital.

At the time of this writing, one of the attackers has been arrested—no names have been released by the authorities, but the victims' daughter has been vocal via social media. The main aggressor caught on camera beating the senior man has retained an attorney, stating that *he's* actually the victim and was only responding to an altercation initiated by the couple. Elton John hasn't released a statement on the incident. ("Sorry Seems to be the Hardest Word," indeed!)

The last couple of stories are only scary to ear doctors.

Anti-audiologist and drummer Keith Moon took it to 11+ at the end of his band's live-on-the-air performance in Hollywood on *The Smothers Brothers Comedy Hour* on September 17, 1967. The Who were already known for their seismic sound and decimating their instruments at the climax of their more rambunctious sets but the notoriously naughty Moony decided to up the ante—and not tell bandmates Pete Townshend, Roger Daltrey, and John Entwistle what he was up to. The drummer, wearing foppish ruffles for the appearance, surreptitiously hid a small canon filled to the brim with theatrical flash powder behind his kit. He detonated it for the grand finale of "My Generation" while Pete clobbered his axe against the stage floor and the live audience cheered.

The surprise explosion resulted in pure chaos, temporarily deafening everyone within range (including guests Bette Davis and Mickey Rooney). Pete, who drove a Packard hearse at the time, reacted like he thought he might be going home in the back of it—after a cinder singed his stylishly-coiffed hair, he furiously grabbed host Tommy Smothers' guitar and bashed it to bits.

"Everyone was so shocked," remembered Tommy, some years later. "When Townshend came over and grabbed my guitar, I was busy just seeing where the bodies were, seeing if anyone was injured. He picked the guitar up, and people kept saying, 'Did he really ruin your guitar? It looked so real!' And I'd say, 'Well, it was real! I was confused as hell!'"

While the big kaboom was the beginning of the end of Pete's perfect sound-perception, he has said that the main reason he was forced to start wearing amplification devices in both ears at a relatively young age was that he liked to drunkenly listen to playback in the studio with blaring headphones plastered to his noggin. (Part of the inner ear, called the cochlea, contains tiny hair cells that vibrate and send sound messages to the brain. Close, loud noise breaks these fragile receptors, causing irreversible damage.)

In a curious case of stage fright synchronicity, on the same night that The Who nearly blew up L.A., L.A.'s most famous band, The Doors, were on the East Coast, causing TV host Ed Sullivan a conniption. At CBS-TV Studio 50 in New York City, The Doors were performing their hit single, "Light My Fire." At some nervous Nellie's behest, frontman Jim Morrison (who was every bit as impish as Keith Moon), had agreed to change the shocking lyric "Girl, we couldn't get much higher" for the live broadcast but emphasized it instead. The Doors were forever banned from the show but their integrity earned them friends in high places.

Back in the shrieking '70s, The Grateful Deaf, er, Grateful Dead, had a literal "wall of sound" that would not only blow Phil Spector's mind but it was also loud enough to split the atom. Theirs was a mountainous sound reinforcement system designed in 1973 specifically for live performances by counterculture engineer Owsley "Bear" Stanley and has the distinction of being the first large-scale line array.

The distortion-free sound system could project perfectly for a least a quarter of a mile. (Far out!) It took four semi-trailers to haul the 75-ton Everest of 600 speakers, and it took no less than 21 crew members to set it up and break it down. Even hearing aid inventor Earl C. Hanson wouldn't have needed his gadget to hear the Dead... from his grave.

CHAPTER NINE: SEX TYPE THING

"Rape is not sex; it's violence."—Gloria Steinem

The theme of rape ran rampant in Nirvana's compositions and filtered down into many interviews with the band's provocative frontman and lyricist, Kurt Cobain. "I don't feel bad about being a man at all," he said when asked if he felt any guilt on behalf of his gender for the male-heavy acts of violence he sometimes sang about. "There are all kinds of men that are on the side of the women and support them and help influence other men. In fact, a man using himself as an example towards other men can probably make more impact than a woman can."

In 1991, the trio was making negative headlines for their song "Polly" which appeared on their blockbuster debut, *Nevermind*. The slow, sludgy dirge was sung from the perspective of a specific sadistic S.O.B., Gerald Friend, who had kidnapped, tortured, and violated a 14-year-old girl in Tacoma, Washington, four years before.

The unnamed minor had just attended a concert and was hitchhiking home when Gerald picked her up, then abducted her. The doomed teen was taken to his trailer home where the 50-year-old trussed, blindfolded, and sexually assaulted her while burning her naked skin with a blowtorch. She managed to escape and the repeat offender, who'd served 20 years for assaulting a 12-year-old girl in the late 1960s, was hauled off to prison where he remains to this day.

Kurt Cobain wrote a note in the liner for the 1992 compilation album *Insecticide* in which he directly addressed Nirvana's less-savory fanbase, who'd added yet another dark footnote to the saga of "Polly."

At this point, I have a request for our fans. If any of you in any way hate homosexuals, people of different color, or women, please do this one favor for us—leave us the fuck alone! Don't come to our shows and don't buy our records. Last year, a girl was raped by two wastes of sperm and eggs while they sang the lyrics to our song 'Polly.' I have a hard time carrying on knowing there are plankton like that in our audience. Sorry to be so anally P.C. but that's the way I feel.

In 1993, Nirvana came out with another controversial offering called, "Rape Me." The violent verb was being used as a metaphor for fame—but the teeming masses and those in business suits aren't generally known for their sensitivity to nuance, so the torches and pitchforks came out.

Any mention of the tune, which appeared on what would become the band's final studio album, *In Utero*, was banned by major U.S. retailers, Wal-Mart and Kmart. The retailers staunchly refused to carry the record unless the title was altered on its cover. The group approved, so "Waif Me" was written on the package's exterior, while the original title remained on the inside. Kurt defended the cave-in, saying, "One of the main reasons I signed to a major label was so people would be able to buy our records at Kmart. In some towns, that's the only place kids can buy records."

Everyone now knows—or *should* know—that there is only one thing that causes a rape, and that is a rapist. Not what the victim said or what they were wearing, not because of being out after dark, or leaving their bedroom window open. But that's not how it was in 1974 when pop singer Connie Francis was raped. The New Jersey native felt ashamed, shunned, and misunderstood after her own horrifying attack—in her 2017 memoir, *Among My Souvenirs*, she recalls that her father called her "damaged goods" in response to the news that she'd survived.

The "Where the Boys Are" singer was staying at a Howard Johnson's following her November 7th performance at the Westbury Music Theater in Long Island, New York. Sometime after she went to sleep, an unknown assailant broke the lock on the door and slipped into her room. When he got to her bedside, he jammed his hand over her mouth and warned, "Scream, and I'll kill you."

Then he raped her. "A searing pain shot through me," she wrote in her book. "I was yanked by my hair and thrown down on my back. I looked up and it took me a moment to understand. My God... this is no dream!"

After a two-hour assault at knifepoint, the rapist tied her trembling, naked body to a chair, then kicked it over on its back, making Connie feel even more vulnerable. He then threw two double mattresses on top of her, using pillows to fill in the gaps, nearly smothering her in the process. He took her mink coat from the closet and ordered her not to make a sound for at least half an hour or, he said, he'd come back to kill her.

Despite her pain and terror, there was one thing that went through her mind: "How are we going to keep this shameful thing quiet? Daddy will go insane; he will never accept this disgrace." That was clearly a result of conditioning from conversations that centered on *women being raped*, not *men raping women*.

The "Stupid Cupid" crooner was finally discovered by motel staff and sent to the hospital, where she was treated, then questioned by the police. Although Connie was married to her third husband, Joe Garzilli, it was her aunt and her father who picked her up in their car when she was released. "On our way home, as I cowered in shame on the floor in the back of the car," she wrote, "Daddy said those incredible words [damaged goods] I would never forget."

After the traumatic experience, Connie became a recluse and suffered a nervous breakdown. The rapist was never caught but she did win $1.5 million in a lawsuit against the motel chain for failing to provide safety locks on the glass door through which her attacker entered. But the money was cold comfort. Her dad said she was no good anymore and apparently her husband believed it—he left her a few years later, saying, "You've become a loser and I don't like losers."

The Runaways were a hot band for a hot minute in the mid-1970s. They were not only an all-girl group that could rock as hard as the boys, they were all teenagers. The Runaways were managed by the Svengali-like Kim Fowley, who'd long been a fixture on the Hollywood music scene. Under his tutelage, they came out with their biggest hit, the cheeky "Cherry Bomb," and he saw that their somewhat sleazy stage costumes consisted of teddys and high heels. The Lolitas of Rock were: Joan Jett, Lita Ford, Cherie Currie, Jackie Fox, and Sandy West. The band toured all over the U.S. in support of headlining groups such as Cheap Trick, Van Halen, Talking Heads, and Tom Petty and the Heartbreakers.

But it wasn't all glitz, glam, garters, and bubblegum. Decades later, following Fowley's death in 2015, Fox came forward for the first time with accounts of the older man sexually assaulting her in the most humiliating way possible. She said it happened right in front of her bandmates and several guests at a 1975 New Year's Eve party following a concert, and nobody did anything to help her. Joan and Cherie responded by saying they had not witnessed the incident, despite Jackie's insistent claims that they had, and even "snickered" while it was happening.

"Anyone who truly knows me understands that if I was aware of a friend or bandmate being violated, I would not stand by while it happened," Joan Jett said in a statement. "For a group of young teenagers thrust into rock stardom, there were relationships that were bizarre, but I was not aware of this incident. Obviously, Jackie's story is extremely upsetting and although we haven't spoken in decades, I wish her peace and healing."

Jackie Fox—who is now a lawyer using her real last name, Fuchs—left The Runaways in 1977 during the band's Japan tour and was replaced by Vicki Blue. They broke up two years later; Joan Jett went on to an extremely successful solo career, while Cherie Currie basically left the biz in 1990 when she married the actor, Robert Hays, and became a mom.

Lady Gaga is another artist who suffered sexual assault at a young age. In December of 2014, she revealed to radio host Howard Stern and his listeners that she had been raped at the age of 19 by an unnamed record producer who was at least 20 years her senior. She added that her 2013 single, *Swine*, was about the incident. "You're just a pig inside a human body/Squealer, squealer, squeal out, you're so disgusting."

Gaga isn't the only one to turn torment into a tune; a 21-year-old Tori Amos, trying to make a name for herself in L.A., was raped by a fan who offered to drive her home after one of her club performances. He assaulted her over the course of several hours, holding her hostage, and forcing her to sing for him, which she did while literally pissing herself. The man threatened to share her with his friends, then kill and mutilate her, but abandoned that idea when he started jonesing for a drug fix. He let her go, and Tori wrote the powerful a cappella song "Me and a Gun" for her debut album, *Little Earthquakes*, which was released in 1992—paving the way for feminist singer-songwriters like Alanis Morrisette and Fiona Apple to dominate the airwaves for the rest of the decade.

Tori also inspired her fellow male performers, including pop singer Rufus Wainwright, who credits her with helping him to heal after his own sexual assault that the age of 14 at the hands of a man he'd met and hoped to date. "I said I wanted to go to the park and see where this big concert was going on. I thought it was going to be a romantic walk in the park but he raped me and robbed me afterward, and tried to strangle me. AIDS was at its height and you were told that this kind of contact could kill you. So I was just put off sex. I didn't sleep with anyone again until I was 21. It took that long to recover." The "Bitter Tears" singer added that when he was touring with Tori Amos in 2001, her advocacy organization, RAINN, taught him how better to cope with what happened to him.

Debbie Harry, the face of the 1970s pop-punk band Blondie, wrote in her 2019 autobiography *Face It* about being stalked by an enraged, seemingly insane ex-boyfriend but it's her tale of being raped by a stranger that really took the public and the press by surprise.

In a chapter recalling the early days of Blondie in New York City, Debbie and then-boyfriend Chris Stein (co-founder and guitarist of the band), returned home to their apartment after a night out and were confronted by a man with a knife. The lowlife forced his way into the home and then demanded money and drugs. The young couple had neither so the assailant tied them both up and ransacked the place. He found their guitars and stacked the instruments by the front door. But he didn't leave.

"Then he untied my hands and told me to take off my pants," she wrote, saying he "fucked" her on the bed, told her to clean herself up, and left with his ill-gotten goods. "I'm very glad this happened pre-AIDS or I might have freaked. In the end, the stolen guitars hurt me more than the rape."

There was a swift and immediate backlash when some readers and journalists felt that

Debbie was too dismissive of the crime—it seemed almost as if they *wanted* her to be destroyed by it. But she wasn't. "Can this be true?" a reporter for the *Guardian* asked the punk princess.

"Yes," she replied. "I mean, I was angry and I felt victimized. I wasn't beaten or harmed physically, it was all emotional or mental. Being raped—or fucked—by some stranger against my will at knifepoint... It wasn't a happy moment in my life, but I really, seriously, empathize with women who are beaten; that would be something that [would lead to] emotional ramifications for the rest of my life. But this doesn't. I went on with my life."

The stunned reporter argued, "But you were tied up at knifepoint."

"Yeah. Not the same [as being beaten during a rape]. It wasn't; for me, anyway." The "Heart of Glass" singer added that "being a victim was really not who I wanted to be." Hence, she didn't have counseling, said Chris Stein was supportive, "and we moved on."

Fame can come fast and feverish to male musicians who are far too immature and starry-eyed to even think of saying "no" to a Byronic free fall into rock-and-roll abandon. But does that give them a free pass to be so crass about it? Apparently so.

In the book *VJ: The Unplugged Adventures of MTV's First Wave*, the famously curly-haired New York rock jock Mark Goodman remembered traveling with Van Halen in the 1980s. The music station sent him to cover their latest tour, and he remembered being both fascinated and repelled by the whole scene and how the boys in the band routinely humiliated their groupies.

"They would have girls do headstands in toilets—they thought it was the funniest thing ever, but it was just gross and sad," he said. "It wasn't lost on me that these girls were there by choice and at any time could have said, 'Fuck off, I'm not doing that!' Still, I couldn't treat another human being that way."

Don Felder of the Eagles wrote in his memoir *Heaven and Hell* about how difficult it was to be a married man while on tour—he and his band brothers "were doing drugs, drinking, and screwing everything that walked; half the time, I was so high I didn't know what I was doing anyway. It was such an extreme situation [and] I defy any man to resist temptation in such circumstances. After every sexual transgression, I was wracked with guilt." The groupies, he said, were in every town they played, throwing themselves at the band backstage, waiting in the hotel lobbies after the shows, and even keeping scorecards about whom they slept with and comparing notes on their bedroom skills.

Don went on to describe special backstage passes that the band's entourage gave out to select female concert attendees, which were marked "3E." Little did the women know, that stood for a "Third Encore" back at the band's hotel. During their 1994 Hell Freezes Over reunion tour, portable video cameras were far more prevalent than they had been in the soft rocker's salad days, and, Don recalled, the crew put together a compilation video for private consumption of the most well-endowed ladies in the audience—they labeled it "The Eagles' Greatest Tits."

Leather-clad tough chick Joan Jett rose to fame in the 1970s as the frontwoman and guitarist of the aforementioned pioneering all-girl group The Runaways, then hit the big-time as a solo artist with her band, the Blackhearts. When the legendary "Bad Reputation" singer signed on for an all-headliner 2022 stadium tour with Def Leppard, Poison, and Mötley Crüe, as the sole female act, a reporter from *Rolling Stone* asked how she felt about sharing the stage with bands who have been accused of longstanding misogyny. "If I had to weed out every band you thought was problematic," she quipped, "there wouldn't be very many left [to work with]. Chill out, it's music."

While Def Lep and Poison were no angels in their heyday, glam metal gods Motely Crüe broke unofficial records for outrageous acts set by the likes of Led Zeppelin and The Rolling Stones in the previous decades. But Robert Plant and Mick Jagger were choirboys compared to Vince Neil, Tommy Lee, Nikki Sixx, and Mick Mars.

The "Girls, Girls, Girls" musicians bragged publicly about deflowering 12-year-old virgins, doing the deed with passed-out partners, and having a point system for their conquests in relation to their physical attractiveness. The least-liked girls were the ones who'd traded sexual favors with the road crew for backstage access; they were given a "Pre-Show Pussy" pass that let everyone know how she'd earned it.

In one stomach-turning tale, the dukes of debauchery recalled making a bet to see who could last the longest without showering and still get chicks—the wager ended a staggering two months later when a groupie, who'd recently eaten a bowl of pasta, puked while fellating the fetid Nikki Sixx. So, he "won." (This saucy story was the inspiration for the title of Guns N' Roses' 1993 album, *The Spaghetti Incident?*)

When the band's biopic *The Dirt* was released in 2019, a long-since clean and sober Sixx was asked if Mötley Crüe should be worried about their past in the wake of the #MeToo movement. "No," the bassist replied. "Here's the thing: if anybody was abusing power, that's one thing. But it was a time when everyone was living a life that is very different from today. That was then and this is now [so] we don't have anything to worry about. But we would have done the wrong thing if we had made a film that worried about presenting us in a way that was politically correct."

Joan Jett shrugged off any insinuation that she was condoning Crüe's behavior by appearing on the same bill with them during the 2022 Stadium Tour. "[Sexism] is very prevalent, all over rock & roll. Look, all I can do as the woman I am is go out there and show an alternative view and do it my way." When asked if she believed rock had become less chauvinistic since the Reagan Era, she replied, "That's a good question. The bands I listened to weren't necessarily at all misogynistic, but I'm talking about guys like Fugazi. I would say [it's] probably not as misogynistic [now], just because of their openness to getting criticized about it, because you get creamed online and people seem to care about that. That doesn't mean that it changes who they are, so maybe that's dangerous. It goes underground. But I think things are changing."

While the master/slave sexual politic was 90% in favor of the male rock star, there was a faction of feminist groupies who had the guys by the gonads—literally. Led by Cynthia Albritton, The Plaster Casters became infamous in the '60s and '70s for making marvelous molds of famous phalluses.

The pixyish blonde was born in Chicago in 1947, putting her at the right age for the Sexual Revolution and the advent of The Pill when she was in college. While attending art school in the mid-'60s, Cynthia was given the assignment to create a plaster cast of "something solid that could retain its shape," and got the idea to preserve the most prized penises she could get her hands on.

The first cast came from Jimi Hendrix, who dove in head-first after meeting the studious 21-year-old fan in front of a Hilton Hotel one chilly night. It was February 25, 1968, and the gifted guitarist had just performed with his band, the Experience, at the Chicago Civic Opera House. Cynthia and her cohorts went with the boys to Room 1628 and whipped out the mix. The band got laid and an avant-garde artist was born.

While the whole idea was seen as sort of a joke, dick after dick lined up for a chance at immodest immortality. Cynthia continued her craft for years, casting the likes of MC5's Wayne Kramer, Jim Croce, Eric Burdon from the Animals, Jello Biafra of Dead Kennedys, and of course, no such collection would have been complete without a wang from The Buzzcocks, so Pete Shelley lent his schlong to the cause.

"Their human flaws make them kind of attractive," Cynthia once said of her appendage-art. She described what it was like getting those larger-than-life rockstars by the short-and-curlies. "I was shocked and delighted to find that they were as insecure as I was. That kind of made me see them in a different light. They're the same as us." The principal Plaster Caster was an equal-opportunity artisan, turning her attention in later years to the breasts of Peaches, Sally Timms of the Mekons, Laetitia

Sadier of Stereolab, and Yeah Yeah Yeahs frontwoman, Karen O.

The all-girl, all-groupie rock band the GTOs included snippets of a conversation with Cynthia on their 1969 album, *Permanent Damage*, and a few years later, singer-songwriter Jim Croce penned "Five Short Minutes" for Cynthia and her troupe. Although KISS' Gene Simmons never had Little Gene immortalized in mortar, he did write a song called "Plaster Caster" for the band's 1977 platinum-selling album, *Love Gun*. Another non-participating supporter was vanguard musician Frank Zappa, who championed the shy young lady's work and put her in the spotlight as best he could. The "Titties & Beer" singer even funded his protégé's brief move from Chicago to L.A.

"Frank was just the most important person in my life, my mentor and my supporter and my dear friend and shoulder to cry on," she recalled in an interview with the *New York Times*. "He was the first person in the world to tell me I was an artist." After Zappa passed away in 1993, Cynthia turned her sculptures over for safekeeping to his business associate Herb Cohen, who subsequently refused to return the molded members. He was convinced to do the right thing only after the head Plaster Caster filed a lawsuit.

The self-proclaimed super-groupie enjoyed a fun reputation over the years, but she never really gained the proper respect for her naughty innovations. The prurient people were more interested in the muses—Jimi's junk was winkingly referred to as the "Penis de Milo"—than the brain behind the boners. (However, pioneering rock journalist Ellen Sanders did compare Cynthia's adults-only artistry to that of Robert Mapplethorpe.)

Except for a smidge of late-in-life accolades and some exhibitions, Cynthia Albritton died a curio on April 21, 2022, from cerebrovascular disease at the age of 74. She never married and didn't leave any heirs—she donated her life's work to various museums.

But her sexy sculpts will live on. "Hers was a revolutionary art in a time that demanded revolutionary work," Wayne Kramer told the *New York Times*. "She smashed the barriers of sexual conversation and helped open up people's minds to the endless possibilities of art."

Another of her models, John Langford of the Mekons, agreed. "I think Cynthia was a brilliant conceptual artist who made her art with great humor, a deep love of music, and a reckless disregard for societal norms. It was fun and deadly serious at the same time—a mad science experiment, really."

CHAPTER 10: HELL IS FOR CHILDREN

"The true character of society is revealed in how it treats its children."—Nelson Mandela

Serge Gainsbourg, one of the most influential singer-songwriters of the French New Wave era, was eulogized upon his death on March 2, 1991, by then-president François Mitterrand as "our Baudelaire, our Apollinaire. He elevated the song to the level of art."

While the controversial, cigarette-smoking, skinny-tie-wearing icon did inspire the likes of Nick Cave, Daft Punk, and Massive Attack, he leaves a problematic legacy. The themes of incest, misogyny, and racism that run throughout his lyrics ring sour in today's hyper-vigilant world—especially with our societal tendency toward presentism (that is, judging past people by today's standards).

While Serge is something of a poster boy for toxic masculinity, he's also a transgressive troubadour who pushed the boundaries in the most titillating of ways—especially when singing with yesteryear's sex kittens, which included Brigitte Bardot, Anna Karina, Catherine Deneuve, and his wife, Jane Birkin. Their daughter, Charlotte Gainsbourg, also shared the mic with daddy dearest, resulting in the most shocking song of them all. The duet is called "Lemon Incest" and was recorded in 1985 when the girl was just 12 years old. Even at the time, the sleazy-sounding electronica tune was criticized for glamorizing pedophilia—yet, it managed to spend eight weeks in the French Top 10.

Talking about "Lemon Incest" with *the Guardian*, the adult Charlotte admitted that even with the current French #FreedomToOffend movement (which is a female-driven #MeToo backlash), the song would not be acceptable today. "My father would be condemned for every move he made. Everything is so politically correct. So boring. So expected. And everyone is so scared of what will happen if they go too far." And to *France Inter* on the 30th anniversary of her father's death, she said she still likes the song. "To me, it's very innocent. My father is playing with provocation, but he is extremely sincere and honest," she observed. "We had a very innocent father-daughter relationship. It's what we say in 'Lemon Incest:' a love that is very pure and very beautiful."

Mackenzie Phillips, the notably troubled former costar of the vintage sitcom *One Day at a Time* released her autobiography, *High on Arrival*, in 2009. In it, she gave appalling, intimate details of her 10-year "consensual" sexual relationship with her father, John Phillips of the iconic '60s rock group, The Mamas and the Papas. (John had been dead for eight years when the memoir came out, so he was unable to confirm or deny these allegations.)

While on her book tour, the reformed drug addict told Oprah Winfrey that she was first raped by her father in a hotel room when she was 18, then passed out following a drug binge. The relationship continued after she married Jeff Sessler (a "gofer" for the Stones) when she was 19 and ended when she became pregnant in her late 20s... and feared her father was the baby's father. (She added that dear old dad gallantly paid for the abortion—whaddah guy!)

In 1980, shortly after she'd been fired from *One Day at a Time* due to flagrant drinking and drugging (which included mainlining heroin), Mackenzie began to travel with her father's then-current band, The New Mamas and the Papas. It was during that time that she began regularly having sex with him. "It didn't happen every day, it didn't happen every week, but it certainly happened and happened many times," she wrote. "It became a consensual relationship over time." But, "No matter what kind of incest, it is an abuse of power ... a betrayal of trust."

Michelle Phillips, Mackenzie's stepmother and a member of the original Mamas and Papas, told the *Hollywood Reporter* she did not believe the claims. She said Mackenzie had "a lot of mental illness" and that "she's had a needle stuck up her arm for 35 years," adding, "Mackenzie is jealous of her siblings, who have accomplished a lot and did not become drug addicts."

In a 2022 interview with *Rolling Stone*, Michelle softened her stance somewhat but remained steadfast in her disbelief. When the mag reached out to Mackenzie for her response, she replied, "I stand by my truth as I always have and as I always will. Plus which, who on Earth would fabricate such a story as mine? To what end? It's not exactly a résumé builder, for God's sake ... [*High on Arrival*] is true, and it was my story to tell. If I had to live it, I had the right to tell it." She added that she takes some comfort in the ways the world's perspective on abuse allegations has changed in the past decade. "Imagine if my memoir had been published during the #MeToo movement. I sometimes wonder what that would've been like."

Former Lynyrd Skynyrd drummer Artimus Pyle, whose real name is Thomas Delmer Pyle, was arrested in Florida in 1992 for sexual battery by an adult on a victim under 12 and lewdly fondling, assaulting, or simulating sexual acts on a child under 16. Pyle protested his innocence and said that law enforcement allegedly targeted him for punishment despite having zero proof of the accusations made against him—he insists that he's the casualty of "false charges" made by a woman with whom he had two children. Artimus maintained the girls had been abused by people who held a grudge against him and also claimed the allegations were made to extort money from the Lynyrd Skynyrd organization. "I fought (the charges) for two years and went through $400,000 in legal fees," he complained. "Then, the week before my trial was to start, my lawyers told me they needed another $100,000 and I had no money left," forcing him to plead "no contest" to the charges.

The former Marine and Rock & Roll Hall of Fame inductee was arrested again a few years later. "Just before Thanksgiving 2007, I went to see the governor of Florida to try and have the charges expunged from my record," he said, only to be charged with failing to register as a sex offender at his then-current residence. "I've spent years clawing my way back," Artimus told reporters. "I have never hurt a child in any way in my life; if I had raped a child, would I have played 27 cities on tour in Europe? I've never missed a child support payment; I bought a house in Asheville where I pay taxes; I've never hidden from the public eye. I'm innocent."

The Who's guitarist, Pete Townshend, is famous for his onstage leaps, windmill strumming, smashing guitars, and, of course, for writing two of the greatest rock operas of all-time, *Tommy* and *Quadrophenia*. Unfortunately, he also became infamous as a registered sex offender in 2003 after using his credit card to gain access to a child pornography website.

Townshend's world came crashing down during the Operation Ore investigation into images of child sex abuse on the internet and he was just one of 1,600 people arrested in the sweeping sting. In his book, *Who I Am*, Townshend said that he himself is a survivor of childhood sexual abuse and that exploring the practice was cathartic. He did it artistically, through a song from *Tommy* called "Fiddle About," and through various non-profit foundations that he worked with.

It was while doing research, Pete said, that he found the deplorable domain. He used his credit card to enter the site but quickly decided to cancel the transaction and did not download anything—unfortunately, "quickly" wasn't quick enough, and the guitarist was caught in the entrapment scheme.

Rather than fight in court, the "Won't Get Fooled Again" songwriter accepted a police caution and was placed on the sex offenders register for five years. He was cleared of possessing indecent pictures transferred from the internet (because he didn't download any). "What I did was wrong and stupid," he said in his book. "My culpability is clear... but my innocence is absolute." The incident still haunts him, and since he remains involved with children's charities, the constant reminder is there. "It's something I think about a lot. I'm very much involved in supporting charities that deal with the consequences of the sexual abuse of children, including those that are photographed."

The King of Pop, Michael Jackson, seems like a prime example of a pedophile: living in a state of arrested development, he fancied himself as "the boy who never grew up" ala Peter Pan—he named his ranch Neverland and said several times that he enjoyed the company of children over adults. The "Man in the Mirror" hosted slumber parties, where all the guests were prepubescent children. So much has been written about his many brushes with the law in regard to his inordinate affection for young boys, and he settled some cases out of court, but it's important to note that when he did go on trial in Santa Barbara, California, in 2005, Michael was acquitted of all charges.

The alleged victims, Wade Robson and James Safechuck, both adults by then, insisted that the Gloved One did not abuse them after all; Robson even testified in Michael's defense. But then, following MJ's death at the age of 50 in 2016, they changed their tune and sued his estate for millions. When that didn't work, they took part in a high-profile, four-hour documentary film made by HBO, *Finding Neverland*.

The "Beat It" singer's family was livid. "We are furious that the media, without a shred of proof or a single piece of physical evidence, chose to believe the word of two admitted liars over the word of hundreds of families and friends around the world who spent time with

Michael, many at Neverland, and experienced his legendary kindness and global generosity," said his biological children, Paris, Prince, and Bigi (formerly known as Blanket), in a statement.

While Michael's rap sheet remains unblemished, that is certainly not the case with '70s-era glam rocker Gary Glitter (whose real name is Paul Francis Gadd). He has been convicted of many various charges ranging from possessing "thousands" of images of child pornography to statutory rape.

The British citizen was deported from Cambodia on suspected child sexual abuse charges in 2002, so he moved to Vietnam where he probably assumed the laws would be looser. He was wrong; just three years later, the "Rock-and-Roll" singer was arrested and charged with molesting two underage girls, aged 10 and 11, at his home in Vũng Tàu. He faced child rape indictments carrying the death penalty but prosecutors did not find enough evidence for those especially severe charges. After several brushes with the law over the ensuing years, Glitter was tarnished again in 2014, racking up eight counts of sexual offenses committed against two girls aged 12-14 between 1977 and 1980. On February 5, 2015, he was convicted of attempted rape, four counts of indecent assault, and one of having sex with a girl under the age of 13, but was acquitted of the three other counts. Judge Alistair McCreath sentenced Gary to 16 years behind bars and at the time of this writing, he's still serving them at Her Majesty's Prison, The Verne.

Pete McNeal, who sat behind the drumkit for the '90s geek-rock outfit Cake from 2001 to 2004 and played on one of their biggest hits— "Short Skirt/Long Jacket"—was sentenced to 15 years to life in California state prison for molesting a three-year-old toddler at a Thanksgiving house party in the Hollywood Hills. (The judge who put him away was Fred Wapner, son of *The People's Court* superstar Joseph Wapner... only in Hollywood, right?) The then-46-year-old father of two had previously been charged and sentenced to three years' probation following a separate incident in which he attempted to molest a six-year-old while volunteering at an L.A. school.

Not to be outdone, Lostprophets frontman Ian Watkins was planning to have sexual intercourse with a one-year-old baby girl when he was arrested in 2012 for possession of child pornography and *"extreme* animal pornography." (Eek.) He'd already taped himself raping other children (the offspring of his girlfriends—in one text, he wrote, "If you belong to me, then so does your baby") and was taken down in an undercover sting operation. A year after he was arrested, the disgraced singer pled guilty and was sentenced to 29 years in the pokey. But he didn't seem overly concerned about what he'd done; an unrepentant Ian referred to his sex crimes as "mega lolz" in a recorded phone call to a female fan made from behind bars. The "For He's a Jolly Good Felon" singer is currently serving his time in H.M. Prison Wakefield in West Yorkshire, England. His two co-defendants, the mothers of his victims, received sentences totaling 31 years of imprisonment.

At the tender age of 10, jazz legend-to-be Billie Holiday was brutally raped by one of her neighbors. Soon thereafter, she was sent to the House of the Good Shepherd, a reform school known for meting out harsh punishments for even minor transgressions. "For years I used to dream about it and wake up hollering and screaming," she wrote in her 1956 tell-all autobiography, *Lady Sings the Blues*. "It takes years to get over it." When she was 14, Billie moved to New York City with her mother and was raped yet again—this time, her attacker paid the price but he was only sentenced to a mere three months in jail.

In an interview in the *Sunday Independent's Life Magazine* in 2013, Cranberries lead singer Dolores O'Riordan revealed details about the horrific molestation she suffered as a child at the hands of an adult neighbor in County Limerick, Ireland. The abuse began in the late 1970s, shortly after the O'Riordan family moved into a low-income housing estate. The seemingly harmless man created a ruse by befriending her father, who was housebound after suffering brain damage from an accident. "My mother worked a lot to pay the bills and my father was oblivious to [what was happening]."

The "Zombie" singer said her abuser "used to masturbate me ... He made me do oral sex for him and ejaculated on my chest when I was eight years old." Dolores, the youngest of seven children, was too ashamed and too traumatized to tell anyone—the awful acts continued until she was 12.

She became world-famous at the age of 18 with the Cranberries and while the band sold 40 million records worldwide over the years, her success did nothing to salve her wounds. The short-haired, pixyish frontwoman couldn't forget "my little dirty secret" she recalled, even though she was "putting on this charade, this perfect face. I had anorexia, then depression, and a breakdown. I knew why I hated myself. I knew why I loathed myself. I knew why I wanted to make myself disappear."

Dolores said she eventually confided in her mother—but not her father, who died in 2011. She told *Life* that her abuser turned up to pay his respects at her father's service. "I didn't see him for years and years, and then I saw him at my father's funeral. I had blocked him out of my life. I was going to talk to the priest about it [that day] but I didn't. I asked him to pray for me as I was about to go on another world tour and I worried that I might not make it through it."

Dolores married Don Burton, a Canadian musician, in 1994 and the couple had three children. "Don showed me love I never knew. I love him and the kids with all of me. They are my salvation. They saved me," she said in a 2013 interview.

But the following year, the couple split, and her husband won custody of their kids after Dolores was arrested for stamping on a flight attendant's foot then headbutting and spitting in the face of a garda in the same air rage incident. Dolores fell back into the abyss and while there were some ups to balance the downs, she overdosed and died from drowning in a hotel bathtub on January 15, 2018.

"Criminal" songstress Fiona Apple was also violated as a child. She was only 12 years old when the unthinkable happened in Harlem, New York, in November of 1989. The defenseless girl was accosted just outside the apartment she shared with her mother and sister, who were, unfortunately, out shopping at the time.

The assailant apparently followed the sixth-grader home from school and got into the building, shadowing her as she rode the elevator to her floor. She had to turn her key in three different locks to get inside and he caught up with her just after the second, threatening her with a screwdriver if she made one more move. He raped her right there in the hallway outside her door, then said, "Happy Thanksgiving. Next time don't let strangers in." After he left, she opened the third lock and went into the apartment, where she called the police.

The man was never caught. Fiona wrote the song "Sullen Girl" about losing her innocence in such a violent, horrific way. (He took my pearl/And left an empty shell of me)

In his 2011 book *Not Dead & Not For Sale* Stone Temple Pilots singer Scott Weiland revealed that when he was 12 years old, "a high school senior [who] rode the bus with me every day to school invited me to his house. The dude raped me. It was quick, not pleasant. I was too scared to tell anyone." He tried to forget all about it. "This is a memory I suppressed until only a few years ago when, in rehab, it came flooding back." Scott died of an accidental drug overdose on December 3, 2015.

Chester Bennington of Linkin Park said that he was also mistreated by an older male friend, the abuse starting when he was just seven years old. "It escalated from a touchy, curious, 'what does this thing do' into full-on, crazy violations," he told *Kerrang!* in 2014. "I was getting beaten up and being forced to do things I didn't want to do. It destroyed my self-confidence. Like most people, I was too afraid to say anything. I didn't want people to think I was gay or that I was lying." Chester took his own life on July 20, 2017.

Dave Holland, Judas Priest's hard-hitting drummer during their commercial peak in the '80s, was convicted by Northampton Crown Court in 2004 for the attempted rape of a 17-year-old male music student of his, who suffered from learning disabilities. While the unnamed minor was allowed by his parents to spend the night at Holland's house on occasion, they never suspected any wrongdoing until their son detailed the abuse in a letter he wrote and gave to them.

Following the verdict and eight-year prison sentence, Judge Charles Wide said that Dave had "deliberately and calculatedly planned a strategy to abuse a boy whom he knew was exceptionally vulnerable." The "Ram it Down" drummer was flabbergasted by the result, telling the court, "There might have been the odd hug or something like that. I know it is politically incorrect nowadays, but kids like to be shown a bit of affection." The power-metal skins man also revealed for the first time that he was bisexual. (Judas Priest's frontman, Rob Halford, had come out as gay during an MTV interview six years earlier.)

After serving his sentence, Dave moved from his native England to Spain and was working on writing his autobiography when he died of lung cancer on January 16, 2018, at Hospital Universitario Lucus Augusti in Lugo. He was 69 years old. "It is with regret that we hear of the passing of Dave Holland," Judas Priest said in a statement. "Despite his actions since working with the band, his time with us was amongst the most productive and successful in our career and Dave was an integral part of that and for that alone, he will be missed."

Rock & roll pioneer Chuck Berry (born Charles Edward Anderson Berry) was arrested for taking a 14-year-old Apache girl, Janice Escalante, across state lines for "immoral purposes." The pair met in Ciudad Juarez, Mexico, in December 1959, and traveled together for a week, through five American states—with Janice being raped daily, she said in court. Since the allegations involved crossing state lines, and the law prohibiting sex with minors was then at a state rather than a federal level, the U.S. Attorney charged the 24-year-old "Sweet Little Sixteen" singer under the Mann Act, sometimes known as the White Slavery Act.

Chuck denied the accusations, stating that he didn't know the girl was that young and he wasn't interested in her for sex—he'd hired her to work as a hatcheck girl in a nightclub he owned, Club Bandstand, in St. Louis, Missouri. His lawyer later stated that Janice was too ugly to be raped. She was "very, very homely, not pretty at all. And that's why I believe Chuck."

After a two-week trial in March 1960, the "No Particular Place to Go" singer went to jail. He was convicted on most of the charges, fined five grand, and sentenced to five years. On appeal, Berry argued that the judge's comments and attitude were racist and prejudiced the jury against him. The appeal was upheld, and he served just two years.

Chuck, who often posed nude for publicity shots (hiding the naughty bits behind his guitar), was no stranger to the system—when he was 18, he was convicted of armed robbery and served three years in prison; in 1958 he faced another Mann Act indictment for "transporting" 17-year-old Joan Mathis Bates; and in the summer of 1959, he was charged with "disorderly conduct" after a white girl in Mississippi told police he asked her for a "date."

Nothing changed after he matured. In 1987, Chuck was charged with beating and assaulting a woman at New York's Gramercy Park Hotel and wound up paying a $250 fine. Three years later, the duck-walking guitarist was sued by several women who claimed that he had installed a video camera and filmed them using the bathroom of his Southern Air restaurant in Wentzville, Missouri. Criminal charges were also brought because some of the recordings were of minors but those were dropped as part of a plea bargain relating to charges of possession of marijuana—still, he had to shell out over a million dollars to quiet the ticked-off tinklers.

"Berry died in 2017, to much fanfare and some controversy," wrote J.P. Robinson in his *Medium* blog. "He perfected rock 'n' roll, people said, he was a great, they said, a lyrical genius. He mythologized teenagers, they said, even invented the very idea of them."

While only a relative few rock stars have been formally charged with statutory rape, singer-drummer Don Henley called the cops on himself—sort of. He was arrested in 1980 after dialling 911 when a 16-year-old prostitute overdosed on quaaludes and cocaine at his house following a big party in "celebration" of his departure from the Eagles. The completely nude teen, who was found seizing, was also arrested. (Talk about kicking someone when they are down!)

While "Don Juan" did ring up the escort service in the first place, he denied sleeping with the girl after finding out how young she was. Regardless, he was fined $2,500 and given a two-year probation for contributing to the delinquency of a minor. The "Life in the Fast Lane" singer claimed he took the fall for the roadies who supplied the drugs and were fooling around with the youngster. "I took complete blame for everything," he later told *GQ*. "I was stupid; I could have flushed everything down the toilet [and done nothing, but] I didn't want this girl dying in my house." Following a barrage of media coverage, Henley wrote his cynical hit, "Dirty Laundry."

Bob Dylan—a Nobel Peace Prize winner and the rare rock star without scandals besmirching his legacy—was named in a shocking 2021 lawsuit for purportedly molesting a 12-year-old girl "multiple times" way back in the mid-'60s. The 80-something elder statesman of pop-folk and his legal team officially fired back against the complaint, describing it as "false, malicious, reckless, and defamatory." The action against him asserted that the "Just Like a Woman" songwriter, who maintained an apartment at New York City's Chelsea Hotel at the time of the alleged abuse, had "exploited his status as a musician" in order to "obtain control over" the plaintiff, who identified herself only as "J.C." to the public.

"This case—based on Plaintiff's alleged interactions with Bob Dylan more than 56 years ago—is a brazen shakedown masquerading as a lawsuit," read the filing from the 10-time GRAMMY-winner (and 38-time nominee). "It was filed in bad faith for the improper purpose of extracting a huge payout on the threat of negative publicity. Mr. Dylan will not be extorted [and he] will vigorously defend himself against these lawyer-driven lies and seek redress against all those responsible, including by seeking monetary sanctions against persons responsible for manufacturing and bringing this abusive lawsuit."

The eight-page-long response to the lawsuit took aim at J.C.'s personal life and professional background. "[She] is a psychic who specializes in 'channeling' the deceased loved ones of grieving families—for a fee" and has made several strange statements over the years that "she has been abducted by aliens and piloted their spaceship, speaks to cats, dogs, and other animals—alive and dead—as well as insects and plants," and "can divine signs from lipstick smudges, coffee grinds, tea leaf residue, crystals, playing cards, and palms." The Tambourine Man's council concluded by saying,

"Mr. Dylan may have seemed like an easy mark for the lawyers who filed and hoped to profit off of this fraudulent lawsuit ... They likely assumed he would not be up for the fight and would instead pay extortion to avoid the burden, publicity, and expense of defending himself."

The case was dismissed *with prejudice* (which means the case cannot be refiled, ever) almost one year later, on July 29, 2022, by U.S. District Judge Katherine Polk Failla for lack of evidence. "We are pleased that [this] lawyer-driven sham [has been] dismissed with prejudice," said Dylan's lead attorney, Orin Snyder, who was one of a formidable team working to quash the clearly baseless complaint. There was no public comment from the "It Ain't Me, Babe" singer.

Here's a strange case of so-called "kiddie porn" in the form of a 2021 lawsuit brought by a man who, as a naked baby, was pictured on Nirvana's *Nevermind* album cover. Spencer Elden alleged that he was a victim of child pornography—despite the fact he has recreated that image in other photoshoots over the years and even sports a tattoo across his entire chest that says "Nevermind" in cursive script.

In case you don't remember the 1991 picture, it shows a nude, four-month-old baby boy swimming underwater grabbing at a digitally-imposed dollar bill impaled on a fishhook—a snide commentary on capitalism.

Kurt Cobain commissioned the shoot after he saw a documentary on babies being born underwater and "thought the image would make a cool cover," Art Director Robert Fisher said in an interview. "That vision was a bit too graphic, so we went with the swimming baby instead."

Photographer Kirk Weddle took the pics in an Olympic-size pool at the Pasadena Aquatic Center in California, and Spencer was one of four tots modeling and vying for the cover that day. (Infants are natural underwater swimmers; when submerged, the soft tissue at the back of the throat [called the larynx] automatically closes to block the entrance to the airway.) Each baby's family was paid a paltry $250.00, according to a 1992 article in *Entertainment Weekly*.

Spencer's father recounted how the shoot came about in a 2008 interview with *NPR*. He said his friend, the photographer, "calls us up and was like, 'Hey Rick, wanna make 200 bucks and throw your kid in the drink?' I was like, 'What's up?' And he's like, 'Well, I'm shooting kids all this week, why don't you meet me at the Rose Bowl, throw your kid in the drink?' And we just had a big party at the pool, and no one had any idea what was going on!" The family didn't hear anything more about the album but three months later, they saw a blowup of the cover painted on the Tower Records façade on Sunset Boulevard. "Two months after that," the *NPR* article stated, "Geffen Records sent one-year-old

Spencer Elden a platinum album and a teddy bear."

Non-sexualized nude photos of infants are not considered child pornography under U.S. Law but Spencer's lawyer, Robert Y. Lewis, alleged that the inclusion of currency in the shot makes the baby "look like a sex worker." The plaintiff demanded "at least" $150,000 from each of the defendants, who include surviving band members Dave Grohl and Krist Novoselic; Cobain's widow, Courtney Love, who is the executor of Cobain's estate; plus the managers of his estate; photographer Kirk Weddle; art director Robert Fisher; and numerous existing or defunct record companies that distributed the album since its initial release. Original Nirvana drummer Chad Channing is also named as a defendant, even though he had been replaced by Grohl in 1990, well before the album was recorded or the cover photography shot!

"Weddle took a series of sexually graphic nude photographs of Spencer," the suit stated. "To ensure the album cover would trigger a visceral sexual response from the viewer, Weddle activated Spencer's gag reflex before throwing him underwater in poses highlighting and emphasizing Spencer's exposed genitals."

Before *Nevermind*'s release, art director Robert Fisher suggested that the baby's genitalia could be censored if anyone thought that it would be an issue. An unedited photo showing early concept art for the album's cover includes a handwritten comment by Fisher: "If anyone has a problem with his dick, we can remove it." Cobain responded, saying if that was the case, the album should be released with a sticker over the genitals saying: "If you're offended by this, you must be a closet pedophile."

According to the lawsuit, Spencer said he "has been and will continue to suffer personal injury" and "permanent harm," including "extreme and permanent emotional distress with physical manifestations, interference with his normal development and educational progress, lifelong loss of income earning capacity, loss of past and future wages, past and future expenses for medical and psychological treatment, loss of enjoyment of life, and other losses."

It should be stressed again that Spencer Elden has repeatedly recreated the pose as a teenager and adult, diving into pools to pose (with swimwear) on *Nevermind*'s 10th, 17th, 20th, and 25th anniversaries. In 2016, the last time the sullen swimmer recreated the pose, he told the *New York Post* he wanted to take the shot naked. "I said to the photographer, 'Let's do it naked.' But he thought that would be weird, so I wore my swim shorts."

He added, "It's strange that I did this for five minutes when I was four months old and it became this really iconic image. It's cool but weird to be part of something so important that I don't even remember." So why be suddenly traumatized? Maybe that dollar bill he's swimming toward as an infant actually had a more profound effect than the nudity on the adult Spencer Elden.

In an eight-page ruling, U.S. District Judge Fernando Olguin dismissed the lawsuit on September 3, 2022, on the grounds that Spencer Elden waited too long to file, based on a 10-year statute of limitations. "Because the plaintiff had an opportunity to address the deficiencies in his complaint regarding the statute of limitations, the court is persuaded that it would be futile to afford [him] a fourth opportunity to file an amended complaint."

But we may not have heard the last of this. "Spencer intends to appeal this ruling. This ruling's interpretation of the statute of limitations on Masha's Law contravenes over 15 years of well-settled precedent and the legislature's intended purpose of the law," Elden's lawyer Margaret Mabie told *Rolling Stone*. (Masha Allen was adopted as a 5-year-old Russian orphan by an American millionaire named Matthew Mancuso, who sexually abused her for years and posted her pictures extensively online until she was rescued by the FBI in 2003. She went on to testify before the U.S. Congress, inspiring then-senator John Kerry to bring "Masha's Law" into effect in 2006 to make it easier for victims of child pornography to sue for civil damages.)

Ex-Nirvana drummer and current Foo Fighter Dave Grohl summed the whole sordid situation up most succinctly when he remarked:

"[Spencer Elden] has a *Nevermind* tattoo. I don't."

Fifteen years before *Nevermind* was released, German metalheads Scorpions put out *Virgin Killer*, an LP featuring a full-color photo of a completely nude 12-year-old girl (some sources say she was 10) on the cover. She's posed provocatively, and a jag of broken glass is superimposed over her crotch.

It was 1976 but despite the looser mores of the era—*Pretty Baby*, a movie about a child prostitute's virginity being auctioned off, starring 11-year-old Brooke Shields, was just around the corner—the cover caused a strong backlash. The presses were stopped and a benign publicity photo of the band replaced it in some countries, while others obscured the offending image with a black sleeve that could only be removed after purchase.

No one thought about the cover of Scorpions' 4th album for years, not even during the band's successful stint in heavy-rotation on *MTV*, but the controversy resurfaced in 2008 when the British Internet Watch Foundation dug it up. The foundation even managed to temporarily block Wikipedia, where the cover photo was available, from internet users.

Over the years, the members of Scorpions spoke out about the *Virgin Killer* controversy. Former guitarist Uli Jon Roth gave an interview to *Classic Rock Revisited* in 2006, saying, "Looking at that picture today makes me cringe. It was done in the worst possible taste. Back then I was too immature to see that. Shame on me—I should have done everything in my power to stop it."

Scorpions founder and rhythm guitarist Rudolf Schenker blamed the band's record company, RCA Records, for the misstep. "We didn't actually have the idea. It was the record company," he told *Blabbermouth*. "The record company guys were like, 'Even if we have to go to jail, there's no question that we'll release that.' In the song 'Virgin Killer,' *time* is the virgin killer. But then, when we had to do the interviews about it, we said 'Look, listen to the lyrics, and then you'll know what we're talking about. We're using this only to get attention.'

"Even the girl, when we met her 15 years later, had no problem with the cover. Growing up in Europe, sexuality, of course not with children, was very normal. The lyrics really say it all," Rudolf emphasized. "Time is the virgin killer; a kid comes into the world very naïve, they lose that naiveness and then go into this life losing all of this and getting into trouble. That was the basic idea about all of it."

Vocalist Klaus Meine talked to *Metal Exiles* in 2010, saying, "Today when you think of child pornography on the net, you would never do something like that. We never did this in the sense of pornography, we did it in the sense of art. ... Looking back from the band point of view it was never an album cover that we took home to our parents and said, 'Look what we just released.' There was always mixed feelings about it and even 30 years later it caused a scandal."

The 2008 censure of Wikipedia, and a look-see from the FBI, brought about an intensive debate about freedom of expression. All of this was seized on by the renowned visual artist, Anneé Olofsson, who bought the album a few years after it was released, when she was about the same age as the model had been. The Swedish designer said that "for some reason, I am still caught by that picture and I have thought a lot about what it actually is in it that is so provocative. I got the urge to get inside that cover, to go back in time and find out more about the girl and about the day the photo was taken."

She wanted to incorporate the image into an exhibit of her own, so Anneé contacted the photographer, Michael von Gimbut—he didn't share much information about the girl because she was promised that her identity would never be revealed but he did give permission for his photo to be used in Anneé's own artistic exploration.

In the resulting 12-minute arthouse film, *A Demon's Desire* (2011), Anneé Olofsson reconstructs the photo shoot: Behind the still camera is Michael von Gimbut, assisted by his wife Parvin, just as it was in 1976. Michael was the only man present at the original session; in addition to the girl's mother and sister, the PR people, stylists, and representatives of the record company were all women. The purpose of the film was to explore "how we decode images and how the gaze changes over time. [Anneé Olofsson] delves through different layers of meaning, dissects and investigates, trying to find new questions and answers."

So much for art changing hearts and minds—in August of 2015, a court in Sweden ruled that it considered the album cover to be "child pornography" and banned it.

CHAPTER 11: YOUR DISEASE

"You only live once. But if you do it right, once is enough."—Mae West

The Black Death was a devastating global outbreak of bubonic plague that struck Europe and Asia in the mid-1300s—and it remains the grand-daddy of all contagions, having caused 75–200 million fatalities when it peaked from 1347 to 1351. (To put that into perspective, the COVID-19 pandemic hit the 6 million mark in mid-2022.) Back then, the ignorant populace believed that the Plague was Divine punishment—retribution for sins against God such as greed, blasphemy, sacrilege, fornication, and book learning.

Silly, right? Surely by the 1980s, citizens of the world had become much smarter and more sophisticated. Nope, not by a long shot. When AIDS hit U.S. shores during the Reagan Era, it was written off as a "Gay Cancer," killing "faggots and drug addicts" who deserved it, anyway—at least, that's what many of the filthy-rich televangelists said. Jerry Falwell publicly and repeatedly declared, "AIDS is not just God's punishment for homosexuals; it is God's punishment for the society that tolerates homosexuals."

"The Reagan administration's unwillingness to recognize and confront the AIDS epidemic has gone down in history as one of the deepest and most enduring scars on its legacy," wrote Karen Tumulty in a 2021 retrospective piece on HIV/AIDS for *The Atlantic*. "What wasn't known at the time was that, as the death toll mounted, a pitched battle ensued within the Reagan White House—and within the Reagan family—as First Lady Nancy Reagan and her son, Ron, tried to shake the President out of his complacency. It was a battle that pitted the two of them and a handful of allies against his hard-right advisers, who believed that AIDS should be dealt with as a moral and religious challenge, rather than a health crisis."

Freddie Mercury biographers Mark Langthorne and Matt Richards noted that things weren't any better in the U.K. "The country was governed through almost all of the worst years of the AIDS crisis by Margaret Thatcher who, while extolling the virtues of human rights and humanism, remained utterly resistant to the suffering of those around her and was indifferent to gay rights."

In the U.S., Republican-and-Christian-Right-backed ads for the Moral Majority advocated wearing medical masks in public—an interesting reverse image of the same political party that became anti-mask in 2020 with the advent of COVID-19.

Regardless of who said what, or why the disease wasn't taken seriously for far too many years as it spread, the fear and the stigmatization of AIDS made the final years of glorious rock gods like Freddie Mercury needlessly shameful and painful, forcing them to die in the shadows.

Before Freddie, there was Jobriath—a self-created glam icon whose stage name was a lofty combo of "Job" and "Goliath." Known briefly as the "American Bowie," Jobriath was born Bruce Wayne Campbell on December 14, 1946, in King of Prussia, Pennsylvania. The highly intelligent and precocious child started playing the piano on his own, then mastered the grand organ that was stationed at the local church.

When he was in his early 20s, Jobriath moved to L.A. and was quickly cast in the wildly popular stage musical, *Hair*. He was Woof, a lead and implied gay, character—which didn't faze him a bit as he was one of the few performers of the day who didn't hide his light under a bushel (so to speak). After several successful shows in the West Coast production at the Aquarius Theater on Sunset Boulevard, he was fired in 1969 for "upstaging" the other actors.

After flitting from gig to gig, and sometimes working as a hustler to make ends meet, Jobriath's talent was finally noticed in 1972 by music mogul Jerry Brandt (retroactively known as the "Svengali of the '70s"). The rest was a whirlwind—the ivory-tinkling singer-songwriter was secured for a two-album deal to Elektra Records for $500,000, the most lucrative recording contract of its time, making him the first openly gay rock musician to be signed to a major record label.

A blitz ensued, with Jobriath gracing the pages of *Vogue*, *Penthouse*, and *Rolling Stone*, plastered across some 250 New York City buses, and a huge 14-by-48-foot nude billboard in Times Square. A glamorous three-night live debut at the Paris Opera was announced, plus a full-on tour of Europe's most storied opera houses. Jobriath told the press that the show would feature him dressed as "King Kong being projected upwards on a mini-Empire State Building. This will turn into a giant spurting penis and I will have transformed into Marlene Dietrich." But as costs spiraled beyond the stratosphere, these fabulous events were canceled and Elektra merely released the first album sans fanfare—it was met with mixed reviews.

The self-identified "True Fairy of Rock & Roll," enjoyed a mere two-year, two-album stint in the spotlight before being let go by Electra. Six months after the release of his debut album, Jobriath's *Creatures of the Street* was released, featuring Peter Frampton, and John Paul Jones of Led Zeppelin, but it stalled on the charts and yielded no hits. He later complained that he was ahead of his time, shunned by the gay community while dismissed by mainstream critics as nothing but flash.

He wasn't wrong—in the early 1970s, bisexuality and the tease of homosexuality were all the swishy rage among trendsetters like Mick Jagger, Marc Bolan, Bryan Ferry, and David Bowie, each of whom wore feminine makeup, women's blouses, satin pants, and high heels onstage and at nightclubs. The pretty boys would purr and wink their glittered eyelids for the cameras at press conferences, then they'd go home to their girlfriends or wives. It was all a provocative game; a persona to don at will, then shed when no longer fun.

When Queen debuted with their self-titled album in 1973, their charismatic, flamboyant lead singer Freddie Mercury was no different—he pretended to pretend that he was gay without admitting anything due to fear of retribution. While it's impossible to imagine now, being gay in those days not only carried criminal consequences, but the American Psychiatric Association even classified it as a mental illness! (This notion was officially dropped in 1973.)

There's a saying that "the pioneers take the arrows" and that sadly rings true in Jobriath's case. While his personal musical preference leaned more toward classical, his piano-playing rivals that of Elton John's and his lyrics are every bit as cutting edge as Iggy Pop's—but because the "I'maman" singer was not willing to compromise his true self, he was shut down.

It was a fairytale without the happily-ever-after. At the dawn of the new year in 1975,

Jobriath left La-La Land and moved into a pyramid-pointed rooftop apartment at the Chelsea Hotel in New York City, where he hoped to resume his acting career. He was disappointed, yet again. The showbiz maven reinvented himself as "Cole Berlin" (Cole Porter meets Irving Berlin) and worked at a restaurant as a cabaret singer; sadly, he was forced to supplement his income as a part-time prostitute. And then he got "the Gay Cancer." Jobriath died a forgotten recluse in his lonely room at the Chelsea on August 3, 1983, at the age of 37.

In the years since his death, young rock and glam fans have discovered his music through Morrissey, Def Leppard, The Pet Shop Boys, and Gary Numan, all of whom have praised the first openly gay pop star as an influence on their music.

Fey art student and 24-year-old aspiring rock star Farrokh Bulsara joined the Middlesex, U.K.-based band Smile in 1970 and quickly took command by changing their name to Queen and his own to Freddie Mercury. The friendly yet sometimes shy fashionista donned skintight, sparkly stage wear, eyeshadow, and nail polish—and peppered his speech with terms of endearment like "darling" and "dearie"—but he wasn't "out." In fact, the Zanzibar-born artist never left the closet. Although he lived with a man, Jim Hutton, in his later years and became ill during the thick of the HIV/AIDS crisis, the "My Fairy King" singer kept mum on the subject of his sexuality. However, he did once respond to a reporter's question about being homosexual by saying, "I'm as gay as a daffodil, my dear!"

He was, at least at the beginning of his rock star days, exploring bi-sexuality. The famously toothy "Fat-Bottomed Girls" singer dated women and even proposed to his longtime lover Mary Austin, whom he described as "the love of my life" and "my wife." In his personal life, Freddie stopped bothering to hide his sexual orientation after a 1973 marriage proposal to Mary fizzled following his admission to her that he'd been sleeping with men. (The pair remained close friends for life and what's more, he provided for her in his will; she received half of his amassed fortune, his portion of Queen's royalties, and the 28-room London mansion where he passed away. She still lives there, and, following the success of the 2018 biopic *Bohemian Rhapsody*, Mary raked in another $50 million.)

In public, the "Somebody to Love" frontman kept them guessing—not only out of respect for his religious Indian family but for his bandmates, who are not gay and whose careers would have been thrown into jeopardy in those scarily homophobic times.

While Mary Austin was the first and forever love of Freddie Mercury, his last relationship was with Jim Hutton, a hairdresser who didn't even recognize the rocker when they first met at a London club called Heaven in 1985. The Irish-born stylist was seeing someone else at the time and refused Freddie's offer to buy him a drink—but fate brought them together at the same spot a year and a half later. The two began dating soon after, and Jim moved into Freddie's London estate, Garden Lodge. The pair were together as partners and exchanged wedding bands although they weren't legally married (same-sex marriage was illegal at the time).

Shortly after meeting Jim, Freddie was diagnosed with HIV, which, despite the latest treatments, mutated into full-blown AIDS. Privately, the other members of Queen—guitarist Brian May, bassist John Deacon, and drummer Roger Taylor—were aware that their bandmate and friend was gravely ill, but it was not public knowledge at the time despite swirling rumors about the "Keep Yourself Alive" singer's health, particularly in tabloids. "Freddie wanted his life to be as normal as possible," Brian recalled. "He was obviously in a lot of pain and discomfort but for him, the studio was an oasis—a place where life was just the same as it has always been. He loved making music. He lived for it."

His final public appearance at the 1990 Brit Awards led to much speculation due to his gaunt, pasty face and skeletal body. He did continue to perform and record with Queen for as long as humanly possible, though. Brian's wife, Anita Dobson, remembered Freddie saying to her, "When I can't sing anymore, darling, then I will die. I will drop dead."

The operatic-style singer was famously betrayed by his former manager and (so-called) friend, Paul Prenter, who announced to the world that it was he who originally thrust the star into the gay world in the 1970s and helped him "not to be ashamed of who he was." However, Freddie fired him in 1986 and the following year Paul sold his vindictive exposé to *The Sun*, describing a lascivious life in which Freddie bedded "hundreds of men."

On November 23, 1991—a scant 24 hours before his death—the public was given the truth about the beloved performer's health. In a statement released by his publicist, Roxy Meades, the illness was finally named, which was groundbreaking at the time and helped to begin to erase some of the associated stigmas. "Following enormous conjecture in the press, I wish to confirm that I have been tested HIV positive and have AIDS. I felt it correct to keep this information private in order to protect the privacy of those around me. However, the time has now come for my friends and fans around the world to know the truth, and I hope everyone will join with me, my doctors, and all those worldwide in the fight against this terrible disease."

The 45-year-old superstar succumbed the next day at home in his bed, surrounded by his loved ones Mary and Jim, plus his personal assistant and friend Peter Freestone, and an ex-boyfriend, Joe Fanelli. He was cremated and

Mary, carrying out Freddie's final wish, scattered the ashes in an undisclosed location.

Just a few years after Freddie Mercury's death, Jim Hutton, who was largely left out of the lion's share of the will, released a kiss-and-tell book about their relationship, called *Mercury and Me*. Jim went into shocking detail about Freddie's final day. "He woke up at six in the morning and uttered what were to be his last two words: 'Pee, pee!' He wanted to be helped to the loo. He looked terribly weak and I had to carry him. As I lowered him back onto the bed, I heard a deafening crack. It sounded like one of Freddie's bones breaking. He screamed out in pain and went into a convulsion" before falling into a coma followed by death. (Jim Hutton died of cancer in 2010 at the age of 60.)

Shortly after Freddie Mercury's memorial service, *Daily Mirror* columnist Joe Haines smashed symbolic nails into the superstar's coffin by taking him to task for not announcing his illness sooner. "It might have been brave to announce he had AIDS the moment that it was diagnosed. It wasn't brave to conceal it until those last few hours. There was nothing flamboyant about catching AIDS and probably spreading it to others. Nothing admirable about touring the streets seeking rent boys to bugger and share drugs with. Mercury died from a disease whose main victims are homosexuals. For his kind, AIDS is a form of suicide." (Wow. Homophobic much, Joe?)

Freddie Mercury and countless others became infected with HIV before anyone even knew about it, and what's more, the concept of "safe sex" wasn't on the public's mind until there was a problem. The egregious excess of the '80s was, at first, a continuation of the sexual revolution and the blithe, hedonistic era of disco and Studio 54.

While he wasn't gay, nor was he an intravenous drug user, Creedence Clearwater Revival co-founder and rhythm guitarist Tom Fogerty got caught in deadly budget cuts when he was given a tainted blood transfusion during back surgery in the mid-1980s—The American Red Cross' willfully negligent failure to adopt expensive blood-screening tests in those days resulted in hundreds of transfusion recipients being infected with AIDS. Tom died at home in Scottsdale, Arizona on September 6, 1990, due to the autoimmune disease, which was exacerbated by tuberculosis. The "Bad Moon Rising" musician was survived by his second wife Tricia, his six children, and brothers John and Bob.

In the years that followed, other music men, including such disparate performers as Liberace and NWA's Eazy-E fell prey to the AIDS scourge. One of the saddest and most shocking losses was that of Robbin Crosby, a once-vital titan of hard rock.

"Robbin had everything kids dream of growing up," said Bill Decker following the death of his former brother-in-law, Robbin

Crosby of RATT. "He was married to a Playboy Playmate, he had a Ferrari, a Laurel Canyon house with a pool that overlooked L.A., a personal assistant... But then he started getting heavily into drugs and his marriage started to fall apart. He lost his way."

RATT's classic lineup consisted of charismatic Stephen Pearcy on lead vocals, tall, blond Robbin Crosby on lead and rhythm guitar, Warren DeMartini on lead and rhythm guitar, Juan Croucier on bass, and Bobby Blotzer on drums. Upon moving to L.A.—the hair-metal mecca—RATT's star rose thanks to catchy hits like "Round and Round," which earned them multi-platinum album sales and the adulation of fans.

Stephen recalled the "twin guitar attack" of Crosby and DeMartini, in an interview with *NoiseCreep*. "Robbin had his own style, but he was definitely influenced by Billy Gibbons [of ZZ Top] and Jimi Hendrix. He played with great feel. Warren was more of a noodler, a guitar hero type of player. They complimented each other so well."

Robbin explained to *the San Diego Tribune* in 1984 how RATT separated themselves from the competition. "We definitely try to be melodic so that we don't get caught up in the heavy metal shuffle, but I think our music is more aimed at a female audience than a lot of contemporary hard rock bands. Part of our plan was to attract a female audience. We try to come off with a lot of sex appeal in our lyrics and our look, rather than having a violent or rebellious image."

Robbin's girlfriend at the time was the redheaded sex-kitten Tawny Kitaen, who not only graced the cover of RATT's breakout 1984 album *Out of the Cellar* but would go on to star in *Bachelor Party* with Tom Hanks and appeared in a now-classic episode of *Seinfeld*, "The Nose Job." The pair were each other's first loves but eventually, they drifted apart. (She would go on to become an *MTV* video vixen in her own right, not to mention O.J. Simpson's mistress, the ex-wife of Whitesnake frontman David Coverdale and MLB pitcher Chuck Finley, before dying under somewhat mysterious circumstances on May 7th, 2021 at the age of 59.)

Part of the reason Tawny and Robbin broke up was due to his enthusiastic indulgences. He not only enjoyed everything RATT's groupies had to offer but he also eddied down into alcoholism and drug addiction—which included shooting heroin. It's been said that Robbin's use of a dirty-needle led to HIV and then AIDS. He married Playboy Playmate Laurie Carr in 1987 but it didn't last. Feeling dejected and minimized by his bandmates, Robbin went into rehab for the first time in 1990. Following his sober stint, Robbin joined the band on tour but staying off the booze and dope in that environment proved too tough. He played his final gig with them in 1991 in Osaka, Japan, and was replaced by former UFO and Scorpions guitarist Michael Schenker. (RATT disbanded soon after, victims of the almighty grunge movement.)

Crosby, whose nickname was "King," publicly disclosed that he had AIDS in July 2001 during an interview with L.A. radio station *KNAC*. He guessed that he contracted the disease when he started using heroin in the mid-1980s. "I have full-blown AIDS," he said. "Basically, it's killing me. I've got a terminal disease. I've been in the hospital for eight straight months, and in and out for over seven years."

During another interview, this time with *VH1's Behind the Music*, the "Lay It Down" strings man seemed to have accepted his fate, saying, "When I die, nobody cry at my funeral; in fact, let's all have a party. I've lived the life of 10 men. I lived all my dreams and more."

In the months leading up to his death, Robbin had changed physically due to a pancreatic condition that altered his metabolism. "Apparently my pancreas has given up and I'm not metabolizing food the way I should. It's really frustrating. I have a roommate that probably weighs 150 pounds and he eats a lot more than I do. It's not like I'm a pig or a slob."

Robbin Crosby died in L.A. on June 6, 2002. The two contributing factors to his death include AIDS-related complications and a heroin overdose. According to the autopsy report, he was six-foot-five and weighed 400 pounds.

Tawny Kitaen later speculated that King had committed suicide in an interview on the *Rock Talk with Mitch Lafon* podcast. "About five or six months before he passed... before he took his life, I would go up and stay with him at the nursing home. He could not stay at Cedars Sinai. He got so big that the beds could not accommodate his size. ... He had already made up in his head what he was going to do. Something he said really struck a chord with me about him wanting to reach out and tell his story and the people that he was around, letting them know that he appreciated them, and so on, and so forth."

She also revealed their regrets. "He said to me in that vein that 'I wish that we would have had children.' And that just broke my heart. I was in a marriage and I had two children. Robb was the love of my life and to not have had a child with the love of my life... His birthday was August 4th, mine was August 5th. We both looked like lions with all the hair that we had going on. It would have been a wonderful time. I can't even put into words what that would mean to me, to have Robb's and my child here, but unfortunately, the cards did not play out that way."

AIDS isn't the only killer disease to be stigmatized by victim-blaming. Over the last several years, severe acute respiratory syndrome (SARS, a coronavirus) has emerged as a feared malady. From xenophobia associated with "strangers" (Asians, particularly Chinese) to its politicization in regards to wearing virus-blocking masks and quickly-made vaccines, COVID-19 has also taken its share of musicians.

One of the most controversial COVID-19-related deaths was that of Marvin Lee "Meat Loaf" Aday, who was rumored to be "anti-vax." Memes related to his 1993 chart-topping power ballad, "I'd Do Anything for Love (But I Won't Do That)" (get vaccinated) flooded social media when the 74-year-old's death was announced on January 21, 2022.

"Meat Loaf first found success on the Broadway stage in the groundbreaking musical *Hair*, and he had a brief, but memorable role in *The Rocky Horror Picture Show* as the ill-fated delivery boy Eddie—but it was his 1977 album *Bat Out of Hell* that turned him into a superstar and rock & roll icon," wrote *Rolling Stone*'s Andy Greene in the obituary. *Bat Out of Hell* went platinum 14 times over and yielded hit singles "Paradise by the Dashboard Light," "You Took the Words Right Out of My Mouth (Hot Summer Nights)," and "Two Out of Three Ain't Bad."

But Meat's career faltered after lawsuits and other setbacks. Try as he might, the brilliant belter who had a three-and-a-half octave vocal range wasn't able to recapture the magic of his glory days. "I felt like a leper," he said in an interview. "I felt like I was on an island with my wife and my two daughters." But in 1993, he released *Bat Out of Hell II: Back Into Hell* and the sequel album went on to sell 14 million copies, giving him a comeback for the record books. Successful tours and film roles (most notably as Bob in 1999's *Fight Club*) followed.

When his musical partner Jim Steinman—whom the *L.A. Times* dubbed "the Richard Wagner of Rock & Roll"—died on April 22, 2021, at the age of 73 from kidney failure, it ripped a huge void into Meat Loaf's heart, who was reduced to Facetiming his longtime friend, "because he [Jim] was afraid of COVID." After the songwriter's death, Aday was wrecked. "I don't want to die, but I may die this year because of Jim. I'm always with him and he's right here with me now," he told *Rolling Stone*. "I've always been with Jim and Jim has always been with me. We belonged heart and soul to each other. We didn't know each other. We *were* each other."

Meat's words proved prophetic—he didn't live even one more year following Jim's demise. He was said to be "seriously ill" with the coronavirus when he died at his Nashville, Tennessee, home. During the pandemic, the vocalist became outspoken in his disdain for quarantines, lockdowns, and mask mandates. Five months before getting the disease, he cavalierly told the *Pittsburgh Post-Gazette*, "If I die, I die, but I'm not going to be controlled."

What's more, he wrote several online posts about the right to "keep on rockin' in the free world," quoting the Neil Young song.

In 1984, when he was 20 years old, a gruff-voiced aspiring vocalist named Mark Lanegan was run over by a tractor and badly injured, halting his plan to leave his native Washington State in hopes of finding fame and fortune in Las Vegas. As the grunge gods would have it, Mark joined the Screaming Trees the following year, setting him on his musical path along with guitarist Gary Lee Conner, bassist Van Conner, and drummer Mark Pickerel.

Despite releasing a string of critically-acclaimed albums that straddled the line between hard psychedelia, punk, and foreshadowed grunge, the band never hit the commercial heights enjoyed by contemporaries like Nirvana or Soundgarden. They broke through to a wide audience when their song "Nearly Lost You" was used in the movie *Singles* (1992) and although they scored a few Top 10 hits on *Billboard*'s Modern Rock chart, Mark quit the band amid acrimony and addiction. Their final album, *Dust*, reached the U.K. Top 40 and produced the hit single "All I Know." Mark went on to join his friend Josh Homme's band Queens of the Stone Age, contributing to five of their seven albums, then meandered with his on-again-off-again solo career.

The "Dying Days" singer hit a few highlights here and there, including co-

composing the theme song for TV chef Anthony "Tony" Bourdain's show, *Parts Unknown*. The personality's suicide in 2018 was particularly hard for Mark, who had already been traumatized by Kurt Cobain's death and the drug overdose death of another close friend, Layne Staley of the Seattle band Alice in Chains.

The redheaded singer, who grappled with alcoholism and drug dependency from the young age of 12, released a memoir in 2020, partially inspired by his friend Tony Bourdain, called *Sing Backwards and Weep*. "[Tony] took his own life, which was stunningly shitty and devastating. He was such a bright light in dark times and such an important person to me. At that point, I said, 'Okay, now I have to finish this book,' even though it was the last thing in the world I wanted to do. I felt an obligation." In the book, he detailed some of the more harrowing moments in his life, not the least of which was an amputation scare while on tour with Screaming Trees—his arm became so badly infected from heroin needles that doctors considered cutting it off. After leaving the band, he became homeless.

Mark cleaned up when Kurt Cobain's widow, Courtney Love, paid to send him to rehab. In a *Rolling Stone* interview to publicize *Sing Backwards and Weep*, he said, "I remember Courtney leaving me a letter saying, 'Kurt loved you as a big brother and would have wanted you to live. The world needs you to live,'" he said. "That was powerful because I hadn't done any good for anybody in years." He subsequently connected with Queens of the Stone Age's Josh Homme, who'd performed as a second guitarist in Screaming Trees, and toured with that group while also painting sets for television shows.

Mark and his second wife Shelley Brien, a Hollywood hairstylist and sometime singer, moved from L.A. to County Kerry, Ireland, in 2020, just as the global pandemic was gaining traction. In March 2021, the *Sweet Oblivion* singer was hospitalized with severe COVID-19 and almost died. The virus rendered him deaf, unable to walk, and drifting in and out of consciousness. Ever the artist, Mark wrote a book of poetry and prose about his experience, *Devil in a Coma*, which was released while he was still ill. In December of that year, he admitted, "I was one of those knuckleheads who was wary of the vaccine. But I learned my lesson. I'll be the first one to get a booster shot when it's available in Ireland."

Unfortunately, his reversal wasn't enough to save his life. Mark Lanegan died at the age of 57 at home in Killarney, on the morning of February 22, 2022.

When Joan Jett and the Blackhearts scored a major hit with "I Love Rock 'N' Roll" in 1981, few fans were aware that the catchy rock tune was first recorded six years before by the Arrows, a British rock band. Twenty-four-year-old New York-born world-traveler Alan Merrill sang the song he wrote (he reportedly gave an erroneous co-writer credit to Arrows bandmate Jake Hooker, to whom he owed money) and enjoyed some success working with various musicians over the years, including Meat Loaf and Rick Derringer.

Alan was honored when Joan covered "I Love Rock 'N' Roll," making it a bona fide anthem, and again the following year, when GRAMMY-winner Lou Rawls recorded his song "When The Night Comes" as the title track of his 1983 album—which was taken into the cosmos by astronaut Guion Bluford (making it the first music taken to and played in outer space).

Alan Merrill continued to work in the music and entertainment industry, releasing his final track, "Your Love Song," in 2019. A year later, the 69-year-old talent was dead, a victim of the coronavirus. He passed away on March 29, 2020, in Manhattan.

His daughter Laura Merrill told *CNN* that her dad was rushed to Mount Sinai Hospital and immediately put on a ventilator because he had a fever and was struggling to breathe. He'd been self-quarantining for about 10 days at home but thought he just had a cold. "He was still playing ball with his dog on his patio [and] doing his usual stuff until he just woke up and couldn't breathe," she said, so he was admitted to the hospital.

That night, her sister texted to say their dad's vital signs were failing and that family members would be allowed to visit him for two minutes to say goodbye. "So, I went in and comforted him and told him that his whole family loved him and rubbed his head. It's just been a big shock to the entire family and you know, you don't think coronavirus is going to happen to you," she said. "You hear about it, it's something people joke about online and, and it's just, you know, it's real, it's real and it's affecting people and people are dying."

Fountains of Wayne wasn't just a scenic backdrop in an episode of HBO's beloved dramedy series, *The Sopranos*—it was once an actual store where New Jersey natives could shop for outdoor cement fountains. It also served as the inspiration for the name of a power-pop geek-rock band that emerged from New York in the mid-1990s with hits like "Stacy's Mom" and "All Kinds of Time."

Fountains of Wayne was founded by Chris Collingwood (lead vocals, keyboards, guitar) and Adam Schlesinger (bass, keyboards, backing vocals, drums, rhythm guitar) and they enjoyed a good run with other band members Jody Porter and Brian Young before disbanding over creative differences in 2013.

The novel coronavirus was acknowledged by the World Health Organization on January 10, 2020, and just a few months later, on April 1st, 52-year-old Adam Schlesinger died from it. The singer-songwriter's girlfriend, Alexis Morley, shared details about their final days together in an Instagram post, saying that his sickness just "seemed like the crappy flu," adding that he told her, "'I'm okay. I have my Alexis.' But seven days later things got worse and I brought him to the hospital." Though she wasn't allowed to see him, she recalled texting back and forth, "making cute jokes, feeling optimistic." Ten days later, he was intubated and his prognosis was grim. Finally, she and his family were allowed to say goodbye. "Adam looked sweet, peaceful, beautiful. I'm so thankful that I got to spend that one final hour with him ... I like to think he could sense us there, but he was deeply unconscious."

A few weeks after Adam Schlesinger's death, the cast of Tom Hanks' directorial debut, "That Thing You Do!" staged a virtual reunion to honor the songwriter who penned the film's theme song, and Fountains of Wayne reunited for one night only on "Jersey 4 Jersey," a benefit live-stream for charity.

When 53-year-old Francis Stueber died on October 17, 2021, while on tour with KISS, the band's roadies publicly blamed them for their lax health protocol. Fran was a longtime figure in the KISS Army, having worked as Paul Stanley's guitar tech for two decades.

Speaking anonymously to *Rolling Stone*, numerous crew members detailed the lack of COVID-19 safeguards enforced on the tour, possibly leading to Fran's untimely passing. "I couldn't believe how unsafe it was, and that we were still going," one person griped, adding that they would never work for KISS again. "We'd been frustrated for weeks, and by the time Fran died, I just thought, 'You have to be fucking kidding me.'"

Another member of the road crew remarked, "Every day during the shows, we weren't tested. And there are so many unknowns. Did we super spread this, did we spread this thing from city to city? It's horrible that Fran passed, and it's horrible if this is our protocol just for us to tour. Is this going to be the new normal, to stick someone in a hotel and if somebody dies, 'Oh, well, on to the next guy?'"

KISS responded to being put on blast by suggesting that crew members may have faked vaccination cards and breached health protocols themselves. "Our End of the Road World Tour absolutely had COVID safety protocols in place that met, but most often exceeded, federal, state, and local guidelines," the band said in its statement. "But ultimately this is still a global pandemic and there is simply no foolproof way to tour without some element of risk."

The band added, "We are profoundly heartbroken at the loss of Francis, he was a friend and colleague of 20 years, and there is no way to replace him. Millions of people have lost someone special to this horrific virus and we encourage everyone to get vaccinated. Please protect yourself and your loved ones." Frontman Gene Simmons and lead guitarist Paul Stanley have both been staunch advocates for vaccinations and mask mandates.

When someone with a mental illness is called "crazy" or "dangerous" rather than "unwell," they tend to try and hide their condition rather than seek help for it. That was truer than ever in the days when rock music was becoming popular and its creators were thrust into the spotlight—they were seen as "eccentric" or as "burnouts" when they tried to self-soothe with booze, pills, and in some cases, hallucinogenics.

While mental illness isn't deadly in and of itself, the condition has caused too many of rock's finest to take their own lives. Those who somehow managed to navigate the slippery slope of their fragile psyches and were able to carry on, serve as inspiration to many.

Brian Wilson of The Beach Boys is perhaps the best-known example of a talented, adroit, and hard-working person who was sidelined by psychosis but managed to find his way back to his reason for being—music.

Brian was born on June 2, 1942, and raised in Hawthorne, California—an area that's mere miles from Manhattan Beach, Redondo Beach, and Rancho Palos Verdes. He formed his upbeat, harmony-heavy band The Beach Boys in 1961 alongside his two younger brothers Dennis and Carl, cousin Mike Love, and school friend, Al Jardine. As a songwriter, he captured the essence of innocence and unrest that characterized his generation—his early tunes rode the waves of fun in the sun, cool cars, and beautiful girls. But his magnum opus is *Pet*

Sounds (1966), a seminal album that garnered him the respect of his peers and caused critics to start using the words "Brian Wilson" and "genius" in the same breath.

In the year following the fanfare of Pet Sounds, the 26-year-old "Good Vibrations" songwriter started feeling bad; he'd take to his bed for days on end, self-medicating with drugs, booze, and food while shutting the world out. Some saw him as a burnout or a malingering rich kid who peaked too soon. But Brian was sick.

He was admitted to a psychiatric ward in 1968 and treated for severe anxiety disorder. After his release, Brian fell prey to an unscrupulous, tyrannical medical professional, Dr. Eugene Landy. The Beach Boy was misdiagnosed with paranoid schizophrenia and eventually, Brian gave the doctor guardianship of himself and access to his personal and business correspondence.

The doctor was an odd duck—a quack, you might say. He started out in showbiz, briefly managing jazz guitarist George Benson and producing a Frankie Avalon single in the '60s. When that profession failed to pan out, Eugene went to school and earned a doctorate in psychology. He was soon a "therapist to the stars," and claimed the likes of Alice Cooper, Rod Steiger, Richard Harris, and Gig Young among his patients. (When the latter died in a gunshot murder-suicide with his wife of three weeks in 1978, his name was quietly taken off the doc's résumé.)

Brian, a once-lauded musical prodigy and multiplatinum artist, was kept doped up on an array of pills and lived in fear while his fortune was being siphoned to the tune of nearly half-a-million dollars a year for "services rendered." While part of Landy's get-well regimen was helpful (developing healthy eating habits and an exercise routine) the bad canceled out the good.

The mid-1970s were tumultuous for Brian, to say the least. On top of his mental illness, he developed a condition called tardive dyskinesia (facial tics) and heard cruel, confidence-killing voices in his head, all day, every day, taunting him. The exact cause of the "God Only Knows" composer's condition is unknown but research suggests a toxic cocktail of physical, genetic, psychological, and environmental factors can make a person more likely to develop psychoses. Brian has said in interviews that his father, Murray, was domineering, and mentally and physically abusive to him.

He also blamed his excessive use of LSD for permanently altering his brain chemistry. Acid is a manmade hallucinogenic that was popular in the 1960s among musicians and artists and was celebrated as being "mind-expanding." Its effects include intensified thoughts, vivid emotions, and enhanced sensory perception, which, for some, brought about improvements in songwriting, artwork, and other creative pursuits. While the drug is made in a laboratory, its base compound is a substance found in ergot, which is a grain-based fungus. These amalgams can cause what is known as "flashbacks"—persistent hallucinations that continue off and on for months or even years, after ingesting the drug.

Oddly enough, it was Brian's first wife, Marilyn Rovell (married in 1964, divorced in 1979), who introduced him to Dr. Landy and it was his second wife, Melinda Ledbetter (married in 1995), who got him away from the greedy Svengali.

Finally in the right hands, Brian was properly diagnosed with schizoaffective disorder and mild bipolar (then known as manic depression). In 2004, Brian Wilson triumphantly released *Smile*, a long-fabled but unfinished Beach Boys project that fell apart at the beginning of his mental health hitches.

Following various medication cocktails and constant therapy, the now 80-year-old multi-instrumentalist has finally found a regimen that allows him to make music, both in the studio and onstage. Brian Wilson co-headlined a U.S. tour with Chicago in 2022 and plans to continue his career for as long as he's able.

Pink Floyd founder Syd Barrett is another musical prodigy who fell prey to mental illness, which was probably precipitated by using experimental psychedelics like LSD. The handsome Brit was never officially diagnosed with any form of mental illness, but historians have speculated that he suffered from schizophrenia and bipolar disorder, which didn't help his acid-related fatigue—a state known as "perma-fried."

Syd recorded only a handful of releases with his band—one that would go on to worldwide fame and acclaim in the 1970s—the frontman was on their debut album *The Piper at the Gates of Dawn* (1967), and portions of their second album *A Saucerful of Secrets* (1968) before descending into irretrievable decline.

"In my opinion, [his breakdown] would have happened anyway," said David Gilmour, who stepped in as Pink Floyd's guitarist just before Syd's exit. "It was a deep-rooted thing. But I'll say the psychedelic experience might well have acted as a catalyst. Still, I just don't think he could deal with the vision of success and all the things that went with it."

Clearly, the decline of their band brother had a profound effect on the remaining members of Pink Floyd, which included co-founder and bassist, Roger Waters. Themes of mental illness pervaded their output, particularly their mega-bestselling *Dark Side of the Moon* (1973) and *Wish You Were Here* (1975), the latter of which was a tribute to Syd, especially the song, "Shine On, You Crazy Diamond," which begins with the lyrics, "Remember when you were young, you shone like the sun/Shine on, you crazy diamond/Now there's a look in your eyes, like black holes in the sky." Pink Floyd's double album *The Wall*

(1979) was also dedicated to their former frontman—it went platinum 23 times over and is one of the Top Five bestselling records of all-time.

After the "Interstellar Overdrive" songwriter left his band, he released two nonstarter solo albums, *The Madcap Laughs,* and *Barrett,* both bowing in 1970. Two years later, the once-jovial and sociable young man went into self-imposed exile and spent the rest of his life focusing on gardening, drawing, and painting at his family home in Cambridge, England.

Roger Waters and David Gilmour did more than just write about Syd Barrett—they made sure that he was paid Pink Floyd royalties and was kept comfortable for the rest of his days (which came to an end in 2006 when he was 60, following a battle with pancreatic cancer).

When Irish songstress Sinéad O'Connor turned 33 on December 8, 1999, she planned on making it her last birthday. Just nine years before, she'd been crowned a pop princess of sorts (albeit a morose one) following the phenomenal success of her version of the Prince-penned song "Nothing Compares 2U." At the time, she was the mother of two children, son Jake, and daughter Roisin. But her life had been one of extreme upset, and she was ready to end it all. Somehow, she managed to hold it together.

In 2007, she described her mental illness as a "gaping hole in the center" of her existence but after being prescribed the right medication, everything changed. "Within half an hour it was like cement going over the hole," she said. But things didn't stay steady for long. On top of reportedly suffering from bipolar disorder as well as complex post-traumatic stress disorder, borderline personality, and agoraphobia, O'Connor is also in constant pain from fibromyalgia, a musculoskeletal disorder that also causes insomnia and mood swings. In 2015, the "War" singer underwent a radical hysterectomy to treat endometriosis which triggered her previous symptoms and rendered her medication useless.

Sinéad, who has changed her name several times and become a devout Muslim, is no stranger to controversy. She has used television, the press, and social media to voice her dislike and disdain for many of her fellow music artists—not to mention major figures like Pope John Paul II, whose photograph she tore to pieces while performing on *Saturday Night Live* in 1992. She did that, she said, to shine a spotlight on the longtime and rampant sexual, physical, and mental child abuse that was perpetrated by the Catholic Church since its inception (a shameful practice that was only then coming to light). Despite her speaking the truth, Sinéad's act of rebellion made her a pop pariah. Two weeks later, she was booed offstage, and while she has never stopped making music, her career never bounced back.

The outspoken artist was born on December 8, 1966, in Glenageary, County Dublin, an area soon to become beleaguered by the Troubles. When she was eight, her parents divorced and Sinéad's mum, Marie, got custody of her. She remembered being beaten and kicked daily, often in her abdomen, which resulted in trips to the hospital. "My mother had this obsession with destroying my womb," she told *PEOPLE* in 2021 while discussing her memoir, *Rememberings*. When she was 13, Sinéad went to live with her father, and five years later, Marie was killed in a car accident.

"You can never predict what might trigger my PTSD (post-traumatic stress syndrome). I describe myself as a rescue dog: I'm fine until you put me in a situation that even slightly smells like any of the trauma I went through, then I flip my lid," she said. "I manage very well because I've been taught brilliant skills. There was a lot of therapy. It's about focusing on the things that bring you peace as opposed to what makes you feel unstable."

Unfortunately, the mother of four lost one of her sons, 17-year-old Shane, to suicide by hanging on January 7, 2022, which caused her to break down again. The heartsick mother posted on social media about the tragedy, saying, "Nevi'im Nesta Ali Shane O'Connor, the very light of my life, decided to end his earthly struggle today and is now with God. May he rest in peace and may no one follow his example. My baby. I love you so much. Please be at peace."

One week after Shane's body was recovered, the *Universal Mother* musician tweeted, "I've decided to follow my son. There is no point living without him. Everything I touch, I ruin. I only stayed for him. And now he's gone." Alarm bells were raised, and she later told her online followers, "I'm sorry. I shouldn't have said that. I am with cops now on way to hospital. I'm sorry I upset everyone. I am lost without my kid and I hate myself. Hospital will help a while. But I'm going to find Shane. This is just a delay."

Marianne Joan Elliot-Said, better-known by her stage name Poly Styrene, pioneered the British punk movement as the frontwoman of her band, X-Ray Spex. While they're not the household names of Sex Pistols or Blondie, the cutting edge band paved the way for many others with its blazing anthems that took on the patriarchy, consumerism, and identity. As a biracial, bisexual woman on the scene, Styrene had a lot to say— even though X-Ray Spex broke up in 1979, the singer's words echo in the still-emerging impact of the riot grrrl feminist punk movement. Hers was a voice once described as "powerful enough to drill holes through sheet metal" but she sang with joy and verve. The dark-haired, braces-faced frontwoman was misdiagnosed with schizophrenia in 1978 and she was actually locked away in a psychiatric hospital the first time she saw herself singing on television.

Years after X-Ray Spex disbanded, she released an easy-listening solo album, *Translucence*, and around that time, 1981, she met the musician Adrian Bell. They married three months later and she gave birth to her daughter, Celeste. But the marriage didn't last and in response, Styrene shunned the material world by joining the Hare Krishna movement and moving with her daughter to Bhaktivedanta Manor, a country house George Harrison donated to the group in 1973. Among her guests were Annie Lennox, Hazel O'Connor, and Boy George, whose 1991 hit "Bow Down, Mister" features her chanting in the background.

Still, her mental health continued to deteriorate. She left the temple, and Celeste, then just eight years old, went to stay with her grandmother. Styrene lived off meager royalties, saying "being broke and famous is the worst of both worlds." Shortly after being correctly diagnosed with bipolar disorder in 1991, she was hit by a fire truck, fracturing her pelvis. Still, the "Oh Bondage Up Yours!" singer continued to make underground music and enjoyed her legacy as a godmother of punk.

Polystyrene is a known carcinogen, so maybe it's only fitting that the sly songstress died of cancer. She passed away on April 25, 2011, at the age of 53. In 2021, her daughter, Celeste Bell, released a documentary, *Poly Styrene: I Am a Cliché*. "My mum believed she was psychic," Celeste said, while on a promotional tour for the flick. "You can see that in her lyrics. She had this uncanny ability to predict what was going to happen."

CHAPTER 12: BOULEVARD OF BROKEN DREAMS

"Bad behavior makes men more glamorous but women get destroyed, thrown out of society, and locked up in institutions."—Marianne Faithfull

Almost as fascinating as the rock god is his chosen goddess—the one woman who is desired by the man everyone else desires. "What has she got that I haven't?" many a Paul McCartney devotee wondered when he married Linda. "Why her and not me?" wailed Mick Jagger's female fans (and some male!) when he walked down the aisle with Bianca. Other wives became targets of scorn and outright hostility, from Yoko Ono to Courtney Love.

While the perks of being with a rock star seem like the stuff of fantasy—mansions, private jets, five-star hotels, and a limitless checkbook—every rose has its thorn, as a wise man once said. (Okay, okay... it was Bret Michaels.) The downside often includes infidelity, drunken rages, stints in rehab, and albums that don't sell... and may never sell again.

And it's not just the wives who suffer. It's the girlfriends, boyfriends, employees, and hangers-on. These planets floating around in a star's orbit can sometimes find themselves void of gravity and spinning helplessly into outer space while the object of their affection moves on to the next. Or worse.

After The Doors' charismatic frontman Jim Morrison died at the age of 27, his longtime love, Pamela Courson, was left to pick up the pieces. He died on her watch, so to speak, leaving a volley of questions and blame—when the "Light My Fire" singer drowned in the bathtub of their rented Paris apartment on July 3, 1971, her life promptly fell apart.

The delicate, fresh-faced, California-born redhead was ill-equipped to deal with the fallout. For one thing, she was only 24 years old and an art school dropout who was more into partying than planning. Jim took care of the woman he called his "cosmic mate" and even financed her first business, a fashion boutique in L.A., on La Cienega Boulevard called Themis. For a second thing, Pamela Courson was hopelessly addicted to heroin, using the drug daily.

While in France with Morrison, Courson was seeing a local drug dealer both as a customer and a lover—but Jean de Breteuil wasn't just any old pusher, he was a blue-blooded aristocrat. Some who knew the Count described him as a handsome jet-setting playboy, while others said he was nothing more than a titled peddler to the vices of the rich and famous. Although Jean was French, he didn't have ties there; he traveled the world and he first started a dalliance with Pamela in L.A. in 1967, when she was two years into her famously volatile (and reportedly open) relationship with Jim.

"The Doors singer was less than impressed by his rival for Courson's affections," wrote *PEOPLE* journalist Jordan Rintagh in 2021. "His 1968 song 'Love Street' is said to reference Courson's shopping excursions with Breteuil, whom he loathed: 'She has robes and she has junkies/lazy diamond-studded flunkies.' (He changed 'junkies' to 'monkeys' in the final version.) Tensions mounted as Courson began sampling Breteuil's deadly wares. Morrison hated heroin, and his burgeoning alcoholism shortened his temper. Shouting matches were frequent between the two. Courson usually stormed out, often finding solace with Breteuil."

Pam and Jean jet-setted, staying in his family's mansions and finding the most potent drugs on the planet—which the young Frenchman sold to high-profile clients in L.A., including singer Janis Joplin, who was found dead of a heroin overdose in her room at the Landmark Hotel on October 4, 1970. Fearing that he would be linked to the "Piece of My Heart" singer, the Count fled the States and settled back into Parisian life. Pamela followed, and then Jim. Jim was fed up with fame, Hollywood, and The Doors—he planned to make a fresh start in the fabled City of Lights. Instead, it was lights out.

While Jim's official cause of death—despite the lack of an autopsy—is a heart attack brought on by booze and hot bathwater, some conspiracy theorists have suggested that Pam or Jean gave him heroin. Jim was strongly against the drug so it's doubtful he would have willingly taken it. But maybe, just maybe, some said, he mistook a line of heroin for cocaine.

Paris in 1971 was overflowing with pure, uncut heroin that was being smuggled into the country through the port city of Marseilles (the so-called "French Connection" in director William Friedkin's Oscar-winning film of the same name). "Shortly before Morrison's death," Rintagh wrote, "he pored over the *Newsweek* cover story 'The Heroin Plague,' which traced the abnormally high number of overdoses across Europe and the United States. The magazine issue was dated July 5, 1971. Morrison wouldn't live to see that date."

After a distraught Pamela Courson returned home to the States, Count Jean de Breteuil frolicked on the French Riviera, doling out drugs like a Pez-dispenser to clients like Keith Richards, heiress Talitha Getty, and Mick Jagger's ex, rock singer Marianne Faithfull.

Marianne wrote about Jean in her self-titled 1994 memoir. "He was a horrible guy, someone who had crawled out from under a stone. He was Talitha's lover, and somehow I ended up with him. It was all about drugs and sex. He was with me only because I'd been involved with Mick Jagger. In that froggy way, he was obsessed with all that. To him, I was *très le type rock 'n' roll*. I knew this species well, but as I said, he had a lot of drugs." Marianne struggled with addiction for years but got clean in 1985 after checking herself into Hazelden Betty Ford, a drug treatment center.

After Jim Morrison died, the rest fell into their own heroin haze. Thirty-year-old Talitha Getty died two weeks later of a suspected smack overdose. Jean himself expired in Tangier on June 25, 1972, at the tender age of 22 with 10 times the lethal dose of heroin in his system. This egregious overage led some to suspect suicide, while others concluded he'd been murdered. Pam OD'd and perished on April 25, 1974, just weeks after a Los Angeles court declared her Jim Morrison's legal heir.

Jim Morrison was the last in a devil's trifecta of 27-year-old American rock stars who'd died within 10 months of each other. Janis Joplin was in the middle. Jimi Hendrix was the first, and like Morrison, he was in a foreign country with his girlfriend.

Jimi met German figure skater Monika Dannemann on January 12, 1969, at a venue where he was performing. The pair hit it off so well that they spent that night together, and she went with him to his next show, which was in Düsseldorf. The pair saw each other on-and-off, until that fateful 18th day of September in 1970 when he overdosed and died in Monika's London flat. The official ruling on the cause of death was asphyxiation through aspiration of vomit due to a barbiturate overdose—Monika's prescribed Vesparax sleeping tablets that she gave him. The "Hey, Joe" singer swallowed nine of them, and never woke up.

While seeing Monika, Jimi also enjoyed the company of several other women. The day before he died, he and Monika ran into Devon Wilson, a "super-groupie" and model whom the guitarist treated as more than just a fling. In fact, it's said that Jimi wrote his song "Dolly Dagger" with Devon in mind. There's a line that goes, "She drinks her blood from a jagged edge" which is in reference to a memory of his birthday party in 1969, which was held at her apartment. Legend has it that Devon sucked the blood off Mick Jagger's finger after he accidentally cut it on a broken wineglass, while he, Hendrix, watched. Devon spent that night with the party guest, not the birthday boy. (Apparently, Mick clapped back with "You Can't Always Get What You Want," singing, "In her glass, was a bleeding man.")

Devon was born on October 20, 1943, in Milwaukee, Wisconsin, and while details about her childhood are sketchy it has been rumored that she ran away from a violent household as a young teen and made her way to Las Vegas, where she supported herself with sex work. But she was smart and she was beautiful—Devon traveled to New York, where she found legitimate modeling gigs and worked at the Playboy Club. It was there that she met music impresario Quincy Jones, who took her under his wing (and into his bed). Along the way, the tall, striking music aficionado hooked up with Brian Jones of The Rolling Stones, guitarist Eric Clapton, Duane Allman, jazz legend Miles Davis, and, of course, Mick and Jimi.

Devon quotes are few and far between, but she did give an interview to *Rags* magazine in 1969 about her conquests (the article was called "Cop of the Year"—'cop' was then-popular sexual slang). When asked what she'd do after bagging the big prize (Mick Jagger), she quipped, "So, what can I do for an encore? I don't know, probably marry Jimi... Will you publish my wedding pictures?"

Devon was one of the few Black women that Jimi dated (the nimble-fingered musician apparently had a thing for Germanic and Scandinavian blondes) after he met her in New York in 1965. The pair played around but there was little sense of a traditional intimate relationship there; whether it was the times, their lifestyles, or a tacit agreement, Devon was known to procure girls, drugs, or whatever Jimi's whim wanted at any given time. She was bisexual, took part in "free love" group sex with him, and was said to be okay with their mutual liaisons... *sometimes*. She could also be extremely jealous and possessive of the Strat-burning rock god. Still, those who knew them and saw them together did say there was a kind of love between them.

There must have been, for Devon was wrecked following her main man's untimely exit. She attended his funeral with her former beau Miles Davis and then-wife Betty, and, witnesses recalled, Devon acted as though she meant to throw herself headlong into Jimi's grave as his casket was lowered into the cold Seattle ground. (Jimi Hendrix was a Washington State native, so even though he lived in L.A. and died in London, his bones lie in Renton, a suburb southeast of Seattle.)

Devon Wilson was never the same, according to her friends and contemporaries. She dove deeper into her already dangerous addictions, which included the flagrant use of heroin. Following the funeral, she settled back in New York and moved into the fabled, historic Hotel Chelsea in Manhattan. According to her friends, she was constantly stoned and high, and barely functional. As her addiction and depression fed each other, she couldn't bear to go on. On February 2, 1971, five months after losing the love of her life, Devon opened the window to her room on the 8th floor and jumped to her death. She was 28 years old.

Devon's friend Betty Davis wrote an upbeat funk song in her memory, growling about the "cutie from her head down to her toes," and called it, "Steppin' in Her I. Miller Shoes." The tune appeared on Betty's self-titled album in 1973 and was released as the B side of Betty's better-known single, "If I'm In Luck I Might Get Picked Up."

Decades later, Monika Dannemann also committed suicide. Following a longstanding "catfight" with one of Jimi's other women, Kathy Etchingham, Monika wound up in court for libeling her rival and was found guilty by a British court—which apparently was more than the former figure skater and rock muse could bear, so she got into her garaged Mercedes, started it up, and poisoned herself on the fumes.

The 50-year-old former wife of Uli Jon Roth of The Scorpions had made something of a career of being Jimi Hendrix's intended bride (there's only her word on this—which she outlined in a 1995 memoir called *The Inner World of Jimi Hendrix by His Fiancée*) by appearing at celebrity signature conventions, giving countless interviews, doing photospreads, and amassing something of a Hendrix artifact museum in her home.

While Monika saw Jimi as a spiritual messiah of music and the cosmos, Kathy painted a completely different portrait, characterizing the man as a boozer and abuser. The two women contradicted each other in every interview they (respectively) did.

Kathy gave an interview to *the Independent* shortly after Monika's death. "I don't like history being altered," she said. "And it's not right that anyone should change the character and essence of a person. Jimi was a really nice bloke but he was not a prophet. At the end, he was a man who had lost his way. If you look at the footage of the final concerts you can see what LSD and cocaine do." What's more, she did not believe that Monika was anything more than one of Jimi's bed buddies. "That's why she could only ever speak about the night he died," Kathy surmised, pointing out that there were only one or two photos of Jimi and Monika together.

While she wasn't happy that Monika committed suicide following the court's ruling, Kathy believed that the verdict exposed deception on Monika's part. "The court case established once and for all that she was not Jimi's girlfriend. Everything was beginning to catch up with her."

A few months after Iron Maiden frontman Bruce Dickinson left his wife of 29 years for a younger woman, she killed herself. Following what was euphemistically referred to as a "tragic accident" by Bruce, 58-year-old Patrice "Paddy" Bowden was found dead at the marital home in the gated community of Chiswick, London on May 18, 2020.

Whatever happened, news footage from that day shows several officials wearing full-on hazmat suits as they went in and out of the multimillion-dollar abode—they were alerted and summoned by a frantic emergency phone call from the housekeeper who found Paddy's lifeless body.

One of the former couple's three children, Austin Dickinson, posted on Instagram: "By now a lot of you have seen the news. My mum has tragically passed away, I haven't even got the words to say right now and I ask for privacy and respect for myself and our family." Even years later, details remain sketchy.

In 2015, Bruce underwent a tongue-cancer scare that nearly ended his singing career and friends say that it was Paddy who nursed him back to health as he endured nine weeks of chemotherapy and 33 sessions of radiation. But just four years later, Bruce allegedly ditched his devoted wife. Around that time, the "Run to the Hills" singer left his London home and began living with Parisian fitness guru Leanna Dolci, who is said to have been a huge Iron Maiden fan, even though she was born in the same year the band formed—1975.

Anita Pallenberg was Keith Richards' common-law wife and the mother of two of his children (plus one that died of Sudden Infant Death Syndrome). In the late 1970s, she was ostracized from the Stones' circle when her drug use and out-of-control behavior were seen as too risky.

She responded by taking up with a very young lover after sorta-kinda parting ways with the "Satisfaction" guitarist; since they shared children together and their lives had been entwined for so long, Keith let Anita and her kids live in one of his houses. Sixteen-year-old Scott Cantrell joined her in the South Salem, New York, home and lived there for about a year before his life was cut short.

When a gunshot rang out from the couple's bedroom at about 10:30 on the night of July 20,

1979, Keith and Anita's 10-year-old son, Marlon, dashed in to see what had happened. "I went my God, Jesus Christ," Marlon said, quoted in Keith Richards' autobiography, *Life*. "I had to have a little peek, so I did go up and saw all this brain matter all over the walls."

State police investigator Douglas Lamanna later said he arrived to find 17-year-old Scott Cantrell on the bed, dressed in a shirt and jeans but barefooted. He was barely breathing but not conscious. A .38 caliber Smith & Wesson pistol was laid on a dresser toward the foot of the bed with one empty chamber. A bullet had entered the teen's right temple, exited from the back of his head, ricocheted off the ceiling, and came to rest on the floor. He died at 12:15 a.m. at a nearby hospital.

Thirty-seven-year-old Anita spent the next seven hours marinating in blood-soaked clothes at police headquarters, shivering under harsh fluorescent lights and fielding a barrage of questions. Detective Lamanna said she was "visibly upset, distraught, and at times felt faint." She told him that she'd known Scott Cantrell for about a year, and let him move in with her because "he said he had no place to stay." As for the shooting itself, she never saw it; Anita "was tidying up" with her back to him when she heard the shot. "He was lying on his back and I turned him over," she said. "I heard a gurgling sound. He was choking on his blood. I picked up the revolver and put it on the chest of drawers. I don't like guns."

She added that the kid was a heavy marijuana user. "There were also indications that he'd been drinking, probably white wine. He had .06 blood-alcohol, which is mild," said Lamanna, noting that Pallenberg's breath smelled of alcohol during the interview. Anita turned over her Italian passport and was released on $500 bail.

Marlon said, "There were all these stories in the press at the time saying that she was a witch, that people were having Black Sabbaths. They were saying all sorts of things. It literally was just bad luck. I don't think he intended to shoot himself, really, just an idiot of 17 who was stoned, angry, playing with a pistol."

The lead detective later claimed he had no idea who Anita Pallenberg was until: "I saw an article in the room. It was from a London paper. December of '78. The headline said, 'What Anita did to Bianca.' I said, 'Is that you?' She said, 'Yes.' I said, 'What'd you do to Bianca?' She said, 'It was all publicity.'" He noted that the once-stunning blonde was heavily overweight and unrecognizable from the days when she graced the silver screen in movies like *Barbarella* (1968) and *Performance* (1970).

Further examination would turn up no identifiable fingerprints on the gun, which turned out to be stolen from a sheriff in Florida (by whom, no one knew). A rumor that Anita and Scott had been playing Russian Roulette started to circulate, but in the end, she was not legally responsible for what the police concluded was a suicide. She was charged with being in possession of two unregistered firearms.

"It was a miracle how that case just disappeared," Keith wrote in his book. "I believe it was to do with the fact that the gun was traced back to the police... suddenly it wasn't an issue. The case was put down as suicide. The boy's parents tried to bring a case for corruption of a minor, which didn't stick. So, Anita moved to New York, to the Alray Hotel, and began a different kind of existence. That was the final curtain for me and Anita, apart from trips to see the children. It was the end. Thanks for the memories, girl."

In 1981, a year after their split, Keith met model Patti Hansen at Studio 54, and the pair have been married since 1983. Around that same time, Anita met and married Gabriel Roux and they remained together until her death from Hepatitis-C in 2017. Less than a year before her passing, Anita told journalist Alain Elkann, "I am ready to die. I have done so much here. My Mum died at 94. I don't want to lose my independence. Now I am over 70 and to be honest I did not think I would live over 40." Upon the news of her death, Keith Richards issued a statement saying, "A most remarkable woman. Always in my heart."

Many of those in the Stones' ambit have been like so much "Tumbling Dice," some coming out winners while others have rolled the dreaded snake eyes. Mick Jagger's longtime girlfriend L'Wren Scott was a successful model, fashionista, designer, and stylist, who seemed to have everything going for her… until the day she inexplicably ended her life.

The leggy, vivacious brunette was born Laura "Luann" Bambrough on April 28, 1964, in Salt Lake City, and was one of three adopted children. She developed an interest in fashion and style from the early age of 12 because her height shot to six feet and she was obliged to sew her own clothes.

As a teen, she was spotted by a modeling talent scout and left home to make her fortune in Paris. Working under the name L'Wren, she soon became the favorite of haute couture icons like Thierry Mugler, Helmut Newton, Guy Bourdin, David Bailey, Jean-Paul Goude, Herb Ritts, Karl Lagerfeld, and the House of Chanel. But more than anything, she wanted to be working behind the scenes in a creative capacity.

She found success in Hollywood, working on several films as a stylist, and eventually crossed paths with Martin Scorsese, whose love of The Rolling Stones is well-known. It was through her work on the Scorsese-helmed documentary, *Shine a Light* (1998), that she met Mick. She'd already suffered through two divorces, but the pair started a love relationship in 2001 and stayed together until her death on March 17, 2014. As to be expected, there was an age gap between them—L'Wren was born in the same year that the Stones released their first album and by most accounts, she didn't even know the names of most of the hits from their heyday.

In the mid-2000s, L'Wren launched her own fashion and accessories line; her ambassadors included everyone from Madonna to First Lady Michelle Obama—in a short time, she was a bona fide brand with clothing, handbags, scents, and more.

Despite her outward success and happiness, L'Wren suffered from bouts of extreme depression, and one spring morning in Manhattan, her mood disorder got the best of her. The night before she hung herself with a black scarf in her glamourous apartment, L'Wren gave a dinner party and although she seemed "a little down" or "preoccupied" according to some of her guests, no one had anticipated that she was about to take her own life.

Mick, who was on tour in Australia at the time, released a public statement about L'Wren's death through his social media platforms, saying, "I am still struggling to understand how my lover and best friend could end her life in this tragic way. We spent many wonderful years together and had made a great life for ourselves. She had great presence and her talent was much admired, not least by me. I have been touched by the tributes that people have paid to her, and also the personal messages of support that I have received. I will never forget her." He later set up a scholarship fund in her name for fashion students at Central Saint Martins, located in London.

Not everyone in the Stones' camp loved L'Wren Scott. An anonymous source quoted Keith Richards as referring to the six-foot-three Amazon as "L'Man." Some said Mick wasn't as easygoing and open with his humor when he was in her presence; she seemed to stifle his effervescence. Making matters worse, the randy rock star had started seeing another woman while on tour—a woman 25 years younger than L'Wren. Mick met Melanie Hamrick, an American ballerina, while performing in Japan just days before his girlfriend back at home hung herself. It was also just six weeks before what would have been the former model's 50th birthday—it seemed, in her mind, that the Big 5-0 was a fate worse than death.

Since L'Wren didn't leave a note and gave no inkling of her awful intentions, no one knows for sure why she did it. Some speculated it wasn't "Love in Vain" or age-related angst, it was business debts in the millions that demoralized her to the point of no return. Others said the liabilities weren't out of line for a business that was "just getting started." A spokesperson for her company stated, "the long-term prospects for the business were encouraging," due to its expanding portfolio of partnerships with Banana Republic and Bobbi Brown Cosmetics, among others.

Her family, friends, and associates all expressed shock and disbelief that a woman who was so kind, compassionate, intelligent, and together would take such a final action in relation to temporary setbacks. But some did admit that L'Wren didn't talk about her problems and wasn't one to confide in or burden those around her. She was a perfectionist who drove herself to that ideal in sometimes unhealthy ways, obsessing over color selections for months or remaking the same pattern dozens of times until it was just right.

A journalist for *the Guardian*, writing in-depth about L'Wren Scott's suicide, noted, "In his book *The Savage God: A Study of Suicide*, the writer Al Alvarez argues that "the decision to take your own life is as vast and complex and mysterious as life itself."

Sometimes chance meetings can lead to wonderful new and nourishing relationships. Other times, not so much. Canadian backup singer Cathy Smith was notorious as a human hurricane, storming in and out of the lives of countless music men; most weathered the blows but one's life was cut short by, well, blow.

When comedian and singer John Belushi died at the age of 33 after indulging in a toxic "speedball" of cocaine and heroin injected by Cathy, the world was collectively stunned. Everything about this tragic tale has the hallmarks of Hollywood's fabled "boulevard of broken dreams" but the story starts long before, in a midsize city 2,500 miles away.

Catherine Evelyn Smith was born an orphan in the port city of Hamilton, Ontario, on April 25, 1947. She was soon adopted but her new parents turned out to have substance abuse issues, which perhaps led to her decision to leave school at the age of 16 to take an office job. But a steady paycheck and four walls couldn't hold the free-spirited young woman from striking out on the road with a multitude of musicians.

Known as a groupie when the term was still cool, Cathy recalled in her 1984 tell-all tome *Chasing the Dragon* that when she went on the road with The Rolling Stones in the mid-1970s, "I was at the top as far as vicarious living went."

Her first love and rock & roll conquest was Levon Helm of The Band (Bob Dylan's backing when he famously went electric at the Newport Folk Festival in 1965, then becoming a formidable force in their own right with songs like "The Weight" and "The Shape I'm In"). Before long, the charming 17-year-old party girl was also loving Levon's band brothers… when she became pregnant, the entourage jokingly called the kiddo "the Band Baby."

The little girl, Tracey Lee, was given up for adoption and her mama moved on to greener pastures with Canadian folk and rock legend Gordon Lightfoot. He wound up writing one of his most iconic songs, a bitter ballad laced with insinuation called "Sundown" about his fiery affair with Cathy Smith who, by then, was drinking, drugging, and carousing 24/7.

The tempestuous two met when he was married to his first wife, Brita Olaisson. Gord and Cathy had a short-lived fling but fate brought them together again in 1971 when they found themselves in the same elevator of the downtown apartment building where the now-separated songwriter lived. Friends recalled his bachelor pad was decked-out with so many seductive bells and whistles, it made Hugh Hefner look like Mister Rogers; the den of decadence boasted red velvet couches, deep pile shag carpets, an aquarium stocked with exotic fish, and a sexy hi-fi that could knock your socks off—not to mention other items of apparel.

"It was one of those relationships [when] a feeling of danger comes into the picture," said the singer-songwriter in the 2020 documentary, *Gordon Lightfoot: If You Could Read My Mind*. After divorcing Brita, Gordon settled in with Cathy, buying a stately mansion in Toronto's rich Rosedale neighborhood, where they partied, carefree, "drunk, and madly in love," Cathy wrote in her book. But there were bad times too, as their arguments turned physical at times, instigated at one time or another by them both.

One night, Cathy went out to a concert with her girlfriends. Alone, jealous, drinking, and overthinking, Lightfoot wrote one of his biggest hits, "Sundown," and soon the Smith-inspired lyrics, "I can see her lookin' fast in her faded jeans/She's a hard lovin' woman, got me feelin' mean" were pouring out of FM radios all over

North America. It reached #1 on the U.S. *Billboard* Hot 100 and Canada's RPM national singles chart.

While his career was on the way up, his relationship with Cathy was breaking down. The final nail in love's coffin came in 1974, when she provided backing vocals on his music rival Murray McLauchlan's song, "Do You Dream of Being Somebody."

Gord kicked Cathy to the curb, and she eventually landed in L.A. While finding her way in the Golden State, she did a little more backup singing and found odd jobs here and there, but her main source of income came from drug-pushing. By the late 1970s, the husky-voiced, chisel-cheeked beauty was known as "Cathy Silverbag" because she carried a dainty metallic purse filled with dope.

She hung out with L.A.'s glitterati, eventually hooking up with John Belushi. The star became an A-lister through his groundbreaking work on *Saturday Night Live*'s inaugural season, leading several blockbuster films, and successfully pursued a career in music as one-half of The Blues Brothers (alongside *SNL* castmate and friend, Dan Ackroyd). Unfortunately, John had a severe substance abuse problem that was putting everything he'd worked for into jeopardy.

He was forging full steam into his determined downward spiral when Cathy became the married superstar's newly-minted companion in the $200-a-day Bungalow 3 at the swanky Chateau Marmont on the Sunset Strip. In the early morning hours of March 5, 1982, the party palace was visited separately by comedian Robin Williams, actor Robert De Niro, and the drug-dispensing Cathy Smith.

John's friend and bodyguard, karate legend Bill "Superfoot" Wallace, arrived at around 12:00 noon that fateful Friday to deliver a typewriter that had been requested the previous day. Inside the otherwise empty bungalow, Bill found John's dead body tucked into a fetal position on the bed. He said he thought Belushi was asleep but called paramedics when he realized his boss was not breathing. "I listened for his heartbeat and there was none ... He had needle marks on his right arm," Wallace later said in court.

Smith was arrested by the Los Angeles Police Department a few hours after the discovery of Belushi's body. She was driving the wrong way into the one-way exit of the Chateau Marmont behind the wheel of John Belushi's rented red Mercedes. The LAPD found a small amount of drugs on her, but they released her after questioning. A few days later, L.A.'s "Coroner to the Stars," Dr. Thomas Noguchi, determined that the comedian had overdosed and no foul play was suspected. Sometime after that, Cathy quietly returned home to Toronto.

Then, in a bizarre June 29, 1982, interview with *the National Enquirer*, Cathy Evelyn Smith admitted to injecting the "Soul Man" singer with the lethal speedball dose before leaving the bungalow and taking off in his Mercedes. The headline screamed, "I Killed John Belushi!" Maybe she needed the money or wanted a claim to fame. After all, before then no one knew who she was. The article blew the lid off: "World Exclusive—Mystery Woman Confesses."

Soon after the interview appeared, the case of Belushi's death was reopened. Thirty-five-year-old Cathy was arrested, extradited from Canada back to the Los Angeles jurisdiction, and charged with first-degree murder.

"I didn't kill John Belushi," she clarified in *Chasing the Dragon*, which was published while her case was still in progress. "I do suffer guilt, but the guilt comes from not being aware of what was really going on." The public wasn't buying her excuses—though they bought the book, in droves—and Cathy was pilloried.

Reviews of the memoir, thought to be too self-serving, were harsh. But one journalist saw something deeper; in his piece, *Globe* writer Mark Breslin noted that although the book contained various pictures of the famous people she had been involved with, Cathy appeared in just one of them. "In all the rest, she is noticeably absent," Breslin wrote. "The message is clear. Stars are forever blessed by the beat, while fans are expendable, ephemeral commodities best suited to holding the bag and taking the rap."

As the case got underway, the prosecutor said, "John Belushi would not have died when he died except for the heroin that was furnished and administered by the defendant." To illustrate that it was Cathy's drugs that killed the funnyman, a coroner's chemist testified that he found traces of heroin and cocaine on a hypodermic needle and spoon found in Smith's purse when she was arrested on March 5th.

The defense pointed to John's long history of drug abuse and reckless self-endangerment. The judge, David A. Horowitz of the Los Angeles Superior Court, said John's own irresponsibility did not absolve Cathy. "You were brought into the action with Mr. Belushi's circle of friends because you were the connection, the source of that poison," the judge said. "You knew how to use the needle."

Meanwhile, Cathy Smith remained free for four years while the legal system's cogs and wheels slowly turned. On June 11, 1986, she pleaded to lesser charges of involuntary manslaughter and three counts of furnishing and administering controlled substances to John Belushi. Despite her admission of some guilt, Horowitz handed down a harsh sentence. "Every time you stuck a needle in someone's arm, you put their life at risk. And as a result of your actions, John Belushi is dead," he intoned. "That behavior, to me, is totally unacceptable. To make it clear to you how unacceptable it is, I believe a prison term is necessary."

While serving her sentence at the Chino Women's Prison, Cathy taught computer skills to her fellow inmates. A few were members of the Manson Family. One of Cathy's closest friends, Lesley St. Nicholas (who was married to Steppenwolf bassist Nick St. Nicholas), gave an interview, saying, "She got along with Patricia Krenwinkel but Susan Atkins freaked her out. Cathy was very tough, and she had a tongue on her. Atkins, though, scared her."

After her release from prison in March of 1988, she was deported to Canada. In Toronto, she did volunteer work speaking to teenagers about the dangers of drugs but three years later, she was arrested with two grams of heroin in her purse—she paid a $2,000 fine and was on probation for a year.

Cathy Smith had her ups and downs before finally succumbing to poor health (the lifelong cigarette-smoker was on oxygen for her remaining few years) at home in British Columbia on August 16, 2020. She was 73 years old. It is worth noting that one other song Gordon Lightfoot wrote with his muse in mind is 1975's "Rainy Day People," which is about "high-stepping strutters who land in the gutters."

A few months before John Belushi died via misadventure, a music journalist whose work he read and loved, Lester Bangs, accidentally overdosed—also at the age of 33. Headlines were small but in the years since the *CREEM* and *Rolling Stone* writer died, his legend has grown.

These days, he is remembered as "the great gonzo journalist, gutter poet, and romantic visionary of rock writing—Hunter S. Thompson, Charles Bukowski, and Jack Kerouac all rolled into one," according to his biographer, Jim DeRogatis. By all accounts, Lester was an acerbic, cynical wordsmith who nevertheless harbored a glimmer of hope in his soul. Actor Philip Seymour Hoffman—who also overdosed and died—portrayed him to great acclaim in the beloved film, *Almost Famous* (2000), which helped introduce him to a whole new generation of fans. As a 2002 retrospective piece on Bangs in *the Guardian* says, "When you watch Hoffman as Bangs—hungover and chain-smoking in a cramped apartment, yet selflessly shepherding a 15-year-old reporter through his first breakthrough feature—you are suddenly face-to-face with the full measure of the man: the tender-hearted, penetratingly intelligent, infuriatingly illogical individual behind the gonzo fright-mask."

Born Leslie Conway Bangs on December 14, 1948, he had a checkered childhood; his mom was a devout Jehovah's Witness who disapproved of education and curiosity, and his ex-con, alcoholic dad was killed in a mysterious house fire in 1957, shortly after abandoning his family. "Your father is dead," Norma Bangs calmly told her son. "He burned in a fire, but don't worry, he had *the Watchtower* and *Awake!* beside his bed. He'll be all right because, in the end, he was with God."

When Lester was 11, he was coerced into sexual relations in exchange for bubble gum and comic books by a middle-aged man living in a trailer park near his school. "Everybody comes from a fucked-up family," Bangs used to say to anyone who blamed their bad luck on bad parenting. "I'm the living example of not using that as an excuse."

Although Lester grew up loving the Beat poets, jazz music, science fiction, and comic books, he was a few years too late to be a "dharma bum" on the road with Kerouac. But he did hang out with the Hells Angels and took so many drugs while with them, that he scared himself into looking for a profession. After dropping out of college, the quick-witted critic started writing album reviews—mostly scathing—for *Rolling Stone*. They published his first negative critique (on MC5's *Kick Out the Jams*) in 1969, and his last in 1973, which derided Canned Heat's *The New Age*. He was fired for "disrespecting music."

Lester was taken on as a freelancer for Detroit-based *CREEM* magazine in 1970 and he was eventually hired as a staff writer. He stayed with them for years, building his reputation as a tough assessor of self-indulgent stadium rock, while praising pared-down proto-punks like Patti Smith and Iggy and the Stooges. He moved to Detroit, calling the depressed but musically-rich area "rock's only hope," and adopted it as his chosen hometown. For a time, he was the guiding editorial force of what was billed as "America's Only Rock & Roll Magazine." Lester was one of the first writers to use the term "punk-rock" and as the 1970s progressed, forward-looking *CREEM* was among the few publications to give credence to hard rock and metal bands like Motörhead, KISS, Judas Priest, and Van Halen.

Lester Bangs' antics were as legendary as his sharp, often vicious, counterculture assessments of the world around him. In one particularly colorful anecdote, the mustachioed scribe hauled himself and his typewriter onstage while the J. Geils Band were performing, and proceeded to type a review of the event, banging the keys in perfect time to the guitar, bass, and drums. As his encore, he smashed his "instrument" to the stage floor, stomping it to bits. "The audience went wild!" remembered vocalist Peter Wolf, decades later.

After leaving *CREEM* in 1976, Lester wrote for *the Village Voice*, *Penthouse*, *Playboy*, *NME*, and others; while he was professionally successful, his personal life left much to be desired. "He was a romantic in the gravest, saddest, best, and most ridiculous sense of that worn-out word," fellow rock writer Nick Tosches said of his friend. "He couldn't merely go to bed with a woman; he had to fall in love with her. He couldn't merely dislike something; he had to rail and rage against it. None of it was real, but in the end, the phantoms of all that crazy love and anger, since they weren't his to command, conquered him."

Or, as Maria Bustillos wrote in a 2012 *New Yorker* retrospective profile of the journalist, "Lester Bangs was a wreck of a man, right up until his death in April of 1982, at the age of 33. He was fat, sweaty, unkempt—an out-of-control alcoholic in torn jeans and a too-small black leather jacket; crocked to the gills on the Romilar cough syrup he swigged down by the bottle. He also had the most advanced and exquisite taste of any American writer of his generation, uneven and erratic as it was."

Though often described as "charismatic," Lester never had so much as one long-term romance and he wound up alone, burned out, washed up, and often broke. His mother and his sister tried to lure him back into the religious fervor of the family fold by mailing him issues of *the Watchtower* but also, despite his black sheep status, they showed their concern by sending cash whenever they could. He bounced around, checked in and out of rehab, and eventually settled into a modest Manhattan apartment, lamenting the loss of his career, and wondering what the seemingly hopeless future would hold for him.

"The last thing anybody should ever consider doing is entering this racket," he wrote in an essay entitled *How to Be a Rock Critic.* "In the first place, it doesn't pay much and doesn't lead anywhere in particular, so no matter how successful you are at it, you'll eventually have to decide what you're going to do with your life anyway."

In 1981 a fire raged through his flat and he narrowly escaped his father's fate; perhaps the scrape scared him into focusing, for he spent the next year writing a book he tentatively titled *Rock Gomorrah*. His mother died of an aneurysm in 1982, and he attended her funeral in El Cajon, California, but soon went home to finish his book.

On the day he completed the final draft and optimistically delivered it to the publisher, he decided to celebrate his accomplishment, despite feeling under the weather with flu-like symptoms. At a party of one in his small abode, Lester put the new Human League album, *Dare*, on the turntable and treated himself to a handful of Valium and Darvon, washed down with over-the-counter cough syrup. The journalist on the skids, now sparked with hope for his new book, never woke up. (Lester Bangs is now considered *the* most influential rock critic of all-time... better late than never?)

When it comes to *Playboy* Playmates who met tragic ends, Dorothy Stratten—blown away by her jealous husband in a gory murder-suicide shortly after grabbing the Playmate of the Year brass ring—gets the headlines. But there's another starry-eyed, small-town girl who posed for the mag and came to a bad end who is all but forgotten now.

She was born Ellen Louise Stowe, on March 19, 1956, and was the typical pretty girl in a go-nowhere town with big dreams—

nothing rare there but she did take that extra step to make those wishes come true. As a teen, she thumbed it to the neon jungle of Las Vegas, where she worked as an exotic dancer under the name Star—she migrated to the so-called City of Angels and was soon spotted by a talent scout for *Playboy* and whisked off to the mansion for her big shot.

The slim-hipped, small-busted blonde was photographed by *Playboy*'s primo shutterbug, Pompeo Posar, and was the Playmate of the Month in February of 1977. She was the first centerfold with a visible tattoo and she showed her love of rock music by posing with a black and white Rickenbacker bass guitar, and a poster of Jimmy Page tacked to the wall of the set. She was adorable and she got an equally cutesy write-up in the text that no one read:

> *Her name is Star Stowe and if she were from Barstow, we'd write a limerick about her, but she's not—she's from Little Rock, Arkansas, and now lives in Los Angeles. Star wasn't the moniker she was given at birth, either; the name was given to her several years ago, when the somewhat precocious Miss Stowe, then a minor, tried to finagle her way into a bar. The doorman wouldn't let her in, which prompted the fellow she was with to quote the title of a song by The Rolling Stones: "Star, Star," he said, "can't get in the door."*

Thereafter, people started to call her Star and she didn't object. "Some people think it's egotistical to call myself Star," she says, "but it's not meant in the Hollywood sense at all." It's meant, and we kid you not, in the celestial sense. Star happens to be fascinated by stars— you know, those twinkly little objects that come out at night. In her spare time, she hangs out at planetaria and studies pictures of nebulae and comets, and, in celebration of her interest in things celestial, she even had an electric-blue star tattooed on . . . well . . . a private part of her anatomy.

Another star that interests her is rock star Gene Simmons, bass-guitar player for the group KISS. They met some years ago in Las Vegas; specifically, at the elevator banks of the Hotel Sahara, where Gene and his group were playing at the time. She didn't recognize him with his make-up off (onstage the group is heavily and rather bizarrely made up), but his laid-back manner attracted her and she's been hanging around with the band ever since. "Once in L.A.," she recalls, "while Gene was onstage, I flashed him—I just opened my jacket for a split second and I wasn't wearing anything underneath. Sometimes, I just love to be naughty."

Star did love to be naughty; in addition to Gene, she was caught by paparazzi on the town with Rod "the Bod" Stewart. She also had a predilection for drinking and drugging. As such, she never had the wherewithal to work on her career, and her star, ahem, faded. Then it fell. Although she did marry and had a son, by the time she was 40, the woman who once had it all had nothing and wound up working the streets of Fort Lauderdale, Florida, as a prostitute.

On March 17, 1997, Star Stowe was found dead—strangled and dumped in a derelict parking lot behind a pharmacy. Another streetwalker had been found dead in much the same way a couple of weeks earlier, and over the next couple of years, more "working girls" were murdered and discarded like debris— probably the work of a serial killer, but then his nefarious activities stopped and that was that. Star's murder remains unsolved.

Star Stowe wasn't the only musician's muse to die at the hands of a serial killer: Tiffany Bresciani, the 22-year-old girlfriend of Reagan Youth frontman Dave "Insurgent" Rubenstein, met her hideous fate on June 24, 1993, in Long Island.

When Tiffany was a teen she dated Rick Wilder, founder of underground punk band The Mau-Mau's, but their relationship was on-off and stormy. Then she met Dave, the deeply troubled son of Holocaust survivors. Reagan Youth were hardcore leftist punkers—their name was a satirical smoosh of Ronald Reagan and the Hitler Youth of WWII—their run only lasted a couple of years. After the band broke up, and before meeting Tiffany, Dave was forced to undergo a life-saving lobotomy after being brutally bashed in the head with a baseball bat by an irate drug dealer. Dave was left with irreparable brain damage and a burgeoning heroin habit.

By the time they met and fell for each other, both Dave and Tiffany had fallen on hard times—her Broadway dreams were punctured at the point of a hypodermic needle, and he would never be able to perform again. Before long, the Louisiana-born, chestnut-haired waif was selling her body on the seedy streets and back alleys to support both of their bad habits.

Tiffany turned out to be the 17th and final victim of the villainous Joel Rifkin and, if there's any silver lining to be found in her tragic demise, it's that she turned out to be his waterloo. The hulking incel had had his eye on the young sex worker for some time—she stripped at a sleazy nightclub and he liked to watch her dance—and one night, Joel got the better of Tiffany. He strangled her in the backseat of his car and then drove the body back to his mother's home to find a tarp and some rope.

But Joel was careless and didn't dump his trophy right away. (His mom even drove her blue sedan to the store, never noticing there was a dead woman in the trunk!) He eventually stashed the body in a wheelbarrow in the garage, where it festered for three days in the humid summer heat. Finally, the 34-year-old washout was on his way to get rid of the evidence when state troopers noticed his pickup truck didn't have a rear license plate (but it did have a bumper sticker that said, "Sticks and stones may break my bones but whips and chains excite me") and started flashing their lights. Instead of pulling over, the driver led them on a high-speed chase. He didn't get away; after he crashed into a light pole, the cops noticed a rancid smell coming from the camper shell and discovered Tiffany.

The killer then confessed and was later sentenced to 203 years in prison. In an interview for an *A&E* documentary on his crimes, Joel joked about Tiffany's putrid body being "nice and ripe," and chuckled at the memory that his mother had never noticed it was in the trunk of her own car while running her errands. He added that he killed sex workers because he believed nobody cared about them and they'd never be missed.

But Tiffany Bresciani had been missed; her family loved her and worried about her but they couldn't help her. They kept in touch as best they could long-distance, and often mailed care packages to her from Metairie to New York. Dave cared about her too, searching the streets and strip clubs for any sign, until he was finally found by authorities and told that his girlfriend was never coming home.

In an almost unreal twist of fate, just two days after being told Tiffany had been killed by New York's most prolific serial slayer, Dave's mother died in a freak car accident when his dad accidentally ran over her in the family's garage. On July 3, 1993, less than a week after losing his girlfriend and his mom, Dave "Insurgent" Rubenstein ended it all by overdosing on heroin.

When skin-flick superstar Savanna was interviewed by *Adult Video News* (*AVN*) in 1990, she gushed, "I love sex and I love sex with rockers more than anything else!" She wasn't kidding. Before her short stint on this earth was over, the busty, lusty lady had had relationships with Gregg Allman, Billy Idol, Van Halen frontman David Lee Roth, Mr. Big bassist Billy Sheehan, Slash of Guns N' Roses, rapper-turned-actor Mark Wahlberg, and Mötley Crüe's blond bombshell, Vince Neil.

Savannah was born Shannon Michelle Wilsey on October 9, 1970, in Laguna Beach, California, but after her parents divorced, she was raised by her mother, Pamela Longoria, in the Lone Star State. That's where she met Gregg Allman, who was dining out with friends.

The rock & blues pioneer with the soulful voice co-founded The Allman Brothers Band in the year *before* his future paramour was born—but that didn't stop Pamela from pushing her barely 16-year-old daughter to go over and introduce herself to the grown man. It worked and he was smitten. The wild child ditched high school for good to go on the road with Gregg, who'd already been married and divorced a few times (and had a daughter just two years younger than Shannon).

Gregg and Shannon rode his tour bus for months, "watching porn," according to an interview she later gave to *Vivid* magazine, and enjoying each other's company. But her boyfriend was a constantly relapsing substance addict who was experiencing a midlife crisis exacerbated by a career nosedive when his 1988 album, *Just Before the Bullets Fly*, tanked. When his teen tart got pregnant, Gregg paid for the abortion but soon sent her on her way. Feeling "old and ugly," he later said, he found solace in the arms of another woman, Danielle Galliano, whom he married the following year. She was wife number five of seven.

Young Shannon was left to figure out life on her own. She stayed with her dad, Mike Wilsey, and his second family, for a while in L.A., but soon fell in with a degenerate crowd. A natural beauty, she found work as a lingerie model to support herself—and her drug habit. That led to more work, and more pay, posing in the nude. (Fans who bothered to look at her less-lascivious body parts would notice a tattoo spelling GREGG on her ankle.) The cash really started flowing following breast enhancement surgery and this, in turn, led to her starring in hardcore films as the newly-minted "Savannah."

She'd gotten the name, she said, from one of her favorite movies, a PG-rated kiddie flick called *Savannah Smiles*, which is about a little girl who runs away from her neglectful father and joins two adult male criminals on the lam, forming a family of sorts. She also worked under the name "Silver Cane," which was a wicked wink to the heroin needle she craved. Sexy Savannah was a sudden sensation, winning *AVN*'s Best New Starlet Award in 1992, and it seemed as though she was on an unstoppable upward trajectory.

While details are sparse regarding contact with her family during this time, there was a handwritten letter, apparently never sent, to her dad found among Savannah's things following her death. In large, teenage-looking print, it read:

> I will never forgive you. You think God has forgiven you, but if there is a God, he has seen the torture and pain I have been through since I was born and can't possibly forgive you! You will die knowing that your 1st-born child hopes you rot in hell with all the pain I have inside of YOU. DO NOT EVER CONTACT ME AGAIN! I HATE YOU!!

Savannah might as well have been the poster girl for daddy issues. When she was 13, she found out that the man who raised her wasn't her biological father; friends later revealed she'd told them that she was sexually molested by her stepfather when she was little. Her first serious relationship was with a man old enough to be her father and she never bothered with so-called good boys. "I don't seem to go out with really normal people. I'm kind of on the wild side. I don't think I ever went out with anybody with short hair. I like musician types," she said. Savannah was always looking for love in the wrong places, giving herself to guys who didn't care about her. (Comedian Pauly Shore may have been the exception; he was the only ex to pay his respects at her funeral.)

While she was a generous person— Savannah helped pay friends' rent, and she supported the Pediatric AIDS Foundation—she also spent her newfound riches with abandon on parties, houses, sports cars, and drugs. As she grew more dependent on alcohol, cocaine, and eventually heroin, the *Legal Tender* star became unreliable at work, making diva-like demands and not delivering on the money shots—her orgasmic moans now had to be dubbed and added in post-production. Her reputation suffered, not to mention her bank account; she died thousands of dollars in debt to the IRS. She tried going bigger in the breasts but sadly, the surgery was botched, leaving her even worse off.

Like many women who were molested as children, Savannah dabbled in same-sex relationships. Her lover Jeanna Fine was a triple-X performer as well. "We had an ongoing, on-again, off-again, volatile, loving relationship," Jeanna said in an interview after Savanna's headline-grabbing leap from the mortal coil. "At that time, I was having a lot of problems myself. Between [male adult actor] Sikki Nixx and Savannah pushing and pulling, I pretty much at one point ran away from them both. I couldn't take it any longer. But I feel I left her behind when she needed me most. It's very sad."

Savannah dated the famously fickle Vince Neil for a time, who remarked on an episode of *E's True Hollywood Story* that when they met, he "knew she was a porn chick but I didn't know she was *the* porn chick." The pair had met through their shared lover, Jeanna Fine, in 1991. "She was beautiful," said the "Too Fast for Love" singer. "I loved everything about her. She was gorgeous, and she was great in bed; there was nothing she wouldn't try or do." According to Jeanna, Vince strung Savannah along, even going so far as to tell her to start looking for a house for them to live in. He took her on a romantic vacation in Hawaii, then lowered the boom—Savannah never saw it coming and was devastated, according to those in her inner circle. "I think she thought we were boyfriend and girlfriend, and that it was more serious than it really was," Vince remarked. "But I was going through a divorce at the time. We were really more like party buddies."

Twenty-two-year-old Savannah then started what she hoped would be a long-term relationship with Slash but, like Gregg Allman, the two-timer blindsided her by marrying someone else. The blonde beauty took the breakup especially hard and her drug addiction worsened—anything to numb the never-ending pain and chaos.

As a result of her need for narcotics and all-around bad behavior, Vivid Video dropped their once-shining star in 1993, but her manager, Nancy Pera, stayed on. She got her client a cameo in a music video for rappers House of Pain, which Savannah did on Sunday, July 10, 1994. Her next gig would be a lucrative national tour as a pole dancer making special appearances at various gentlemen's clubs. Could this be a turn in the right direction, finally? The burnt-out young woman was grasping at straws, hoping to dig herself from her ever-increasing IRS debt and other financial burdens.

After shooting the music video, Savannah and Jason Fine, who worked as a personal assistant to House of Pain, took off in her white Corvette to celebrate her exotic dance tour, which was set to kick off the next day, Monday. At around 2 a.m., they headed back to her place in Burbank. She took a turn too fast and, less than a block from home, the coffin-shaped car smashed head-on into a fence, crumpling the hood. Savannah and Jason weren't badly hurt, but Savannah did bash her face into the steering wheel. With a broken nose, she'd have to postpone the best chance at getting her debts in order.

She was bereft but didn't show it—she and Jason got the 'Vette to her house and into the garage. Savannah asked Jason to take her Rottweiler, Daisy Mae, for a walk, and while he was at it, would he double-check the damage to her neighbor's fence? Once he was off, she phoned her manager. "Nancy," she said, "I've just had a horrible car accident. I broke my nose. It's bleeding really bad and I've hit my head. You have to take me to the hospital."

Jason was still out with the dog and Nancy was on her way over when Savannah's darkest thoughts compelled her to walk into her bedroom to get the pistol a friend had loaned her for personal protection. Was she thinking back to her traumatic childhood? The string of broken promises from the rock & roll men she'd given herself to and gotten nothing in return? Her ever-increasing debts? That she was only 23 and already washed up in her film career? We'll never know for sure what Savannah was thinking; all we are left with is the fact that after getting the .40 caliber semi-automatic blue-steel Beretta, she walked into her garage, put the muzzle to her temple, and pulled the trigger.

When Nancy found her, she was lying in a pool of blood in the garage, and she was still breathing. The exit wound "looked like she had a big flower on the side of her head," Nancy recalled in an interview. "I said, 'Stay with us, Shannon.' I thought she would make it."

She didn't make it. The grievously injured patient was in a coma and on life support at St. Joseph's Medical Center in Burbank for hours on end when her family decided it was best to pull the plug. They were with her and so was her ex, Pauly Shore, when Shannon Michelle Wilsey died at 1:20 p.m. on July 11, 1994.

Shannon's family blamed the adult film industry; her biological father, Mike, said, "People ask me if pornography is wrong. I say you can judge a tree by its fruit." Paul Fishbein of *AVN* disagreed, saying, "Porn didn't do this." Following her suicide, friend and fellow film actor Bill Margold founded Protecting Adult Welfare, a non-profit organization that provides counseling for performers in need of help and guidance.

Perhaps fittingly, Shannon's first love, Gregg Allman, died in the Georgia city of Savannah. It was much, much later, on May 27, 2017. He'd had a hard life as well—from his father being murdered when he was a toddler, to losing his brother Duane in a motorcycle accident just when their band was taking off, severe substance abuse issues, a string of broken marriages, and two wrongful-death lawsuits brought against him (one from

Shannon's parents, and another from the family of a young camera assistant who was working on uncleared train tracks while an Allman Brothers Band biopic was being filmed; neither action came to fruition). While he should have been old enough and experienced enough to avoid having a relationship with Shannon in the first place, it's clear that Gregg was a damaged soul as well—it's a sad story all around.

Judy Wong was so beloved by Fleetwood Mac that they wrote the song "Jewel-Eyed Judy" for her, and dedicated entire albums to her. She was a tireless assistant and secretary to the band for 18 years; she introduced them to Bob Welch (who was their lead guitarist for a few years), and she ran their Penguin production offices. But, as Fleetwood Mac says, "Players only love you when they're playing," and when Judy was no longer useful, out she went, reportedly without so much as a severance check.

Singer Christine McVie said in an interview, "Judy was Mac's secretary for 18 years, but now we have closed the Mac offices [aka, Penguin] and so Judy became redundant. Because of our solo careers, we all have our own managers, secretaries, and lawyers."

Sometime around April 8, 2005, Judy died alone in her apartment—sick, toothless, and broke, and, according to some accounts, her body lay undiscovered for over a week. Suffering from a heart condition and without insurance or help, the ailing former Fleetwood Mac insider made ends meet by selling her rock memorabilia on eBay.

Ken Caillat, who worked as a producer on Mac's hit album *Rumors*, said in an interview, "There was no responsibility for anybody to take care of anybody else, but they are rich and some of the people like Judy Wong ... she was found in her apartment after being dead for a week. Judy did everything for Christine McVie and the band, and for her not to be given whatever she needed [is reprehensible]."

Although it ended sadly, Judy's life began with promise. The San Francisco-born young lady married Jethro Tull bassist Glenn Cornick in 1970 and that same year, Fleetwood Mac released their ode to her on the album *Kiln House*, featuring Danny Kirwan on vocals and lead guitar. He left the band in 1972, while Judy divorced Glenn and went to work for Fleetwood Mac, becoming a seemingly indispensable fixture in their offices.

Judy was a student of UC Berkley in the '60s, and she went on to own and operate Passionflower, a fashion boutique in the North Beach area of San Francisco; Janis Joplin was a customer who became a friend. While running the shop, she also became friends with British fashion models Jenny and Patti Boyd (rock & roll muses in their own rights) and shared a house with them in the city before marrying Glenn. Her friends and associates included Eric Burdon, Paul McCartney, and The Kinks.

While she did a myriad of things for Fleetwood Mac, Judy was able to channel her former fashionista for them in 1987 with their Tango in the Night Tour merch, including designing a special edition tee-shirt that was sold to fans.

A few years later, thanks to Fleetwood Mac's famous feuding, everything fell apart and Judy was on her own. Details on the rest of her life are vague, but after the heart attack victim was found dead at the age of 61, a representative from the band posted the following statement on a Fleetwood Mac fan site:

> We wanted to confirm that longtime friend and associate of the band, Judy Wong, passed away last week. She'd had heart problems for years, and had a massive heart attack 10 years ago, and was having some health issues as of late. She was hospitalized but checked herself out against doctor's advice, and unfortunately died at home. Judy was responsible for introducing Bob Welch to Fleetwood Mac, and worked for them 'behind the scenes' for many years, in their offices and on their tour books. Bob Welch says Mick Fleetwood is in the process of trying to get a memorial together for her, as she really had no family.

We here at the Penguin [Fleetwood Mac's nickname, after their mascot] would like to say how sorry we are to hear of her passing, and we thank her for her role in looking after the people in the band we all love so much. Our condolences to all who knew and loved her; she will certainly be missed.

A member of Judy's family responded, saying (in part):

Judy Wong does indeed have a family. I am her cousin, Candy Jung, and I live in Sacramento. We were first cousins and grew up together. Her brother, Corby, also lives in Sacramento, and we were notified by the Coroner's office on Saturday of her death. We are contacting the Coroner's office on Monday to bring Judy home if we can. She also leaves several surviving cousins and an aunt. I am writing this to correct the assumption that she was without family.

Her association with Fleetwood Mac was one of the happiest and most fulfilling periods in her life, both professionally and personally. Judy was kind, spiritual, and an exceptionally loyal friend. Our family is grateful for your poster in Second Hand News in bringing public attention and recognition to someone we greatly loved and treasured. —Candy Jung

Others jumped in to confirm that Mick Fleetwood had been supportive of his old friend and employee over the years since her dismissal, having stepped in to pay her rent on more than one occasion. What's more, he was the only member of her Fleetwood Mac family to attend and speak at her memorial, which was held on May 12, 2005, at the Hollywood Forever Cemetery.

Grunge has spawned its share of sadness and, while only a flash in the proverbial pan in the 1990s, its legacy and legends have endured. Of all the Seattle bands, Alice in Chains shone with a blush of glam touched with metal and a sense of style. They came together in 1987—with Jerry Cantrell on guitar, drummer Sean Kinney, bassist Mike Starr, and vocalist Layne Staley—and burst onto the scene with their first album, *Facelift*.

Due in no small part to Layne's powerful, agile voice, the band soared into star territory with their sophomore album, *Dirt*. He achieved a unique effect by layering his vocals onto two or three vocal tracks in multiple intervals and took those a step further by creating complementary harmonies by singing with Jerry, blending their distinctive voices. Layne took everything to the limit—whether it was love, drugs, money, or everything else all at once, no one could say he did things without gusto.

Before finding fame, the 19-year-old singer met a vivacious, part-Cherokee brunette, Demri Lara Parrott, and fell for her immediately. She was 17 but her parents approved of the relationship and accepted Layne as one of their own. Like any young couple, the pair had their growing pains but those ups and downs were complicated by fame and addiction.

Layne and Demri started taking heroin at about the same time and they both got hopelessly hooked on the insidious opiate. They split up and each circled their own drain, yet their love for one another remained; she visited him in rehab, and he went to her bedside at the hospital. Over and over, they tried and failed to get better; better at love, better at life... but it never happened.

Following "cotton fever"—which is caused by bacteria from reused cotton to wipe hypodermic needles—Demri's heart was so compromised by 1994 that it had to be helped along with a pacemaker. That was also the year that Nirvana's Kurt Cobain, another heroin addict, committed suicide by shotgun. Layne was shaken into sobriety but soon relapsed.

Meanwhile, Demri was released from the hospital but no matter how many wake-up calls she got, she was steadfast on her path to self-destruction. The once-vital aspiring model was reduced to trading sex for drugs; she was arrested for petty theft and prostitution and ended up homeless, sometimes sofa-surfing. She carried her few worldly possessions in a suitcase and hitchhiked to get from place to place because she couldn't even afford bus fare.

Described as a "sweet girl," she had many friends, including Jane's Addiction guitarist Dave Navarro, who went to visit her in rehab and at the hospital. Alice in Chains' manager Susan Silver also kept tabs on Demri, and as ever, so did Layne Staley.

Demri's mother, Kathleen Austin, recalled, "Demri was sick and dying for those last two and a half years. Layne would come and stay with her in the hospital at night." Kathleen worked at Harborview Medical Center, where Demri was a patient, and would let the "No Excuses" singer into a side door of the building with her pass. He would spend the night, then slip away in the predawn hours.

Demri Lara Parrott died on October 29, 1996, after passing out in a friend's car. The coroner concluded that she died of acute intoxication caused by the combined effects of opiate, meprobamate, and butalbital. She was only 27 years old.

According to some friends, Layne was placed on a 24-hour suicide watch after he found out that Demri was gone forever. He then fell into a deep depression and could barely function. In an interview with *Rolling Stone*, he said, "Drugs worked for me for years, and now they're turning against me, now I'm walking through hell, and this sucks. I didn't want my fans to think that heroin was cool. But then I've had fans come up to me and give me the thumbs up, telling me they're high. That's exactly what I didn't want to happen."

After a two-year break, the members of Alice in Chains came together to record songs for what would become their final album, *Music Bank* (1999). Layne Staley wrote a song in memory of his first love, calling it "Died." "My heart is tired of beating slow/It's been depleting since you died/Died..."

The Austin Chronicle gave the boxed set a glowing review: "*Music Bank* is an exceptional collection that bears the unmistakable sentiment of an epitaph. As one of the best bands of the '90s, Alice in Chains are the ultimate Seattle band, shrugging off the hipper trappings of punk for pure love of a minor chord. They were metalheads who rode the grunge wave via *MTV* and relentless fan support, never as self-conscious as Nirvana nor as faux eccentric as Pearl Jam, and much darker than the bluesy Soundgarden. They released a string of excellent radio hits and toured until they couldn't."

The hard-rocking, remorseful "Died" turned out to be the last song recorded, and hence, it was Alice in Chains' final song with Layne Staley before he himself died two years later.

Layne's death came following the amputation of an arm turned gangrenous from constant dirty-needle jabs and extended periods of self-imposed hibernation in his Seattle apartment. Alice in Chains' drummer, Sean Kinney, recalled, "It got to a point where he'd kept himself so locked up, both physically and emotionally. I kept trying to make contact. Three times a week, like clockwork, I'd call him, but he'd never answer. Every time I was in the area, I was up in front of his place yelling for him. Even if you could get into his building, he wasn't going to open the door. You'd phone, and he wouldn't answer. You couldn't just kick the door in and grab him, though there were so many times I thought about doing that. But if someone won't help themselves, what, really, can anyone else do?"

On April 19, 2002, police were called and visited the "Rain When I Die" singer's apartment with his mother, Nancy McCallum, where they found his decomposed body. The autopsy revealed that the skeletal 34-year-old Layne Staley had been dead for about two weeks and the cause was a self-administered speedball.

Fans are the furthest on the fringes of those boulevards of broken dreams, but their suffering is no less acute—when Kurt Cobain pulled the trigger on himself, it was a shot heard around the world, sending shockwaves as far as the crossroads of the Balkans, Caucasus, Middle East, and eastern Mediterranean. According to a short news blip in *Rolling Stone*, "In southern Turkey, a 16-year-old fan of Cobain's locked herself in her room, cranked Nirvana music, and shot herself in the head."

Following the public vigil near Seattle's Space Needle on April 10, 1994, some of the mourners were so overwrought, they went into hysterics. The Seattle Crisis Clinic took roughly 300 calls that day—a hundred more than usual, according to Dr. Christos Dagadakis, director of emergency psychiatry at Harborview Medical Center. One fan, 28-year-old Daniel Kaspar, shot himself in the head upon returning home from the wake, dying immediately.

A certain *60 Minutes* curmudgeonly commentator showed zero empathy for Kurt's heartbroken fans during his segment the following Sunday night. "What would all these young people be doing if they had real problems like a Depression, World War II, or Vietnam?" the elderly Andy Rooney groused, scowling while knitting his prodigious bushy white brows. "No one's art is better than the person who creates it. If Kurt Cobain applied the same brain to his music that he applied to his drug-infested life, it's reasonable to think that his music may not have made much sense either." (Smells like senior spirit; or, to quote the man himself: "Bah!")

CHAPTER 13: RUNNING ON EMPTY

"I can't die now—I'm booked!"—George Burns

Generally speaking, a young person's body can take a lot of abuse. But with each passing year, ingesting those blizzards of cocaine, greenhouses of weed, and vats of alcohol becomes akin to mainlining napalm. After a certain age, you just can't party like you used to and even a small indulgence can cause your long-suffering organs to say sayonara.

Steven Hyden, author of *Twilight of the Gods: A Journey to the End of Classic Rock*, says that in our current "decadence-adverse" times, he's found many people think that if a rock star used drugs and alcohol in their lifetime, they will be dissed in death because it's "their fault" they died. "This very non-classic rock idea has taken hold in these very non-classic rock times. A core tenet of classic rock mythology is that using drugs and alcohol forges a pathway to understanding what it means to be alive, even if it kills you. Maybe *especially* if it kills you."

Most rockers have hopped on-and-off the sobriety train at least a few times in their lives but when the Stones' second-lead guitarist Ronnie Wood decided to try playing straight in

2005, he was ridiculed by the band's numero-uno strings man, Keith Richards. Ronnie recalled the incident in an interview with *Mojo*. "I do remember going on stage clean for the first time, it was at this club in Canada for the start of a tour in August." He was terrified, shaking like a leaf because apparently, he'd never been onstage without a shot of liquid courage. Mick Jagger patted him on the back with words of encouragement but, "Keith's going, 'Rehab's for quitters!' Trying to make out I was the weakling."

Apparently, even Keef, who is 79 years old as of this writing, decided to curtail his legendary habits a few years back. Not that he said as much; Ronnie "outed" him to the press. While not exactly saying, "I told you so!" he did reveal that his bandmate was "done and dusted" with drinking and smoking... but Keith did admit to having "the occasional glass of wine. And beer."

It is something of a miracle that the "Sway" guitarist is still alive—and thriving. Keith killed it (and not himself) on The Stones Sixty 2022 Tour but back in the early days when he was famously hooked on heroin there were several occasions in which he seemed done for.

Eagles guitarist Don Felder remembered the exciting moment when he thought he'd get to meet the legend. In his autobiography, *Heaven and Hell*, Don talked about mega tours in the '70s that featured his band, Tina Turner, and the Stones.

"The Stones were pretty wild boys, especially Keith Richards, who played real dirty, neanderthal guitar and was a walking human chemistry set. I remember arriving at our first hotel in Kansas City, a Holiday Inn or a Marriott, and being taken to meet the boys," by the tour manager. When he was escorted into Keith's suite, a loud party was going on and Don saw piles of heroin, Jack Daniels bottles, beer bottles, and clothes strewn about. But he didn't see Keith. "Maybe he's in the bedroom," said the manager, looking around. "Just then, out of the corner of my eye," Don wrote, "I saw a man's foot sticking out of the open bathroom door. 'Jesus!' I said. I ran around to find what nobody wants to discover—Keith Richards doing a very good impersonation of a corpse. His skin was gray, and he was completely motionless, face-down on the bathroom floor. I thought he was dead. Barely batting an eye, the road manager called the tour doctors."

Don said he watched the news that night for a report on the death of the Rolling Stone but there was none. "The following evening, at the Kansas City Stadium, a very much alive Keith Richards, looking none the worse for his brush with death, pranced around the stage cranking out his raunchy rock & roll guitar for all he was worth. Now that's what I call stamina."

The Eagles themselves all had habits in the snorty '70s but they stuck with cocaine, which was referred to in euphemisms like California cornflakes, the devil's dandruff, booger sugar, or hitch up the reindeer. Not that cocaine was much healthier but heroin was considered too scary for most, even back in those carefree days.

Jerry Lee Lewis was one of the hardest-living, long-lived rock & rollers of all-time. He breathed his last on October 28, 2022, at the age of 87 but he had plenty of close calls before that, including drunken car wrecks, arrests, and a whole lot of hell-raising. While no specific cause of death was announced, Jerry Lee Lewis' wild lifestyle took its toll but his sheer force of will allowed him to stick around on "borrowed time" (to quote a John Lennon song) for decades longer than expected.

Raised in the Bible belt, he expressed concern about going downstairs after he died but not enough to bother changing his ways. "Look, we've only got one life to live," he said in 1977. "We don't have the promise of the next breath. I know what I am. I'm a rompin', stompin', piano-playin' sonofabitch. A mean sonofabitch. But a *great* sonofabitch. A good person. Never hurt nobody unless they got in my way. I got a mean streak.... I gotta lay it open sometimes."

In 1981, the "Whole Lotta Shakin' Goin' On" pianist was admitted to a Memphis, Tennessee, hospital in sorry shape—it was the culmination of decades of nonstop drinking and drugging. He was there for three months. In 1984, doctors diagnosed him with perforated ulcers and had no choice but to cut away a third of his stomach;

he was given a 50/50 chance of survival. But survive he did. (The same can't be said of some of his wives. There were seven in all but it wasn't a very lucky number; wives four and five died under iffy circumstances—but the man nicknamed "The Killer" for his prowess on the piano, was never so much as questioned by police in either case.)

Maybe the writing was always on the wall; when he was 14, the boogie-woogie singer got a taste of performing before a live audience with a cover of Stick McGhee's "Drinkin' Wine Spo-Dee-O-Dee." His life was on a fast track from there on, and despite his attitude, alcoholism, and addictions, Jerry Lee outlived all his fellow rock & roll pioneers.

Most notably, he outlasted his biggest rival (and frenemy) Elvis Presley, who died at the age of 42 in 1977, following extreme drug and alcohol abuse exacerbated by overeating and an awful diet. When asked for his take on The King's demise, Jerry Lee was dismissive, telling a reporter he was "glad" to hear the news. "Just another one outa the way. I mean, Elvis this, Elvis that."

Despite his self-abuse, Elvis' death might be attributed to medical malpractice. After all, Dr. George C. Nichopoulos (aka, "Dr. Nick") admitted to the Tennessee Board of Health that he had knowingly prescribed addictive medications and slyly gave the "Hound Dog" singer useless sugar pills for other conditions. Following Elvis' death, the doctor-feelgood was questioned and admitted to writing prescriptions for more than 10,000 doses of opiates, amphetamines, barbiturates, tranquilizers, hormones, and laxatives for his most famous patient between January and August of 1977. Shockingly, he was still allowed to practice medicine. In 1980, the fast and loose physician was accused of getting Jerry Lee Lewis hooked on prescription drugs but... you guessed it: he was acquitted of all charges. Fifteen years later, Dr. Nick's medical license was *finally* permanently suspended. He himself lived a long life, passing away peacefully at the age of 88.

Another rock & roll pioneer who lived on borrowed time was Ike Turner. Born in 1931 in Clarksdale, Mississippi, he grew up poor and was subjected to horrible abuses as a child—not only at the hands of violent, alcoholic family members but two female neighbors that molested him.

Music was Ike's only salvation—playing the piano and guitar, he formed a working band when he was a teenager. His 1951 single "Rocket 88" is thought by some historians to be the *first* rock & roll song. Not only did Little Richard borrow the piano intro for his own hit "Good Golly, Miss Molly," but "Rocket 88" was inducted into three halls of fame: Blues, GRAMMY, and Rock & Roll, respectively.

Ike found his greatest renown through his protégé and wife, Tina Turner. Songs like "River Deep, Mountain High," and their cover of

Creedence Clearwater Revival's "Proud Mary" catapulted the team into fame's peak zeniths... but Ike's vicious temper and his serious dependence on paranoia-producing cocaine ultimately brought them down.

While Tina rose to even greater fame, Ike's star faded with every passing year and each line that went up his nose. The "Poor Fool" songwriter's addiction to the intoxicant exhausted his finances and led to several stints behind bars; he did not attend his own 1991 Rock & Roll Hall of Fame induction because he was serving time. He did make a brief comeback in 2001, winning a GRAMMY for his album *Here and Now*, but just a few years later he relapsed and never got better.

Ike claimed to have been married 14 times, but only five can be proven. His last wife, a young Tina look-and-soundalike named Audrey Madison, was with the 76-year-old R&B legend when he died from a cocaine overdose in his rented San Marcos, California, home on December 12, 2007.

Jerome "Jerry" Garcia was the anti-Ike Turner—he was an easygoing, well-liked, stoner hippie who found immortality through his music with The Grateful Dead. The bearded, buddha-like guitarist only lived until the age of 53, but he packed more living—and longer jam sessions—into that relatively short time than many of his peers.

The Dead epitomized the San Francisco psychedelic rock scene and the Summer of Love—they performed at the Monterey Pop Festival in 1967 and at Woodstock in 1969—but their popularity did "Not Fade Away." Over the years, legions of fans affectionately known as Deadheads followed their favorite band no matter where their tours took them, then those fans' kids took up the torch. During the final decade of Jerry's freewheeling life, following his recovery from grave heroin withdrawls and a five-day diabetic coma in 1986, the Dead played some 150 gigs a year, frequently to sold-out college-age audiences clad in tie-dyed tees.

Jerry Garcia was born August 1, 1942, in San Francisco, and had a few juvenile delinquent brushes with the law before the Dead started to get noticed as the house band at Ken Kesey's famous Acid Tests, while Jerry earned the nickname "Captain Trips" by taking tons of LSD. Throughout his life, the "Friend of the Devil" guitarist consumed copious amounts of cocaine, heroin, Seconal, opium, and marijuana.

Surprisingly, he wasn't much of a drinker—unless you count the old "electric Kool-Aid"—but his bandmates more than made up for it with their own alcoholism issues. Twenty-seven-year-old Ron "Pigpen" McKernan, the band's organist and singer, was found dead in his apartment on March 8, 1973, having succumbed to cirrhosis of the liver. The group's keyboardist hired in 1979, Brent Mydland, 37, was also no stranger to the bottle but he died of a cocaine overdose on July 26, 1990.

When Dead contemporary and San Francisco scenester Grace Slick of Jefferson Airplane released her memoir, Somebody to Love? she wrote about the prevalent use of heroin in the music business, saying, "I was interested in drugs as a means to enjoy or alter the waking state. I simply couldn't figure out why anyone would take the trouble to get the money, get the dealer, get all the paraphernalia, get sick, go into a coma—and then consider it an experience they'd want to repeat."

Jerry Garcia's own "Long Strange Trip" came to an end on August 9, 1995, when he died of a heart attack while checked into a residential drug treatment facility in Forest Knolls, California. Just before dawn, a counselor peeked into his room and saw the singer lying on top of his bed in sweatpants and a tee-shirt, "cuddling an apple like it was a baby, with a smile on his face."

The furry frontman's death came a month after yet another successful Grateful Dead tour and following lifelong on-and-off dalliances with two women, Merry Prankster Carolyn Adams (better-known as "Mountain Girl"), and filmmaker Deborah Koons. (He was married to a couple of others as well, and had four daughters.) While Jerry Garcia didn't live all that long, he did live his life to the fullest.

Bob Dylan, who was a longtime friend, spoke at the memorial service: "There's no way to measure his greatness or magnitude as a person or as a player. I don't think eulogizing will do him justice. He was that great—much more than a superb musician with an uncanny ear and dexterity. He is the very spirit personified of whatever is muddy river country at its core and screams up into the spheres. He really had no equal."

John Entwistle, the thunderous bassist of The Who, died a true rockstar's death—in a Las Vegas hotel room with hookers and blow. (All right; it was actually just one stripper and a few lines. Must've been a slow night.)

"The Ox" (as he was called because of his immobile stance onstage) had been with the "My Generation" band from the start, which formed in London in 1964 with singer Roger Daltrey, guitarist Pete Townshend, and drummer Keith Moon (who died of a drug overdose in 1978). They were still toward the top of their game and the 57-year-old bass man showed no signs of slowing down—though it may have been hard to tell with him. Following his death, Entwistle's only son, Christopher, told the inquest his father had been in high spirits and seemed healthy, with no symptoms of chest pain. While he seemed serene and steady, the old saying about it being the "quiet ones you have to watch out for" proved true in John's case.

The Who was about to kick off a big U.S. extravaganza and they were living it up in the bar of their hotel, the Hard Rock. After a final toast to the tour with his band brothers, John retired to the boudoir of Suite #658 with exotic dancer and hard-partying groupie Alycen Rowse at about 3 a.m.

Alycen, who was 32 at the time, shook her stuff under the stage name Sianna at the Deja Vu nude revue in Las Vegas. The night of June 27, 2002, wasn't the first time the pair had hooked up; a self-proclaimed "Who groupie," the bouncy brunette told authorities that she looked forward to being with the "Bargain" bassist whenever he was in town.

A report from the Clark County coroner's office in Nevada stated that Alycen heard John snoring during the night and he had rolled over at 6 a.m. But when she got up about four hours later, her bed buddy was "unresponsive and cold to the touch." She tried to resuscitate him and called paramedics but they were not able to revive him either. The medical examiner determined that his death had been due to a heart attack induced by cocaine; he already had severe heart disease and usually smoked a pack of cigarettes per day, so he was pushing his luck that night.

Shortly after the autopsy, the body was repatriated and buried in the village church in Stow-on-the-Wold, Gloucestershire. The Who canceled the opening night of their tour but quickly brought in a replacement: session player Pino Palladino. The first show kicked off at the Hollywood Bowl on July 1. "Tonight, we play for John Entwistle," Roger told the crowd. "He was the true spirit of rock & roll, and he lives on in all the music we play."

Meanwhile, Alycen Rowse told the press that she had no regrets about being with John Entwistle. "I don't want this to sound egotistical," she said, "but he couldn't have gone [died] with a better woman, because I know how to keep the privacy." Whatever that means— after all, the seductress sold her story to the tabloids just a few months later, then she self-published a kiss-and-tell book, *We've Got Tonight: The Life and Times of Notorious Groupie, Alycen Rowse* (2014).

John Entwistle's romantic entanglements didn't end with his death, believe it or not. Not only was he still married to stylist Maxine Harlow at the time of his death, but the bass-playing bad-boy also had a long-term girlfriend, Lisa Pritchett-Johnson, to whom he left millions in his will. Sometime after John's burial, Lisa ran off with the married vicar, Colin Wilson, who'd officiated at the funeral. The randy reverend resigned and apologized to his parishioners for "going off the rails." Sadly, Lisa went off the rails, too. Or *on* them, depending on how dark your sense of irony is—the 43-year-old died three years later due to an overdose of cocaine aggravated by heart disease.

The founding bassist and songwriter for the legendary New York punk band The Ramones, Douglas Glenn Colvin (Dee Dee Ramone), died June 5, 2002, of a heroin overdose at the age of

50. Punk pundit Legs MacNeil described him thusly: "Dee Dee was the archetypical fuck-up whose life was a living disaster. He was a male prostitute, a would-be mugger, a heroin dealer, an accomplice to armed robbery, and a genius poet who was headed for prison or an early grave—but was side-tracked by rock & roll." And film director Joe Dante, who wrote the foreword to Dee Dee's 2001 novel, *Chelsea Horror Hotel*, said the author was a "punk-rock Lovecraft."

The Ramones had a fairytale beginning and career—guitarist John William Cummings (Johnny Ramone) and Dee Dee met in NYC, and one day, fed up with their day jobs, they both decided to cash their paychecks and go all-in on guitars; Johnny got a Mosrite, and Dee Dee bought a Danelectro. The Ramones—Dee Dee came up with the name after learning that Paul McCartney often used the alias "Paul Ramon" when he checked into hotels—debuted live on March 30, 1974, and soon became an in-demand club act.

"Using just three and four chords, The Ramones mixed their love for bubblegum girl pop with the hard rock of the Who and the MC5 and the proto-punk of The Stooges, then put the blender on full-speed, creating a wall of primal, melodic, abrasive and bouncy sound that was both visceral and infectious," wrote Jon Weiderhorn in a *Loudwire* retrospective. "The Ramones quickly became leaders of the New

York punk-rock scene and in 1976 released their seminal self-titled debut."

The "I Wanna Be Sedated" songwriter was found unconscious on the couch by his wife, Barbara. He died in their L.A. apartment surrounded by drug paraphernalia, including a used syringe. It was supposed that Dee Dee's body just couldn't take it anymore and he died while doing something he'd gotten away with for most of his five decades.

Danny Joe Brown, the long-haired, hell-raising lead singer of the hard-driving Southern rock band Molly Hatchet, was literally "Flirtin' With Disaster" every time he drank or took drugs—he'd lived with diabetes his entire adult life, and he had Hepatitis-C as well as failing kidneys when he died at the age of 53.

The energetic, Florida-born vocalist with a deep voice and distinctive raspy growl, joined Molly Hatchet—named after a murderous historical figure—in 1975 and was the frontman for the band's self-titled first album, released in 1978, and its second the following year, *Flirtin' With Disaster*, which sold more than two million and spawned another hit, "Whiskey Man," also penned by Brown.

Danny had his ups and downs over the next few years, in and out of Molly Hatchet but sadly, the singer was forced to retire from the music business after he suffered a massive stroke in 1998. He passed away on March 10, 2005, less than an hour after returning to his home after a month-long hospitalization. He was survived by his wife of 20 years, Crystle, their children, and children from his first marriage.

Kevin DuBrow, Quiet Riot's full-blast glam metal frontman, was 52 years old when he died on November 19, 2007, at his home in Las Vegas. The Hollywood-born musician rose to fame in the 1980s with the band, whose early members included Randy Rhoads on guitar and Kelly Garni on bass (with Rudy Sarzo later stepping into the four-string spot), and was known for his gravelly voice, curly hair, flamboyant antics, suspenders, and hats. Sometimes during concerts, he dressed up in a straitjacket and metal face mask to appear as Quiet Riot's mascot, which graced the covers of almost all the group's albums.

As Quiet Riot mixed up their membership over the years, the "Cum On, Feel the Noize" singer was the persistent driving force, whose "decibel-tolerant fans" supported him through his ups and downs. Sadly, there were a lot of downs as Kevin's substance abuse became the stuff of legend—making some of Quiet Riot's album titles *Metal Health* (1983), *Condition Critical* (1984), and *Rehab* (1986) ring all too true.

Kevin never married, nor had children; he died alone in his bed and no one raised an alarm bell until almost a week had passed. When his former band brother, Kelly Garni, who also lived in Las Vegas, was asked to check on him, it was far too late.

"The last time I saw him was on our mutually shared birthday, October 29, he gave me a big hug and a really great present," Kelly said in a statement. "The best present, though, was the hug."

Poet, songwriter, author, and provocateur Jim Carroll was something of a Jurassic punk when he died at the age of 60 on September 11, 2009, in Manhattan; many of his contemporaries had perished decades before. Perhaps best-known for his 1978 memoir *The Basketball Diaries*, which detailed how he got hooked on heroin when he was just 13 years old, Jim also fronted a critically-acclaimed self-titled band. His most enduring hit, "People Who Died," is an upbeat tune that belies its tragic lyrics.

Jim Carroll was admired by artists with street cred like Patti Smith, who recalled, "I met him in 1970, and already he was pretty much universally recognized as the best poet of his generation. The work was sophisticated and elegant; he had beauty." The punk poets were an item, for a while. Other friends and admirers included Keith Richards and Allen Ginsberg.

While he lived fast, he didn't die young. According to Rosemary Carroll, his former wife who remained a close friend, Jim Carroll's trademark flaming red locks had thinned and gone gray, so he hid them under a wool beanie, and he concealed his skeletal face with a bushy white beard, making him unrecognizable to all but those who knew him well. His once-lithe, six-foot-three basketball player's body was weakened by pneumonia and hepatitis-C, preventing him from leaving his apartment for days or even weeks at a time. "Jim would often sit home with these heavy curtains drawn shut," said Martin Heinz, a friend and one of the few to be among the last in his inner circle. Although he'd been sober since the '70s, Jim did still venture out whenever possible to attend local Narcotics Anonymous meetings.

While he'd lived many lives, it seemed his number was finally up on the chilly fall day that marked the eighth anniversary of the Twin Towers tragedy. "Jim was really in love with the concept of his own phoenix-like rise, which had happened repeatedly in his life," Rosemary told the *New York Times*, "bottoming out, then transcending his negative circumstances with an undeniably brilliant work of art."

He was working on a novel when he died but other than royalty checks, the former rock star had little income and was forced to move back to the rough neighborhood in which he'd been brought up—in fact, he was living in the same building (585 Isham Street in Inwood).

An email Jim sent to his friend Martin is particularly telling. "My self-sabotaging tendencies in all aspects of my life, along with the validation needs you referenced, go without saying. There are deep seeded reasons for both, but the latter is also an outcome of the way you are spoiled and coddled by managers, women and media et al when you are on top, and the quickness with which everyone scatters when you recede a moment."

Jim Carroll died alone, just like the hero of the novel he'd been working on. *The Petting Zoo* was released in 2010. It ends, as you might have guessed, poetically.

Finally, a last sigh of consciousness rocked him gently on the deck of an old schooner ship. Billy's body, dark blue like the storm clouds preceding the storm, shuttered and his eyes closed dull and loosely. Sensing young Wolfram had given up the ghost, the raven glided back down aside the dead artist, whispering a last demand.

"It's time your eyes remain shut, Billy Wolfram. Now is the time, so get on with it. Take that single step and fly."

And the beat went on.

Mike Starr (April 4, 1966 – March 8, 2011) was the original bassist for Alice in Chains when they formed in 1987 until he left the band in 1993. Eighteen years later he left this world altogether, following an overdose. Even though he was only 44, it's a wonder he lasted as long as he did; in a band of drug addicts, Mike was fired due to his rampant addictions. Layne Staley saved his life when Alice in Chains was on tour in January 1993 with Nirvana in Brazil. According to the "Man in a Box" bassist, both Layne and Kurt Cobain gave him shots of heroin in his hotel room. Right after the second fix, Mike saw stars and passed out. Layne revived him by giving him CPR; just two months later, he was out of the band.

Mike meandered personally and professionally for years, occasionally surfacing for stints on TV's *Celebrity Rehab with Dr. Drew* and *Sober House* between arrests and the occasional new music release. Although he did survive Layne Staley by nine years, the bassist's body finally gave out in Salt Lake City, on March 8, 2011. Mike Starr overdosed on prescription medication while at his home, which he shared with fellow Days of the New bandmates, Spencer Roddan and Travis Meeks.

Most ironic song title: "We Die Young," Alice in Chains.

Jani Lane (born John Kennedy Oswald; February 1, 1964 – August 11, 2011) had the face, the voice, and the vibe you couldn't miss if you were watching MTV any day of the week in the early '90s. Warrant's song "Cherry Pie" is a sweet, tart, upbeat hair-metal ditty that goes tongue-in-cheek with the iconic video featuring blonde-haired, blue-eyed *vixen du jour* Bobbie Brown dancing around with blond-haired, green-eyed Jani. (The pair were such a perfectly matching set, they even got married—then had a daughter, and divorced, in the span of two years.) While Jani expressed appreciation for "Cherry Pie" he also blames it—and the advent of grunge—for the demise of his career. He wanted to be taken seriously as a songwriter, but being "the Cherry Pie guy" was his claim to fame.

Jani left Warrant in the mid-'90s and, following a few DUI warrants, two more marriages, several songs, and half-finished tours, the "Heaven" singer was at the end of his tether. On August 10, 2011, the once-bestselling artist checked himself into a Comfort Inn in Woodland Hills, California, locked the door, and proceeded to pop pills and guzzle straight vodka. The 47-year-old was found dead the next day, sans I.D. or money—all he had was a note, not written by him, tucked inside his jeans pocket which stated, "I am Jani Lane" along with a phone number. While that sounds like the start of a murder mystery, it's not—an unidentified friend of the rocker rented the room (because he had lost his license due to DUIs) and left the note, fearing the worst. Jani's family later expressed anger and disappointment that the person had left the troubled 47-year-old on his own.

<u>Most ironic song title</u>: "The Bitter Pill," Warrant.

Michael "Mikey" Welsh (April 20, 1971 – October 8, 2011) got famous as a replacement bassist for the pop-punk geek-rock band, Weezer, but after a mental breakdown, and later reportedly attempting suicide, he parted ways with the band after a few years. In a 2007 interview, Mikey admitted, "Basically, a lifetime of doing drugs and being undiagnosed as having bipolar disorder, post-traumatic stress disorder, and borderline personality disorder finally caught up with me when I was 30 years old." Mikey recounted a particularly scary overdose when his "heart stopped beating."

As the years went on, he seemed content and was making strides as an experimental painter. While his online persona was mostly upbeat, Mikey did use social media to predict his own death with a tweet posted on September 26, 2011, saying, "Dreamt I died in Chicago next weekend (heart attack in my sleep). Need to write my will today." (Shortly after, he corrected the date of his impending demise to "the weekend after next.") Mikey had expressed excitement about seeing the upcoming Weezer show in Chicago and catching up with his former bandmates. "So I'm going on my first vacation in quite a long time... very stoked," he wrote one week before his death on his public Facebook. As scheduled, Mikey flew from Vermont to Illinois for the RIOTfest concert but he never made it to the venue.

After failing to check out at 1 p.m. on October 8, 2011, and not answering his phone, a Raffaello Hotel staff member went to the room. The 40-year-old "Hash Pipe" bassist didn't respond to the knocking, so they opened the door, only to find it blocked by his body inside. Prescription pills and a white powder thought to be heroin tucked into a zip-lock baggie were found but toxicology reports came back as "inconclusive."

Most ironic song title: "Vacation," Weezer.

David Murray Brockie (August 30, 1963 – March 23, 2014) was the founder, front-monster, and creative force behind GWAR, a punk and metal-infused shock-rock band formed by a group of misfit artists in Richmond, Virginia in 1984. Dave performed as Oderus Urungus, an intergalactic Scumdog who was banished to Antarctica and forced to perform onstage for lowly humans. One of Oderus' sickest and most beloved stunts involved dousing the adoring audience in jets of jizz that he shot from the "Cuttlefish of Cthulu" fastened between his legs. One of their long-form videos, "Phallus in Wonderland," celebrated the absurdity and was nominated for a GRAMMY. Stacey Anderson of the *New York Times* described the group as "less a band of blood-spewing, priapic demon beasts than a darkly hilarious spoof on death metal—though they are certainly a band of blood-spewing, priapic demon beasts."

Despite the accolades and a loyal following, they were never taken seriously and the gig wasn't exactly a cash cow—low brow and low budget, it wasn't an easy existence to maintain and as a result, there were many, many personnel changes over the years—but Dave stayed the course despite his ups and downs with drugs.

When Dave's turn came to leave the band, he was 50 years old. The once-outrageous performer was found sitting upright in a chair at home by a bandmate, the victim of an accidental and fatal heroin overdose. Lamb of God frontman Randy Blythe, a friend and colleague whose band also came from Richmond, wrote on social media, "Dave TRULY WAS ONE-OF-A-KIND. I can't think of ANYONE even remotely like him," Blythe said. "My band learned how to become a real touring band from GWAR. They gave us our first shot at this thing. I learned many things from Dave, many of which I am eternally grateful for, and some of which I am deeply ashamed of."

Most ironic song title: "The Road Behind," GWAR.

Jimmy "Jimi" Wayne Jamison (August 23, 1951 – August 31, 2014) who was dubbed "The Voice" by legendary DJ Casey Kasem, joined the radio-friendly pop-rock band Survivor post-"Eye of the Tiger" success (that hit was sung by Dave Bickler). Jimi made his debut on their 1984 album *Vital Signs* and while he enjoyed success with them, he left seven years later to go solo. The Memphis-born belter also sang backup for ZZ Top, Joe Walsh, and was invited to join Deep Purple following singer Ian Gillian's departure. As the group's guitarist, Jim Peterik, said, "Very few bands can survive a lead singer transplant [but] Jimi had the most magical voice I'd ever heard."

The year 2000 would see him get back on tour with Survivor, plus other comings and goings, and the night before he died, Jimi, who was a generous philanthropist, performed at a benefit for charity backed by his Survivor brethren.

The rocker expired at home, just a few days after his 63rd birthday, due in part to the effects of his lifestyle. According to the coroner's report, Jimi's passing was partly the result of substance abuse. Although he suffered from 90% blockage in his coronary arteries, he experienced a "hemorrhagic stroke of the brain with acute methamphetamine intoxication contributing." But "Because meth was determined to be a contributor, and the circumstances leading up to the death were not suspicious, the coroner ruled Jamison's death as an accident."

<u>Most ironic song titles</u>: "High on You," Survivor, and "I'm Always Here," *Baywatch* TV theme.

Wayne Richard Wells (November 4, 1965 – November 1, 2014), aka **Wayne Static**, was the lead vocalist, guitarist, keyboardist, and primary lyricist for the industrial nu-metal band, Static-X. The brilliant, ear-bruising band formed in California in 1994 and while there were some personnel changes, their frontman never faltered. Wayne was an all-in performer, whose distinctive look—sprayed-stiff shocks of spiky black hair, and a long chin-tail—almost overshadowed his command of instruments (he favored modified flying-V guitars). During the 2007 Ozzfest tour, Wayne met his wife-to-be, Tera Wray, an "alternative porn star" (who'd aspired to the er, position, since she was in the fourth grade, she said in an interview). The couple tied the knot on January 10, 2008, in Las Vegas, and were still happily married when Wayne died at home in his sleep.

The 48-year-old "Love Dump" singer mixed oxycodone, hydromorphone, alprazolam, and alcohol, before going to bed with Tera, who woke up sometime later to find him cold to the touch and in full rigor. The coroner declared that there was no foul play or intent; it was an accidental overdose. (Fourteen months later, 33-year-old Tera Static intentionally committed suicide with drugs.)

Most ironic song title: "Cold," Static-X.

Scott Richard Weiland (October 27, 1967 – December 3, 2015) was the charismatic, chameleon-like frontman for the groundbreaking hard rock grunge pioneers, Stone Temple Pilots. The Gen-X superstar was seen as the voice of his peers along with Kurt Cobain, Layne Staley, and Chris Cornell. Scott was just 22 years old when Stone Temple Pilots—long for "STP" which is a synthesized, hallucinogenic drug comprised of mescaline and amphetamine—formed and from there he was on a never-ending rocket of sex, drugs, and rock & roll.

The multiplatinum-selling artist's egregious drug use led to an on-again-off-again relationship with his band brothers and led to him going on to front Slash's supergroup, Velvet Revolver, in 2003. He went on to drift in and out of other musical alliances and claimed he'd finally kicked his habits for good following a sincere and concentrated effort to get clean.

Scott's heroin addiction was well-known, but the "Dead & Bloated" singer hadn't used the opioid in over a decade. While he seemed together on the outside, with a new band (The Wildabouts) and a loving wife (number three, Jamie Wachtel), a series of stormy episodes rocked his final year—these setbacks included a close friend's death (guitarist Jeremy Brown), cancer diagnoses for both his mother and father, separation from his children, severe financial setbacks, and self-medication.

Forty-eight-year-old Scott Weiland died on December 3, 2015, while sleeping on his tour bus in Bloomington, Minnesota. The medical examiner later determined that the cause was an accidental overdose of cocaine, alcohol, and methylenedioxyamphetamine (MDA, aka, "Sally"). The M.E. also noted atherosclerotic cardiovascular disease, a history of asthma, and prolonged substance abuse. (Sadly, not all of Scott's problems died with him—the financial devastation led Jamie to put her 14-diamond engagement ring up for auction on eBay.)

<u>Most ironic song title</u>: "Still Remains," Stone Temple Pilots.

Prince Rogers Nelson (June 7, 1958 — April 21, 2016) A flashy, sex-fueled showman and lover of all things purple, Prince hit international superstardom in 1982 after his breakthrough album *1999* tore up the charts. Over his career, the gifted guitarist and singer earned 30 GRAMMY nominations (winning seven) and received an Academy Award for Best Original Song Score for Purple Rain. His 2007 Superbowl performance is considered one of the best of all-time, and he sold more than 100 million records in his lifetime.

While Prince's music remained rock steady, his personal life was a rollercoaster. His early output of funky-beat, guitar-driven songs extolled a life of freewheeling sexual vice, but over the years the "Gett Off" singer became increasingly religious and his health was in decline.

Although he was staunchly anti-drugs from a recreational standpoint, Prince was forced to take prescription pills for most of his adult life, following a bizarre bathtub accident that nearly killed him early in his career. According to the 2021 oral history book, *Nothing Compares 2 U*, when The Purple One was prepping for his 1984 tour, he was rehearsing one of the most spectacular stunts—he planned on singing When Doves Cry while sitting in a bathtub 10 feet off the ground, in a nod to the iconic music video—the apparatus broke, sending the singer hurtling to the floor.

"After that," said tour manager Alan Leeds, "his back hurt day after day. Then in L.A., he slipped and hurt his knee. He got some meds and finished the tour, but I don't think his hip and his leg were ever completely normal after that."

On April 14, 2016, just after what would be his final concert (in Atlanta) Prince's private Dassault Falcon 990 jet made an emergency landing after an "unresponsive male" was reported aboard. Prince was given a shot of Narcan (a medication that offsets opioid overdoses) but refused a blood transfusion due to his Jehovah's Witness beliefs; after being hospitalized for just three hours, Prince left against medical advice and returned to his Minneapolis, Paisley Park Estate. The next night, he threw a huge party at his home and by all accounts seemed just fine.

But just a few days later, the 57-year-old "Dirty Mind" singer was found dead, lying on his back just outside the elevator of his mansion by employees. The cause of death was an accidental overdose of the opioid fentanyl, which had not been prescribed to him (his doctor, who was fined by the state medical board, doled out the drugs under another patient's name). The synthetic painkiller has been described as "highly addictive" and "50 times more powerful than heroin." Prince was divorced, his only child had died as an infant, and he left no will, so a major fight for control of his estate ensued. Paisley Park was turned into a museum and paid tours include a look at the small urn that contains the cremains of the once larger-than-life superstar.

<u>Most ironic song title</u>: "I Would Die 4 U."

Thomas Earl Petty (October 20, 1950 — October 2, 2017). Florida-born Tom Petty was writing songs, singing, and playing guitar from a very young age but it took moving to L.A. and forming the Heartbreakers for him to hit major commercial success. Released in 1976, the eponymous debut LP introduced the world to Tom's unique blend of hard-edged rock and story-driven '60s-influenced pop with songs like "Breakdown" and "American Girl."

When *MTV* hit the airwaves, the video-driven music channel made the angular blond frontman a superstar, as well as an offbeat sex symbol. Tom rose to even higher heights in the late '80s with a side-project supergroup, The Traveling Wilburys, in which he shared the spotlight with Bob Dylan, George Harrison, Roy Orbison, and ELO's Jeff Lynne. Their first album reached #3 on the charts, went triple-platinum, and won a GRAMMY for Best Rock Performance.

Tom Petty admitted he drank a little and experimented with fashionable drugs like coke over the years, but he avoided the major pitfalls that took down so many of his contemporaries... until he didn't. Oddly enough, he waited until his late 40s to try heroin. He was soon hooked, blaming a bitter divorce from his childhood sweetheart, Jane Benyo, for his addiction... but the strong-willed "Learning to Fly" singer sought treatment, remarried in 2001, and got himself back on track. Tom Petty and the Heartbreakers were inducted into the Rock & Roll Hall of Fame in 2003 (and just a year later, bassist Howie Epstein died of a heroin overdose).

In 2017, the 66-year-old frontman enjoyed a successful 40th Anniversary tour with the Heartbreakers, selling out the Hollywood Bowl three nights in a row before taking a short break. It was during that break that Tom Petty suffered cardiac arrest after an accidental drug overdose in his Malibu home on the morning of October 2, 2017. He was rushed to UCLA Santa Monica Hospital, where he died later that night, surrounded by his loved ones. An autopsy found a mixture of oxycodone, fentanyl, Xanax, and other medications in his system—it came out later that he'd valiantly performed 53 concerts with a painful fractured hip, an old injury to his hand (he'd "pulverized" it by punching a wall in the studio in the '80s) flaring up, plus he had pneumonia.

<u>Most ironic song title</u>: "End of the Line," The Traveling Wilburys.

Dolores Mary Eileen O'Riordan (September 6, 1971 — January 15, 2018) was born in County Limerick, Ireland, to a Catholic working-class family but the gifted singer had higher aspirations—and despite some major setbacks, alcoholism, and mental illness, she achieved her dreams and beyond. As the lead singer of the alternative rock band The Cranberries, she went multiplatinum and was named Top Female Artist of All-Time on *Billboard*'s Alternative Songs chart.

At the height of her fame, Delores *was* The Cranberries—everyone knew her name and could instantly pick her beautiful mezzo-soprano voice on a '90s rock radio otherwise littered with sludgy grunge or guttural metal screams. Their 1993 debut album *Everybody Else Is Doing It, So Why Can't We?* generated the massive hit "Linger," which led to anthems like "Zombie," and "Dream."

The Cranberries broke up in 2002 but reunited briefly a couple more times over the next decade. In 2014, Delores split from her husband of 20 years, former Duran Duran tour manager Don Burton; the couple had three children. Toward the end of her life, she had a new band, a new love, and seemed to be making positive strides with her bipolar disorder—but it all came to a sad, lonely end at the London Hilton Hotel on Park Lane on January 15, 2018.

Forty-six-year-old Dolores was alone, drinking everything from the minibar when, for some reason, she decided to take a bath while fully clothed in her pajamas. She was found by hotel employees submerged "face-up" in the water, surrounded by empty bottles—five mini-vodkas, a full-sized magnum of champagne, and half-empty pill containers.

Police found the minibar was activated around 2 a.m., and she phoned her mother at around 3 a.m. She was found unresponsive and confirmed dead at 9:16 a.m. Police constable Natalie Smart, who was at the scene, testified at the inquest, saying, "I saw Mrs. O'Riordan submerged in the bath with her nose and mouth fully under the water. We did a full skin and body check; no marks, no blood in the water, and no injuries. There were no signs of disturbance and the door was locked from the inside." She added that no suicide note was found.

The "Yeats' Grave" singer's psychiatrist, Seamus O'Ceallaigh, told the court that he had last seen Delores less than a week before, and she seemed in "good spirits, no thoughts of suicide, no evidence of self-harm." The inquest concluded that Delores had died of accidental drowning while drunk.

<u>Most ironic song title</u>: "When You're Gone," The Cranberries.

Vincent "Vinnie" Paul Abbott (March 11, 1964 – June 22, 2018) was the drummer and co-founder of the heavy metal band Pantera, and later went on to form Damageplan with his younger brother, "Dimebag" Darrell—who was murdered onstage as the band performed in a small nightclub on December 8, 2004. But Vinnie didn't give up music or performing—the hard-hitting, lightning-fast sticks man was with the hard-rocking supergroup Hellyeah from 2006 until his untimely death at the age of 54 in 2018.

Vinnie's final performance took place just five days before his death, at The Vinyl at The Hard Rock Hotel and Resort in Las Vegas. He passed away at home (also in Las Vegas) due to severe coronary artery disease and a malady of the heart muscle called dilated cardiomyopathy—both of which were blamed on his devil-may-care rock & roll lifestyle.

While he was gone too soon, the drummer's death did serve to make his Hellyeah band brothers reassess their own habits. "Vinnie's passing was a wake-up call for us all," said guitarist Tom Maxwell. "I really sat back and looked at my mortality and said, 'You know what? I've got to quit smoking and exercise more and stop eating garbage.' I have a little boy who needs his dad. I have a wife who needs her husband."

Vinnie Paul was buried beside his mother and his brother at Moore Memorial Gardens Cemetery in the Abbott's hometown, Arlington, Texas. He left the bulk of his estate to his longtime girlfriend, Chelsey Yeager, and his best friend, Charles Jones.

Most ironic song title: "Cemetery Gates," Pantera.

Oliver "Taylor" Hawkins (February 17, 1972 — March 25, 2022) was best-known as the drummer of the rock-pop band Foo Fighters founded by Nirvana's former drummer, Dave

Grohl, but he first gained traction as an essential part of Alanis Morissette's touring band during the "Jagged Little Pill" years.

Taylor didn't just drum—he was a talented vocalist and songwriter. Although the blond, California surfer-type was always seen smiling, and was friendly and gregarious, there was a hidden side that harbored struggles with stage fright and self-medication. In 2001, Taylor OD'd so seriously on heroin that he was hospitalized and kept in a coma for two weeks. His bandmate and best friend, Dave Grohl, never left his side. Hawkins later said, "I was partying a lot. I wasn't a junkie, per se, but I was partying. There was a year when the partying just got a little too heavy."

He got married in 2005 and had three children, and by all accounts seemed to be drug-free and living a healthy lifestyle. In an interview with Rolling Stone magazine in 2021, he confirmed this belief, saying, "I'm healthy … I just found out from my doctor, got all my blood tests and my heart everything checked and he goes, 'Dude, you're in amazing shape. Your heart's big, because you exercise a lot. It's like a runner's heart.' And that's fine."

But it wasn't fine. The enlarged heart and his previous over-indulgences led to his death at the age of 50, while he was on tour in Bogotá, Columbia, with the Foos. The GRAMMY-winner was alone in his hotel room when he started suffering chest pains and called for help, but it was too late by the time someone got to him. The post-mortem analysis indicated Hawkins' heart was "about double... normal size," indicating that "it could have collapsed" apart from any contribution of drugs in his system—however, 10 substances were noted in the toxicology report, including opioids, benzodiazepines, tricyclic antidepressants, and THC (the psychoactive component in cannabis).

There was an all-star, six-hour tribute concert held in Taylor's memory. Those paying their decibel-defying respects were: Def Leppard, Queen, the James Gang, Rush, Soundgarden, Mötley Crüe, Pretty Reckless' Taylor Momsen, Kesha, P!nk, Heart's Nancy Wilson, Joan Jett, Miley Cyrus, and Alanis Morissette; plus Taylor's own former bands Chevy Metal, the Coattail Riders, and of course, Foo Fighters.

The guest drummers included Lars Ulrich of Metallica, Travis Barker of blink-182, Stewart Copeland of the Police, Brad Wilk of Rage Against the Machine, Chad Smith of Red Hot Chili Peppers, John Theodore of Queens of the Stone Age, Rufus Taylor of Darkness, Patrick Wilson of Weezer; and Hawkins' teenage son, Shane, whose performance brought tears to the eyes of everyone watching, whether it was in person or at home watching on television.

Most ironic song title: "(There Goes) My Hero," Foo Fighters.

Sometimes quitting while you're ahead helps, sometimes it doesn't. Whenever a 50-something rocker checks into rehab, it brings to mind a tall tale about the legendary old-timey comedian, W.C. Fields:

Throughout his showbiz life, W.C. professed an unabashed fondness for whiskey and women. The professional drunk was certainly not known as a pious man but as his death was nigh, he was admitted to the hospital with a shot liver and a grim prognosis. When a friend arrived for a final goodbye, she was surprised to see the red-nosed comedian thumbing through the pages of a Bible and asked what on earth he was doing. W.C. replied, "Looking for loopholes!"

AFTERWORD

That's it for this round of *Rock & Roll Nightmares: True Stories*. If you haven't done so yet, circle back to Volume One, which tells sordid tales of suicide, freak accidents, plane crashes, overdoses, the 27 Club, and so much more.

If you're into horror fiction, do pick up the first three books in the series: *Along Comes Scary, Do You Fear Like We Do*, and *Gory Days*. I have a podcast, too! It's called—you guessed it—Rock & Roll Nightmares.

There are several more *Rock & Roll Nightmares* books planned, so if you'd like to be kept in the loop, please subscribe to my monthly news bulletin through my website, StaciLayneWilson.com (BONUS! all new subscribers receive free exclusive eBooks not available anywhere else.)

Special thanks to Oriel Collins, Linda Rose, and the erudite members of the Rock & Roll Nightmares Facebook Group.

Lastly, if you liked this book, please kindly rate and review... indie authors depend on word of mouth (or word of fingertips, as the case may be). Thank you!

SOURCES

Books

Baby, Let's Play House: Elvis Presley and the Women Who Loved Him, Alanna Nash

Black Diamond Queens: African American Women and Rock and Roll, Maureen Mahon

Boys in the Trees, Carly Simon

Delta Lady, Rita Coolidge

Gold Dust Woman: A Biography of Stevie Nicks, Stephen Hopkins

Heaven and Hell, Don Felder with Wendy Holden

Heavy Duty: Days & Nights in Judas Priest, KK Downing

I'm with the Band, Pamela Des Barres

Just a Shot Away: Peace, Love, and Tragedy with the Rolling Stones at Altamont, Saul Austerlitz

Love Until Death: The Sudden Demise of a Music Icon and a Trail of Mystery and Alleged Murder, Mark Seal

Nöthin' But a Good Time, Tom Beaujour & Richard Bienstock

Petty: The Biography, Warren Zanes

Scary Monsters & Super Freaks, Mike Sager

Somebody to Love: The Life, Death, and Legacy of Freddie Mercury, Matt Richards & Mark Langthorne

Somebody to Love? Grace Slick with Andrea Kagan

The True Adventures of the Rolling Stones, Stanley Booth

Traveling Soul: The Life of Curtis Mayfield, Todd Mayfield with Travis Atria

Twilight of the Gods, Steven Hyden

VJ: The Unplugged Adventures of MTV's First Wave, Collective

Who I Am, Pete Townshend

Movies/TV

Biography: The Nine Lives of Ozzy Osbourne
Crime Scene: The Vanishing at the Cecil Hotel
Dream Deceivers: Heavy Metal Goes on Trial
Gordon Lightfoot: If You Could Read My Mind
King 5 News: Alan White's Drum Kit Stolen
ReMastered: The Miami Showband
Tear the Roof Off: The Untold Story of Parliament
Funkadelic
Tom Petty: Runnin' Down a Dream
VH1: Behind the Music

Print

Billboard
Circus
CREEM
Entertainment Weekly
Goldmine
GQ
Irish Times
Mail on Sunday
Melody Maker
Playboy
Rolling Stone
Star
Sydney Morning Herald
The Denver Post
The Los Angeles Times
The New York Times
The Seattle Times
Vanity Fair
VSiN.com
Wired

Online

ABCNews.go.com
AllThatIsInteresting.com
AutoWeek.com
BestsellingAlbums.org
Blender.com
Britannica.com
Caselaw.findlaw.com
ClickOnDetroit.com
DailyMail.co.uk
Dan Patrick Podcast
DesertUSA.com
Diffuser.fm
DigitalMusicNews.com
FarOut.com
FloydianSlip.com
Grunge.com
Insider.com
Internet Journal of Criminology
Islingtontribune.co.uk
KelleyLynchFactCheck.com
LiverpoolEcho.co.uk
Loudersound.com
LouderThanWar.com
Loudwire.com
MaximumRockNRoll.com
MetalHammer.com
MTV.com
Musicholics.com
NoTreble.com
OnThisDayMusic.com
PopDose.com
RetroCulturati.com
RockCelebrities.net
Snopes.com
SocietyOfRock.com
TheDay.com

TheStacksReader.com
ThisDayInMusic.com
thjkoc.net/
ThunderRoadsOhio.com
UltimateClassicRock.com
VickiSheff.com
WeAreClassicRockers.com
Wikipedia.org

This book has been researched using the original declassified police investigation files, court records, press reports, and as many authentic sources as possible, which are freely available in the public domain, including eyewitness testimony, confessions, autopsy reports, first-hand accounts, and independent investigation, where possible. It is not a full and complete representation of any of the cases, the people involved, or the investigation, and therefore should not be taken as such.

Made in the USA
Las Vegas, NV
23 July 2023

75134748R00292